A LABORATORY COURSE IN
WORDPERFECT 5.0

HEATH LABORATORY COURSE SERIES

A Laboratory Course in DOS, WordPerfect 5.0, Lotus 1-2-3, and dBASE IV

A Laboratory Course in DOS, WordPerfect 5.0, Lotus 1-2-3, and dBASE III PLUS

A Laboratory Course in DOS, WordPerfect 4.2, VP-Planner Plus, and dBASE III PLUS

A Laboratory Course in WordPerfect 5.0

A Laboratory Course in WordPerfect 4.2

A Laboratory Course in Lotus 1-2-3

A Laboratory Course in VP-Planner Plus

A Laboratory Course in dBASE IV

A Laboratory Course in dBASE III PLUS

A LABORATORY COURSE IN
WORDPERFECT 5.0

ERNEST S. COLANTONIO

D. C. HEATH AND COMPANY
LEXINGTON, MASSACHUSETTS TORONTO

Acquisitions Editor: John Carter Shanklin
Developmental Editor: Katherine T. Pinard
Production Editor: Kathleen A. Savage
Designer: Cornelia L. Boynton
Production Coordinator: Mike O'Dea
Composition and pre-press: Graphic Typesetting Service
Photo Researcher: Martha L. Shethar
Cover: John D. Kramer/ImageSet Design

Published simultaneously in Canada.

Printed in the United States of America.

International Standard Book Number: 0–669–21752–2

10 9 8 7 6 5 4 3 2 1

PREFACE

The microcomputer has become standard equipment in most schools, offices, and businesses. A wealth of exceptional software is available to apply this versatile tool to a wide range of tasks. *A Laboratory Course in WordPerfect 5.0* has been written for the novice end-user of microcomputers and application software.

Many microcomputer users work with operating systems and word processing software. This text teaches students how to use such software in their everyday lives. In particular, this text concentrates on the most recent versions of DOS and WordPerfect.

Text Content and Organization

A Laboratory Course in WordPerfect 5.0 has been carefully designed for use in any first course in microcomputer application software.

Computer Skills   The text is designed for use in courses with microcomputer laboratory facilities. Specifically, the text teaches DOS 3.3 and 4.0 and WordPerfect 5.0. We assume that students have access to these software packages and a computer that can run them.

Appendixes   The text's three appendixes provide additional material that may be of interest to students and instructors. Appendix A, Selecting a System, provides valuable tips for those individuals faced with the daunting task of purchasing hardware and software. Appendix B, Software Installation, briefly summarizes how to set up DOS and WordPerfect on a computer. Appendix C presents comprehensive command summaries for DOS and WordPerfect 5.0.

Text Learning Aids

A Laboratory Course in WordPerfect 5.0 combines a relaxed writing style with an outstanding array of pedagogical features to facilitate understanding and encourage reader enthusiasm.

Chapter Outline   Each chapter opens with *In This Chapter*, an outline of the chapter's headings.

Chapter Preview   Students learn more effectively if they are presented with clear learning objectives. Each chapter's *Preview* section introduces the material and provides learning objectives.

Readability   The text's engaging writing style ensures that concepts are explained clearly and simply. Editors, course instructors, and reviewers have carefully monitored the reading level to maintain accessibility for students.

Design and Illustrations   Students prefer a textbook that will hold their interest. We have created a design that is simple, but that effectively presents the material. High-resolution computer screen views are liberally inserted throughout each chapter to help illustrate major topics.

End-of-Chapter Materials   A carefully graded set of review materials is provided at the end of each chapter. First, the *Summary* briefly reviews the information that parallels the learning objectives stated in the chapter's *Preview*. Next, the *Key Terms* presents all of the chapter's boldfaced glossary terms. Twenty *Multiple Choice* and twenty *Fill-In* questions test students' understanding of the material. Ten *Short Problems* and ten *Long Problems* provide computer exercises that let students apply their new skills.

Glossary   A complete glossary includes clear definitions for all the boldfaced terms in the text.

Command Summaries   Appendix C contains comprehensive command summaries for DOS and WordPerfect 5.0 that serve as quick-reference guides to the software packages.

Keyboard Templates   Color-coded keyboard templates for DOS and WordPerfect 5.0 are included just inside the back cover of the book. Designed to be detached from the book and placed on top of the keyboard, these invaluable reminders list the important keyboard commands of each software product. The color-coding indicates at a glance whether the Shift, Control, or Alternate key should be pressed in conjunction with another key to execute a command.

Acknowledgments

Many people helped make *A Laboratory Course in DOS and WordPerfect 5.0* possible. I would like to thank Robert Hendersen and Nancy Sampson of the University of Illinois Department of Psychology Instructional Computer Laboratory for the use of various microcomputer hardware and software. Paul W. Ross of Millersville University provided many helpful suggestions throughout the development of this project. In addition to her work as copyeditor, Ann Hall helped extensively with the *Insight* and *Real World* features.

I would like to thank all of my colleagues who reviewed the manuscript:

- Professor Harvey Blessing, Essex Community College
- Professor Walter Bremer, California Polytechnic University
- Professor Frank S. Butash, University of Hartford
- Dr. William J. Engelmeyer, Anne Arundel Community College
- Professor Clinton P. Fuelling, Ball State University
- Professor C. Brian Honess, University of South Carolina
- Professor Susan Karian, Denison University
- Professor Gladys Norman, Linn-Benton Community College
- Dr. J. Douglas Robertson, Bentley College
- Professor Jerry Sitek, Southern Illinois University at Edwardsville
- Professor Karen Watterson, Shoreline Community College

Thanks also to WordPerfect Corporation for its support.

Finally, my special gratitude and appreciation go to all the people at D. C. Heath who worked long hours and sweated endless details to make this text the best that it could be, especially Kathleen Savage, Cia Boynton, and Mike O'Dea.

E.S.C.

 ## About the Author

Ernest S. Colantonio brings combined teaching, technical, and writing skills to this textbook. He received his undergraduate degree in psychology and completed several semesters of graduate work in computer science at the University of Illinois at Urbana-Champaign. While in graduate school, he taught introductory courses in computer science for nontechnical majors. Since 1982, Mr. Colantonio has developed microcomputer software for various organizations, including the Illinois State Geological Survey, the University of Illinois Department of Psychology, the Office of Naval Research, Psychology Software Tools Corporation, and SubLOGIC Corporation. He is the author of several data processing and microcomputer textbooks. Currently, Mr. Colantonio spends most of his time writing new textbooks from his home north of Green Bay, Wisconsin. He also develops and teaches introductory computer courses for Lakeland College and Northeast Wisconsin Technical College.

Contents

3   *Intermediate DOS*   71

PREVIEW   72

GETTING STARTED   72

4   *Beginning WordPerfect*   **123**

5   *Intermediate WordPerfect*   **175**

6 *Advanced WordPerfect*   233

A LABORATORY COURSE IN
WORDPERFECT 5.0

THE MICROCOMPUTER SYSTEM

In This Chapter

Preview

We begin this first chapter by introducing IBM and IBM-compatible microcomputers, their hardware components, and popular types of software. (By *IBM-compatible* we mean any computer that works like a comparable IBM model and can run the same software.) Then we discuss a few helpful hints for working with microcomputers.

After studying this chapter, you will understand

- what is meant by the term *microcomputer*.
- the basic operations performed by all computers.
- the four major hardware components of a typical microcomputer system.
- the major components inside a microcomputer's system unit.
- the three major types of microcomputer displays.
- how the various special-purpose keys on a microcomputer keyboard are used.
- the four most popular types of microcomputer printers.
- the three major categories of microcomputer software.
- how to turn on a microcomputer.
- how to operate a microcomputer printer.
- how to care for floppy disks.

What Is a Microcomputer?

Its very name tells us that a **microcomputer** is a small computer. A **computer** is an electronic device that performs calculations and processes data. Most people think of a microcomputer as being small enough to fit on top of a desk. Although some powerful models can serve several users simultaneously, most microcomputers are used by only one person at a time. For this reason, microcomputers are also often called **personal computers.**

Another characteristic of microcomputers is that their "brain" or **central processing unit (CPU)** consists of a single electronic device known as a **microprocessor.** This device, a marvel of miniature engineering, controls the microcomputer, performs its calculations, and processes data. A microprocessor is just one type of **integrated circuit chip,** which is a thin slice of semiconductor material, such as pure silicon crystal, impregnated with carefully selected impurities. These chips are commonly used in computers and many other modern electronic devices.

One way to define microcomputers is by what they do. They can be used to help accomplish many different tasks. At the lowest level, however, a microcomputer performs the same basic operations as all computers. This can be summed up as *input, processing,* and *output* (see Figure 1).

First, a **program** is needed to tell the computer what to do. This is a set of instructions that controls a computer's operation. The program lets you enter raw **data,** which can consist of numbers, text, pictures, and even sounds. These data entered into the computer are called **input.** The program instructs the computer to process the data by doing calculations, comparisons, and other manipulations. The final result is processed data or **information,** hopefully a more organized and useful form of the original input. This information produced by the computer is called **output.** Keep in mind that there is no magic here—a program is needed to tell the computer what to do and the output information is only as valid as the original input data.

Figure 1 What a Computer Does

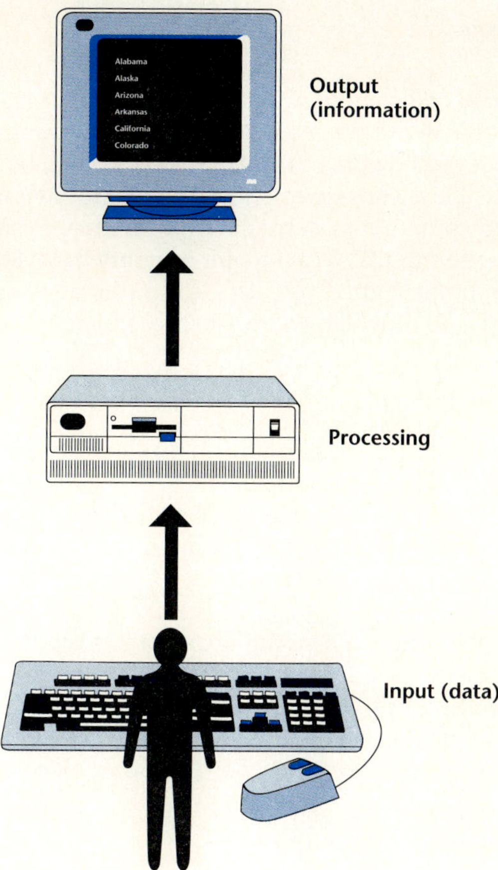

Although microcomputers perform the same basic operations as larger computers, they differ in speed and capacity. Larger computers can generally process data faster than microcomputers. They can also internally store more data at a time than microcomputers. These factors make larger computers better for performing lots of extremely complex and time-consuming computations. Microcomputers are also less adept than larger computers at handling several different users or tasks at the same time. On the other hand, microcomputers are superbly adapted to help with many work-a-day tasks like typing papers, figuring taxes, maintaining mailing lists, sending messages, drawing charts, managing finances, and even playing games.

Finally, microcomputers generally fall within a given price range. This can be as little as $100 or as much as $15,000. Today the average price of a typical microcomputer used in business is around $2500. This is, however, a good deal less than the cost of much more powerful computers, which may run into many thousands or millions of dollars. Although microcomputers are by no means cheap, their prices have been generally dropping even as their capabilities have increased. For example, in late 1983 the list price of a basic IBM Personal Computer XT was $5675. The list price of its successor, a similarly-equipped IBM Personal System/2 Model 30, was only $2545 when first released in mid-1987. Even though the newer Model 30 costs less than half as much as the old XT, it still has more than twice the speed and storage capacity, along with many other improvements.

Hardware

The **hardware** of a computer system is the electronic and mechanical equipment that make it work. Like a stereo system, microcomputer hardware generally consists of several distinct components connected by cables. Although there are several possible arrangements and many different models, Figure 2 shows a typical microcomputer system, the IBM Personal System/2 Model 30 and an IBM Personal Pageprinter. The four major parts are the system unit, display, keyboard, and printer. In this figure, you also can see the power switch, a floppy disk drive, and a mouse, all of which will be discussed later.

System Unit

From the outside, the system unit looks like a shallow box about the size of a portable typewriter. Figure 3 shows what the system unit of an IBM Personal System/2 Model 50 looks like on the inside. This central component houses important elements such as the computer's motherboard, microprocessor, memory, disk drives, and power supply.

Motherboard   The main circuit board of a computer is called the **motherboard** or **system board** (see Figure 4). Among other components, the motherboard holds the computer's CPU, some memory, and much of its control circuitry. In addition, the motherboard contains the **bus,** a set of wires and connectors that link the CPU to memory and other computer components.

Figure 2 A Microcomputer System

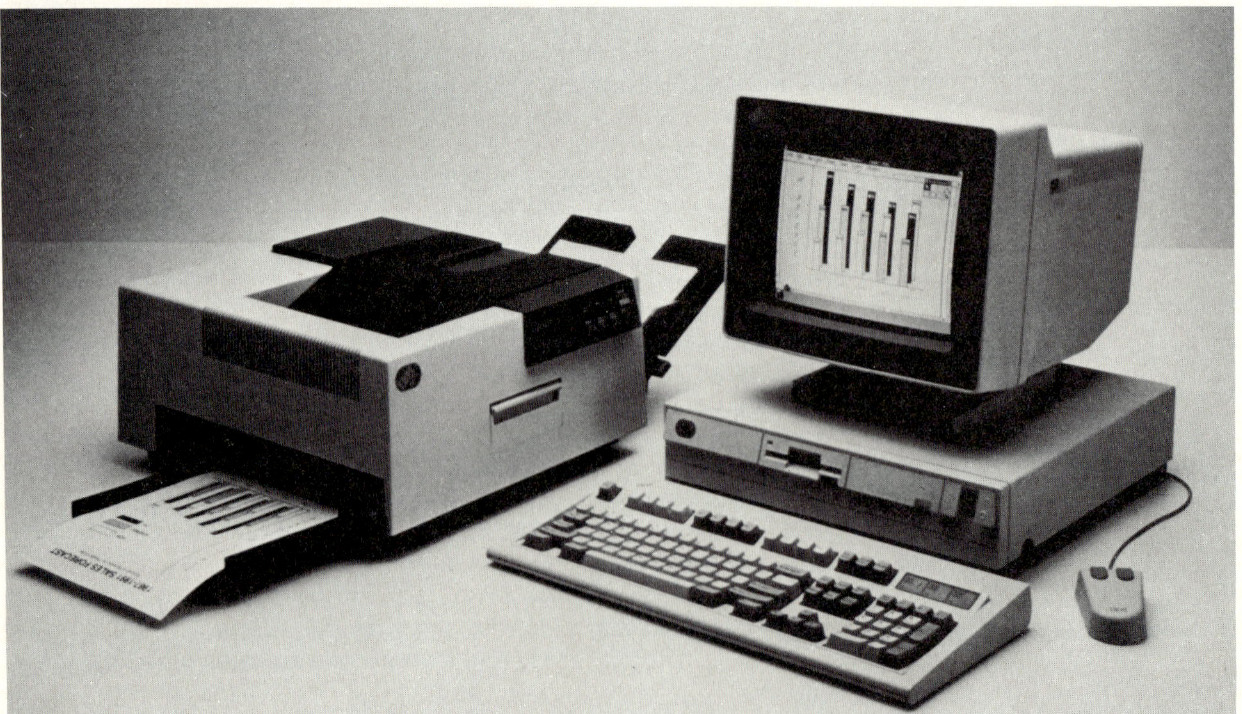

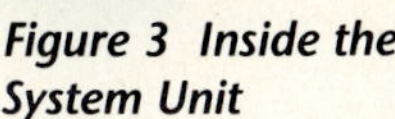

Figure 3 Inside the System Unit

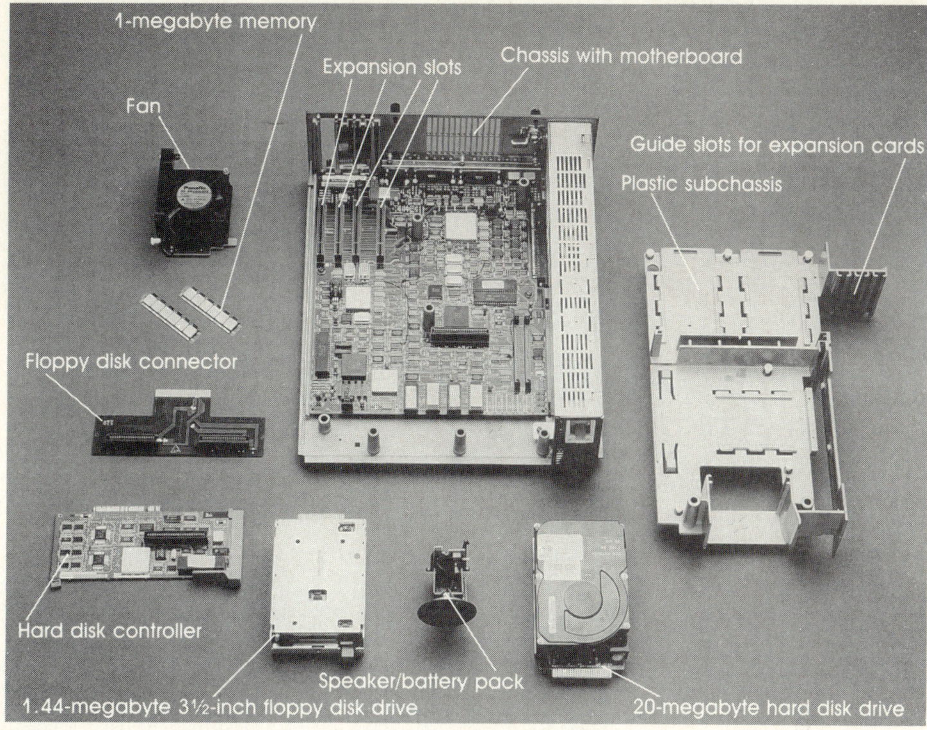

In most microcomputers, the bus is accessible through a series of **expansion slots.** Each expansion slot is an internal connector that allows you to plug an additional circuit board into the motherboard. The IBM Personal System/2 Model 50, for example, has four expansion slots, which can be seen in Figure 4. Some computers come with eight or more expansion slots. A circuit board that plugs into an expansion slot is called an **expansion board, card,** or **adapter.** Such circuit boards make it possible to connect a wide variety of extra equipment to a computer, thus *expanding* its capability.

The motherboard or expansion boards also contain device controllers. A **device controller** is a set of chips or a circuit board that operates a piece of computer equipment such as a disk drive, display, keyboard, mouse, or printer. Recently, there has been a trend toward building device controllers onto microcomputer motherboards. The IBM Personal System/2 Model 50 shown in Figure 4, for example, has most of its device controllers on the motherboard.

Microprocessor   As we said, the microprocessor is a microcomputer's central processing unit (CPU). It consists of a single integrated circuit chip that is usually soldered or plugged into a socket on the motherboard (see Figure 4). IBM and IBM-compatible microcomputers use microprocessors from the Intel 8088 family, which includes the 8088, 8086, 80286, 80386, and 80486 chips. The 8088 is used in older IBM and IBM-compatibles such as the original IBM Personal Computer and PC/XT. The slightly more efficient 8086 chip is used in IBM's newer low-end models, such as the IBM Personal System/2 Models 25 and 30. The more capable 80286 chip is used in mid-range microcomputers, such as the original IBM Personal Computer AT and the newer IBM Personal System/2 Models 50 and 60.

Figure 4 A Motherboard or System Board

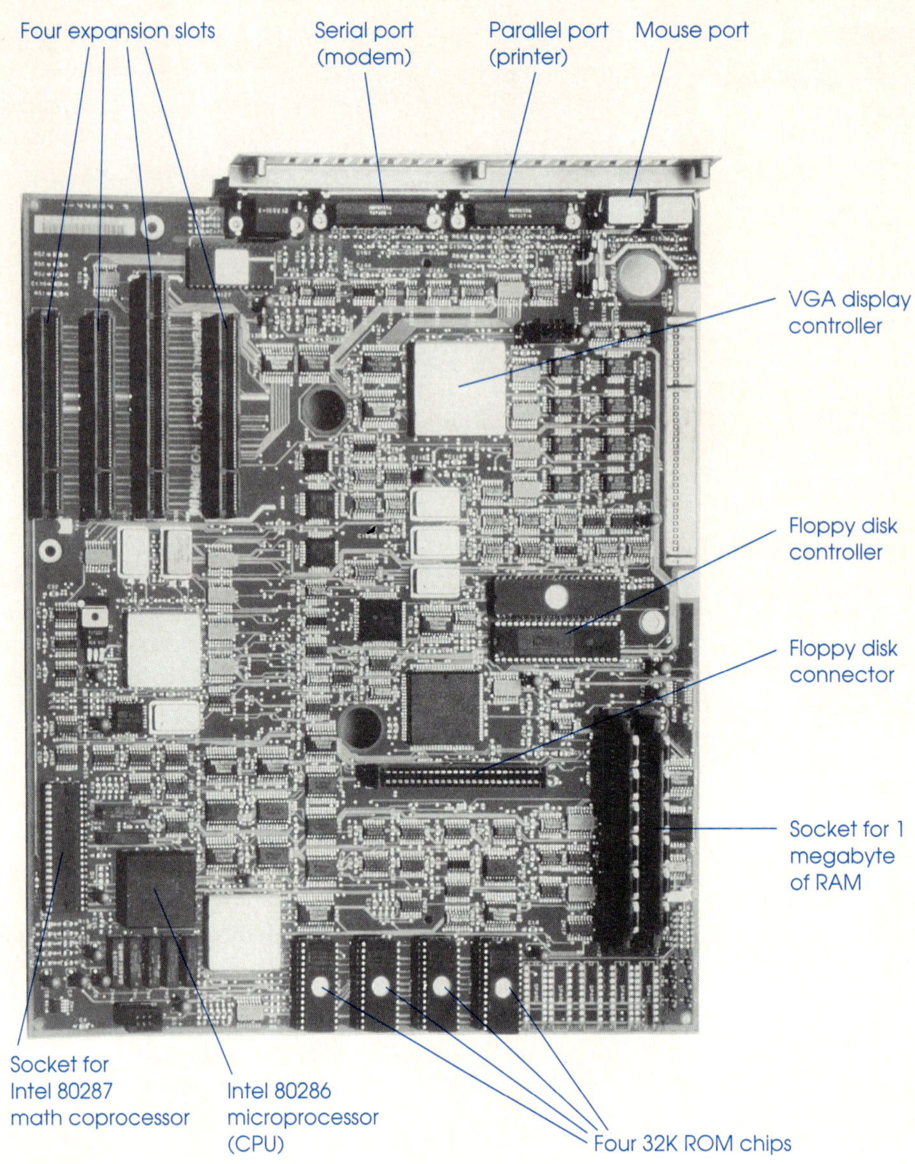

The fast and powerful 80386 chip is used in high-end models, such as the IBM Personal System/2 Models 70 and 80. Finally, the faster and even more powerful 80486 is used in IBM's Power Platform upgrade for the Personal System/2 Model 70 and high-performance computers such as the Apricot VX FT Server and the Hewlett-Packard Vectra 486 PC.

Memory   **Memory** is a computer's internal storage, used to hold programs and data. Also called **primary storage,** memory is measured in bytes. A **byte** is the amount of storage needed to hold a single character, such as the letter *A*, or a number between 0 and 255. Since computers can store thousands, millions, or even billions of bytes, the terms kilobyte, megabyte, and gigabyte are often used. One **kilobyte (K)** is equal to 1024 bytes, one **megabyte (M)** is equal to 1,048,576 bytes, and one **gigabyte (G)** is equal to 1,073,741,824 bytes. In general, microcomputer memory is made up of two types of integrated circuit chips: RAM and ROM.

RAM, which stands for **Random Access Memory,** is temporary storage. Programs and data can be kept there while they are being used and then overwritten by other programs and data later. When the computer is turned off, RAM loses its contents. Most microcomputers can now have at least 640K of RAM on the motherboard. Many can have much more installed on expansion boards. For example, the IBM Personal System/2 Model 80 can be equipped with up to 16 megabytes of RAM.

ROM, which stands for **Read Only Memory,** is permanent storage. The contents of ROM chips, which are encoded at the factory, remain intact when the computer is turned off. The programs and data permanently stored in ROM can be read and used, but never erased, changed, or augmented. Many microcomputers use ROM to store programs and data that are used frequently but need never be changed, such as portions of the operating system. Most microcomputers contain at least one ROM chip as part of their primary storage. The IBM Personal System/2 Model 50, for example, uses four 32K ROM chips on the motherboard to store essential programs and data (see Figure 4).

Disk Drives   A **disk drive** is a piece of equipment that can read and write programs and data on magnetic disks. A **magnetic disk** is a semi-permanent storage medium that can be erased and rewritten over and over again. Most microcomputers can be equipped with two basic kinds of disk drives: floppy disk drives and hard disk drives.

A **floppy disk drive** works with **floppy disks** (also called **diskettes**), which are inexpensive, flexible magnetic disks encased in plastic (see Figure 5). Floppy disks can be inserted and removed from their disk drives. The IBM Personal System/2 Model 50, for example, comes standard with one floppy disk drive. This drive accepts a 3½-inch floppy disk which can hold up to 1.44 megabytes

Figure 5 Floppy Disks

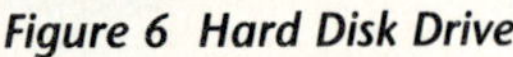

Figure 6 Hard Disk Drive

of programs and data. Although most newer microcomputers now come with 3½-inch floppy disk drives, many microcomputers still use 5¼-inch floppy disk drives. A typical 5¼-inch floppy disk holds 360K, but many drives can use 5¼-inch disks that hold 1.2 megabytes.

A **hard disk drive** uses one or more rigid, magnetic platters to hold programs and data (see Figure 6). Most hard disk drives have their magnetic disks permanently sealed inside. These disks spin much faster and have much greater capacity than floppy disks. Hard disk drives come in sizes ranging from 10 megabytes to several hundred megabytes. The most popular sizes are now 20, 30, and 40 megabytes. The IBM Personal System/2 Model 50, for example, comes standard with a 20-megabyte internal hard disk. On a microcomputer with a hard disk, programs are usually run from the hard disk. The floppy disk drive is generally relegated to copying software to or from the hard disk and making backup copies of important programs and data.

Display

A **display,** also called a **monitor,** is similar in many ways to an ordinary television screen. The display is used to present text and **graphics,** which are simply any kind of pictures, drawings, charts, or plots. Almost all computer monitors create text and graphics on the screen with tiny dots called **pixels** (short for picture elements). The number and size of these pixels determine a monitor's sharpness or **resolution.** There are three basic types of displays:

- **Monochrome Text** These monitors can display only letters, numbers, punctuation, and a limited set of other symbols in just one color, usually green on black, amber on black, white on black, or black on white.
- **Monochrome Graphics** In addition to text, these monitors can also display graphics on the screen. Only one color can be presented, but different shades of that color may be used.
- **Color Graphics** These monitors can display text and graphics in more than one color.

The capabilities of a particular display system are dependent on both the monitor itself and its device controller. The device controller for a display is called a **display adapter.** Several display adapters are available for IBM and IBM-compatible microcomputers:

- **Monochrome Display Adapter (MDA)** This is the controller used with early low-end IBM microcomputers. It can display only text on a monochrome screen, but it generates crisp, easy-to-read characters.
- **Color Graphics Adapter (CGA)** This is IBM's first microcomputer color graphics adapter. It can produce color graphics, but the quality is rather poor. In other words, its low resolution makes text and graphics look rather fuzzy. Furthermore, the CGA is limited to a maximum of only 16 different colors, of which only four can be on the screen at the same time.
- **Hercules Graphics Adapter** This adapter, made by Hercules Computer Technology, acts as a monochrome display adapter, but adds monochrome graphics capability.
- **Enhanced Graphics Adapter (EGA)** This color graphics adapter from IBM can do everything the CGA can do, yet is much better than the CGA. The resolution is significantly higher and the maximum number of different colors on the screen is 16 out of 64 possible choices.
- **Multi-Color Graphics Array (MCGA)** This is the display adapter built onto the motherboards of the IBM Personal System/2 Models 25 and 30. It can be used with either a monochrome graphics or color graphics monitor. Its maximum resolution is better than the EGA and can display a maximum of 256 different colors on the screen at once out of 262,144 possible choices.
- **Video Graphics Array (VGA)** This is the display adapter built onto the motherboards of the IBM Personal System/2 Models 50, 60, 70, and 80. It can also be purchased as a separate expansion board for other types of IBM and IBM-compatible computers. Slightly more advanced than the MCGA, the VGA can also do everything the EGA can do.

Keyboard

The keyboard is the primary device for entering text and telling the computer what to do. It is similar, in many respects, to a typewriter keyboard. Many microcomputers also have an auxiliary input device known as a **mouse.** This little box, which is slid across the table top, allows the user to manipulate objects on the display screen, draw pictures, and select actions to be performed by pressing one or more buttons.

Three basic keyboard designs are used on IBM and IBM-compatible microcomputers: the original IBM Personal Computer keyboard, the original IBM Personal Computer AT keyboard, and the new IBM Enhanced keyboard. Figure 7 shows all three of these keyboards. Besides the usual letters and punctuation marks found on any typewriter, a computer keyboard has other important keys:

- **Enter** (or **Return**) Analogous to the carriage return on a typewriter, this key is used to signal the end of an entry. Basically, it tells the computer to go ahead and process what was just typed.
- **Backspace** Like the Backspace key on a typewriter, this key is used to go back and type over a previously typed character.
- **Shift** Located at either side of the keyboard, one of the Shift keys is held down while pressing another key to produce a capital letter or the symbol shown on the top part of the key.

Figure 7   IBM Keyboard Designs
*(top) Original IBM PC Keyboard,
(center) ''AT-Style'' Keyboard, and
(bottom) IBM Enhanced Keyboard*

- **Caps Lock** This key is like the Caps Lock key on a typewriter, except that it works for only letter keys. When the Caps Lock key is pressed, capital letters will appear when you press letter keys. When Caps Lock is pressed again, small letters will appear when their keys are pressed.
- **Tab** Like the Tab key on a typewriter, this key is used to advance to the next tab stop.
- **Escape** The Escape key (abbreviated **Esc**) is often used to cancel a previously typed entry or to prematurely end a program.

- **Break** This key is much like the Escape key and is used by some programs in a similar fashion.
- **Control** Somewhat like a Shift key, the Control key (abbreviated **Ctrl**) is pressed in conjunction with other keys. It's used to control a program's actions by sending certain codes to the computer.
- **Alternate** Similar to the Control key, the Alternate key (abbreviated **Alt**) is also pressed in conjunction with other keys. It's used to give an alternate meaning to the keys pressed along with it.
- **Insert** This key (abbreviated **Ins**) is often used to insert a new entry between existing entries.
- **Delete** This key (abbreviated **Del**) is often used to erase an entry or a single character.
- **Function Keys** These are keys that are pressed to activate frequently used operations within a program. They are used differently by different programs. IBM-compatible keyboards have either 10 function keys along the left side or 12 function keys across the top. The function keys are labeled with an F followed by a number, like this: F1, F2, F3, and so on.
- **Cursor Movement Keys** Most programs use these keys to let you move the **cursor** (a little blinking underscore or box) around the screen. In a word processing program, for example, the cursor marks the place where text is inserted, deleted, or otherwise manipulated. The cursor movement keys include Up Arrow, Down Arrow, Left Arrow, Right Arrow, Home, End, Page Up, and Page Down.
- **Numeric Keypad** This is an array of keys at the right side of a keyboard that resembles the layout of a calculator's keys. It includes the ten digits and other symbols that facilitate the entry of numbers and formulas. On the IBM PC and AT keyboards, the numeric keypad is superimposed on the cursor movement keys.
- **Num Lock** This key is used to switch the function of the numeric keypad. In one state, the numeric keypad acts as number keys. In the other state, the numeric keypad acts as cursor movement keys. You press the Num Lock key to switch between these two states.
- **Print Screen** If you have a printer, this key is pressed to send a copy of the current screen to your printer. On some keyboards, it is abbreviated **PrtSc.**
- **Pause** This key is used to temporarily suspend the operation of the current program.
- **Scroll Lock** This key is used by few programs and it has no standard function. Some programs use it to switch the Cursor Movement keys into a state in which they can move (or scroll) the whole screen up, down, left, or right.

Printer

A **printer** is a device that produces permanent copies of text and graphics on paper. Although a printer is not absolutely necessary to run most programs, it is handy because microcomputers are commonly used to produce letters, reports, books, tables, figures, charts, graphs, diagrams, maps, and pictures. Paper output, or *hard copy,* is a convenient medium for distributing text and graphics to others. The four kinds of printers most frequently used with microcomputers are dot-matrix printers, daisy-wheel printers, ink-jet printers, and laser printers.

Dot-Matrix Printers   A **dot-matrix printer** is an output device that uses tiny dots to create text and graphics on paper (see Figure 8). Just as graphics monitors use pixels to construct characters and pictures on a screen, dot-matrix printers

Figure 8 Dot-Matrix Printer
(a) The printhead of a dot-matrix printer,
(b) The process of printing a dot-matrix char-
acter, (c) The pattern of dots within the matrix
that form the character, and (d) The IBM Pro-
printer XL24, a dot-matrix printer

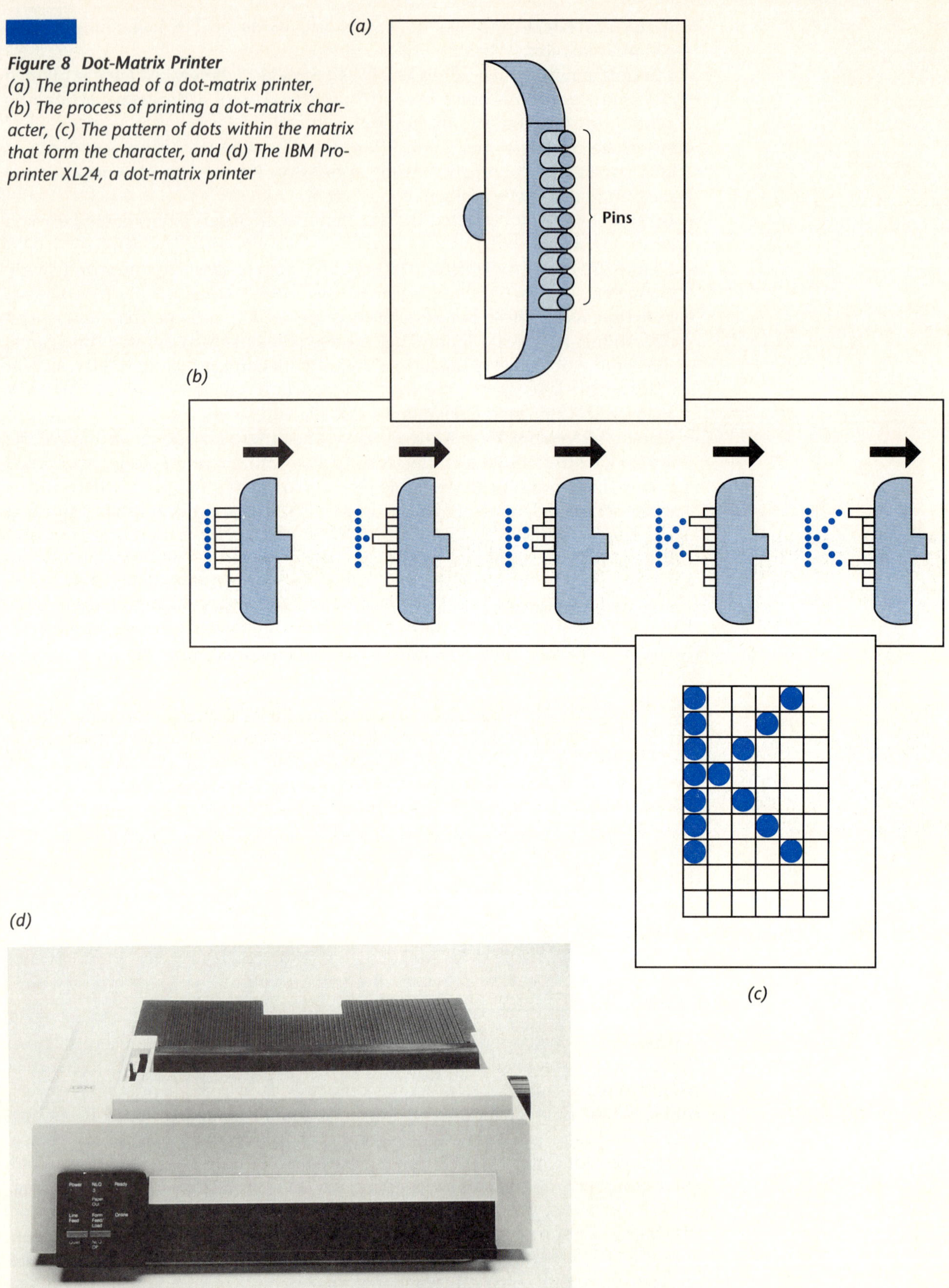

similarly use dots of ink on pages of paper. Inside the dot-matrix printer a **print-head** is moved across the paper from left to right, and sometimes also from right to left (see Figure 8). This printhead may contain anywhere from 7 to 27 pins arranged in a vertical column. While most dot-matrix printers use 9 pins, more expensive printers with 24 pins are also common. As the printhead moves horizontally, it constructs a character by repeatedly striking these pins against an inked ribbon and the paper. Electrical signals cause the appropriate pins to be thrust out at the proper moment to form the successive columns of dots that make up a character's image. Each column of the character is struck in turn against the ribbon and paper until the complete image has been formed. Dot-matrix printers are sometimes described as being impact printers because of the way the pins hit the ribbon and paper. This printing mechanism is most often used for text, but dot-matrix printers can usually produce graphics, too.

Dot-matrix printers are the most popular type of microcomputer printer. They are reasonably priced, fairly quick, and pretty reliable. Prices range between $150 and $3000, but the typical cost of a 9-pin dot-matrix printer is about $500. The speed of a dot-matrix printer depends upon what print mode it is using. The fastest mode is called **draft mode,** in which characters are formed by just a single pass of the printhead. Some expensive dot-matrix printers are able to achieve speeds of 400 characters per second in draft mode. Many dot-matrix printers also have a **near letter-quality (NLQ) mode.** In this mode, the printhead makes two or more passes over each character, slightly shifting its position each time. This tends to fill in the gaps between the dots and makes text appear more like it was produced by an electric typewriter. Using NLQ mode may slow some printers down to only 15 characters per second. Generating graphics with a dot-matrix printer can also be time-consuming. Depending upon how dark the images are, it may take several minutes per page to produce graphics on a dot-matrix printer.

Daisy-Wheel Printers   A **daisy-wheel printer** uses a circular printing mechanism called a **daisy wheel.** Solid, raised characters are embossed on the ends of little "arms" arranged in a circle like the spokes of a wheel or the petals of a daisy. As this daisy wheel spins, a tiny, stationary hammer strikes the back of the proper character when it passes (see Figure 9). This impact drives the character pattern, which is embossed in reverse, against an inked ribbon and the paper. Daisy-wheel printers are true **letter-quality** printers because they produce well-defined text just like electric typewriters. Their prices are comparable with that of dot-matrix printers. Unlike dot-matrix printers, however, daisy-wheel printers cannot produce graphics. They are also noisier and slower than dot-matrix printers. The typical daisy-wheel printer can only print about 10 characters per second, and even the most expensive models generally cannot do better than 100 characters per second. Daisy-wheel printers are still common, but they are being supplanted by 24-pin dot-matrix printers and laser printers.

Ink-Jet Printers   An **ink-jet printer** has a mechanism that squirts tiny, electrically-charged droplets of ink out of a nozzle and onto the paper (see Figure 10). No pins or hammers strike the paper, so ink-jet printers are classified as non-impact printers. Ink-jet printers are fast, quiet, and can produce high-quality print, but they are slightly more expensive than dot-matrix printers. Some ink-jet printers require special paper to avoid smearing. On the other hand, many ink-jet printers can print in color, a capability most other types of printers lack.

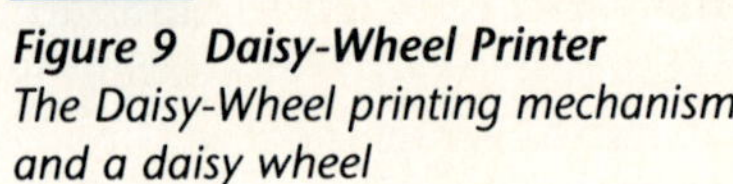

Figure 9 Daisy-Wheel Printer
The Daisy-Wheel printing mechanism
and a daisy wheel

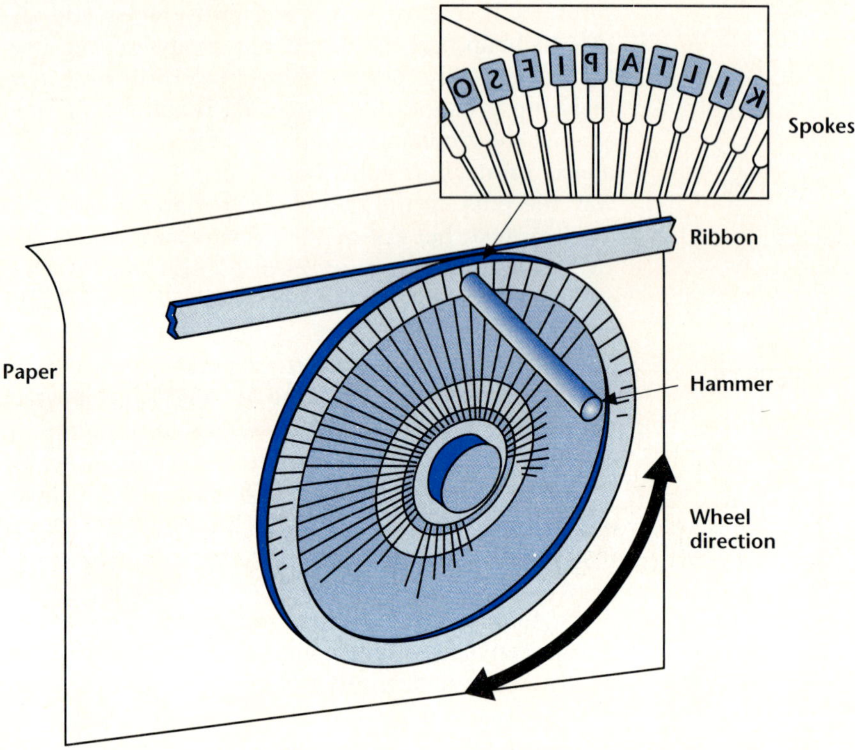

Laser Printers   A **laser printer** is an output device that uses tightly focused beams of light to transfer images to paper (see Figure 11). A tiny laser emits pulsating pinpoint bursts of light that are reflected off a special spinning mirror. This mirror reflects light onto a rotating drum. Light striking the drum causes it to become charged with electricity. An inklike toner is attracted to the drum in these electrically charged spots. When the drum is rolled over a piece of paper, the toner is transferred to the paper and an image is permanently fixed through a combination of heat and pressure. This image transfer process is similar to that found in a plain-paper photocopy machine. The result is high-quality text and graphics that almost look as if they were typeset. Like ink-jet printers, laser printers are classified as nonimpact printers.

Laser printers represent the most advanced printing technology. Although the images they produce are made up of dots, these dots are much smaller and more densely packed than the dots created with a dot-matrix printer. The typical microcomputer laser printer is capable of printing at a resolution of 300 dots per inch, both horizontally and vertically. This means 90,000 dots per square inch. Besides printing high-quality images, laser printers are also fast and quiet. The

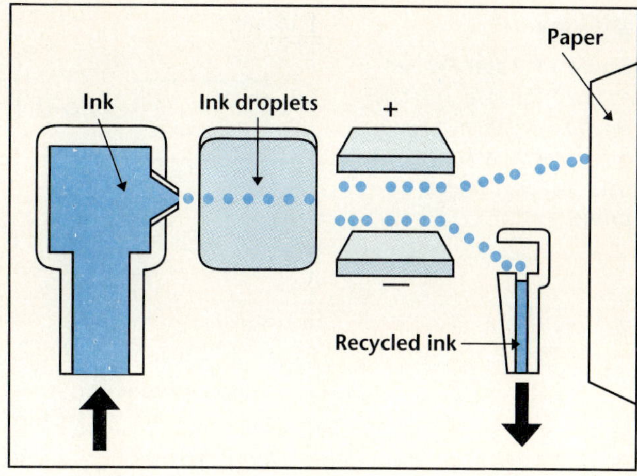

Figure 10 Ink-Jet Printer
(above) Ink jet printing, and (below)
the Hewlett-Packard PaintJet color
graphics printer

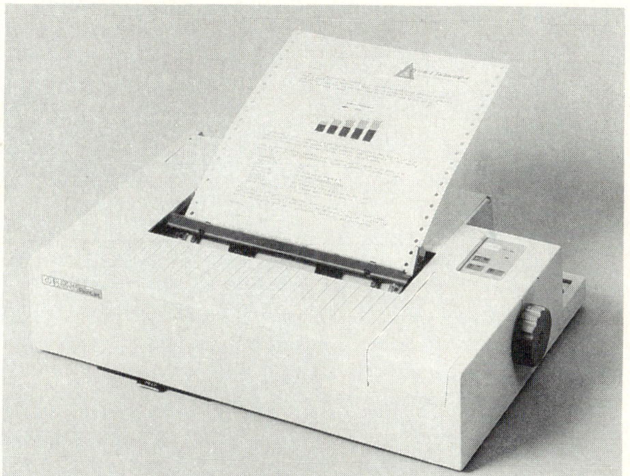

average speed of most laser printers is 8 pages per minute. This is equivalent to about 400 characters per second. Because laser printers don't use impact methods like dot-matrix and daisy-wheel printers, they are very quiet by comparison. The major disadvantage to laser printers is their cost. Prices generally start at around $1000. Despite the cost, more and more laser printers are being used with microcomputers every year. They are especially popular in office situations where the printer can be shared among several users.

Software

By itself, computer hardware is useless. Programs are needed to operate the hardware. As we mentioned earlier, a program is simply a sequence of instructions that tells a computer what to do. **Software** is a general term that refers to any single program or group of programs. In contrast to hardware, which is

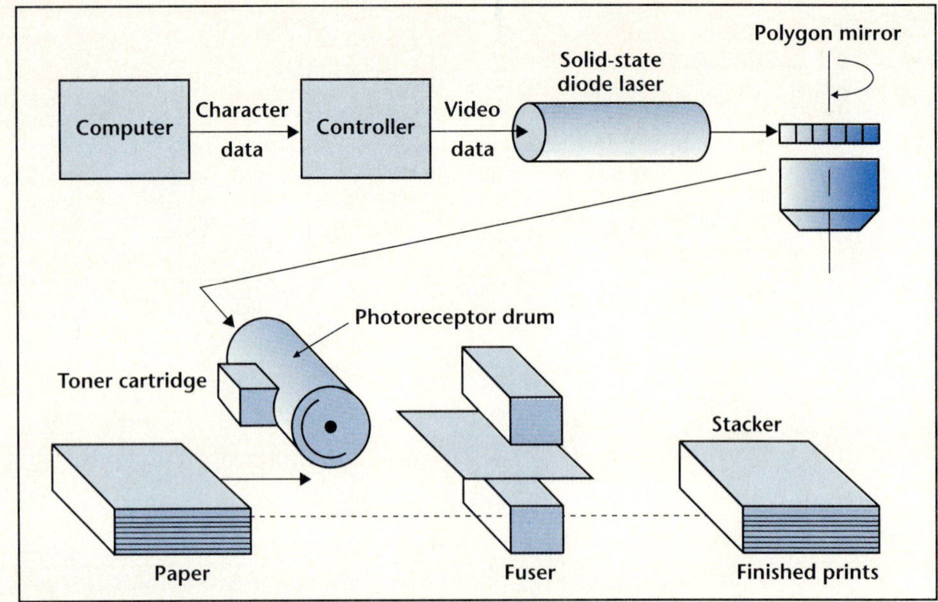

Figure 11 Laser Printer
(above) The laser printing mechanism, and (below) the Hewlett-Packard LaserJet Series II laser printer

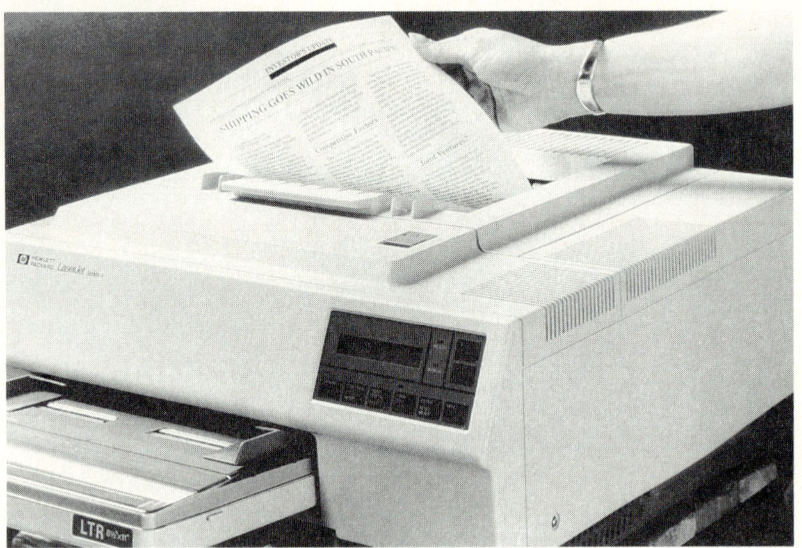

constructed from physical materials like metal and plastic, software is built from knowledge, planning, and testing. A person who creates programs is called a **programmer.** Programmers use their knowledge of how a computer works to plan sets of instructions that accomplish useful tasks. These instructions are entered into the computer and repeatedly tested and modified until they achieve the desired results. Programs and data are generally kept on magnetic disks, where they can be accessed and used over and over again. Note that the disks themselves aren't the software, they are just the medium on which software is stored.

As an analogy, think of a stereo system. The amplifier, compact disc player, and speakers are the hardware. The amplifier is like the central processing unit and memory, the compact disc player is like a disk drive, and the speakers are like the display, except they present audio instead of video output. The music, which is stored on compact discs, is like software, which is stored on floppy disks. Just as you can amass a huge music collection by buying more compact discs, you can build a bigger software library by purchasing additional programs on floppy disks. The stereo system is of little use without the compact discs and the compact discs are useless without the stereo system. Similarly, a computer system is useless without software and software is useless without a computer system on which to run it.

Just as there are different types of hardware, there are also different types of software. Basically, there are three major categories: system software, programming languages, and application software.

System Software

System software handles the many details of managing a computer system. A computer's **operating system** makes up most of its system software. This is the set of programs that controls a computer's hardware and manages the use of software. One small part of the operating system, for example, is a program that identifies which key you've pressed, determines the character that corresponds to that key, and forms that character on the display screen. Another example is a program that lets you erase the contents of a magnetic disk. Some system software is built into a computer's ROM chips, while other system software comes on magnetic disk and must be purchased separately.

Programming Languages

Computer programs are developed with programming languages. A **programming language** is simply a set of symbols and rules to direct the operations of a computer. There are many different programming languages in common use, each designed to develop certain types of programs. A few of the most popular programming languages are BASIC, Pascal, C, FORTRAN, COBOL, and Ada. Although it can be helpful to learn a programming language for some very specific applications, most people who use computers don't actually program them. They just use programs, such as operating systems and application software, that have been developed by professional programmers.

Application Software

Application software is the software that applies the computer to useful tasks such as helping you create documents, figure your taxes, maintain mailing lists, and draw charts. Also called **application packages** or simply **applications,** these programs are the real reason most people buy and use microcomputers. The three most widely used applications are word processing, spreadsheet, and data base management.

- **Word Processing** A **word processing package** is software that helps you prepare documents by letting you enter, store, modify, format, copy, and print text.
- **Spreadsheet** A **spreadsheet package** is software that lets you manipulate tables of columns and rows of numbers, text, and formulas. It is an extremely flexible tool that can be used to handle typical accounting chores, monitor investments, balance a checkbook, and work out a budget.
- **Data Base Management** A **data base** is an organized collection of one or more files of related data. A **file** is a mass of individual data items kept together on

a disk. A **data base management package** is software that lets you create, add to, delete from, update, rearrange, select from, print out, and otherwise administer data files such as mailing lists and inventories.

Besides these "big three" application packages, there are many other types of popular software, including the following:

- **Communications** Using an auxiliary device called a **modem,** a computer can transmit and receive programs and data over ordinary telephone lines. Communications software makes it possible for a computer to use a modem to call other computers and access on-line information services.
- **Graphics** Graphics packages let you use a computer to create all kinds of pictures including graphs, charts, maps, paintings, drawings, diagrams, blueprints, simulated slide shows, and animated presentations.
- **Desktop Publishing** Combining the results of word processing and graphics, desktop publishing or page layout software lets you use a computer and laser printer to produce near-typeset quality documents.
- **Integrated Software** Integrated software combines word processing, spreadsheet, data base management, communications, and graphics applications in a single package.
- **Windowing Environment** Working closely with the operating system, a windowing environment allows you to divide your screen into a number of different boxes, or *windows*, and run a separate program in each one.
- **DOS Shell** A DOS shell is a program that enhances PC-DOS or MS-DOS, the operating system used with IBM and IBM-compatible microcomputers. Basically, it is an easy-to-use front-end to DOS that helps you execute commands and manage disk files.
- **Utilities** There are a host of small, specific programs called utilities that add handy features and functions to a particular operating system or application package. These include disk and file utilities, printer utilities, keyboard utilities, and desk accessories such as calculators, calendars, and address books.
- **On-Line References** Software to help you check your spelling, find a synonym, or look up a word's definition are all examples of on-line references.
- **Statistics and Math** Many programs exist for performing statistical analyses and helping solve mathematical equations.
- **Project Management** A project management package is software that helps you formally plan and control complex undertakings, such as the construction of a building, the development of a new product, or the installation of a large computer system.
- **Accounting** Accounting software lets you use a computer to record, analyze, and report business transactions.
- **Personal Finance and Taxes** Many programs exist for helping you manage your money and prepare your federal and state income tax returns.
- **Education** There is a wide range of programs for teaching skills and concepts, from learning the alphabet to designing physics experiments.
- **Entertainment** An amazing variety of microcomputer software exists for playing games, simulating cars and planes, and playing music.
- **Hypertext** A hypertext package is software that lets you store and retrieve all kinds of information in a nonsequential manner. In other words, you can randomly jump from topic to related topic, accessing any kind of information the computer can store, including text, graphics, audio, and video.
- **Expert System** An expert system is a computer program that contains a collection of facts and a list of rules for making inferences about those facts. Such software can use these facts and rules in a particular field to advise, analyze, categorize, diagnose, explain, identify, interpret, and teach.

Key Terms

As an extra review of this chapter, try defining the following terms.

application package (application)	kilobyte (K)
bus	laser printer
byte	letter-quality
central processing unit (CPU)	Line Feed button
computer	magnetic disk
cursor	megabyte (M)
daisy wheel	memory
daisy-wheel printer	microcomputer (personal computer)
data	microprocessor
data base	modem
data base management package	motherboard (system board)
device controller	mouse
disk drive	near letter-quality (NLQ) mode
display (monitor)	On Line button
display adapter	operating system
dot-matrix printer	output
draft mode	pixel
expansion board (card, adapter)	power switch
expansion slot	primary storage
file	printer
floppy disk (diskette)	printhead
floppy disk drive	program
Form Feed button	programmer
gigabyte (G)	programming language
graphics	random access memory (RAM)
hard disk drive	read only memory (ROM)
hardware	resolution
information	software
ink-jet printer	spreadsheet package
input	word processing package
integrated circuit chip	

Multiple Choice

Choose the best selection to complete each statement.

1. A microcomputer is a computer in which the central processing unit consists
   of
   - (a) a RAM chip.
   - (b) a ROM chip.
   - (c) a microprocessor chip.
   - (d) a device controller chip.

2. A set of instructions that controls a computer's operation is
   - (a) a program.
   - (b) data.
   - (c) input.
   - (d) output.

3. The main circuit board of a computer is called the
   - (a) expansion board.
   - (b) device controller.
   - (c) bus.
   - (d) motherboard or system board.

4. IBM and IBM-compatible microcomputers use microprocessors from the
   (a) Motorola 68000 family.   (b) Intel 8088 family.
   (c) Zilog Z80 family.   (d) GTE G65SC816 family.

5. A byte is the amount of storage needed to hold a
   (a) single character.   (b) single page.
   (c) single line.   (d) single file.

6. Which of the following does NOT describe random access memory (RAM)?
   (a) It is temporary storage.   (b) It loses its contents when the power is turned off.
   (c) It is permanently encoded at the factory.   (d) It can be read and written over again and again.

7. The two most popular floppy disk sizes are
   (a) 3½-inch and 8-inch.   (b) 5¼-inch and 8-inch.
   (c) 3½-inch and 5¼-inch.   (d) 3-inch and 12-inch.

8. Which of the following types of display systems can present text and pictures on the screen, but only in a single color?
   (a) monochrome text display   (b) monochrome graphics display
   (c) color graphics display   (d) monochrome display adapter

9. Which of the following microcomputer keyboard keys is used to tell the computer to go ahead and process what was just typed?
   (a) Enter key   (b) Escape key
   (c) Control key   (d) Function key

10. The most advanced and expensive type of printer in the following group is the
    (a) dot-matrix printer.   (b) daisy-wheel printer.
    (c) ink-jet printer.   (d) laser printer.

11. A set of programs that controls a computer's hardware and manages the use of software is called
    (a) an operating system.   (b) a programming language.
    (c) an application package.   (d) a data base management package.

12. Which of the following types of software lets you manipulate tables of numbers, text, and formulas?
    (a) word processing package   (b) spreadsheet package
    (c) data base management package   (d) operating system

13. Which of the following types of software lets you use a modem to transmit and receive programs and data over ordinary telephone lines?
    (a) communications package   (b) graphics package
    (c) desktop publishing package   (d) windowing package

14. Which of the following types of software lets you use a computer to record, analyze, and report business transactions?
    (a) graphics package   (b) accounting package
    (c) DOS shell   (d) utilities

15. Small, specific programs that add handy features and functions to a particular operating system or application package are called

    (a) on-line references.　　(b) hypertext programs.

    (c) spreadsheets.　　(d) utilities.

16. Which of the following types of software would be the best choice for maintaining a mailing list?

    (a) word processing package　　(b) spreadsheet package

    (c) data base management package　　(d) accounting package

17. Which of the following types of programs would you use to help plan and control the construction of a new office building?

    (a) word processing package　　(b) spreadsheet package

    (c) integrated software package　　(d) project management package

18. Which of the following types of software lets you store and retrieve all kinds of information in a nonsequential manner and then randomly jump from topic to related topic?

    (a) word processing package　　(b) spreadsheet package

    (c) hypertext package　　(d) expert system

19. Which printer button determines whether the printer is connected to and controlled by the computer?

    (a) Power　　(b) On Line

    (c) Line Feed　　(d) Form Feed

20. Which of the following should you NOT do to a floppy disk?

    (a) Keep it in its sleeve when not in use.　　(b) Keep it away from extreme heat.

    (c) Keep it near a magnet when not in use.　　(d) Keep it dry.

Fill-In

1. An _______ microcomputer works like a comparable IBM model and can run the same software.

2. At the lowest level, the basic operations of all computers can be summed up as input, _______, and output.

3. The _______ of a computer system is the electronic and mechanical equipment that make it work.

4. A microcomputer's motherboard contains the _______, which is a set of wires and connectors that link the CPU to memory and other computer components.

5. _______ is temporary storage for programs and data, which can be used and then overwritten by other programs and data. _______, on the other hand, is permanent storage encoded at the factory with frequently used programs and data that need never be changed.

6. Most microcomputers can be equipped with two basic types of disk drives: floppy disk drives and _______.

7. The number and size of a monitor's _______ determine its sharpness, or resolution.

8. The ________ is the display adapter that comes built onto the motherboards of high-end IBM Personal System/2 microcomputers.

9. Many microcomputers have an auxiliary input device known as a ________, which is a little box with one or more buttons that is slid across the table top.

10. On an IBM keyboard, the ________ Movement keys include Up Arrow, Down Arrow, Left Arrow, Right Arrow, Home, End, Page Up and Page Down.

11. ________ printers are by far the most popular type of microcomputer printer.

12. ________ is a general term that refers to any single program or group of programs.

13. BASIC, Pascal, C, FORTRAN, COBOL, and Ada are all examples of popular programming ________.

14. ________ software is the software that applies the computer to useful tasks such as helping you create documents, prepare a budget, or maintain a mailing list.

15. ________ packages let you use a computer to create all kinds of graphs, charts, maps, paintings, drawings, diagrams, slide shows, and presentations.

16. Combining the results of word processing and graphics software, ________ software lets you use a computer and laser printer to produce near-typeset quality documents.

17. ________ software combines word processing, spreadsheet, data base management, communications, and graphics applications in a single package.

18. A ________ environment allows you to divide your screen into a number of different boxes and run a separate program in each one.

19. A ________ management package is software that helps you formally plan and control complex undertakings.

20. An ________ system is a computer program that contains a collection of facts and a list of rules for making inferences about those facts.

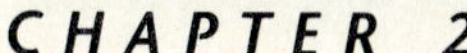

CHAPTER 2

BEGINNING DOS

In This Chapter

DOS Versions

Getting Started

Preview

According to *Business Week,* some 10 million IBM and IBM-compatible micro-computers were being used in businesses around the world by the middle of 1987. Joseph R. (Rod) Canion, president of Compaq Computer Corporation, figures that customers have spent $80 billion on IBM PCs, IBM-compatibles, and the hardware and software that work with them. IBM sold approximately 2.7 million microcomputers in 1988. Compaq, the leading "clone" manufacturer and number 2 business computer maker in the United States, sold around 500,000 that same year. The number 3 business computer manufacturer is Apple, which makes machines that are not IBM-compatible unless they are fitted with special equipment. Frederic E. Davis, editor-in-chief of *MacUser* magazine, estimates that IBM and IBM-compatibles outnumber Apple Macintoshes in the marketplace six to one. Clearly, IBM and IBM-compatibles are by far the most popular class of microcomputer. The overwhelming majority of these machines are running DOS.

After the original IBM Personal Computer was unveiled in 1981, DOS quickly became popular in offices, large corporations, and other businesses where IBM has traditionally wielded a great deal of influence. As soon as various hardware manufacturers started selling lower cost IBM-compatible computers, DOS also began popping up in small businesses, organizations, and institutions, as well as in schools, libraries, and homes. Because of this "hardware explosion," many software developers began to write application packages to run under DOS. This attracted even more users, who attracted still more software developers. At the same time, hardware manufacturers began to develop expansion boards and peripheral devices to be used with computers that run DOS. Today, a huge body of application software and a multitude of hardware devices are devoted to DOS microcomputers. Despite more advanced operating systems, such as OS/2 and XENIX, designed for high-end IBM and IBM-compatible machines, DOS is still the most popular microcomputer operating system in the world. In 1988 alone, IBM and Microsoft shipped 9.8 million copies of DOS, and approximately 75 percent of all microcomputers sold used DOS. This percentage is expected to increase until at least 1991.

After studying this chapter, you will know how to

- start up DOS with the computer turned off.
- start up DOS with the computer turned on.
- obtain a directory of the files on a disk.
- use the special DOS keys.
- change the default disk drive.
- obtain a disk and memory status report.
- clear the display screen.
- format a diskette.
- format a system diskette.
- copy files.
- copy an entire diskette.
- change file names.
- erase files.
- protect a diskette from accidental erasure.
- display on the screen and print text files.
- run an application package.

Insight

Will PC-DOS Be Replaced by Another Operating System?

Watch out, PC-DOS—there are a couple of hounds nipping at your heels.

PC-DOS (or MS-DOS) has been enjoying a fairly safe and secure life as a leader of the operating system pack since the microcomputer population explosion of the 1980s. But time is taking its toll, and the gray hairs are starting to show.

DOS was originally designed to be a single-user, single-tasking operating system, allowing only one program to be run at a time. Today, there are some clever applications packages that seem to let you do two things at once, such as print a file in the background while you're still working with the word processor. DOS doesn't handle this well.

When you want to perform more involved tasks, such as processing a large number of accounting transactions while still working on a spreadsheet, DOS is definitely inadequate. In large business, scientific, and engineering applications, these kinds of tasks are almost required today.

More elaborate *multitasking* operating systems can run several programs at the same time. Actually, they switch back and forth between tasks, giving each program a small slice of time. The switching is so fast that it's not apparent to the user.

People who use their IBM-compatible microcomputers for multitasking have two main choices in operating systems today—UNIX and OS/2. UNIX is a very powerful and flexible operating system that was developed by Bell Laboratories and originally ran on minicomputers. OS/2 was developed jointly by Microsoft and IBM. It is a memory-hungry system that runs only on the more powerful IBM-compatible microcomputers that use the Intel 80286, 80386, and 80486 processors.

UNIX and OS/2 are being groomed as the operating system leaders of the next generation of powerful microcomputers. But it's unlikely that DOS will just slink off into the woods. DOS has a huge, installed base and many devoted users. For many simple computing needs, it will undoubtedly remain on top.

DOS Versions

DOS stands for **Disk Operating System.** It was originally written for IBM by Microsoft, which kept the right to sell DOS under its own name. Today, DOS is developed jointly by both IBM and Microsoft. When it is sold by IBM for IBM microcomputers, it is called PC-DOS or IBM DOS. When it is sold by Microsoft for IBM-compatibles, such as those made by Compaq, Tandy, or Zenith, it is called MS-DOS. Although a few minor differences exist between the system software sold by IBM and Microsoft, from the user's standpoint PC-DOS and MS-DOS are almost identical. So, they are often both referred to generically as DOS.

Computer technology advances quickly. To remain popular, an operating system must be continually upgraded to accommodate new computers and new capabilities for existing models. Several versions of DOS have been released by IBM and Microsoft. In each release, bugs have been worked out and improvements have been made to previous versions. The driving force behind each new version of DOS, however, has been new hardware capabilities, usually related to disk drives.

It is important to know which version of DOS you are using, because some hardware and software can only be used with more recent releases. Fortunately, each new DOS version is **upwardly compatible** with former versions. This means, at least in theory, that every official command that worked with previous versions should work with the new version. In most cases, this is so. However, there always seems to be at least one command that doesn't work quite the same in the new release. Nevertheless, for the most part you probably don't have to change the way you did things before unless you want to take advantage of the added capabilities of a new DOS version.

If you don't need these additional capabilities, you don't have to buy the latest version of DOS each time a new release is issued. As long as the version you have works well with your hardware and software, you can continue using it. Keep in mind that although a new DOS version may add certain capabilities, you must pay for the upgrade and that new DOS versions typically use more memory and more disk space. In many cases, upgrading is simply not worth it. Unless you're buying a new machine or adding a different disk drive, you may not need the latest DOS version.

DOS versions are identified by numbers such as 1.00, 3.30, and 4.01. The number to the left of the decimal point reflects a major classification; the numbers to the right represent more minor differences. The larger the number, the more recent the version. This table summarizes the major DOS versions that have been released so far, along with the primary reason for each upgrade:

Version	Date	Reason for Upgrade (New Capabilities)
1.00	8/81	5¼" 160K single-sided floppy disk drives
1.10	5/82	5¼" 320K double-sided floppy disk drives
2.00	3/83	5¼" 360K floppy, 10M hard disk drives
2.10	10/83	5¼" 360K half-height floppy drives
3.00	8/84	5¼" 1.2M floppy, bigger hard disk drives
3.10	3/85	Network disks and file sharing
3.20	12/85	3½" 720K floppy disk drives
3.30	3/87	3½" 1.44M floppy disk drives
4.00	7/88	Hard disks larger than 35M, DOS Shell
4.01	10/88	Corrected errors in version 4.00

We will be using MS-DOS 4.01 for the examples. Most of what we cover, however, also applies to DOS 2.00 and newer versions. Versions 1.00 and 1.10 are now considered obsolete. If you are using a version of DOS other than 4.01, the screens you see on your computer may be slightly different than the ones shown in this book.

Getting Started

Although DOS is a powerful microcomputer operating system, you can easily learn its most commonly used features. DOS might be set up at your particular computer site in any of several different ways. You are most likely to use DOS in one of the following arrangements:

1. On a microcomputer with two floppy disk drives and DOS installed on one or more diskettes.

2. On a microcomputer with a hard disk drive and DOS installed on the hard disk.

3. On a microcomputer connected to a local area network with DOS installed on the network file server. Some DOS commands do not work over a network, as we will point out.

You may need additional direction from your instructor to run DOS at your computer installation. You should then be able to complete the following lessons. If DOS has not already been installed on your hard disk (with a path to the DOS subdirectory) or on floppy disks for you, see Appendix B.

Lesson 1: Booting DOS

DOS stands for Disk Operating System. Although some low-level parts of the operating system programs are stored in ROM chips, the higher level programs of the operating system are kept on a floppy or hard disk. Like any program, the operating system must be loaded into the computer's memory before it can start working. The operating system, however, is what loads programs into memory and sets up the computer to execute them. If this is so, how does the operating system itself get started? Does it load itself? In a way, yes. Basically, a small program in ROM is automatically invoked every time the computer is turned on or reset. After loading itself into memory, this program then loads the rest of the operating system into memory and begins execution. In a sense, the computer pulls itself up by its own bootstraps. The process of initially loading and executing the operating system is often called **booting up.** In the particular case of IBM and IBM-compatibles, this is also called booting DOS, loading DOS, or simply starting DOS. At this point, your computer should be turned off.

Step 1: Insert the DOS Startup Disk

If your computer has a hard disk, skip this step and go directly to Step 2. If your computer is connected to a local area network, you may have to complete this step. If your computer does not have a hard disk and is not connected to a network, you must insert a diskette containing DOS before you can turn it on. In most cases, this diskette will be labeled "DOS Startup."

If your computer has two or more floppy disk drives, the A drive is the one on top or to the left. This is the floppy disk drive from which you boot DOS.

If drive A accepts 5¼-inch diskettes, grasp the DOS Startup disk by the label and remove it from the paper sleeve. Be careful not to touch the exposed parts around the oval slot and circular hole. Hold the disk with the label side up and the oval slot pointing toward the computer. Slide the diskette all the way into the drive slot, where it may click into place, and close the door or lever (see Figure 1).

If drive A accepts 3½-inch diskettes, grasp the DOS Startup disk with the label up and the metal shield pointing toward the computer. The arrow embossed or printed on the disk should point toward the computer. Slide the diskette all the way into the drive slot, where it will click and drop into place (see Figure 1).

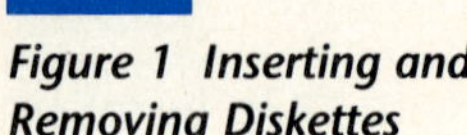

Figure 1 Inserting and Removing Diskettes

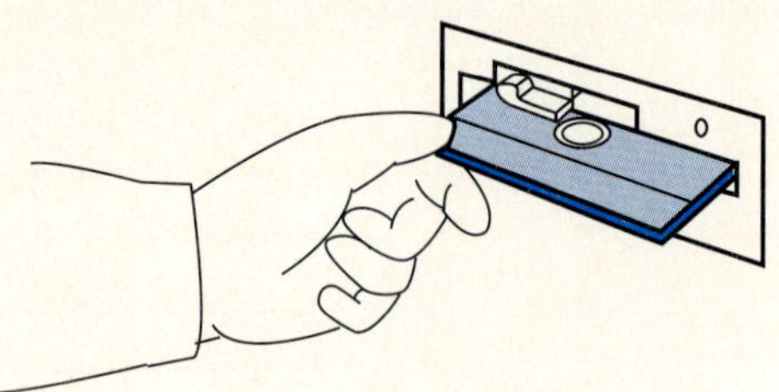

Insert diskette with arrow side up and arrow pointing to diskette drive. Press gently on diskette until it clicks and drops into place.

Remove by pressing eject button on lower right of diskette drive.

Insert diskette into drive until it clicks into place; label must be facing up with write-protect notch on left. Close drive door.

Remove by opening drive door and gently pulling out diskette.

Step 2: Turn On the Computer

If your display has its own power switch, turn it on first. Then turn on the computer. Older IBM microcomputers have a big red toggle switch on the right side of the system unit toward the rear; the newer Personal System/2 models have the switch right up in front (see Figure 2). Some IBM-compatibles have the power switch on the back side of the system unit. Flip the power switch. On many computers you will hear the cooling fan begin to hum.

Step 3: Watch the Display and Wait

After the power has been turned on, the computer completes some self-tests to ensure that it is working properly. One of these tests checks out all of the memory installed in the computer. This test could take several minutes, so don't be alarmed if nothing seems to be happening. After the power-on self-tests are complete, the computer will beep and check drive A to see if it contains the DOS Startup disk. If your computer has a hard disk and no diskette in drive A, it will boot up from the hard disk. Assuming the computer is in working order, the Startup diskette has been inserted correctly (if you need it), and DOS has been correctly installed on the Startup diskette or hard disk, you will see a message on the display screen. The exact contents of this message will depend on the type of computer and the way DOS was installed on the disk. If your computer does not have a built-in battery-maintained clock, DOS may ask you to enter the current date and time.

Step 4: Enter the Date and Time

If you don't see the following message on your screen, skip this step:

```
Current date is Tue 01-01-1980
Enter new date (mm-dd-yy):
```

Type today's date in the form of mm-dd-yy or mm/dd/yy. In other words, type in the month number, a dash or slash, the day of the month, another dash or slash, and the last two digits of the year.

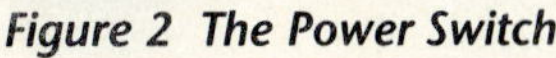

Figure 2 The Power Switch

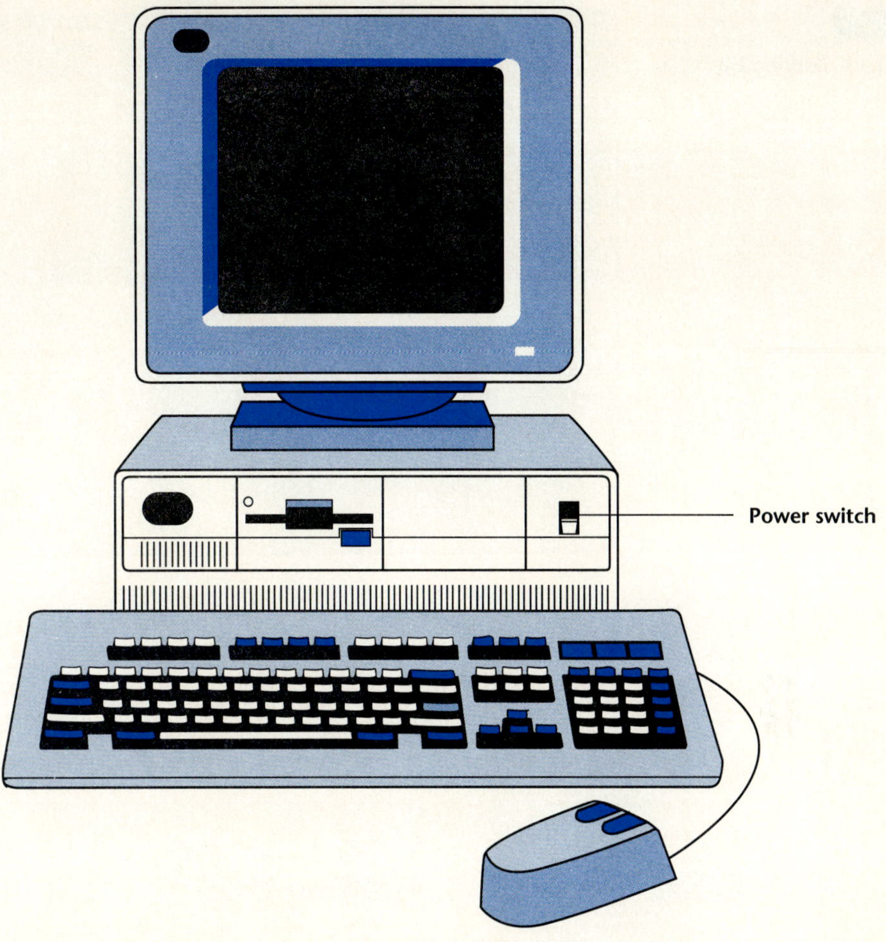

> Press   **Enter**

Next, a message like this may appear:

```
Current time is 12:00:39.05a
Enter new time:
```

Type the hour, a colon, and the minute. If it is afternoon, add twelve to the hour as in the 24-hour clock format. For example, if it is 2 P.M., you would enter 14:00. You can also enter the second and hundredths of a second if you happen to carry a stop watch and feel so inclined. Just the hour and minute are sufficient, however.

> Press   **Enter**

At this point, your screen may look like Figure 3. The C> on the last line is the **DOS prompt.** In this case, it indicates that disk drive C, the hard disk, is the default drive. The **default drive** is the disk drive that DOS assumes you want to use unless you specify otherwise. If you booted up from drive A, then drive A would be your default drive and the DOS prompt would be A>. The prompt tells you that DOS is waiting for a command.

Practice   Turn off the computer. Wait ten seconds. Turn it back on again. If it asks you to enter a new date, just press **Enter** without typing a date. If it asks you to enter

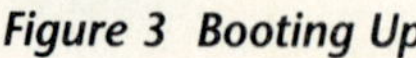

Figure 3 Booting Up

```
Current date is Tue 01-01-1980
Enter new date (mm-dd-yy): 7-10-89
Current time is 12:00:39.05a
Enter new time: 12:42


Microsoft(R) MS-DOS(R) Version 4.01
          (C)Copyright Microsoft Corp 1981-1988

C>_
```

a new time, just press **Enter** without typing a time. You don't have to enter a new date and time, but if your computer doesn't have a battery-maintained clock, it is best to enter the correct date and time when you boot up.

Lesson 2: Rebooting DOS

Occasionally, something goes wrong in a program and the computer may seem to be "stuck." Or after working with a program you may have to "reinitialize," or bring the computer back to the way it was when you first turned it on. You could, of course, just turn off the computer and boot it up as you learned in Lesson 1. There is another way to reboot the computer without shutting it off, however.

Step 1: Press Ctrl-Alt-Del

DOS has a special combination of keypresses that will reboot the computer without having to shut it off first. All you have to do is press the keys marked Control (or Ctrl), Alternate (or Alt), and Delete (or Del), and hold them down at the same time for a moment.

Press   **Ctrl-Alt-Del**

Step 2: Watch the Display and Wait

In most cases, the screen will go blank, the computer will beep, and the disk drive will spin and blink its red access light just as it did when you first turned it on. If all this doesn't happen, a serious program error has probably overwritten a crucial part of DOS in memory, and you will have to turn off the computer and boot it up as you did in Lesson 1. If all is well, DOS will again ask you to supply the date and time if your computer does not have a battery-maintained clock.

Step 3: Enter the Date and Time

If DOS asks you to enter a new date and time, do so as you did in Lesson 1. DOS will once again display its copyright message and the prompt, as shown in Figure 3.

Reboot your computer without turning it off. Enter the correct date and time if asked to do so.

Lesson 3: Listing a Disk File Directory

In most cases, you tell DOS what to do by entering commands or responding to prompts that ask you to supply more information. Some DOS commands are loaded into memory when the computer is booted up and kept there until the power is turned off. These **internal commands,** also called **resident routines,** are kept in memory because they are the most essential or most frequently used parts of the operating system. For example, one of the simplest and most commonly used DOS internal commands is DIR, which displays a file directory. After you boot up, internal commands are always available from any disk. The remaining DOS commands are called **external commands** or **transient routines,** because they are kept in disk storage and temporarily loaded into memory only when they are needed or specifically requested. CHKDSK, for example, is an external DOS command that displays information about a disk and the memory installed in your computer.

Programs, data, and text are kept on disks in files. Every file has a name, size, creation date, and creation time associated with it. The DIR command lets you see what files you have on a particular disk or in a particular subdirectory. A **subdirectory** is a group of files on a disk organized under a single name.

Step 1: Enter DIR

To execute the DIR command:

    Type **dir**
    Press **Enter**

It doesn't matter whether you type DOS commands in lowercase letters, uppercase letters, or a combination of both. For example, DIR, dIr, and Dir are all equivalent.

DIR, which is short for DIRectory, displays information about the files on a disk or in a subdirectory. When the command is entered by itself, it will produce a directory listing on the screen of the default disk or current subdirectory. Figure 4 shows the screen after executing the DIR command. Your screen is probably different because your default disk most likely has different files on it.

Step 2: Examine the Directory Listing

Examine the screen in Figure 4. First it reveals the volume label of the disk. The volume label is just the name of the disk, which in this case is HARD DISK. Next is the volume serial number, which is just a code number assigned to the disk when it is formatted. DOS versions prior to 4.00 do not have volume serial numbers. Then DOS says that this is a directory of the disk in drive C, and it

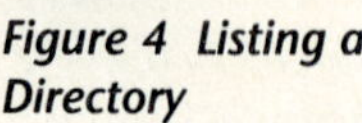

Figure 4 Listing a Directory

```
C>dir

 Volume in drive C is HARD DISK
 Volume Serial Number is 3324-07CC
 Directory of  C:\

CONFIG   SYS        146 07-09-89   1:22p
AUTOEXEC BAT        145 07-09-89   1:22p
COMMAND  COM      37557 12-19-88  12:00a
DOS          <DIR>      07-09-89   1:23p
         4 File(s)   19701760 bytes free

C>_
```

lists the names, sizes, dates, and times of the files. Notice that the first three file names have two parts. We'll have more to say about this file name format shortly. The last file name in the list, DOS, is the name of a subdirectory. The <DIR> designation next to the name tells you that it is a subdirectory and not an ordinary file. This subdirectory, which we'll look at later, contains the files that make up most of DOS. It was created when DOS was installed on the hard disk.

Each file name, except for the DOS subdirectory, has a number to its immediate right. This is the size of that file in bytes. A byte, you'll recall, is basically equivalent to a single character. Finally, listed to the right of each file size is the date and then the time at which the file was created or last changed. The first file in the list, for example, is named CONFIG.SYS, occupies 146 bytes, and was created on July 9, 1989, at 1:22 P.M.

At the bottom of the listing, the DIR command tells you that four files are in this directory and there are 19,701,760 "bytes free." This means that 19,701,760 bytes of storage are still unused on the disk. Since it's important to know what files are on a disk and how much room is left, DIR is one of the most frequently used DOS commands.

Step 3: Examine Another Disk's Directory

The DIR command can also be used to list the directory of a disk in a drive other than the current default drive. You can do this by specifying the disk drive letter after DIR. For example, if your computer has a hard disk, you can examine the directory of a disk in floppy drive A. If you have a diskette with files on it, insert the diskette into drive A.

Type   **dir a:**
Press **Enter**

The **a:** is the designation for the A disk drive. If you have a computer with two floppy drives, you can examine a disk in the second drive by entering DIR B:. Note that the hard disk is usually referred to as the C drive, regardless of whether a B floppy drive is installed.

Step 4: Examine the Contents of a Subdirectory

The DIR command can also be used to list the files in a subdirectory. All you have to do is type the name of the subdirectory after the DIR. For example, if your computer has a hard disk with a subdirectory named DOS, try the following command:

Type   **dir dos**
Press   **Enter**

Figure 5 shows the result. Since 68 files are in this directory listing but only 25 lines can be shown on the screen, many of the names have moved up and disappeared off the top of the screen. Figure 5, therefore, shows only the bottom part of the listing. For the rest of this chapter, we will assume you have a computer with a hard disk that has a DOS subdirectory.

Step 5: Look For a Specific File

Frequently, you'd like to be able to check if a particular file is on a disk or in a subdirectory without having to look at the entire directory listing. The DIR command can do this for you if you give it the name of the file you're looking for. All you have to do is enter the name of the file after the DIR. If you want to look in a subdirectory, type the subdirectory name, a backward slash (\), and then the name of the file. DOS will either list an abbreviated directory with only that file in it or tell you the file is not there. For example, if your computer has a DOS subdirectory, execute this command:

Type   **dir dos\format.com**
Press   **Enter**

This command tells DOS to look in the DOS subdirectory for a file named FOR-MAT.COM. Figure 6 shows the result. If your computer doesn't have a DOS subdirectory, try this command instead:

Type   **dir format.com**
Press   **Enter**

Figure 5 Looking at a Subdirectory

```
GRAPHICS COM     16693 10-06-88   12:00a
GRAPHICS PRO      9397 10-06-88   12:00a
HIMEM    SYS      6261 10-06-88   12:00a
MODE     COM     22968 10-06-88   12:00a
NLSFUNC  EXE      6878 10-06-88   12:00a
PRINTER  SYS     18914 10-06-88   12:00a
RECOVER  COM     10588 10-06-88   12:00a
4201     CPI      6404 10-06-88   12:00a
4208     CPI       720 10-06-88   12:00a
5202     CPI       370 10-06-88   12:00a
README   TXT     14148 10-12-88    9:13p
BACKUP   COM     36880 10-06-88   12:00a
EGA      CPI     49068 10-06-88   12:00a
LCD      CPI     10703 10-06-88   12:00a
RESTORE  COM     36946 10-06-88   12:00a
PCIBMDRV MOS       263 10-06-88   12:00a
SHELL    CLR      4406 10-06-88   12:00a
SHELL    HLP     66527 10-06-88   12:00a
SHELL    MEU      4588 10-06-88   12:00a
SHELLB   COM      3894 10-06-88   12:00a
SHELLC   EXE    153855 10-06-88   12:00a
DOSUTIL  MEU      6660 10-06-88   12:00a
       68 File(s)    19701760 bytes free

C>_
```

Figure 6 Looking for a Specific File

```
C>dir dos\format.com

 Volume in drive C is HARD DISK
 Volume Serial Number is 3324-07CC
 Directory of  C:\DOS

FORMAT   COM     22859 10-06-88  12:00a
        1 File(s)   19701760 bytes free

C>_
```

For the rest of this chapter, we will assume you have a DOS subdirectory on your default disk. If you do not, omit the dos or dos\ designations from the instructions given.

DOS File Names   This is a good time to digress a bit and discuss DOS file names in more detail. First of all, notice that each file in the directory you listed has a unique name. No two files in the same directory can have the same name because DOS wouldn't be able to tell them apart. Two files on different disks or in different subdirectories, however, can have the same name. A file name can consist of two parts: a primary filename and an optional extension. The first part, or **filename** as IBM calls it, can be from one to eight characters long. It can include any of the characters you see on the keyboard except for the following, which are considered invalid in filenames:

. " / \ [ ] : | < > + = ; ,

The second part, an optional short name, is called an **extension.** It is separated from the primary filename by a period and has from one to three characters in it. These characters also can be any of the keyboard characters except those we just listed. If a file's name does have an extension, you may have to use both parts when telling DOS to do something with that file. Extensions are most often used to classify files. For example, here are some of the more common file name extensions, along with the types of files they usually designate:

COM	DOS external command or an executable program
EXE	DOS external command or an executable program
BAT	Batch file
SYS	System setup file
ASM	Assembly language program
BAS	BASIC language program
PAS	Pascal language program
TXT	Text file
BAK	Backup copy of some other file
DOC	Document file of some word processing programs
WKS	Worksheet file of some spreadsheet programs
DBF	Data base file of some data base managers

Finally, a file name can be prefaced with the designation of its disk drive and subdirectory. For example, C:\DOS\FORMAT.COM is the full specification for the file FORMAT.COM on the hard disk C in the DOS subdirectory. Note that the colon must be used after the disk drive letter and the backslash must be used before and after the subdirectory name. If you don't enter part of the specification, such as the disk drive letter or subdirectory, DOS will assume you mean the default drive or current subdirectory.

Step 6: Look for a Specific Group of Files

Not only can the DIR command find a single file on a disk, it can also be used to list a group of files if their names have some characters in common. The DOS **global file name characters,** * and ?, can be included in a filename or extension to give you greater flexibility in designating DOS files. The * character can be used in a file specification to symbolize any character or group of characters. For example, *.SYS means "any file with an extension of SYS." The ? character is used to symbolize any single character. For example, MO?E.COM means "any file that has an extension of COM and a four-letter filename beginning with MO and ending with an E." Both global file name characters can be used together in the same specification, too. For example, ????.* means "any file with at most four characters in its first part." Try each of the following commands:

Type   **dir dos*.sys**
Press   **Enter**
Type   **dir dos\mo?e.com**
Press   **Enter**
Type   **dir dos\????.***
Press   **Enter**

Figure 7 shows what you should see on your screen after entering the command DIR DOS*.SYS.

Figure 7 Looking for a Group of Files

```
C>dir dos\*.sys

 Volume in drive C is HARD DISK
 Volume Serial Number is 3324-07CC
 Directory of  C:\DOS

COUNTRY  SYS     12806 10-06-88  12:00a
DISPLAY  SYS     15692 10-06-88  12:00a
KEYBOARD SYS     23328 10-06-88  12:00a
EMM386   SYS     87776 10-06-88  12:00a
RAMDRIVE SYS      8235 10-06-88  12:00a
SMARTDRV SYS     10224 10-06-88  12:00a
XMA2EMS  SYS     29211 10-06-88  12:00a
ANSI     SYS      9105 10-06-88  12:00a
DRIVER   SYS      5241 10-06-88  12:00a
HIMEM    SYS      6261 10-06-88  12:00a
PRINTER  SYS     18914 10-06-88  12:00a
       11 File(s)   19701760 bytes free

C>_
```

1. List a directory of your default disk drive.

2. List a directory of the DOS subdirectory.

3. Try this command:

   Type **dir *.***
   Press **Enter**

   What does it do?

4. Try this command:

   Type **dir dos*.exe**
   Press **Enter**

   What does it do?

5. Create a listing of the DOS subdirectory that shows only those files that begin with the letter S.

6. Create a listing of the DOS subdirectory that shows only those files with primary filenames less than four characters long.

7. Notice that subdirectory names have no extensions. Try this command (follow the asterisk with a period):

   Type **dir *.**
   Press **Enter**

   What does it do?

Lesson 4: Using Special DOS Keys

Like most software, DOS assigns special meanings to certain keys and combinations of keypresses. You've already learned some of these. For example, you know that you must press the Enter key after typing in a command. This tells DOS to go ahead and process that command. The Backspace key can be used to correct typing errors on a line before the Enter key has been pressed. In Lesson 2 you learned that pressing the Control (Ctrl), Alternate (Alt), and Delete (Del) keys at the same time will reboot DOS without having to shut off the power and turn it back on. Let's explore some of the other keys DOS uses (see Figure 8).

Step 1: Press the Escape Key to Cancel a Line

As you've probably already discovered, it's pretty easy to make typing mistakes when using a keyboard. If the command you're typing is short and you haven't pressed the Enter key yet, the easiest way to fix a mistake is to backspace over it and retype it. If the command is long or if you really messed it up, you can cancel the entire line and start over. To do this, press the Escape (Esc) key. For example, type the following line at the DOS prompt (but don't press the Enter key):

   Type **This line is really messed up!**

Suppose what you really meant to type in was DIR DOS, and you realized your mistake before you pressed the Enter key.

   Press **Escape**

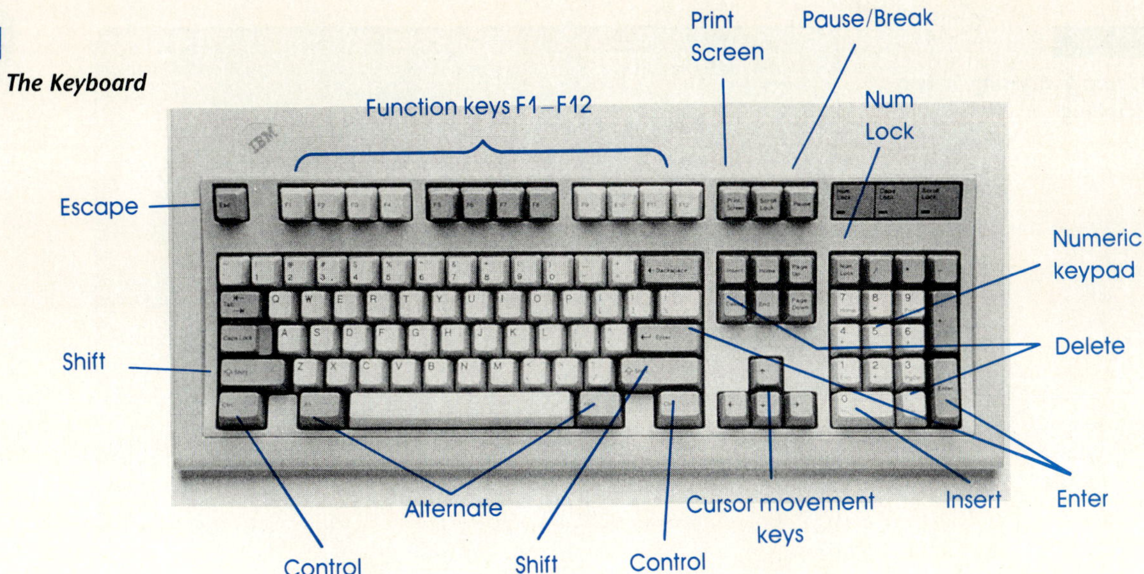

Figure 8 The Keyboard

Pressing the Escape key cancels the current line. When you do this, DOS will display a / (slash) to signal that the line has been canceled, and it will skip down to the next line so you can start over. Now execute the following command to see the familiar DOS directory:

Type **dir dos**
Press **Enter**

Step 2: Press Ctrl-Num Lock to Pause Screen Scrolling

As you watch the DOS directory scroll by on the screen, the first part of it disappears off the top. Sometimes, information scrolls by before you get a chance to read it all. It would be nice if you could temporarily stop the screen so that you wouldn't have to take speed-reading lessons to use the computer. Fortunately, DOS will pause for you if you hold down the Control key and press the Num Lock key. On the newer IBM Enhanced-style keyboards, you press the Pause key instead of Ctrl-Num Lock. In either case, this action will immediately pause any screen that is scrolling by. To resume scrolling, press any key (except a Shift, Lock, Ctrl, or Alt key). For example, execute the following commands:

Type **dir dos**
Press **Enter**
Press **Ctrl-Num Lock** (or **Pause**)

Figure 9 shows what can happen. You can pause and resume scrolling as many times as you wish.

Step 3: Press Ctrl-Break to Cancel a Command

Suppose that you've entered DIR DOS or DIR by mistake and you don't want to wait for the whole directory to scroll by on the screen. Or perhaps you've seen enough and you just want to stop it. You can cancel a DOS command by pressing

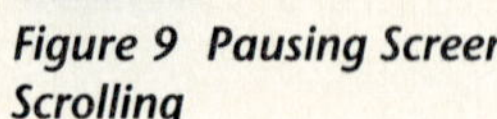

Figure 9 Pausing Screen Scrolling

```
C>dir dos

 Volume in drive C is HARD DISK
 Volume Serial Number is 3324-07CC
 Directory of  C:\DOS

 .            <DIR>      07-09-89   1:23p
 ..           <DIR>      07-09-89   1:23p
 DOSSHELL BAT      196 07-09-89   1:22p
 COMMAND  COM    37557 12-19-88  12:00a
 COUNTRY  SYS    12806 10-06-88  12:00a
 DISKCOPY COM    10396 10-06-88  12:00a
 DISPLAY  SYS    15692 10-06-88  12:00a
 FDISK    EXE    60935 12-19-88  12:00a
 FORMAT   COM    22859 10-06-88  12:00a
 KEYB     COM    14727 10-06-88  12:00a
 KEYBOARD SYS    23328 10-06-88  12:00a
 REPLACE  EXE    19415 10-06-88  12:00a
 SYS      COM    11456 10-06-88
```

the Control and Break keys at the same time. This stops a command from finishing its job. In many cases, Ctrl-Break will also terminate programs other than just DOS commands. To see how this works, follow these directions:

Type   **dir dos**
Press   **Enter**
Press   **Ctrl-Break**

Pressing Ctrl-Break will terminate the directory command before it finishes. Figure 10 shows how this might appear on your screen. The ^C at the bottom stands for Ctrl-C, which means that the command has been canceled.

On IBM PC- and AT-style keyboards, the Break key is right next to the Num Lock key, and is also labeled Scroll Lock. On the newer IBM Enhanced-style keyboards, the Break key is the same as the Pause key. On all types of keyboards, you can also cancel a command by holding down the Control key and typing a C. Note that Ctrl-Break (or Ctrl-C) is different from the Escape key. Escape will cancel a line typed at the DOS prompt before the Enter key is pressed. Ctrl-Break cancels a command after the Enter key has been pressed and while the command is executing.

Step 4: Press Shift-PrtSc to Print the Screen

Frequently there is a sequence of commands or some information on the screen that you would like to save. If you have a printer connected to your computer, DOS can produce a hard copy of everything that is currently on the display screen. On IBM PC- and AT-style keyboards, you press one of the Shift keys along with the key marked PrtSc (Print Screen). On the newer IBM Enhanced-style keyboards, you simply press the key labeled Print Screen. If you have a printer, make sure it's turned on.

Press   **Shift-PrtSc (or Print Screen)**

You should get a copy of what's on your screen right now.

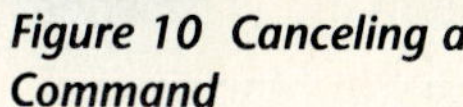

Figure 10 Canceling a Command

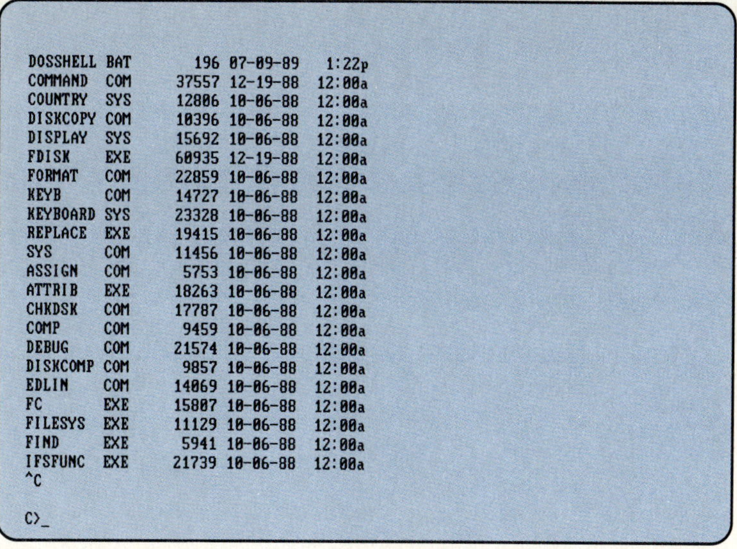

Step 5: Press Ctrl-PrtSc to Echo to the Printer

The printout you got from the previous step contains only one screen of text. This output would not help much if you wanted a hard copy of the entire DOS directory, because the whole directory doesn't fit on the screen at once. Pressing Control and PrtSc (or Control and Print Screen on the Enhanced-style keyboards), however, will cause whatever you type and the computer's responses to be displayed both on the screen and sent to the printer. This echoing will continue until you press Ctrl-PrtSc again. So, you could, for example, get a hard copy of your entire computer session.

To get a hard copy of the DOS disk directory, follow these directions:

Press   **Ctrl-PrtSc**
Type   **dir**
Press   **Enter**

You should see the directory information being displayed on the screen a bit slower as it is also being sent to the printer. When it's finished and you see the DOS prompt, execute this command again to turn off printer echoing:

Press   **Ctrl-PrtSc**

Practice

1. Create a hard copy listing of this Practice session if you have a printer.

   Press   **Ctrl-PrtSc (or Ctrl-Print Screen)**

2. Start typing a command, but don't press the Enter key:

   Type   **dir a:**

   Suppose you meant to type just **dir**, but made a mistake. Cancel the command:

   Press   **Escape**

   Now execute the command you meant to enter:

   Type   **dir**
   Press   **Enter**

3. Generate a directory listing of your DOS subdirectory or Startup disk. Pause and restart the screen scrolling at least twice before the command is finished.

4. Again, generate a directory listing of your DOS subdirectory or Startup disk. This time, however, cancel the command before it finishes by using Ctrl-Break or Ctrl-C.

5. Turn off printer echoing.

6. If you have a printer, make sure it is turned on.

Type **dir**
Press **Enter**

Create a hard-copy listing of just the current contents of your screen.

Lesson 5: Changing the Default Disk Drive

IBM and IBM-compatible computers without hard disks boot up from the diskette in drive A, which is the default disk drive. Computers that have a hard disk with DOS installed on it boot up from drive C, which is considered the default drive. You will recall that the current default drive is indicated by the DOS prompt, for example, A> or C>. This means that whenever you enter a command that doesn't explicitly specify a particular disk drive, the current default drive is assumed. For example, when you enter DIR by itself, you get the directory of the current default drive. If your computer has more than one disk drive, like most IBM and IBM-compatible computers, you may occasionally want to change your default drive from A or C to another installed drive. This is a common procedure, sometimes called **switching drives.** Let's look at how and why you would change the default disk drive.

Step 1: Enter the Designation of the New Default Drive

If you have a computer with a hard disk and one floppy drive, put a disk with files on it into drive A. Then execute this command to change your default drive from C to A:

Type **a:**
Press **Enter**

If you have a computer with two floppy disk drives, put a disk with files on it into drive B. Then execute this command to change your default drive to B:

Type **b:**
Press **Enter**

DOS will respond with a prompt indicating the new default drive.

Step 2: Use the New Default Drive

Now when you execute a command, DOS will assume you are referring to the new default drive unless you specify otherwise. For example, try this command:

Type **dir**
Press **Enter**

You will get a directory listing of the new default drive, A or B (see Figure 11). Although this might not seem terribly exciting at the moment, being able to

Figure 11 Changing the Default Disk Drive

```
A>dir

 Volume in drive A has no label
 Volume Serial Number is 0E1E-1BE0
 Directory of  A:\

COMMAND  COM    37557 12-19-88  12:00a
AUTOEXEC BAT       39 10-06-88  12:00a
CONFIG   SYS       96 10-06-88  12:00a
COUNTRY  SYS    12806 10-06-88  12:00a
DISKCOPY COM    10396 10-06-88  12:00a
DISPLAY  SYS    15692 10-06-88  12:00a
FDISK    EXE    60935 12-19-88  12:00a
FORMAT   COM    22859 10-06-88  12:00a
KEYB     COM    14727 10-06-88  12:00a
KEYBOARD SYS    23328 10-06-88  12:00a
REPLACE  EXE    19415 10-06-88  12:00a
SELECT   COM     3642 10-06-88  12:00a
SELECT   HLP    28695 10-06-88  12:00a
SELECT   PRT     1329 10-06-88  12:00a
SYS      COM    11456 10-06-88  12:00a
        15 File(s)      18432 bytes free

A>_
```

change the default drive enables you to make full use of all of your installed disk drives. As you become more proficient with DOS and application packages, you'll find yourself switching disk drives often. For example, on systems with two floppy drives, you may leave the DOS Startup disk in drive A and a disk containing a particular application package in drive B. Then, after booting up, you could switch to drive B to run your application program.

Step 3: Switch Back to the Original Default Disk Drive

If your computer has a hard disk, execute this command to switch back to it:

    Type   **c:**
    Press   **Enter**

If your computer has no hard disk, execute this command to make A your default drive:

    Type   **a:**
    Press   **Enter**

Practice

1. If your computer has a hard disk, put a diskette with files on it in drive A. If your computer has no hard disk, put a diskette with files on it in drive B. Change your default disk drive to A or B. Use the DIR command to generate a directory listing. Now switch back to your original drive.

2. Try switching to a disk drive that doesn't exist, such as Z. What happens?

3. Try switching to your current drive. For example, if C is your default drive, do this:

    Type   **c:**
    Press   **Enter**

    What happens?

Lesson 6: Checking Disk and Memory Status

You've already learned how one DOS command, DIR, can be used to list information about the files on a disk or in a subdirectory. Another DOS command, CHKDSK, can be used to display further information about a disk and the memory installed in your computer. CHKDSK is an external command, which means that it is kept in a separate file named CHKDSK.COM in the DOS subdirectory on a hard disk. External commands are available only when they are located on your default disk or in your current subdirectory, or when a path has been set up to the subdirectory that contains them. You will learn about paths in the next chapter. If DOS has been installed correctly on your hard disk, a path should already be set up to the DOS subdirectory so that the DOS external commands are always available. Note: the CHKDSK command does not operate when DOS is running on a local area network.

Step 1: Enter CHKDSK

To check the disk in your default drive, execute this command:

> Type   **chkdsk**
> Press   **Enter**

Your screen should look like Figure 12, although the numbers probably will be different.

Step 2: Examine the Status Report

The CHKDSK status report supplies several useful items of information. First, it tells you that the total capacity of the hard disk is 21,204,992 bytes (a little more than 20 megabytes). This is roughly equivalent to about 6,575 pages of single-spaced typewritten text. **Hidden files** are special files used by DOS and some other programs. They're hidden because they do not appear in the disk directory so that you won't rename, change, or delete them. Next the CHKDSK command tells you how many subdirectories and ordinary user files are on the disk and how much space they occupy. It will also say whether any bytes on the disk are in "bad sectors," although there aren't any on the disk shown in Figure 12. Bad sectors occur when some of the disk is unusable due to manufacturing flaws—a fairly common occurrence with hard disks. The unusable areas are discovered when the disk is formatted and are marked so that DOS won't use them. The disk shown in Figure 12 has 19,701,760 bytes of empty space.

The CHKDSK command also reveals information about **allocation units,** which relate to how DOS assigns disk space to files. This is technical information that most users don't really need to know. Finally, CHKDSK reports that this particular computer has 655,360 bytes (or 640K) of RAM installed, of which 521,248 bytes are free to be used by application programs. The difference between these two figures, 134,112 bytes, is the amount of RAM taken up by the parts of DOS that remain in memory, such as the internal commands, and any memory-resident programs that have been loaded.

Practice   Like many DOS commands, CHKDSK can be used on a disk other than the default disk. Put a diskette with files on it into drive A. Then execute this command:

> Type   **chkdsk a:**
> Press   **Enter**

Figure 12 The CHKDSK Report

```
C>chkdsk

Volume HARD DISK    created 01-01-1980 12:28a
Volume Serial Number is 3324-07CC

 21204992 bytes total disk space
    73728 bytes in 3 hidden files
     4096 bytes in 1 directories
  1425408 bytes in 69 user files
 19701760 bytes available on disk

     2048 bytes in each allocation unit
    10354 total allocation units on disk
     9620 available allocation units on disk

   655360 total bytes memory
   521248 bytes free

C>_
```

Lesson 7: Clearing the Screen

By now, you've probably accumulated quite a collection of commands and directory listings on your screen. Although this does no harm, it can be a bit distracting. Or, perhaps you want to type a sequence of commands and then do a print screen, and you would like to start off with a clean slate. It's easy to tell DOS to clear the screen with an internal command called CLS.

Step 1: Enter CLS

To clear the screen, execute the clear screen command:

> Type   **cls**
> Press **Enter**

DOS will erase everything from the screen and start you off again with the system prompt on the first line in the upper left corner.

Use the DIR command to generate a directory listing of your default disk drive. Now clear the screen.

Lesson 8: Formatting a Diskette

Every new disk must undergo an initial preparation known as formatting before it can be used to store programs and data files. Many manufacturers and retailers format the hard disks that are installed in the computers they sell. This initialization for diskettes, however, is not commonly done at the factory, so generally you must format each new floppy you're going to use with your own computer. You also can reformat a previously formatted disk to completely erase all the files that are stored on it. But you should be very careful whenever you format a previously used disk. Make sure that it doesn't hold any files that you want to save. Basically, DOS performs the following procedures when you format a disk:

- Checks the disk for bad or damaged spots that cannot reliably store data and marks these as unusable
- Completely erases any programs and data that might be on the disk
- Builds a directory to hold information about the files that eventually will be stored on the disk
- Marks off the empty space on the disk into equal-sized portions called **sectors**
- Creates a DOS startup disk if instructed to do so

The DOS FORMAT command, which is an external command, performs all of these functions. Note: the FORMAT command does not operate when running DOS on a local area network. This is a safety precaution to prevent users from reformatting shared hard disks.

Step 1: Get a Floppy Disk to Format

The most common and simplest use of the FORMAT command is to set up diskettes that will not be used to boot up the computer. Since the operating system is not installed on these diskettes, they can devote all of their space to holding programs and data files. For this lesson you'll need a new floppy disk or a previously used disk that can be completely erased. If you are going to format a diskette that's not new, double-check to make sure it doesn't have any programs or data files on it that you want to keep. Formatting a disk erases everything on it.

Step 2: Enter the FORMAT Command

To format a diskette in the A drive, execute the following command:

```
Type   format a:
Press  Enter
```

Step 3: Insert the Disk to Be Formatted

The FORMAT command will then tell you to insert the new diskette into drive A. Insert the disk as indicated, and then press the Enter key.

```
Press  Enter
```

Step 4: Enter a Volume Label

The procedure takes about a minute for a 5¼-inch double-sided, double-density diskette, during which time DOS displays a percentage that shows how much it has formatted so far. When it is finished, the FORMAT command will prompt you to enter a volume label, or name, for the newly formatted disk. (Older versions of DOS don't automatically ask you to do this.) You can choose any name you like, but it must be no longer than eleven characters. If you don't want to enter a name, you can just press the Enter key. Name your disk like this:

```
Type   my disk
Press  Enter
```

Step 5: Examine the Screen

After you enter a volume label, FORMAT will tell you how much room is on the disk and whether it contains any bad sectors (see Figure 13). If the diskette has no bad sectors and DOS has not been installed on it, these two numbers will be the same: 362,496 bytes for a 5¼-inch double-sided, double-density diskette. The FORMAT command also displays information about the disk's allocation units and reports the volume serial number.

Step 6: Terminate the FORMAT Command

Finally, the FORMAT command asks you if you want to format another diskette. You can answer "no" like this:

> Type   **n**
> Press   **Enter**

You'll then get the DOS prompt back again, as shown in Figure 13.

Format another blank diskette or reformat the disk you have just formatted. This time, however, press **Enter** without typing a volume label.

Lesson 9: Formatting a System Diskette

The diskette you formatted in Lesson 8 can be used to store programs and data files. It cannot, however, be used to boot up the computer, because it doesn't have DOS installed on it. If you want to format a DOS startup diskette that can be used to boot up your computer from drive A, you must follow a slightly different procedure.

*Figure 13 Formatting a
Diskette*

```
C>format a:
Insert new diskette for drive A:
and press ENTER when ready...

Format complete

Volume label (11 characters, ENTER for none)? my disk

    362496 bytes total disk space
    362496 bytes available on disk

      1024 bytes in each allocation unit
       354 allocation units available on disk

Volume Serial Number is 354B-0BD4

Format another (Y/N)?n
C>_
```

Step 1: Use the /S Parameter

A **parameter** is a specification that designates an alternate action for a command. Many DOS commands can be given one or more parameters to specify a slightly different way of performing their tasks. The FORMAT command, for example, can be instructed to install the operating system on the disk it's preparing. To do this, you add the /S parameter after the specification of the disk to be formatted. The /S tells FORMAT to put the DOS internal commands and the command processor on the disk being formatted. You can try this out by reformatting the disk you formatted in Lesson 8. To prepare a DOS startup disk, execute this command:

Type   `format a:/s`
Press   **Enter**

Step 2: Insert the Disk to Be Formatted

The FORMAT command will then tell you to insert the new diskette into drive A. Insert the disk you formatted in Lesson 8 into drive A and then press the Enter key.

Press   **Enter**

Step 3: Enter a Volume Label

When the formatting procedure is complete, the FORMAT command will report that the system has been transferred to the disk. It will then prompt you to enter a volume label for the disk. Name your disk like this:

Type   `startup`
Press   **Enter**

Step 4: Examine the Screen

After you enter a volume label, FORMAT will tell you how much room is on the disk, whether the disk contains any bad sectors, and how much space is being used by DOS. Figure 14 shows a 5¼-inch double-sided, double-density diskette with MS-DOS 4.01 installed on it. The disk holds 362,496 bytes, DOS takes up 109,568 bytes, and 252,928 bytes of empty space are available. The FORMAT command also displays information about the disk's allocation units and reports the volume serial number.

Step 5: Terminate the FORMAT Command

Finally, the FORMAT command asks you if you want to format another diskette. You can answer "no" like this:

Type   **n**
Press   **Enter**

You'll then get the DOS prompt back again.

Step 6: Examine the Disk's Directory

Now, let's look at the directory of the disk you just formatted. Execute this command:

Figure 14 Formatting a System Diskette

```
C>format a:/s
Insert new diskette for drive A:
and press ENTER when ready...

Format complete
System transferred

Volume label (11 characters, ENTER for none)? startup

    362496 bytes total disk space
    109568 bytes used by system
    252928 bytes available on disk

      1024 bytes in each allocation unit
       247 allocation units available on disk

Volume Serial Number is 0308-07D1

Format another (Y/N)?n
C>_
```

Type   **dir a:**
Press   **Enter**

Your screen should look like Figure 15. Notice that only the file COM-MAND.COM is on the new system disk. It does not contain any of the external command files that are on the DOS disk. So, although you could boot up with this new disk and you could execute internal commands such as DIR, you could not use any external commands such as CHKDSK or FORMAT unless you copied their command files onto it.

Hard Disks   The FORMAT command also works for hard disks. Once a hard disk is initially formatted, however, it may seldom, if ever, be formatted again. Since computers with hard disks often have many important and sometimes irreplaceable files on them, you should be extremely cautious with them. Don't

Figure 15 Directory of the New System Diskette

```
C>dir a:

Volume in drive A is STARTUP
Volume Serial Number is 0308-07D1
Directory of  A:\

COMMAND  COM      37557 12-19-88  12:00a
        1 File(s)      252928 bytes free

C>_
```

attempt to format a hard disk unless you know exactly what you're doing and you're sure that all files on the hard disk have backup copies on other disks. As we said, many computers now come with their hard disks already formatted by the manufacturer or retailer.

Practice

1. Try booting up from your new system diskette. Make sure the newly formatted diskette is in drive A. If the drive has a door or lever, make sure it is closed.

   Press   **Ctrl-Alt-Del**

   Skip entering the date and time:

   Press   **Enter**
   Press   **Enter**

2. Use DIR to list a directory of your default disk, which should be the new system diskette in drive A. As you can see, internal commands like DIR always work after you boot up because they are kept in a hidden DOS file and automatically loaded into memory, where they remain.

3. Use CHKDSK to try to get a status report of your default disk. DOS will say "Bad command or file name." CHKDSK does not work on your new system disk because it is an external command, stored in its own file named CHKDSK.COM, and it has not been copied to the new disk. Similarly, FORMAT will not work from your new system disk either unless its file is copied to the disk first.

4. Remove the new system diskette from drive A. If your computer does not have a hard disk, put the original DOS Startup diskette back into drive A. Reboot your computer:

   Press   **Ctrl-Alt-Del**

   Enter the correct date and time if necessary.

Lesson 10: Copying Files

One of the reasons computers are so useful is that they make it simple to copy programs and data. Once information is entered into a computer, any number of copies usually can be made very easily and quickly. An important function of any operating system is duplicating files. DOS provides several methods of copying files. One of the most popular DOS commands is COPY, which reproduces one or more individual files.

Step 1: Copy a Single File (the Long Way)

Once a diskette has been formatted, it can be used to store program and data files. Let's use the COPY command to copy a single file from the DOS subdirectory onto your newly formatted diskette. First, we'll do it the longhand way, and then we'll show you a shortcut. To copy the file FORMAT.COM from the DOS subdirectory onto your formatted diskette, make sure the diskette is in drive A. Then execute this command:

   Type   **copy c:\dos\format.com a:format.com**
   Press   **Enter**

The first file specification after the COPY command is the **source,** or what you're copying from—the file FORMAT.COM on the hard disk C in the DOS subdirectory. The second file specification is the **target,** or what you're copying to—a file named FORMAT.COM on the diskette in drive A. The source and the target can have the same name because they are on separate disks. After you execute the COPY command, DOS will tell you that one file was copied. Now execute this command to see the contents of the diskette:

> Type　**dir a:**
> Press　**Enter**

You should see the file FORMAT.COM in the directory of the diskette in drive A, as shown in Figure 16.

Step 2: Copy a Single File (the Short Way)

In most cases, if you omit certain information from a command, DOS will make an assumption about what you mean. For example, if you don't supply a disk drive or subdirectory designation in front of a file name, DOS will assume that you mean the default drive and current directory. Similarly, if you don't specify a name for the target file, the COPY command will assume that it is to use the same name as the source. This assumption will work as long as the source and the target files are on different disks or in different subdirectories. Now try this shorter command to copy FORMAT.COM to the diskette:

> Type　**copy dos\format.com a:**
> Press　**Enter**

This command tells DOS to copy the file FORMAT.COM on the default disk in the DOS subdirectory to the diskette in drive A and give it the same name.

Note that you have just copied the FORMAT.COM in the DOS subdirectory to the FORMAT.COM that already existed on the diskette in drive A from the copy operation performed in Step 1. If you choose a name that already exists on the target, DOS will simply copy over it, destroying whatever was in that file

Figure 16　Copying a File

```
C>copy c:\dos\format.com a:format.com
        1 File(s) copied

C>dir a:

 Volume in drive A is STARTUP
 Volume Serial Number is 0308-07D1
 Directory of  A:\

COMMAND  COM     37557 12-19-88  12:00a
FORMAT   COM     22859 10-06-88  12:00a
        2 File(s)     229376 bytes free

C>_
```

before. Since you copied the same file, there's no problem here. As a rule, however, you should be very careful about the name you choose for a target file. If it already exists on the disk you're copying to, the original version will be overwritten. Make sure you no longer need any file on the target disk or subdirectory with the same name as a copy to be created.

Step 3: Copy a Group of Files

By using the global file name characters * and ? introduced in Lesson 3, you can copy several files at once with a single COPY command. For example, execute this command:

> Type   **copy dos*.com a:**
> Press   **Enter**

This command will try to copy every file in the DOS subdirectory with an extension of COM to the diskette in drive A. If you have only a 360K diskette in drive A, it will probably run out of room, as shown in Figure 17. Nevertheless, DOS will copy as many files as it can to the diskette.

Step 4: Copy a File to the Same Directory

You cannot have two files in the same directory with identical names. The COPY command simply will not allow you to duplicate a file in the same directory unless you provide a different name for the target file. So, the COPY command can reproduce a file on the same disk or in the same subdirectory, but the source and the target must have different names.

A common reason for duplicating a file in the same directory is for backup purposes. Let's say that you're going to change an existing file. If that file is especially important, you might want to keep a copy of the original version before you make any alterations. Then if some problem occurs, you will still have the original version intact. So, before you change a file, it might be a good idea to make a copy of it, but with a slightly different name. For example, suppose you

*Figure 17 Copying a
Group of Files*

```
C>copy dos\*.com a:
DOS\COMMAND.COM
DOS\DISKCOPY.COM
DOS\FORMAT.COM
DOS\KEYB.COM
DOS\SYS.COM
DOS\ASSIGN.COM
DOS\CHKDSK.COM
DOS\COMP.COM
DOS\DEBUG.COM
DOS\DISKCOMP.COM
DOS\EDLIN.COM
DOS\LABEL.COM
DOS\MORE.COM
DOS\TREE.COM
DOS\PRINT.COM
DOS\GRAFTABL.COM
DOS\GRAPHICS.COM
DOS\MODE.COM
DOS\RECOVER.COM
DOS\BACKUP.COM
Insufficient disk space
        19 File(s) copied

C>_
```

wanted to somehow change the file AUTOEXEC.BAT, but wanted to keep a copy of the original. You could make a backup copy of the original version on the same disk if you change its name slightly. For example, execute these commands:

Type   **copy autoexec.bat autoexec.bak**
Press   **Enter**
Type   **dir**
Press   **Enter**

The COPY command creates a copy of the AUTOEXEC.BAT file on the default disk and names it AUTOEXEC.BAK (the BAK is for backup), as shown in Figure 18. Now you could go ahead and safely make modifications to AUTOEXEC.BAT, because you've retained a copy of the original file in AUTOEXEC.BAK.

<table>
<tr><td>Practice</td><td>

1. You can use the COPY command to duplicate every non-hidden file on a disk or in a subdirectory. For example, execute this command:

Type   **copy dos*.* a:**
Press   **Enter**

You will probably quickly run out of room on the diskette in drive A, but this command would work if the target disk were large enough.

2. To see how the COPY command will not allow you to duplicate a file with the same name in the same directory, try this command:

Type   **copy autoexec.bak**
Press   **Enter**

Because you omitted the target file name, DOS assumed you meant the same name as the source. Since two files in the same directory cannot have the same name, DOS aborts the command and displays the error message, "File cannot be copied onto itself."

</td></tr>
</table>

Figure 18 Copying a File to the Same Directory

```
C>copy autoexec.bat autoexec.bak
        1 File(s) copied

C>dir

 Volume in drive C is HARD DISK
 Volume Serial Number is 3324-07CC
 Directory of  C:\

CONFIG   SYS      146 07-09-89   1:22p
AUTOEXEC BAK      256 01-01-80   5:52a
COMMAND  COM    37557 12-19-88  12:00a
DOS          <DIR>     07-09-89   1:23p
AUTOEXEC BAT      256 01-01-80   5:52a
        5 File(s)   19699712 bytes free

C>_
```

3. You should be careful with the COPY command. It is up to you to make sure you are copying the file you want and that the target name is correct. For example, execute this command (be sure you type *.bak* and not *.bat*):

> Type   **copy command.com autoexec.bak**
> Press   **Enter**

DOS will copy the file COMMAND.COM to the file AUTOEXEC.BAK, overwriting the previous contents of AUTOEXEC.BAK. It does not ask you if this is really what you want to do.

Lesson 11: Copying an Entire Diskette

DOS has a more specific copy command that lets you duplicate an entire diskette all at once. The DISKCOPY command formats the target diskette, if necessary, and copies all files, hidden or otherwise, exactly as they are on the original source diskette. DISKCOPY may be used to duplicate only floppy disks, not hard disks. Furthermore, DISKCOPY works only if the source and target are the same type of diskette. For instance, you cannot use the DISKCOPY command to duplicate the contents of a 5¼-inch diskette on a 3½-inch diskette. Fortunately, you can use DISKCOPY even if you have only one floppy drive. To see how the DISKCOPY command works, you can make an exact copy of the formatted system diskette you've been working with. You will need another diskette of the same type, either new and unformatted, or containing files you are sure you no longer need. Note: the DISKCOPY command does not operate when running DOS on a local area network.

Step 1: Execute the DISKCOPY Command

If your computer has two identical floppy disk drives, execute this command:

> Type   **diskcopy a: b:**
> Press   **Enter**

If your computer has only one floppy drive or two drives that are of different types, such as a 5¼-inch drive and a 3½-inch drive, execute this command instead:

> Type   **diskcopy a: a:**
> Press   **Enter**

Step 2: Follow the Directions

The DISKCOPY command will tell you which drive to put your source and target diskettes into and when to do so. Remember: the diskette you want to copy is the source, and the new diskette is the target. If your computer has only one floppy drive, you may have to swap the source and target diskettes in drive A several times, depending on how much memory is installed.

Step 3: Terminate the DISKCOPY Command

When it is finished, DISKCOPY will ask you if you want to copy another diskette. If the answer is no, do this:

> Type   **n**
> Press   **Enter**

If you have only one floppy drive, Figure 19 shows what you should see on your screen when DISKCOPY is finished.

DISKCOPY is a very useful command for making backup copies of important diskettes. In fact, the documentation that comes with many software packages suggests that you use the DISKCOPY command to duplicate all of your original diskettes as soon as you get them. Furthermore, you should put the originals away for safekeeping and only use your copies. Then, if you accidentally erase something or if a diskette you use daily becomes damaged or wears out, you will still have your original diskettes from which to make additional copies. These are good suggestions, and DISKCOPY will work fine as long as your software is not copy-protected.

Practice   Use DISKCOPY to duplicate some other diskette that you have.

Lesson 12: Changing File Names

When you create a file, either using a DOS command such as COPY or from within an application package such as a word processor, you assign it a name. This name need not be permanent, however. DOS lets you change file names very easily. There are several reasons why you might want to change an existing file name. Perhaps you've thought of a more appropriate name or maybe you would like to shorten the name. You may want to copy a file onto a disk that already contains another file with the same name. In this case, you could change the name of the file already on the disk so that its contents will not be overwritten by the file you want to copy. The RENAME command, which is an internal command, lets you change the name of one or more files.

Step 1: Rename a Single File

Changing a single file's name is quite easy. Just type RENAME (or its abbreviation, REN), followed by the file name you want to change and then the new

Figure 19 Copying an Entire Diskette

```
C>diskcopy a: a:

Insert SOURCE diskette in drive A:

Press any key to continue . . .

Copying 40 tracks
9 Sectors/Track, 2 Side(s)

Insert TARGET diskette in drive A:

Press any key to continue . . .

Volume Serial Number is 08E3-3224

Copy another diskette (Y/N)? n

C>
C>_
```

name that file is to have. For example, suppose you want to copy a new version of the file FORMAT.COM to the system diskette you created in Lesson 9, but you want to keep a copy of the original FORMAT.COM. You could rename the original FORMAT.BAK and then copy the new FORMAT.COM to your disk. Make sure your formatted system diskette is in drive A. Then execute these commands:

```
Type   a:
Press  Enter
Type   rename format.com format.bak
Press  Enter
Type   dir format.*
Press  Enter
```

Your screen should look like Figure 20. The directory shows that you've successfully changed the name of FORMAT.COM to FORMAT.BAK.

Before you go on, change FORMAT.BAK back to FORMAT.COM to restore your disk to the way it was. This time, however, try using the abbreviated form of the RENAME command:

```
Type   ren format.bak format.com
Press  Enter
```

Step 2: Rename Several Files at Once

Using the global file name characters * and ?, you can rename several files at once. For example, with a single command you can rename each file on your system diskette with an extension of COM and give it an extension of BAK. Make sure the system diskette you formatted in Lesson 9 is in drive A and that drive A is your default drive. Then execute this command:

```
Type   ren *.com *.bak
Press  Enter
```

Figure 20 Renaming a File

```
C>a:

A>rename format.com format.bak

A>dir format.*

 Volume in drive A is STARTUP
 Volume Serial Number is 0308-07D1
 Directory of  A:\

FORMAT   BAK     22859 10-06-88  12:00a
        1 File(s)      2048 bytes free

A>_
```

Now execute this directory command to see what you've done:

>Type   **dir *.bak**
>Press   **Enter**

Your screen should look something like Figure 21. There are now no files on your disk with COM extensions. They all have BAK extensions instead. Before you go on, change them all back to the way they were with this command:

>Type   **ren *.bak *.com**
>Press   **Enter**

Practice   Change the name of the file AUTOEXEC.BAK, which you created in Lesson 10, to JUNK. Remember, this file is on your hard disk or DOS Startup disk.

Lesson 13: Erasing Files

Just as you accumulate old memos, notes, letters, clippings, and other scraps of paper on your desk, disks also can become cluttered with files that are no longer needed. Occasionally, you may have to clean up a disk and discard unnecessary files. Once you erase a file, however, it may be difficult or even impossible to retrieve its contents. In fact, DOS includes no utility for "unerasing" files, although such programs are sold by some independent software publishers. Before you erase any file, make sure you no longer need it. DOS makes it very easy to erase files, so you should be careful. Many instances of people losing files can be attributed to accidents or carelessness with the DOS ERASE command, also known as DEL. ERASE (or DEL) is an internal command.

Step 1: Erase a Single File

To erase a single file, just type ERASE or DEL (for delete) and follow it with the name of the file you want to erase. Make sure that the system diskette you

Figure 21 Renaming a Group of Files

```
    Volume Serial Number is 0308-07D1
    Directory of  A:\

    COMMAND  BAK     37557 12-19-88  12:00a
    FORMAT   BAK     22859 10-06-88  12:00a
    DISKCOPY BAK     10396 10-06-88  12:00a
    KEYB     BAK     14727 10-06-88  12:00a
    SYS      BAK     11456 10-06-88  12:00a
    ASSIGN   BAK      5753 10-06-88  12:00a
    CHKDSK   BAK     17787 10-06-88  12:00a
    COMP     BAK      9459 10-06-88  12:00a
    DEBUG    BAK     21574 10-06-88  12:00a
    DISKCOMP BAK      9857 10-06-88  12:00a
    EDLIN    BAK     14069 10-06-88  12:00a
    LABEL    BAK      4458 10-06-88  12:00a
    MORE     BAK      2134 10-06-88  12:00a
    TREE     BAK      6302 10-06-88  12:00a
    PRINT    BAK     14131 10-06-88  12:00a
    GRAFTABL BAK     10239 10-06-88  12:00a
    GRAPHICS BAK     16693 10-06-88  12:00a
    MODE     BAK     22960 10-06-88  12:00a
    RECOVER  BAK     10588 10-06-88  12:00a
         19 File(s)      2048 bytes free

    A>_
```

formatted in Lesson 9 is in drive A and that drive A is your default drive. Because you know this diskette holds only copies of DOS files that you have on the hard disk or on the original DOS Startup disk, you can safely erase files from it. Nevertheless, you should always be careful when erasing files. Data and programs are more frequently lost as the result of an accidentally or carelessly entered ERASE command than from any other cause. Suppose you want to erase the file FORMAT.COM from the diskette. Execute this command:

Type   **erase format.com**
Press   **Enter**

Now execute this directory command to see what you've done:

Type   **dir format.com**
Press   **Enter**

The file is now gone, so your screen should look like Figure 22.

Step 2: Erasing Several Files All at Once

By using the global file name characters * and ?, you can tell DOS to erase several files with a single ERASE command. In fact, you can even wipe out every file on a disk. Although this is often done to clear off a disk, it should be used with care. Make sure that the system diskette you formatted in Lesson 9 is in drive A and that drive A is your default drive. Then execute this command:

Type   **erase *.***
Press   **Enter**

Because this is a potentially disastrous command if entered by mistake, DOS will ask if you are sure you want to do this. If you answer yes, DOS will go ahead and erase everything. If you answer no, DOS will immediately cancel the ERASE command. You will get this chance to back out, however, only if you use the *.* designation. If you enter ERASE *.EXE, for example, DOS will not ask if you are sure and will immediately delete all files with an extension of EXE. So again, *be*

Figure 22 Erasing a File

```
A>erase format.com

A>dir format.com

 Volume in drive A is STARTUP
 Volume Serial Number is 0308-07D1
 Directory of  A:\

File not found

A>_
```

careful with the ERASE command! Answer yes and then list a directory to see what you have done:

Type **y**
Press **Enter**
Type **dir**
Press **Enter**

Your screen should look like Figure 23.

Practice

Switch back to the hard disk or the DOS Startup disk you used to boot up the computer. Remember the AUTOEXEC.BAK file you created in Lesson 10 and that you renamed JUNK in the Practice section of Lesson 12? Erase it, but this time use DEL instead of ERASE. DEL and ERASE are two names for the same DOS command.

Lesson 14: Protecting Diskettes

In certain situations, commands such as FORMAT, COPY, DISKCOPY, RENAME, and ERASE won't work. Most diskettes have a feature that prevents them from being altered. This feature, called **write-protection,** is similar to the tabs on audio and video cassette tapes that you can remove to prevent accidentally recording over material you want to save.

Step 1: Write-Protect a 5¼-inch Diskette

Most 5¼-inch diskettes have a small rectangle cut out of one side, called the **write-protect notch** (see Figure 24(a)). This notch can be covered with a gummed tab or tape to write-protect the diskette. Files on a diskette protected in this manner can be read but not written or altered as long as the notch remains covered. Diskettes that are write-protected cannot be formatted, have files renamed

Figure 23 Erasing All the Files

```
A>erase *.*
All files in directory will be deleted!
Are you sure (Y/N)?y

A>dir

 Volume in drive A is STARTUP
 Volume Serial Number is 0308-07D1
 Directory of  A:\

File not found

A>_
```

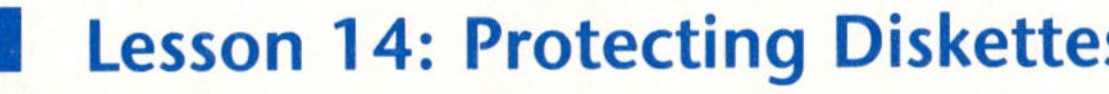

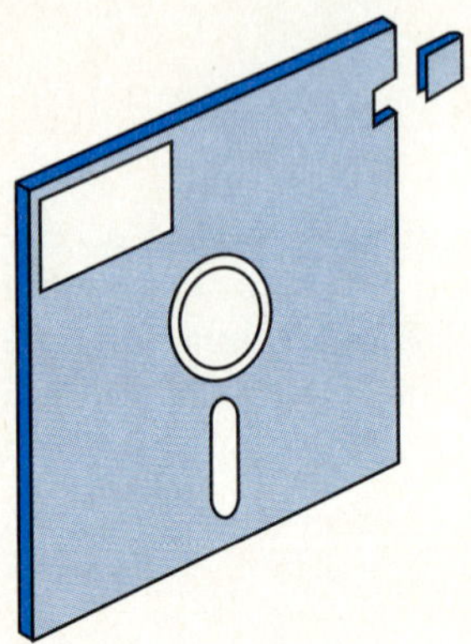

Figure 24 Write-Protecting Diskettes

(a)

5 ¼ - inch diskette

(b)

3 ½ - inch diskette

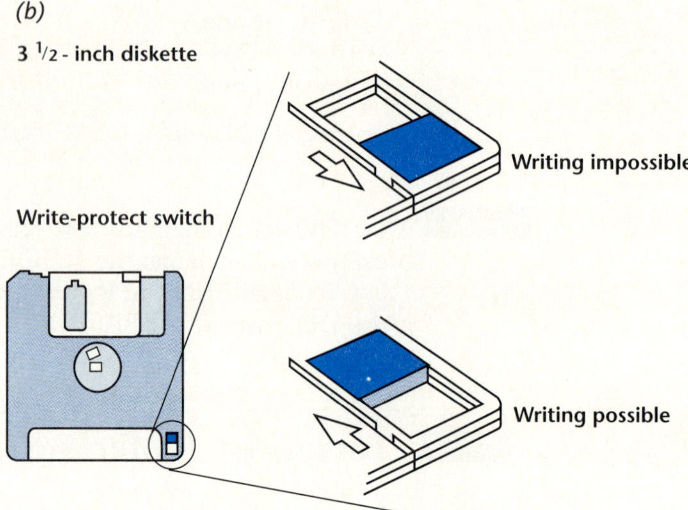

on them, have files copied onto them, or have files erased from them. If you attempt to do so, DOS simply issues a write-protect error message. Some 5¼-inch diskettes don't have a write-protect notch. These diskettes are permanently write-protected.

If you have a gummed tab or piece of tape, try write-protecting a 5¼-inch diskette. Then try copying a file to the diskette, or renaming or erasing a file already on the diskette.

Step 2: Write-Protect a 3½-inch Diskette

The smaller, 3½-inch diskettes also can be write-protected, but the mechanism is slightly different. These diskettes have a **write-protect switch** on the reverse side in the lower right corner (see Figure 24(b)). This switch is a tab that can be slid to open or close a little hole in the disk's plastic case. When the hole is open, the diskette is write-protected. When it is closed, files can be written and altered on the diskette.

If your computer uses 3½-inch diskettes, try write-protecting one. Then try copying a file to the diskette, or renaming or erasing a file already on the diskette.

Copy-Protection   With write-protection, you can safeguard programs and data that are stored on diskettes from accidental erasure. Some software developers use **copy-protection** to discourage you from duplicating their packages and illegally selling or giving away copies. Copy-protected diskettes are prepared in a manner that makes it difficult or impossible to copy them with ordinary DOS commands such as COPY and DISKCOPY. Since it is so easy to duplicate diskettes, some manufacturers feel that they must copy-protect their software to prevent widespread distribution to people who don't rightfully pay for it. Unfortunately, copy-protected software is often inconvenient for rightful owners to use or back up. Although manufacturers of most major application packages have since dropped copy-protection from their products, many game programs are still copy-protected.

If you try to use COPY or DISKCOPY on a diskette that is copy-protected, any one of several results might occur. The attempt could simply fail and cause an error message to be displayed. In other cases, the copy procedure might seem to successfully complete, but when you try to run the software it just won't work. Trying to duplicate copy-protected diskettes can be an effort in futility; to spare the user unnecessary frustration, manufacturers should clearly state whether their packages are copy-protected. The safest course is to follow the instructions for using and making backup copies of original diskettes.

Practice

Write-protect a new diskette or one containing files you don't need. Then try to format it.

Lesson 15: Displaying and Printing Text Files

So far, you've learned quite a bit about manipulating files with DOS. You haven't, however, looked inside one. The DOS TYPE command, which is an internal command, lets you display the contents of a file on the screen. The DOS PRINT command, which is an external command, lets you send the contents of a file to the printer. Although TYPE and PRINT will work with almost any file, unless it's a text file all you'll see is gibberish. A **text file** contains only ordinary letters, numbers, and punctuation marks. It is usually produced by a text editor or word processing program. AUTOEXEC.BAT and CONFIG.SYS, which we will explain further in the next chapter, are text files that tell DOS how to set up your computer when you boot up. Although these files are not absolutely necessary for booting up, they are created on most hard disks and DOS Startup diskettes when DOS is installed. If you don't have AUTOEXEC.BAT or CONFIG.SYS on your hard disk or DOS Startup disk, just read through this lesson.

Step 1: Execute the TYPE Command

Make sure the disk you booted up from is your default disk. Use the DIR command to see if AUTOEXEC.BAT and CONFIG.SYS are present on the disk. To examine the contents of the AUTOEXEC.BAT and CONFIG.SYS text files on your screen, execute these commands:

```
Type    type autoexec.bat
Press   Enter
Type    type config.sys
Press   Enter
```

DOS will display the contents of the files, as shown in Figure 25, although your screen will probably look somewhat different. The exact contents of the AUTO-EXEC.BAT and CONFIG.SYS files may vary quite a bit, depending on how DOS was installed and what options are being used. In the next two chapters, you will learn what all of the statements in these two files mean.

Step 2: Prepare the Printer

Many text files eventually wind up on paper, especially if they are produced by a word processing or text editing program. The DOS PRINT command lets you send a text file directly to the printer instead of displaying it on the screen.

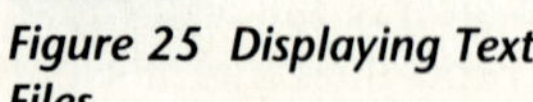

Figure 25 Displaying Text Files

```
C>type autoexec.bat
@ECHO OFF
SET COMSPEC=C:\DOS\COMMAND.COM
VERIFY OFF
PATH C:\DOS
APPEND /E
APPEND C:\DOS
C:\DOS\GRAPHICS
VER
PRINT /D:LPT1

C>type config.sys
BREAK=ON
BUFFERS=20
FILES=20
LASTDRIVE=E
SHELL=C:\DOS\COMMAND.COM /P /E:256
DEVICE=C:\DOS\ANSI.SYS
INSTALL=C:\DOS\FASTOPEN.EXE C:=(50,25)

C>_
```

Before you can print a file, your printer must be turned on. Make sure that the power is on and that the printer is on-line, that is, connected to your computer.

Step 3: Execute the PRINT Command

To use the PRINT command, type PRINT followed by the name of the file you want to print. Print the AUTOEXEC.BAT file by executing this command:

Type   **print autoexec.bat**
Press   **Enter**

DOS may ask you to supply the following (if it doesn't, don't worry):

    Name of list device [PRN]:

This rather cryptic request allows you to tell DOS which printer to use if you have more than one connected to your computer. The expression [PRN] means that unless you tell it otherwise, DOS will send the output to the default printer, which has the device name PRN. If you have only one printer, then it is the default printer. All you have to do is press the Enter key.

    Press   **Enter**

DOS will ask you to supply the list device only the first time you use PRINT for any given computer session. After you do so, DOS will tell you the file is currently being printed.
To print the CONFIG.SYS file, execute this command:

Type   **print config.sys**
Press   **Enter**

DOS will tell you the file is currently being printed and will present the DOS prompt again (see Figure 26). From the printer you will get copies of the AUTO-EXEC.BAT and CONFIG.SYS files, each on their own page.

Figure 26 Printing Text Files

```
C>print autoexec.bat

  C:\AUTOEXEC.BAT is currently being printed
C>print config.sys

  C:\CONFIG.SYS is currently being printed
C>_
```

Practice

1. You can use TYPE to display nontext files, although what you see on the screen won't make much sense. For example, execute this command and see what happens:

   Type   **type command.com**
   Press   **Enter**

2. Get a directory listing of your DOS subdirectory or Startup disk and examine it for any files with the extension BAT or TXT. If you are running MS-DOS 4.01, for example, the files DOSSHELL.BAT and README.TXT may be in your DOS subdirectory. Examine the contents of these files, or any others from the DOS subdirectory or Startup disk, with the TYPE command. You can preface the file name with the disk drive or subdirectory specification. For example, execute this command to view the README.TXT file from the DOS subdirectory:

   Type   **type dos\readme.txt**
   Press   **Enter**

3. Use the PRINT command to get a hard copy of the files you just examined.

Lesson 16: Running a Program

This lesson won't really teach you anything new, because you've been running programs throughout this chapter. Every time you used an external DOS command, you were running a program. Remember: files with an EXE or COM extension are stand-alone, executable programs that you can run.

Step 1: Switch to the Appropriate Disk

First, you must make sure a program you want to run is stored on a disk in one of your drives when you want to run the program. For example, to run an application program such as WordPerfect, Lotus 1-2-3, or dBASE IV, you must

Real World

Microsoft Branches Out

Microsoft Corp., one of the patriarchs of the software industry, believes there's strength in numbers.

The Redmond, Washington-based company could have sat back and watched profits roll in from its highly successful MS-DOS operating system software, but founder Bill Gates decided the company needed more than one star product.

After developing PC-DOS and OS/2 in conjunction with IBM, Microsoft moved into the UNIX field by buying a stake in The Santa Cruz Operation, Inc. and working to bring graphical applications to the UNIX environment.

Microsoft has been heavily involved in applications software for the Macintosh, as well. Gates saw something in the Macintosh long before other software developers did. The result was that Microsoft became the number one software company for Macintosh products. It has three Macintosh best sellers: Excel, a spreadsheet package; Word, a word processor; and Works, an integrated software package.

Microsoft is also pushing its Windows operating environment, which has been described as a "halfway house for DOS users not ready to move to OS/2." Windows uses the experience that Microsoft's programmers gained from working with the Macintosh.

But the road has not been completely smooth for Microsoft. Apple sued Microsoft in 1988 over similarities between Windows and the Macintosh operating system. The court case could drag on for years.

Delayed shipping is another bump in Gate's road. Both Microsoft Word 4.0 for the Macintosh and Microsoft Word 5.0 for DOS were not shipped when promised. The glitches haven't hurt Microsoft's profits, however. In 1988, they jumped almost 63 percent, to $151 million. Diversity apparently pays well.

Source: "New Conquests for the MS-DOS Master," *Datamation*, June 15, 1989, p. 131.

have it installed in a subdirectory on your hard disk or have it on a diskette in a floppy drive. If your computer is connected to a local area network, you could run the program if it's stored on your network's file server disk. DOS must be able to find a program before it can run it. You may have to change your default drive to the one containing the program to be run. An alternative is to preface the program name with the disk drive letter.

Step 2: Switch to the Appropriate Subdirectory

Some programs stored in a subdirectory may need to be run from inside that subdirectory. You will learn how to switch subdirectories in the next chapter. An alternative to switching subdirectories is to preface the program name you enter with the drive and subdirectory in which the program's file is stored.

Step 3: Type the Program Name and Press the Enter Key

As you now know, you invoke an external DOS command by entering its name along with any necessary file names and other information. In this sense, application programs such as WordPerfect, Lotus 1-2-3, and dBASE IV are the same as DOS external commands; all you have to do to run them is type the name of the EXE or COM file in which they're stored and press the Enter key. So, for example, to run WordPerfect from your default drive, you would execute this command (don't do it now):

Type **wp**
Press **Enter**

When you do this, DOS will load the WordPerfect program into primary memory and begin executing it.

Practice Running an application package is just like running a DOS external command such as CHKDSK. You can run a program from a disk other than the one in your default drive. For example, copy the CHKDSK.COM file from your DOS subdirectory to a formatted diskette in drive A. With the hard disk as your default drive, execute this command:

Type **a: chkdsk**
Press **Enter**

Summary

- *Starting up DOS with the computer turned off.* Insert the DOS Startup diskette in drive A if the computer has no hard disk and then turn the computer on.

- *Starting up DOS with the computer turned on.* Press Ctrl-Alt-Del.

- *Obtaining a directory of the files on a disk.* Use the DIR command.

- *Using the special DOS keys.* Press Escape to cancel a line. Press Ctrl-Num Lock or Pause to interrupt screen scrolling. Press Ctrl-Break to cancel a command. Press Shift-PrtSc to print the screen. Press Ctrl-PrtSc to echo to the printer.

- *Changing the default disk drive.* Enter the new drive letter followed by a colon.

- *Obtaining a disk and memory status report.* Use the CHKDSK command.

- *Clearing the display screen.* Use the CLS command.

- *Formatting a diskette.* Use the FORMAT command.

- *Formatting a system diskette.* Use the FORMAT command with the /S parameter.

- *Copying files.* Use the COPY command.

- *Copying an entire diskette.* Use the DISKCOPY command.

- *Changing file names.* Use the RENAME (REN) command.

- *Erasing files.* Use the ERASE (DEL) command.

- *Protecting a diskette from accidental erasure.* Cover the notch with a gummed tab or piece of tape on a 5¼-inch disk. Slide open the write-protect switch on a 3½-inch diskette.

- *Displaying and printing text files.* Use the TYPE command to display text files on the screen and the PRINT command to send them to the printer.

- *Running an application package.* Switch to the proper disk drive and subdirectory, if necessary, and then enter the name of the program.

Key Terms

As an extra review of this chapter, try defining the following terms.

allocation unit	parameter
booting up	sector
copy-protection	source
default drive	subdirectory
Disk Operating System (DOS)	switching drives
DOS prompt	target
extension	text file
external command (transient	upwardly compatible
routine)	write-protect notch
filename	write-protect switch
global file name character	write-protection
hidden file	
internal command (resident	
routine)	

Multiple Choice

Choose the best selection to complete each statement.

1. An operating system is a(n)
   - (a) hardware component of a mainframe computer system.
   - (b) application program that produces text files.
   - (c) set of programs that lets you use your computer's hardware and software resources.
   - (d) system of procedures for operating a computer.

2. Transient routines or external commands are
   - (a) kept in primary memory until the computer is shut off.
   - (b) kept on disk and loaded into memory only when needed.
   - (c) kept in ROM (read-only memory) chips.
   - (d) used once then deleted.

3. The driving force behind each new DOS release has usually been
   - (a) the addition of a new disk drive capability.
   - (b) an effort to improve the user interface.
   - (c) an attempt to eliminate all bugs.
   - (d) an effort by IBM and Microsoft to make more money.

4. Upwardly compatible means that
   - (a) you cannot take advantage of the new version's abilities.
   - (b) all old software versions must be upgraded.
   - (c) new hardware must be purchased to use the new version.
   - (d) operations that worked with former versions work with the new version.

5. A command is a(n)
   - (a) combination of hardware switch settings.
   - (b) operating system directive issued to a user.
   - (c) application package instruction.
   - (d) word or abbreviation that tells DOS to run a program.

6. To boot DOS with the power off

   (a) insert the DOS Startup disk (if necessary) and turn on the power.

   (b) hold down the Control, Alternate, and Delete keys at the same time.

   (c) turn the power on and issue the boot command.

   (d) turn the power on and kick the computer.

7. Pressing Ctrl-Alt-Del will

   (a) invoke a DOS transient routine.

   (b) delete a file.

   (c) reboot DOS without having to shut off the computer.

   (d) execute an application program.

8. The DOS directory command is

   (a) DIRECT.

   (b) LIST.

   (c) DIR.

   (d) CATALOG.

9. The two parts of a DOS file name are

   (a) a disk drive designation and a disk sector number.

   (b) a primary filename and an optional extension.

   (c) a primary filename and a creation date.

   (d) a primary extension and the size in bytes.

10. Files with COM and EXE extensions usually designate

    (a) external commands and executable program files.

    (b) command files and extension files.

    (c) configuration files and batch files.

    (d) BASIC and FORTRAN files.

11. Pressing Ctrl-Num Lock or Pause will

    (a) echo input and output to the printer.

    (b) print the screen.

    (c) cancel a command.

    (d) temporarily halt screen scrolling.

12. To change the default disk drive

    (a) put a new disk in drive A.

    (b) type the new disk drive designation and press Enter.

    (c) open up the computer and replace the faulty drive.

    (d) issue the DIR command.

13. To display a disk and memory status report, use

    (a) STATUS.

    (b) DIR.

    (c) CHKDSK.

    (d) DISKCOPY.

14. Formatting a diskette does not do the following:

    (a) check the diskette for bad sectors.

    (b) wipe out all data on the diskette.

    (c) mark off the space into sectors.

    (d) sort files in the directory.

15. To format a system diskette you must

    (a) reboot the system.

    (b) use the /S parameter with the FORMAT command.

    (c) enter the COPY command.

    (d) purchase a master diskette from IBM.

16. Which command would you use to copy every file from disk drive A to B?

    (a) COPY A:*.* B: (b) DIR A: B:

    (c) COPY A: B: (d) REN

17. To make an exact copy of an entire diskette, use

    (a) COPY.   (b) DISKCOPY.

    (c) DIR.   (d) Ctrl-Alt-Del.

18. Entering the command DEL *.* will

    (a) reboot the system.   (b) copy all files to the disk in the
                                             default drive.

    (c) rename all files on the disk in (d) erase all files from the disk in the
        the default drive.   default drive.

19. To display a text file on your screen, use the

    (a) PRINT command.   (b) DISKCOPY command.

    (c) TYPE command.   (d) Ctrl-Num Lock key.

20. To run a program you must

    (a) type its filename and press the (b) reboot DOS.
        Enter key.

    (c) press Ctrl-Break.   (d) first make a backup copy.

Fill-In

1. A disk operating system has many utilities for dealing with the _______ that are stored on disks.

2. _______ is usually used with IBM computers while _______ is usually used with compatible computers such as those made by Compaq, Tandy, and Zenith.

3. Booting DOS refers to the process of loading the disk operating system into _______.

4. In some cases, when you first boot DOS it asks you to enter the _______ and the _______.

5. The _______ command can be used to list the names, sizes, and creation dates and times of all the files on a disk.

6. A file's primary filename can have from one to _______ characters in it.

7. File name extensions are often used to _______ files.

8. You can press the _______ key to cancel a command if you haven't pressed the Enter key yet.

9. You can press _______ to cancel a command before it finishes executing.

10. The DOS _______ indicates the current default disk drive.

11. The _______ command can tell you how much memory is installed in your computer.

12. A diskette must be _______ before it can be used to store program and data files.

13. The _______ command can be used to duplicate one or more files on the same or on different disks.

14. _______ file name characters can be used to refer to several files at the same time.

15. The DISKCOPY command will automatically _______ the target diskette if it's brand new.
16. The REN command can be used to _______ one or more file names.
17. To remove a file from a disk, you would enter _______ or _______ followed by the file's name.
18. The TYPE command lets you display _______ files on your screen.
19. You could use the _______ command to produce a hard copy of a text file.
20. To run a program, you must type its _______ and then press _______.

Short Problems

1. If you have access to a diskette other than DOS Startup, produce a directory listing of the files on it. If you have a printer, try using Ctrl-PrtSc to turn on printer echoing before you issue the directory command so that you can get a hard copy.

2. When you booted DOS, you may have been asked to supply the date and time. Two DOS commands, DATE and TIME, tell you the current date and time and let you change these settings. Try the DATE and TIME commands. If you don't want to change the date and time settings, just press the Enter key when asked for the new date or time. Notice how DOS automatically figures out and displays the day of the week.

3. Use the * global file name character to produce a directory listing of all the files in the DOS subdirectory or on the DOS Startup disk with an EXE extension.

4. Use the * global file name character to produce a directory listing of all the files in the DOS subdirectory or on the DOS Startup disk whose names begin with the letter K.

5. Use the ? global file name character to produce a directory listing of all the files in the DOS subdirectory or on the DOS Startup disk that have an *E* as the second letter of their primary filename.

6. DOS versions 3.0 and newer have a command that lets you supply or change a volume label without having to reformat a disk. If you have DOS 3.0 or newer try using the LABEL command on a diskette that you have formatted for a lesson in this chapter.

7. If you don't know what DOS version you have, enter **ver**. This command displays the number of the DOS version you are using.

8. Another way to find out the volume label of a disk is to use the VOL command. Enter **vol**. This command displays the volume label (if there is one) of the default disk.

9. It is possible to display a text file on your screen by using the COPY command instead of the TYPE command. In certain cases, DOS can refer to its peripheral devices as if they were files. There are several file names that have a special meaning to DOS. These are called DOS device names. For example, CON refers to the console, or the keyboard and screen. If your disk has a file named AUTOEXEC.BAT on it, execute this command:

    Type   **copy autoexec.bat con**
    Press   **Enter**

    You should see the text of file AUTOEXEC.BAT displayed on your screen just as if you used the TYPE command.

10. Just as CON is a DOS device name that refers to the keyboard and screen, PRN is a DOS device name that refers to the printer. Try using the COPY command to get a printout of the AUTOEXEC.BAT file.

11. The DIR command has two optional parameters that can be useful when looking at disks with lots of files on them. The /P parameter will automatically pause the display when the screen is full and let you press a key to continue. The /W parameter will display the directory in a wide format across the screen, omitting the sizes and creation dates and times so that more file names will fit at once. Obtain a directory listing of the DOS subdirectory or DOS Startup disk using these options:

    Type   **dir /p**
    Press   **Enter**
    Type   **dir /w**
    Press   **Enter**

INTERMEDIATE DOS

In This Chapter

 **Preview**

In the previous chapter you learned the basics of DOS, the operating system used on millions of IBM and IBM-compatible microcomputers. This chapter continues your exploration of DOS with slightly more advanced topics.

After studying this chapter, you will know how to

- use the DOS editing and function keys.
- set the BREAK option.
- work with subdirectories.
- use the PATH and APPEND commands.
- change the DOS prompt.
- back up and restore disks and files.
- recover files from damaged disks.
- use the prompt option when erasing files.
- append files and copy files to devices.
- set the VERIFY option.
- change file attributes.
- copy groups of files.
- update sets of files.
- transfer the DOS system files.
- compare files and disks.
- change volume labels.
- change the current date and time.
- display a memory report.
- reassign, join, and substitute drives.
- print multiple files.

 **Getting Started**

You've already learned how to start DOS and use its most common features and commands. This chapter assumes you have completed all of the lessons and exercises in Chapter 2. Furthermore, it assumes that you have a computer with a hard disk and DOS 3.30, 4.00, or 4.01 installed on it in a subdirectory named DOS. All of the screens in the following lessons were created with MS-DOS 4.01. To work the following lessons, boot up or reboot your computer if you have not already done so.

Lesson 1: Using the DOS Editing and Function Keys

As you learned in Chapter 2, DOS assigns special meanings to certain keys. By now you should know how to use Enter, Ctrl-Alt-Del, Escape, Ctrl-Num Lock (or Pause), Ctrl-Break, Shift-PrtSc (or Print Screen), and Ctrl-PrtSc. In addition, DOS has other key presses that can help you enter commands and save time. These are known as the DOS editing and function keys.

Step 1: Retrieve the Previous Command

Every time you enter a command, DOS saves what you have typed in a special area of memory. You can retrieve the previous command by pressing the F3 function key. For example, follow these instructions:

```
Type    dir
Press   Enter
Press   F3
```

When the directory command is finished, DOS will copy the previous command, which was DIR, to your screen at the cursor location, as if you had typed it again.

```
Press   Enter
```

DOS will execute the DIR command again. The F3 command is especially convenient for repeating the same command several times in a row, or for repeating an especially long command.

Step 2: Edit the Command Line

When you press F3, DOS only copies the previous command to the command line. You still have to press Enter to actually execute the command. You can, however, alter the command line if you like. For example:

```
Press   F3
Press   Space Bar
Type    c:
Press   Enter
```

This sequence of actions will retrieve the previous command, which was DIR, and add the disk drive specification C: onto the end. Once the previous command is retrieved, you can also use the Backspace or Left Arrow key to delete characters to the left of the cursor.

Step 3: Copy the Next Character from the Previous Command

Pressing F3 retrieves all of the previous command and presents it on your screen. You can also retrieve one character at a time from the previous command by pressing the F1 key. For example:

```
Press   F1 (3 times)
Press   Enter
```

This sequence of commands will retrieve and then execute only the first three characters (DIR) of the previous command. The F1 key allows you to retrieve some of the previous command or make modifications to it.

Step 4: Retrieve Some of the Previous Command

Put a formatted diskette in drive A if it does not already contain one. Execute this command:

```
Type    dir a:
Press   Enter
```

Suppose you now want to examine disk drive C or B.

```
Press   F2
Type    a
```

This tells DOS to retrieve the previous command, but only up to the *a* character you've specified. So, now you can type a different end to the command:

```
Type    c:
Press   Enter
```

Step 5: Examine the Other Editing Keys

The editing and function keys we have discussed are probably the most frequently used. A few other keys, however, are available. The following table lists all of the DOS editing keys.

Key	Action
F1	Retypes one character at a time from the previous command.
F2	Retypes all characters up to the next character you type from the previous command.
F3	Retypes all of the previous command.
F4	Deletes all the characters from the previous command up to the next character you type.
F5	Saves the contents of your current command line as if it were the previous command.
F6	Inserts an end-of-file code (Ctrl-Z).
Delete	Skips over a character from the previous command.
Insert	Switches insert/overwrite mode in the command line.
Escape	Cancels the current line.

Practice

1. Try the F4 function key.

   Type   **garbage dir**
   Press **Enter**

   Don't worry about the error message. To throw out the garbage, and execute the remaining DIR command, do this:

   Press **F4**
   Type   **d**
   Press **F3**
   Press **Enter**

2. Try the F5 function key. Suppose you are typing a long command and realize you have made an error. You have not yet pressed the Enter key. For example, do this (but don't press Enter):

   Type   **ytpe autoexec.bat**
   Press **F5**

   Pressing F5 will save what you have typed as if it were the previous command. Now, follow these instructions to correct your error, retrieve the rest of the command, and execute the correct TYPE command:

   Type   **ty**
   Press **F3**
   Press **Enter**

3. Try the Del editing key.

   Type   **xxdir**
   Press **Enter**

Suppose you meant to type *dir*. To fix your mistake, do this:

Press   **Del** (2 times)
Press   **F3**
Press   **Enter**

4. Try the Ins editing key.

Type   `dir os`
Press   **Enter**

Suppose you meant to type *dir dos*. To fix your mistake, follow these instructions:

Press   **F1** (4 times)
Press   **Ins**
Type   **d**
Press   **F3**
Press   **Enter**

Lesson 2: Setting the BREAK Option

In Chapter 2 you learned that you can press Ctrl-Break to cancel a program that is running. Normally, Ctrl-Break works only when DOS is checking the keyboard or sending characters to the screen or printer. You can also tell DOS to check whether Ctrl-Break has been pressed during disk reads and writes.

Step 1: Execute the BREAK Command

The BREAK command allows you to check or change the status of the BREAK option, which controls when Ctrl-Break will cancel a program. To see the current setting of the BREAK option, execute this command:

Type   **break**
Press   **Enter**

DOS will tell you whether BREAK is on or off.

Step 2: Change the BREAK Option

You can change the current setting of BREAK by entering the BREAK command followed by ON or OFF. For example, if BREAK is OFF, turn it on with this command:

Type   **break on**
Press   **Enter**

Now check what you have done:

Type   **break**
Press   **Enter**

Your screen should look like Figure 1.

Practice   Switch the BREAK option back to the way it was before you changed it.

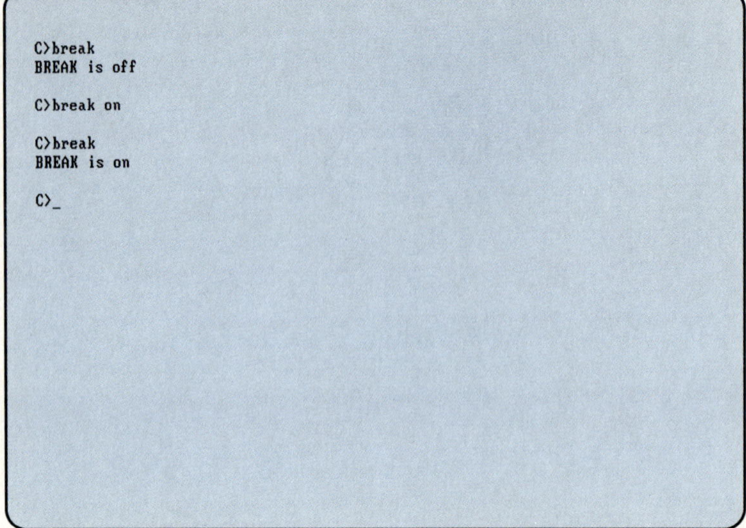

Figure 1 Setting the BREAK Option

Lesson 3: Working with Subdirectories

As you can imagine, people who use microcomputers extensively often generate large numbers of files. Before hard disks became common, users stored their files in many different floppy disks. Organizing files meant physically organizing diskettes by keeping them well-labeled and storing them in subdivided boxes, racks, or cabinets. Once hard disks became common, however, operating systems had to devise a better method of organizing large numbers of files. Even a modest 20-megabyte hard disk can store thousands of different files. Looking for a particular file among hundreds or thousands of files is time consuming and tedious. Consequently, most microcomputer operating systems, including DOS, have evolved a **hierarchical** method of organizing files into groups. A hierarchical system allows you to cluster files into orders or ranks, each subordinate to the one above. These groups of files, called subdirectories, are like file folders that can be nested within one another. Disks can be organized into subdirectories, each of which can contain files and other subdirectories.

Subdirectories are an invaluable tool for organizing programs and data files on high-capacity storage devices. In addition, subdirectories make it easier for the operating system to locate a particular file, because large numbers of files are divided into smaller groups. Although subdirectories are most often, indeed almost always, found on hard disks, they are occasionally used on floppy disks, too. DOS includes commands that let you create, access, and remove subdirectories.

With DOS, every disk has a single main directory, known as the **root directory.** DOS automatically creates a root directory on every disk you format. This is the directory you are in when you first boot up DOS or when you first change your default drive. The root directory itself has no name, but it's represented by a backslash (\).

Step 1: Create a Subdirectory

The internal DOS command MD or MKDIR (short for "make directory") is used to create a new subdirectory. It is followed by the **path** of the new subdirectory. A path is an optional disk drive specifier followed by a list of subdirectory names, separated by backslashes. The rules for naming subdirectories are the same as the rules for naming files. The simplest path is a single backslash \, which represents the root directory of your current default drive. Let's create a new subdirectory on your hard disk. Execute this command:

> Type   **md c:\myfiles**
> Press   **Enter**

The command you just entered creates a subdirectory named MYFILES on the hard disk C. This subdirectory is one level below the root directory. To see the result, execute this command:

> Type   **dir**
> Press   **Enter**

You should see MYFILES followed by the <DIR> designation in the directory listing as shown in Figure 2.

Step 2: Change to the Subdirectory

Think of the subdirectory as a separate "sub-disk" on your disk. You use the change directory (CD or CHDIR) command, which is an internal command, to move into your new subdirectory. Execute these commands:

> Type   **cd c:\myfiles**
> Press   **Enter**
> Type   **dir**
> Press   **Enter**

Your screen should look like Figure 3, showing the directory listing inside the MYFILES subdirectory.

Figure 2 Using MD to Create the MYFILES Subdirectory

```
C>md c:\myfiles

C>dir

 Volume in drive C is HARD DISK
 Volume Serial Number is 3324-07CC
 Directory of  C:\

CONFIG   SYS       146 07-09-89    1:22p
MYFILES       <DIR>     07-12-89    2:10p
COMMAND  COM     37557 12-19-88   12:00a
DOS           <DIR>     07-09-89    1:23p
AUTOEXEC BAT       256 01-01-80    5:52a
        5 File(s)   19699712 bytes free

C>_
```

*Figure 3 Using DIR Inside
the MYFILES Subdirectory*

```
C>cd c:\myfiles

C>dir

 Volume in drive C is HARD DISK
 Volume Serial Number is 3324-07CC
 Directory of  C:\MYFILES

 .           <DIR>      07-12-89    2:10p
 ..          <DIR>      07-12-89    2:10p
       2 File(s)    19699712 bytes free

C>_
```

Step 3: Copy a File to the Subdirectory

Right now, the MYFILES subdirectory has no ordinary user files in it. You can, however, copy files into this subdirectory just as if it were a separate disk. For example, let's copy the AUTOEXEC.BAT file from the root directory into the MYFILES subdirectory. Execute this command:

Type   **copy c:\autoexec.bat**
Press **Enter**

This command copies the file AUTOEXEC.BAT from the root directory of the hard disk C into your current subdirectory, which happens to be MYFILES. Execute this command to see the contents of your subdirectory:

Type   **dir**
Press **Enter**

A copy of AUTOEXEC.BAT now also exists in the MYFILES subdirectory. It's important to realize that there are two separate copies of AUTOEXEC.BAT now on the disk: one in the root directory and one in the MYFILES subdirectory.

Step 4: Display the Directory Structure

A hard disk can hold a great many subdirectories and files. DIR will list the subdirectories and files of only one directory at a time; it cannot show the structure beneath that level. TREE, an external DOS command, can list all of the subdirectories on a disk. It can also list all of the files in each subdirectory. With DOS versions 4.00 and newer, TREE depicts the structure of the disk graphically. Older DOS versions simply list the paths and subdirectories. Execute this command to get a TREE listing of the root directory of your hard disk:

Type   **tree c:**
Press **Enter**

Figure 4 shows the result. You can also tell the TREE command to list all files in all directories by using the /F parameter. Execute this command to see how it works:

Type **tree c:\ /f**
Press **Enter**

Step 5: Remove the Subdirectory

Once you are in a subdirectory, you can almost think of it as a separate disk. You can run programs from within a subdirectory. Many DOS commands that deal with files will operate only on the files in your current subdirectory unless you specify otherwise. For example, you can delete every file in a subdirectory without affecting any of the files in the root directory or any other subdirectory. For example, make sure you are in the MYFILES subdirectory and then execute these commands:

Type **erase *.***
Press **Enter**
Type **y**
Press **Enter**
Type **dir**
Press **Enter**

DOS will erase every file in your current directory, the MYFILES subdirectory. The DIR command should reveal that this is true. Now change back to the root directory and check its contents by executing these commands:

Type **cd c:**
Press **Enter**
Type **dir**
Press **Enter**

As you can see, the AUTOEXEC.BAT file in the root directory is still intact.

Figure 4 Using TREE to Display the Directory Structure

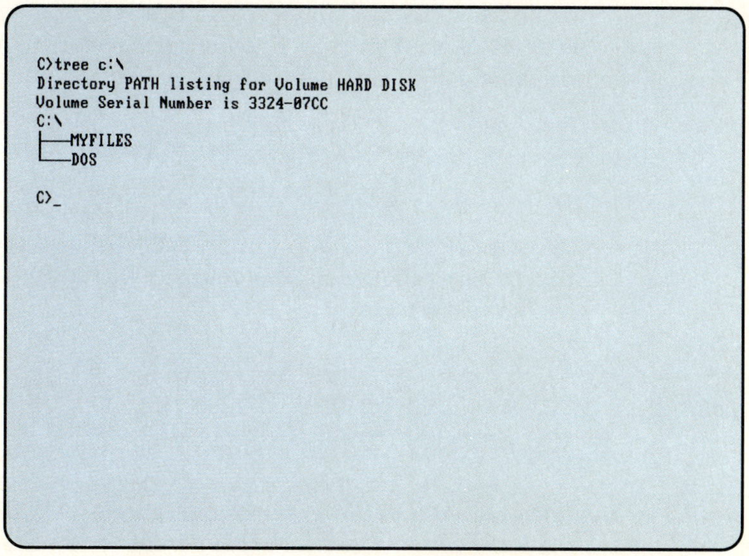

Just as you must occasionally delete unneeded files, sometimes you must remove subdirectories too. Suppose that you are finished with the MYFILES subdirectory and you want to remove it from your disk. To do this you must first erase any files inside the subdirectory and move out of the subdirectory. You have already done this. Now execute the remove directory command (RD or RMDIR) to remove the empty MYFILES subdirectory from your disk:

Type   **rd c:\myfiles**
Press   **Enter**
Type   **dir**
Press   **Enter**

You will see that the MYFILES subdirectory has indeed been removed, and your disk is the same as it was when you began this lesson. Like MD and CD, RD is an internal DOS command.

1. Create a new subdirectory on your disk and name it after yourself (eight characters or less). Change to your new subdirectory. Now create three additional subdirectories inside your new subdirectory and name them ONE, TWO, and THREE. Change to the ONE subdirectory and copy the AUTOEXEC.BAT file from the root, or some other file from the DOS subdirectory into the ONE subdirectory.

2. Use the DIR command to examine the contents of your ONE subdirectory. Notice the first two entries in the directory listing. The . (single period) is a special DOS designation that symbolizes your current directory. The .. (double period) symbolizes the directory above your current directory. For example:

Type   **dir .**
Press   **Enter**

See what happens. Now try this command:

Type   **dir ..**
Press   **Enter**

You will get a listing of the directory above ONE.

3. DOS pros often use the . and .. designations as shortcuts. The . is equivalent to *.*. Use it to erase all the files in your current subdirectory, which should be ONE. Now, change back to the subdirectory above ONE, the subdirectory you named after yourself:

Type   **cd ..**
Press   **Enter**

Try using the .. designation again to return to the root directory.

4. Remove the ONE, TWO, and THREE subdirectories and then remove the subdirectory you named after yourself, leaving your disk the way it was before this practice session.

Lesson 4: Using the PATH and APPEND Commands

In many ways, a subdirectory is like a separate disk. Unless you give DOS special instructions, you can access the files within a subdirectory only when you have switched to that subdirectory with the CD command. In order to fully realize the benefits of DOS subdirectories, you must also understand the PATH and APPEND commands.

Step 1: Execute the PATH Command

By default, you cannot gain access to the programs or data files in a subdirectory unless you are in that subdirectory. Alternatively, you can precede the name of every command or data file with its full path. For example, if you want to use the CHKDSK command (which is an external command kept in the file CHKDSK.COM), and you are not in the DOS subdirectory on the hard disk C, you could enter the command this way:

> Type   **c:\dos\chkdsk**
> Press   **Enter**

Typing the disk drive and path before every command, however, can be tiresome. Fortunately, the PATH command can eliminate the need to do this.

Use the PATH command to tell DOS which subdirectories to search through if it cannot find a program or batch file you request in your current directory. (You will learn about batch files later in this chapter.) For example, in most cases you want the commands in the DOS subdirectory to be accessible no matter which disk or directory you are using. Usually, DOS is installed so that a PATH command granting access to the DOS subdirectory is executed every time the computer is booted up. As you will learn later in this chapter, this is typically done by putting a PATH command in the AUTOEXEC.BAT file.

Execute the following command to see the current command search path that has been set up for you:

> Type   **path**
> Press   **Enter**

You can also use the PATH command to change the command search path. For example, suppose you want programs and batch files in the root directory and the DOS subdirectory to be accessible from any disk or directory. To set this up, execute the following PATH command:

> Type   **path c:\; c:\dos**
> Press   **Enter**

The PATH command is followed by a list of paths you want DOS to search whenever it cannot find the command you have entered. The paths are separated by semicolons. This PATH command has two search paths, c:\, the root directory of the hard disk C, and c:\dos, the DOS subdirectory beneath the root directory on the hard disk C. To see what you have done, execute this command again:

> Type   **path**
> Press   **Enter**

Your screen should look like Figure 5.

You need only enter the PATH command once, unless you want to change the list of subdirectories. Consequently, it is usually placed in the AUTOEXEC.BAT file to be executed every time you boot up your computer.

Step 2: Execute the APPEND Command

The PATH command works only for files with extensions of BAT, COM, or EXE. In other words, PATH will allow DOS to find only programs and batch files in other directories. Users of DOS 3.3 and newer versions, however, can use the APPEND command, which can find other types of files.

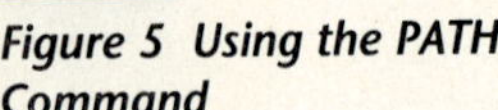

Figure 5 Using the PATH Command

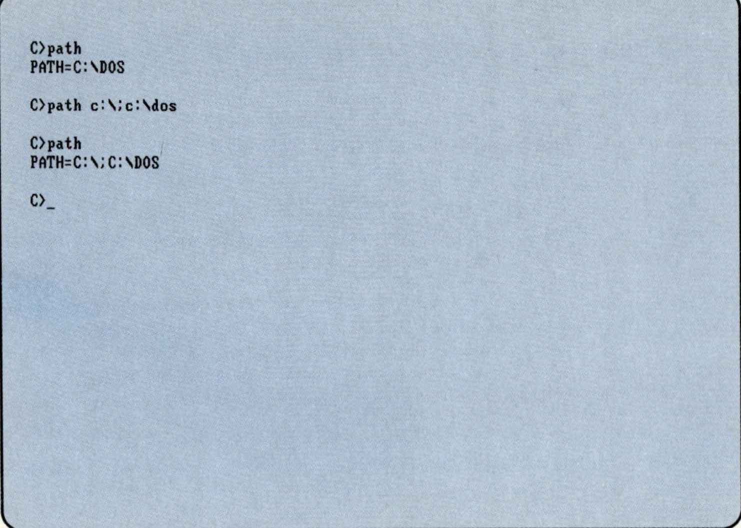

For example, create a subdirectory called LESSONS on your hard disk and change to it with these commands:

Type   **md c:\lessons**
Press **Enter**
Type   **cd c:\lessons**
Press **Enter**

Now, execute these commands to create a sample text file you can use:

Type   **copy con sample.txt**
Press **Enter**
Type   **This is a sample text file.**
Press **Enter**
Press **F6**
Press **Enter**

To see what you have created, execute this command:

Type   **type sample.txt**
Press **Enter**

The text file you have just created should be presented on your screen. As you can see, it is accessible from within the LESSONS subdirectory. Now, move back to the root directory and try to type the file by executing these commands:

Type   **cd c:**
Press **Enter**
Type   **type sample.txt**
Press **Enter**

DOS should say "File not found," as shown in Figure 6, because you are at the root and the file SAMPLE.TXT is in the LESSONS subdirectory.

Now suppose that you want data files in the root directory, the DOS subdirectory, and the LESSONS subdirectory to be accessible from all other disks and directories. Like the PATH command, APPEND can be followed by a list of sub-

Figure 6 SAMPLE.TXT Is Not Found in the Root Directory

```
C>md c:\lessons

C>cd c:\lessons

C>copy con sample.txt
This is a sample text file.
^Z
        1 File(s) copied

C>type sample.txt
This is a sample text file.

C>cd c:\

C>type sample.txt
File not found - SAMPLE.TXT

C>_
```

directories separated by semicolons. Execute the following APPEND command:

> Type   **append c:\;c:\dos;c:\lessons**
> Press   **Enter**

This command tells DOS the directories you want to search for files that have extensions other than BAT, COM, and EXE. Now try this command again:

> Type   **type sample.txt**
> Press   **Enter**

The file should be displayed on your screen, as shown in Figure 7. DOS was able to find SAMPLE.TXT because the APPEND command you entered told it where to search.

Like PATH, the APPEND command is usually put in the AUTOEXEC.BAT file to set up the search paths for data files every time the computer is turned on.

Practice

1. You can also use the APPEND command to see the current search path for data files.

   > Type   **append**
   > Press   **Enter**

   If you enter this command without a list of subdirectories, DOS will display the search paths, if any, that have been established by the most recent APPEND command on your computer.

2. Use the TYPE command to examine the AUTOEXEC.BAT file in the root directory of your disk. Does it contain a PATH and APPEND statement?

Lesson 5: Changing the DOS Prompt

By default, the DOS prompt consists of the current drive letter followed by a > (greater than sign). For example, if hard disk C is your current drive, then the default DOS prompt is

> C>

*Figure 7 APPEND Enables
DOS to Find SAMPLE.TXT*

```
C>md c:\lessons

C>cd c:\lessons

C>copy con sample.txt
This is a sample text file.
^Z
        1 File(s) copied

C>type sample.txt
This is a sample text file.

C>cd c:\

C>type sample.txt
File not found - SAMPLE.TXT

C>append c:\;c:\dos;c:\lessons

C>type sample.txt
This is a sample text file.

C>_
```

You can, however, change the appearance of the DOS prompt with the PROMPT command.

Step 1: Change the Prompt to a Text String

Suppose you want your DOS prompt to be Hello> instead of A> or C>. Execute this command:

> Type   **prompt Hello$g**
> Press   **Enter**

As soon as you enter this command, the DOS prompt will be changed to Hello>. The $g in the command is a special code that stands for the > (greater than sign).

Step 2: Change the Prompt to Show the Disk and Directory

You can probably think of any number of cute prompts such as Hello>. A more useful prompt would show your current disk drive and directory. This is especially handy if you frequently use subdirectories, because it's easy to forget your current path. To change your prompt to display your current path, execute this command:

> Type   **prompt pg**
> Press   **Enter**

If you are at the root directory of your hard disk, the prompt will immediately change to C:\>. Now change to your LESSONS subdirectory by executing this command:

> Type   **cd \lessons**
> Press   **Enter**

Your DOS prompt should now be C:\LESSONS>.

Step 3: Explore the Other Prompt Options

The PROMPT command allows several options besides $g and $p. The following table lists all of the special codes you can use with the PROMPT command. These codes can be combined and mixed with text to create an unlimited number of prompts.

Prompt Code	Action
$q	Presents the = (equal sign) character.
$$	Presents the $ (dollar sign) character.
$t	Presents the current time of day.
$d	Presents today's date.
$p	Presents the current path.
$v	Presents the version of DOS being used.
$n	Presents the current drive letter.
$g	Presents the > (greater than sign) character.
$l	Presents the < (less than sign) character.
$b	Presents the | (vertical bar) character.
$_	Starts a new line.
$e	Presents a left arrow symbol.
$h	Performs a Backspace.

Practice   Try as many of the prompt options in the preceding table as you like. When you are finished experimenting, execute the following command to change the DOS prompt to the current disk drive and directory:

Type   **prompt pg**
Press   **Enter**

Lesson 6: Backing Up and Restoring Disks and Files

Floppy disks and hard disks, though quite reliable, are not infallible. Eventually, every disk or disk drive will fail. In addition, almost every computer user mistakenly erases important programs or data on occasion. It is essential, therefore, to keep backup copies of all files that may be difficult, if not impossible, to replace. DOS includes two external commands, BACKUP and RESTORE, that help you keep extra copies of your software and data files.

Step 1: Back Up the Entire Hard Disk

Although the DOS BACKUP command can be used to make extra copies of floppy disks on other floppy disks, it is most often used to back up all or part of a hard disk onto floppy disks. BACKUP is better than using the COPY command to back up a hard disk, because most hard disks contain too many files to fit on a single floppy disk. Unlike COPY, the BACKUP command will automatically use as many diskettes as needed to save the files from a hard disk. The BACKUP command will fill each diskette as much as possible, even if it means splitting a single file between two disks. Then, BACKUP will prompt you to insert additional floppy disks until it copies all of the files. Furthermore, the BACKUP command of DOS versions 3.3 or newer will even format the backup floppy disks if necessary.

Suppose you want to make a backup copy of your entire hard disk. Assume that you have never backed up your hard disk before. First, you would switch back to the root directory and use DIR or CHKDSK to estimate how many floppy disks you will need. For example, if your hard disk contains 10 megabytes of files, you would need 29 or 30 360K floppy disks. Don't do this on your computer (it might require too many diskettes and take too long), but here is the command you would enter:

backup c: a: /s

This command tells DOS to back up the C drive onto the floppy disks that you will put into drive A. The /S parameter tells DOS to back up all the subdirectories as well. If you are using DOS 4.00 or newer, the BACKUP command can automatically format new diskettes if necessary. If you are using DOS 3.3, you should tell the BACKUP command to format new diskettes (if yours are not already formatted) by including the /F parameter after the /S parameter. Finally, if you are using a DOS version previous to 3.3, you have to format all of your backup diskettes *before* you execute the BACKUP command.

The BACKUP command will then beep and present the message shown in Figure 8. It is up to you to make sure that the floppy disks you use for the backup do not contain any files you need. You would insert the first diskette into drive A, close the door, and press any key. DOS will then list the files as it copies them to the first diskette. When no more room is left on the diskette, DOS will beep and prompt you to enter the second diskette. This will continue until all the files are backed up. As DOS fills the diskettes, you should label them consecutively as backup disk 1, backup disk 2, and so on.

Step 2: Do an Incremental Backup

If you make it a practice of backing up your hard disk at regular intervals, say every day or week, there is no need to copy those files that have not changed. You do, however, want to make sure that you back up any new or modified files.

Figure 8 Using the
BACKUP Command

```
C:\>backup c: a: /s

Insert backup diskette 01 in drive A:

WARNING! Files in the target drive
A:\ root directory will be erased
Press any key to continue . . .
```

This is known as an **incremental backup.** Fortunately, you can tell DOS to do an incremental backup with two additional parameters to the BACKUP command. The /M parameter tells the BACKUP command to copy only new or changed files. The /A parameter tells the BACKUP command to add the selected files to the existing backup diskettes and not erase their contents. So, this would be the command you enter to do an incremental backup (don't do it now):

```
backup c: a: /s/m/a
```

DOS would then tell you to insert the last backup diskette into drive A and press any key when you are ready. Any new or changed files would then be added to this diskette, and additional diskettes, if needed.

In addition to /S, /M, /A, and /F (for DOS 3.3), the BACKUP command also accepts the following parameters:

/D:*date*	Backs up only those files that were created or modified on or after the specified *date*.
/T:*time*	Backs up only those files that were created or modified at or after the specified *time*.
/L:*file*	Creates a backup log in the specified *file*.

Step 3: Restore the Backed Up Disk

Hopefully, you'll never have to use the backup diskettes of your hard disk. Suppose the worst has happened, however, and you must copy the files from your backup diskettes back onto your hard disk. This is done with the RESTORE command. First, you would make sure that you are at the root directory of the hard disk. Again, don't do this now, but the command to restore the entire hard disk would be:

```
restore a: /s
```

This command will restore the files from the backup diskettes in drive A to your current directory, which should be the root directory of the hard disk C. It will prompt you to insert the backup diskettes in the same order in which they were created. The /S parameter tells DOS to restore subdirectories as well.

Step 4: Back Up a Subdirectory

It is also possible to use the BACKUP command to save a copy of a single subdirectory. This is often done when the contents of a hard disk subdirectory will not fit on a single floppy disk. Although your LESSONS subdirectory is very small, let's create a backup of it to illustrate the procedure. Get a formatted floppy disk that is either empty or contains files that can be erased. Then execute this command:

Type   **backup c:\lessons a: /s**
Press   **Enter**

Insert the floppy disk into drive A and press any key. DOS will back up the contents of the LESSONS subdirectory onto the diskette in drive A. Your screen should look like Figure 9.

*Figure 9 Backing Up the
LESSONS Subdirectory*

```
C:\>backup c:\lessons a: /s

Insert backup diskette 01 in drive A:

WARNING! Files in the target drive
A:\ root directory will be erased
Press any key to continue . . .

*** Backing up files to drive A: ***
Diskette Number: 01

\LESSONS\SAMPLE.TXT

C:\>_
```

Step 5: Restore a Subdirectory

Suppose that you accidentally erased the contents of the LESSONS subdirectory. Simulate this accident by executing this command:

> Type   **erase c:\lessons*.***
> Press **Enter**
> Type   **y**
> Press **Enter**

Now, execute the following command to restore the LESSONS subdirectory from the backup diskette:

> Type   **restore a: c:\lessons*.* /s**
> Press **Enter**

DOS will ask you to insert backup diskette 1 in drive A and press any key when you are ready. After you do this and the RESTORE command is finished, your screen should look like Figure 10.

In addition to /S, which ensures the restoration of subdirectories, the RESTORE command also accepts the following parameters:

/P	Prompts you for permission to restore files.
/B:*date*	Restores only those files that were last modified on or before the specified *date*.
/A:*date*	Restores only those files that were last modified on or after the specified *date*.
/E:*time*	Restores only those files that were last modified at or earlier than the specified *time*.
/L:*time*	Restores only those files that were last modified at or later than the specified *time*.
/M:*file*	Restores only those files modified since the last BACKUP.
/N	Restores only those files that no longer exist on the target disk.

*Figure 10 Restoring the
LESSONS Subdirectory*

```
C:\>restore a: c:\lessons\*.* /s

Insert backup diskette 01 in drive A:
Press any key to continue . . .

*** Files were backed up 07-13-1989 ***

*** Restoring files from drive A: ***
Diskette: 01
\LESSONS\SAMPLE.TXT


C:\>_
```

Step 6: Back Up and Restore One or More Files

BACKUP and RESTORE can also be used for individual files and groups of files
specified with the DOS global file name characters ? and *. Simply insert the file
specification instead of just the drive letter or subdirectory of the disk to be
backed up. For example, suppose you wanted to back up only those files with
an extension of TXT on your hard disk. Make sure you are at the root directory
of hard disk C and execute this command:

Type   **backup c:*.txt a: /s**
Press   **Enter**

Insert your floppy disk into drive A and press **Enter** again. All TXT files in all
subdirectories on disk C will be backed up to drive A. To restore the files, enter
this command:

Type   **restore a: c:*.txt /s**
Press   **Enter**

1. If you have several blank diskettes you can use, backup the DOS subdirectory
   from your hard disk onto them. If you have only one diskette available, back
   up only one file or a group of files (such as *.SYS) that will fit on a single
   diskette.

2. Use the DIR command to examine the backup diskette you have created.

Lesson 7: Recovering Files from Damaged Disks

Every hard disk and floppy disk will eventually wear out or become physically
damaged or magnetically corrupted in some way. When one of these unfortunate
events occurs, DOS may not be able to read the files stored in or around the bad
spots. This is one reason why you should try to maintain up-to-date backup

copies of all of your important files and disks. If you don't do this, however, and DOS cannot read one of your files or perhaps even an entire disk, the RECOVER command may be able to help. This external command should be used only as a last resort. RECOVER does not work when DOS is run from a local area network.

Step 1: Recover a Single File

Suppose you try to retrieve a file from a floppy disk in drive A and DOS reports that it cannot read that file. You may get one of the following messages from DOS:

```
Disk error reading drive A:
General failure reading drive A:
Read fault error reading drive A:
Sector not found error reading drive A:
Track 0 bad - disk unusable
Unrecoverable read error on drive A:
```

First, take out the disk, make sure it is inserted correctly, and close the disk drive door or lever again. Then try using the CHKDSK command on that disk. If the CHKDSK command reports that a sector on the disk is bad, RECOVER might be able to read all or part of the file by skipping over the bad spots. Suppose the file you are trying to read is SAMPLE.TXT. You would enter this command (don't do this now):

```
recover a:sample.txt
```

RECOVER would then try to read SAMPLE.TXT, part by part, ignoring the bad spots. Then it would try to rewrite the file without the bad spots, possibly allowing you to read at least some of the original SAMPLE.TXT.

Step 2: Recover an Entire Disk

If you cannot gain access to any files on a disk, then you can tell the RECOVER command to try and reconstruct the entire disk. Again, this should only be done as a last resort. Here is the command you would enter to recover all the files on the disk in drive A (don't do it now):

```
recover a:
```

Practice

1. Take a diskette with files on it that you don't need, such as the backup diskette you created in Lesson 6, and insert it into drive A. Suppose that it is a damaged disk. Execute the following command to try to get back readable information on the damaged disk:

   Type **recover a:**
   Press **Enter**

   Press any key when the RECOVER command asks you to do so. When it is finished, RECOVER will report how many files it recovered.

2. RECOVER is to be used only as a last resort. When it recovers files, it changes their names to FILE0001.REC, FILE0002.REC, and so on. So, you have to examine and rename the recovered files to get them into usable form again. You don't need the files you recovered on the diskette in drive A, so reformat it:

> Type   **format a:**
> Press **Enter**

Lesson 8: Using the Prompt Option When Erasing Files

You have already learned how to use the ERASE (or DEL) command to remove files from a disk. If you try to erase every file on a disk or in a subdirectory, DOS will ask you if you are sure this is what you want to do before it discards the files. The ERASE command, however, does not automatically ask this question when you erase several files at once with the global file name characters * or ?. Fortunately, an optional parameter is available that lets you have DOS prompt you before erasing each file. This option is also handy for selectively erasing some files from a group of many.

Step 1: Specify the /P Parameter

Copy some files from the DOS subdirectory into your LESSONS subdirectory so that you have some files you can erase safely. Execute the following commands:

> Type   **cd c:\lessons**
> Press **Enter**
> Type   **copy c:\dos*.com**
> Press **Enter**

Use the DIR command to make sure that you are in the LESSONS subdirectory. Execute this command to erase the COM files from your LESSONS subdirectory with a prompt before erasing each file:

> Type   **erase *.com /p**
> Press **Enter**
> Type   **y**
> Press **Enter**

As Figure 11 shows, DOS will prompt you with "Delete (Y/N)?" before it actually deletes each file. For the remaining files, answer yes for some files and no for others. When the ERASE command has finished, execute this command to examine the LESSONS subdirectory:

> Type   **dir**
> Press **Enter**

The files for which you answered no will still be present.

Step 2: Don't Specify the /P Parameter

To delete the remaining COM files from your LESSONS subdirectory, execute this command:

> Type   **erase *.com**
> Press **Enter**

Practice

Make sure you are in your LESSONS subdirectory. Use the ERASE command with the /P parameter to tell DOS to delete every file in the subdirectory, but to prompt you first. Answer **n** for no to each prompt so that you don't erase any

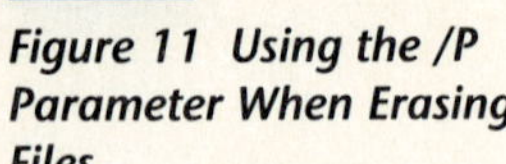

Figure 11 Using the /P Parameter When Erasing Files

files. To be extra safe, you can make it a practice to always use the /P parameter with the ERASE or DEL command.

Lesson 9: Learning More About the COPY Command

COPY is a versatile command that can be used in several different ways. You have already learned how to use COPY to duplicate one or more files from one disk or subdirectory to another. By specifying different names for the source and the target files, you can also duplicate files in the same subdirectory.

Step 1: Copy from the Console to Create a Text File

The COPY command can create a new text file without using a word processing or text editing program. Actually, you already did this in Lesson 4, but let's go over it again.

DOS can refer to certain hardware devices as if they were files. These devices are given special file names called DOS device names. For example, CON refers to the console, or the keyboard and the screen. Similarly, PRN refers to the printer. You can use device names such as CON and PRN as if they were file names in commands such as COPY. Make sure you are in your LESSONS subdirectory and then execute this command:

Type   **copy con sample2.txt**
Press   **Enter**

This command tells DOS to take every character you now type at the keyboard and copy it into a new file named SAMPLE2.TXT. Type the following text, pressing **Enter** at the end of each line:

```
A text file contains only letters, numbers,
punctuation marks, and other symbols that
appear on the keyboard.
```

An end-of-file mark is the Ctrl-Z character; it is the last character in a text file. When you are finished entering the text, you must insert an end-of-file mark into the file by doing this:

> Press   **F6**
> Press   **Enter**

To see what you have done, execute these commands:

> Type   **dir**
> Press   **Enter**
> Type   **type sample2.txt**
> Press   **Enter**

Your screen should look like Figure 12.

Step 2: Use COPY to Append Files

The COPY command is sometimes used to append or combine files. Suppose you wanted to create a new file named SAMPLE3.TXT that contained the contents of SAMPLE.TXT followed by the contents of SAMPLE2.TXT. Execute this command:

> Type   **copy sample.txt+sample2.txt sample3.txt**
> Press   **Enter**

Any number of source files can be combined by listing their names separated by plus signs. The last file name in the COPY command is the target file that will contain the combination of the source files. If you omit the name of a target file, DOS will combine the source files and copy them to the first source file listed. To see what you have done, enter these commands:

> Type   **dir**
> Press   **Enter**
> Type   **type sample3.txt**
> Press   **Enter**

Your screen should look like Figure 13.

Figure 12 Using COPY to Create a Text File

```
C:\LESSONS>copy con sample2.txt
A text file contains only letters, numbers,
punctuation marks, and other symbols that
appear on the keyboard.
^Z
        1 File(s) copied

C:\LESSONS>dir

 Volume in drive C is HARD DISK
 Volume Serial Number is 3324-07CC
 Directory of  C:\LESSONS

.            <DIR>       07-15-89  11:06a
..           <DIR>       07-15-89  11:06a
SAMPLE   TXT         29 07-15-89  11:06a
SAMPLE2  TXT        113 07-15-89  11:08a
        4 File(s)   19691520 bytes free

C:\LESSONS>type sample2.txt
A text file contains only letters, numbers,
punctuation marks, and other symbols that
appear on the keyboard.

C:\LESSONS>_
```

***Figure 13 Using COPY to
Append Files***

```
C:\LESSONS>copy sample.txt+sample2.txt sample3.txt
SAMPLE.TXT
SAMPLE2.TXT
        1 File(s) copied

C:\LESSONS>dir

 Volume in drive C is HARD DISK
 Volume Serial Number is 3324-07CC
 Directory of  C:\LESSONS

.              <DIR>      07-15-89  11:06a
..             <DIR>      07-15-89  11:06a
SAMPLE   TXT         29 07-15-89  11:06a
SAMPLE2  TXT        113 07-15-89  11:08a
SAMPLE3  TXT        143 07-15-89  11:09a
        5 File(s)   19689472 bytes free

C:\LESSONS>type sample3.txt
This is a sample text file.
A text file contains only letters, numbers,
punctuation marks, and other symbols that
appear on the keyboard.

C:\LESSONS>_
```

Step 3: Use the /V Parameter

The COPY command has three optional parameters, /V, /B, and /A. The /V parameter tells DOS to verify that the copy has been made successfully with no errors. Each time data is written to the disk, a confirmation procedure will be performed to ensure that data can be read without error. The /V parameter is used only when making copies to disk files, not device names. Verifying a copy takes longer and is usually not necessary, but you may want to do it when copying especially important files, such as programs in which the scrambling of a single byte can cause a bug. For example, try this command:

Type   **copy c:\command.com command.bak /v**
Press   **Enter**

You won't see any difference on the screen when the COPY command is used with the /V parameter, except that it works a little slower.

Step 4: Use the /B and /A Parameters

By default, the COPY command creates a target file that is the same type of file as the source. If you copy a text file, COPY produces a text file. Another term for text file is **ASCII file.** ASCII, which stands for American Standard Code for Information Interchange, is the most common scheme used to encode characters as numbers so that they can be manipulated by computers. A **binary file** is a file that contains programs or data that are not encoded as ASCII characters. Files with extensions of EXE and COM, for example, are binary files. If you copy a binary file, COPY normally produces a binary file.

The other two parameters of the COPY command, /B and /A, are used when the type of file you want to produce is different than the source. The /B parameter, when specified after a source file name, tells DOS to copy the entire file, including any end-of-file marks. When used with a target file name, the /B parameter tells DOS not to add an end-of-file mark to the end of the file. The /A parameter tells

DOS to treat the file as an ASCII file. If a source file name is followed by /A, only data up to and including the first end-of-file mark will be copied. If a target file name is followed by /A, an end-of-file mark will be added as the last character of the file.

In most cases, you don't have to use /B or /A. You can, however, use the /B command to view the entire contents of a binary file on your screen. First, try the following COPY command without the /B parameter:

Type   **copy command.bak con**
Press   **Enter**

Remember, COMMAND.BAK is a copy of COMMAND.COM, the DOS command processor, which is a binary file. When you copy it to the screen, the display will stop when the first end-of-file mark is encountered. Now, try this command to display the entire COMMAND.BAK binary file on your screen (the computer will beep quite a bit, so skip this command if you don't want to disturb others around you):

Type   **copy command.bak /b con**
Press   **Enter**

Don't be alarmed if your computer seems to be going crazy. All the strange characters and beeps occur because binary programming code is being displayed on the screen. Occasionally, you will see words or phrases that you can read, usually messages embedded in the command processor. It will take a couple of minutes for the entire COMMAND.BAK file to be copied to the screen, and Ctrl-Break won't stop it, so just be patient and wait.

Practice
1. Use the COPY command with the CON device name to display the contents of SAMPLE2.TXT on your screen.
2. Use the COPY command with the PRN device name to send SAMPLE2.TXT to your printer.
3. Use the COPY command with the /B parameter and CON device name to examine an EXE or COM file from the DOS subdirectory on your hard disk.

Lesson 10: Setting the VERIFY Option

In Lesson 9 you learned that the COPY command's optional /V ensures that files copied to the disk can be read without error. The VERIFY command lets you turn this option on or off whenever any files are copied to a disk, not just for a single COPY command like the /V parameter.

Step 1: Execute the VERIFY Command

To see the current setting of the VERIFY option, execute this command:

Type   **verify**
Press   **Enter**

The default setting of the VERIFY option is off.

Step 2: Change the VERIFY Option

You can change the current setting of the VERIFY option by following the command with ON or OFF. For example, execute these commands:

```
Type    verify on
Press   Enter
Type    verify
Press   Enter
```

Turn the VERIFY option off again.

Lesson 11: Changing File Attributes

A **file attribute** is a characteristic of a file. DOS has several attributes that can be associated with files. The two most commonly encountered by the average user are the read-only and the archive attributes.

When a file's **read-only attribute** is turned off, the default state, it can be read, written, modified, or deleted. If the file's read-only attribute is turned on, it cannot be changed in any way. The only way to modify or delete the file is to turn the read-only attribute back off again.

The **archive attribute** indicates whether a file has been changed since it was last saved with the BACKUP command. The archive attribute is turned on whenever a file is rewritten to disk (that is, changed in some way). When the BACKUP command saves a file, its archive attribute is turned off. This is how DOS can tell if a file has been changed since you last backed it up.

Step 1: Change the Read-only Attribute

Suppose the SAMPLE.TXT file was an extremely important file that you did not want to accidentally delete. One way to help ensure that it would not be deleted would be to turn on its read-only attribute. This can be done with the ATTRIB command.

Make sure you are in the LESSONS subdirectory, and then execute this command:

```
Type    attrib +r sample.txt
Press   Enter
```

This command turns on the read-only attribute for the file SAMPLE.TXT. Now, this file cannot be changed or deleted. Try the following three commands:

```
Type    type sample.txt
Press   Enter
Type    erase sample.txt
Press   Enter
Type    dir
Press   Enter
```

As you can see from Figure 14, you can read the file, but you cannot delete it after the read-only attribute has been turned on. DOS replies with "Access denied" when you try to delete a read-only file. Entering the DIR command confirms that the file SAMPLE.TXT has not been deleted.

Figure 14 Using ATTRIB to Set the Read-only Attribute

```
C:\LESSONS>attrib +r sample.txt

C:\LESSONS>type sample.txt
This is a sample text file.

C:\LESSONS>erase sample.txt
Access denied

C:\LESSONS>dir

 Volume in drive C is HARD DISK
 Volume Serial Number is 3324-07CC
 Directory of  C:\LESSONS

 .            <DIR>       07-15-89  11:06a
 ..           <DIR>       07-15-89  11:06a
SAMPLE   TXT          29 07-15-89  11:06a
SAMPLE2  TXT         113 07-15-89  11:08a
SAMPLE3  TXT         143 07-15-89  11:09a
COMMAND  BAK       37557 12-19-88  12:00a
         6 File(s)   19650560 bytes free

C:\LESSONS>_
```

Step 2: Change the Archive Attribute

The ATTRIB command can also be used to change the archive attribute. You could, for example, turn off the archive attribute for a file, even though it has been changed, to prevent it from being saved by the next BACKUP command. Execute the following command:

> Type **attrib -a sample.txt**
> Press **Enter**

This turns off the archive attribute for the SAMPLE.TXT file. Unless you change the file or the attribute again, it will not be saved by the next BACKUP command.

The ATTRIB command can also be used to view the current attributes of a file. Execute the following command:

> Type **attrib sample.txt**
> Press **Enter**

As Figure 15 shows, if you omit the R and A switches between the ATTRIB and the file name, DOS will report which attributes are turned on for that file. Since the read-only attribute is turned on and the archive attribute is turned off, DOS replies with only R before the full file name C:\LESSONS\SAMPLE.TXT.

You can also set both attributes at once with a single ATTRIB command. Turn the read-only attribute back off and the archive attribute back on by executing this command:

> Type **attrib -r +a sample.txt**
> Press **Enter**

Practice

1. Use the ATTRIB command to examine the file attributes of SAMPLE2.TXT.

2. Turn on the read-only attribute of SAMPLE2.TXT and then try to delete the file.

3. Turn off the read-only attribute of SAMPLE2.TXT.

```
C:\LESSONS>attrib -a sample.txt

C:\LESSONS>attrib sample.txt
      R      C:\LESSONS\SAMPLE.TXT

C:\LESSONS>_
```

Lesson 12: Copying Groups of Files

In Chapter 2 you learned that you can copy groups of files with the COPY command by using the global file name characters ? or * in your file specifications. Starting with version 3.2, however, DOS included XCOPY, a more sophisticated command for copying files. While the COPY command reads and then writes a single file at a time, XCOPY reads as many files as it can into memory first and then writes them. This makes XCOPY faster than COPY in some cases. In addition, XCOPY accepts more optional parameters, making it more flexible than COPY. On the other hand, unlike COPY, XCOPY is an external command. This means that XCOPY must be accessible on your disk if you want to use it.

Step 1: Copy a Group of Files with XCOPY

To see how XCOPY works, make sure you are in the LESSONS subdirectory on your hard disk and put a formatted diskette in drive A. Then execute this command:

Type   **xcopy *.* a:**
Press   **Enter**

Your screen should look like Figure 16. XCOPY read all of the files in the LESSONS subdirectory into memory first, and then copied them to the diskette in drive A.

Step 2: Copy Subdirectories

Unlike the COPY command, XCOPY can be instructed to copy files from all the subdirectories in the source disk or directory. In the process, it will create new subdirectories on the target disk if necessary. For example, change to the root directory of your hard disk and try the following XCOPY command:

Type   **cd **
Press   **Enter**
Type   **xcopy sample.* a: /s**
Press   **Enter**

Figure 16 Using XCOPY to Duplicate a Group of Files

```
C:\LESSONS>xcopy *.* a:
Reading source file(s)...
SAMPLE.TXT
SAMPLE2.TXT
SAMPLE3.TXT
COMMAND.BAK
        4 File(s) copied

C:\LESSONS>_
```

XCOPY will look for all files with a primary filename of SAMPLE no matter what subdirectory they might be in. It will create corresponding subdirectories on the floppy disk in drive A and copy the files into the appropriate subdirectories. Execute the following two commands to see what you have done to your floppy disk:

Type **dir a:**
Press **Enter**
Type **dir a:\lessons**
Press **Enter**

Your screen should look like Figure 17.

Figure 17 Using XCOPY to Duplicate a Subdirectory

```
C:\>dir a:

 Volume in drive A has no label
 Volume Serial Number is 1A3F-12C9
 Directory of  A:\

SAMPLE   TXT        29 07-15-89  11:06a
SAMPLE2  TXT       113 07-15-89  11:08a
SAMPLE3  TXT       143 07-15-89  11:09a
COMMAND  BAK     37557 12-19-88  12:00a
LESSONS      <DIR>     07-15-89  11:39a
        5 File(s)     319488 bytes free

C:\>dir a:\lessons

 Volume in drive A has no label
 Volume Serial Number is 1A3F-12C9
 Directory of  A:\LESSONS

.            <DIR>     07-15-89  11:39a
..           <DIR>     07-15-89  11:39a
SAMPLE   TXT        29 07-15-89  11:06a
        3 File(s)     319488 bytes free

C:\>_
```

Step 3: Examine the Other XCOPY Parameters

Several other parameters can be used with the XCOPY command in addition to
/S. The following table lists all of them.

Parameter	Action
/A	Copies only those files whose archive attribute is turned on. Does not change the archive attribute after copying.
/D:*date*	Copies only those files created or last modified on or after the specified *date*.
/E	Copies any subdirectories beneath the specified source disk or directory, even if they contain no files. This parameter, if used, must be used with /S.
/M	Same as /A, but turns off the archive attribute after copying.
/P	Prompts you for confirmation before each file is copied.
/S	Copies nonempty subdirectories beneath the specified source disk or directory.
/V	Verifies each copy to be identical to the original.
/W	Waits for you to press a key before copying files.

Practice

1. Try each of the following commands and explain exactly what they do. Answer
   n for no to each prompt to leave your diskette in drive A unchanged.

   Type   **xcopy *.* a: /p /a**
   Press **Enter**
   Type   **xcopy *.* a: /p /d:01-01-89**
   Press **Enter**
   Type   **xcopy *.* a: /w /p /m**
   Press **Enter**

2. The XCOPY command can copy an entire diskette to another diskette, even
   if the source and target diskettes are different types, as long as the target
   diskette has enough room. For example, if you have a 5¼-inch floppy drive
   A and a 3½-inch floppy drive B, you would have to use XCOPY instead of
   DISKCOPY to duplicate a 5¼-inch diskette on a 3½-inch diskette. Even if you
   have only one floppy drive, you can use XCOPY to duplicate an entire diskette.
   Unlike DISKCOPY, however, XCOPY cannot automatically format a diskette.
   To copy an entire diskette with XCOPY, get an extra formatted diskette and
   execute the following command:

   Type   **xcopy a: b: /s /e**
   Press **Enter**

   Note that this command will work even if you don't have a floppy drive B
   installed in your computer. DOS has the ability to "pretend" that drive A is
   temporarily drive B to complete such commands. It will prompt you when to
   insert the diskette for drive A or for drive B. Just swap the source and target
   diskettes in drive A. When you are finished, use DIR to examine the disk in
   drive A.

Lesson 13: Updating Sets of Files

Suppose you have identical copies of the file SAMPLE.TXT in various subdirectories on your hard disk and you want to update them all with a new copy of SAMPLE.TXT stored on a floppy disk. Although you cannot do this with a single COPY command, you can use a single REPLACE command. REPLACE is an external DOS command that is used to update previous versions of files.

Step 1: Prepare the Floppy Disk

Let's create an updated version of the file SAMPLE.TXT on the diskette in drive A. Then execute the following command to create a new SAMPLE.TXT:

Type   `copy con a:sample.txt`
Press   **Enter**

Now, do the following to add the text to SAMPLE.TXT in drive A:

Type   `This is the new sample text file.`
Press   **Enter**
Press   **F6**
Press   **Enter**

Step 2: Replace the Hard Disk Files

Suppose you had several copies of SAMPLE.TXT on the hard disk in different subdirectories. (You don't, but it doesn't matter for this example.) Execute the following command to replace all copies of SAMPLE.TXT on the hard disk with the new version from the floppy disk in drive A:

Type   `replace a:sample.txt c:\ /s`
Press   **Enter**

The /S parameter tells the REPLACE command to search through all subdirectories of the target for files to replace. To see what you have done, execute this command:

Type   `type c:\lessons\sample.txt`
Press   **Enter**

Your screen should look like Figure 18.

Step 3: Add Files to the Target Disk

The REPLACE command can also be used to copy files that exist on the source disk, but not on the target disk, to the target disk. Execute the following commands to move back into the LESSONS subdirectory on the hard disk and rename a few of the files:

Type   `cd lessons`
Press   **Enter**
Type   `ren sample.txt part1.txt`
Press   **Enter**
Type   `ren sample2.txt part2.txt`
Press   **Enter**
Type   `ren sample3.txt example.txt`
Press   **Enter**

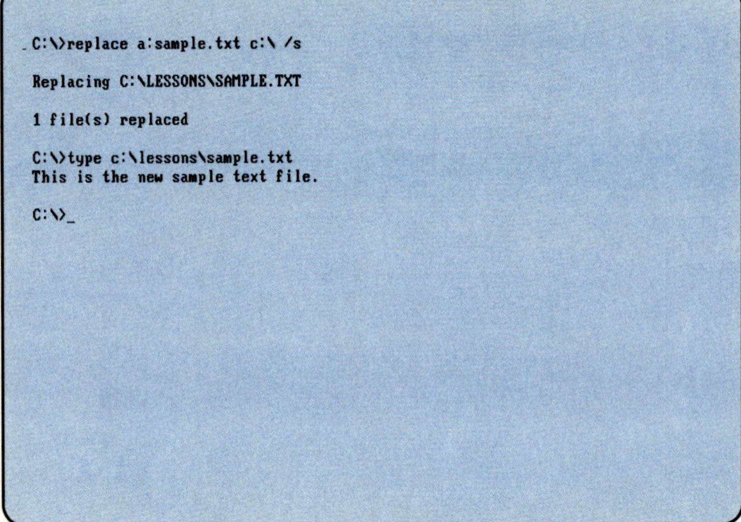

Figure 18 Replacing Files on the Hard Disk

Now your LESSONS subdirectory on the hard disk contains the files PART1.TXT, PART2.TXT and EXAMPLE.TXT. The floppy disk in drive A does not contain files with these three names. Suppose you wanted to copy *only* those files with different names from C to A. Execute this command:

> Type   **replace *.* a: /a**
> Press   **Enter**

The /A is a parameter that tells the REPLACE command to add files from the source to the target, but only those that don't already exist in the target. To see the result, execute this command:

> Type   **dir a:**
> Press   **Enter**

Your screen should look like Figure 19.

Step 4: Examine the Other REPLACE Parameters

Several other parameters can be used with the REPLACE command. The following table lists all of them.

Parameter	Action
/A	Adds new files to the target instead of replacing existing files. Cannot be used with /S or /U.
/P	Prompts you for confirmation before each file is replaced.
/R	Replaces read-only files as well as regular files.
/S	Searches all subdirectories on the target disk to replace matching files. Cannot be used with /A.
/U	Replaces only those target files that are older than their matching source files. Cannot be used with /A.
/W	Waits for you to press a key before replacing or adding files.

Figure 19 Using REPLACE to Add Files

```
Adding A:\PART1.TXT

Adding A:\PART2.TXT

Adding A:\EXAMPLE.TXT

3 file(s) added

C:\LESSONS>dir a:

 Volume in drive A has no label
 Volume Serial Number is 1A3F-12C9
 Directory of  A:\

SAMPLE   TXT       35 07-15-89  11:45a
SAMPLE2  TXT      113 07-15-89  11:08a
SAMPLE3  TXT      143 07-15-89  11:09a
COMMAND  BAK    37557 12-19-88  12:00a
LESSONS      <DIR>     07-15-89  11:39a
PART1    TXT       35 07-15-89  11:45a
PART2    TXT      113 07-15-89  11:08a
EXAMPLE  TXT      143 07-15-89  11:09a
        8 File(s)    316416 bytes free

C:\LESSONS>_
```

Practice

Make sure you are in the LESSONS subdirectory on the hard disk and execute the following command to change the EXAMPLE file:

> Type **copy part1.txt+part2.txt example.txt**
> Press **Enter**

Execute this command and explain what it does:

> Type **replace *.* a: /w /p /r /u**
> Press **Enter**

Press any key to continue and answer **y** for yes to the prompt.

Lesson 14: Transferring the DOS System Files

When you format a system diskette with the /S parameter as you learned in Lesson 9 of Chapter 2, DOS copies two hidden system files to the newly formatted disk. These files, along with the command processor, COMMAND.COM, let you boot up your computer from that disk. It is also possible to format a diskette and leave space for the system files to be transferred later. This is sometimes done by individuals and companies that transfer software or data to others. It is not legal to give away or sell DOS without a license from IBM or Microsoft, so you are not supposed to distribute boot-up disks. You can, however, format a disk so that the recipient can transfer his or her own copy of DOS to that disk. The SYS command makes this possible. The SYS command is also used for upgrading to a new version of DOS. SYS, which is an external command, will not work if you are running DOS from a network.

Step 1: Format a Diskette with the /B Parameter

Execute this command to format a diskette to which DOS can be transferred later:

> Type **format a: /b**
> Press **Enter**

Insert the diskette you have been using into drive A and press the **Enter** key. When the format procedure is finished, press **Enter** to skip typing a volume label and enter **n** for no in response to the prompt asking if you want to format another disk. As you can see from Figure 20, DOS reserved 73,728 bytes for the system. The hidden system files, however, have not yet been transferred to this space.

Step 2: Transfer the Hidden System Files

To transfer the hidden system files, execute this command:

Type   **sys a:**
Press   **Enter**

When DOS is finished, it will display the message "System transferred," but if you examine the disk with the DIR command, no files will appear in the directory. This is because the system files are hidden.

Step 3: Copy the File COMMAND.COM

One more step is necessary in order to be able to boot up your computer from this diskette. Execute the following command to copy the DOS command processor from the root directory of your hard disk to the diskette in drive A:

Type   **copy c:\command.com a:**
Press   **Enter**

The diskette in drive A can now be used to boot up the computer.

Practice

1. Reboot your computer from the system diskette you just created. Enter the current date and time. Use DIR to examine the directory of your diskette. The procedure you followed in this lesson achieves the same result as using the /S parameter with the FORMAT command.

*Figure 20 Using the /B
Parameter with FORMAT*

```
C:\LESSONS>format a: /b
Insert new diskette for drive A:
and press ENTER when ready...

Format complete

Volume label (11 characters, ENTER for none)?

    362496 bytes total disk space
     73728 bytes used by system
    288768 bytes available on disk

      1024 bytes in each allocation unit
       282 allocation units available on disk

Volume Serial Number is 283D-13CC

Format another (Y/N)?n
C:\LESSONS>_
```

2. Now, reboot your computer from the hard disk. Enter the date and time if necessary. Change the DOS prompt so it displays the current drive and directory, if it does not already do so.

Lesson 15: Comparing Files and Disks

Keeping one or more copies of important files or disks is prudent. After you make a copy of an especially important file or diskette, you might want to check it to make sure that it is identical to the original. Although errors are rare, a bit or byte can get scrambled during the copy procedure if the VERIFY option is turned off. DOS has two external commands, COMP and DISKCOMP, that compare files and diskettes, respectively. These commands can also be used if you forget whether two files or disks are identical. Note: DISKCOMP will not work if you are running DOS from a network.

Step 1: Compare Two Files

Change to your LESSONS subdirectory if you are not already there. Use the directory command to examine the files inside LESSONS. It should contain a file named COMMAND.BAK, which you created in Lesson 9. Let's see if COMMAND.BAK in the LESSONS subdirectory is identical to COMMAND.COM in the root directory of your hard disk. Execute this command:

> Type   **comp command.bak c:\command.com**
> Press   **Enter**

Your screen should look like Figure 21. The files are identical, so DOS reports that the "Files compare OK." Press **n** for no in response to the prompt asking if you want to compare more files. If the files had been different sizes or if any bytes had been different, DOS would have told you.

Figure 21 Using COMP to Compare Two Files

```
C:\LESSONS>comp command.bak c:\command.com


C:COMMAND.BAK and C:\COMMAND.COM

EOF mark not found
Files compare OK
Compare more files (Y/N) ?_
```

Step 2: Compare Two Diskettes

The DISKCOMP command is used to compare the contents of two diskettes. For example, if your computer has two floppy drives, A and B, that are the same type, put a diskette in each one and compare them with this command:

Type   **diskcomp a: b:**
Press   **Enter**

If your computer has only one floppy disk drive, like many hard disk systems, try this command instead:

Type   **diskcomp a: a:**
Press   **Enter**

DOS will then prompt you when to insert each diskette. If the two diskettes are identical, then DOS will display "Compare OK." Otherwise, "Compare error" messages will be displayed that report where mismatches were found. When it is finished, DISKCOMP will ask you if you want to compare another diskette. Type **n** for no.

Practice

1. Let's see what COMP does if two files are different. Try this command:

   Type   **comp part1.txt part2.txt**
   Press   **Enter**

   The COMP command determines immediately that the files are different sizes, so they cannot be identical. It doesn't examine them any further.

2. Now let's try comparing two files that are the same size, but different in some other way. Follow these instructions to create a file similar, but not identical, to PART1.TXT:

   Type   **copy con partx.txt**
   Press   **Enter**
   Type   **This is the old sample text file.**
   Press   **Enter**
   Press   **F6**
   Press   **Enter**

   Compare PART1.TXT with PARTX.TXT with this command:

   Type   **comp part1.txt partx.txt**
   Press   **Enter**

   Since COMP is typically used by programmers, the results are given in hexadecimal (base 16) ASCII codes. For example, the letter "n" is represented as 6E and "o" is 6F. COMP shows three differences between the two files: the letters "n e w" versus "o l d."

Lesson 16: Displaying and Changing a Volume Label

DOS calls the name of a disk the **volume label.** This name, which is optional, can be helpful when trying to identify a disk.

Step 1: Display a Volume Label

One way to see the volume label of a disk is to use the DIR command. Another way is to use the internal command VOL. Try this:

> Type　**vol**
> Press　**Enter**

DOS will display the volume label of the disk in your default drive. You can get the volume label of a disk other than the one in your default drive by specifying the disk drive letter. For example, put a formatted diskette into drive A and execute this command:

> Type　**vol a:**
> Press　**Enter**

DOS will respond with the volume label of the diskette in drive A.

Step 2: Change a Volume Label

DOS versions 4.0 and newer automatically ask you to supply a volume label whenever you format a disk. With earlier DOS versions, you can use the /V parameter to have the FORMAT command prompt you for a volume label. You can also specify a new volume label or change an existing one with the LABEL command. LABEL is an external command; it does not work if you are running DOS from a network. To see how it works, put a formatted diskette in drive A and execute this command:

> Type　**label a:**
> Press　**Enter**

DOS will report the current volume label and allow you to enter a new name, which can be up to 11 characters long.

> Type　**sample**
> Press　**Enter**

To see the new volume label of the diskette, execute this command:

> Type　**vol a:**
> Press　**Enter**

Figure 22 shows the result.

Practice

1. If you specify the new volume label right after the LABEL command, DOS won't prompt you. Try this command:

   > Type　**label a:example**
   > Press　**Enter**

   Use DIR or VOL to examine the new volume label.

2. You can also delete an existing volume label. Try the following:

   > Type　**label a:**
   > Press　**Enter**
   > Press　**Enter**
   > Type　**y**

Figure 22 Using LABEL to Change a Disk's Name

```
C:\LESSONS>label a:
Volume in drive A has no label
Volume Serial Number is 283D-13CC
Volume label (11 characters, ENTER for none)? sample

C:\LESSONS>vol a:

 Volume in drive A is SAMPLE
 Volume Serial Number is 283D-13CC

C:\LESSONS>_
```

3. VER is an internal DOS command similar to VOL. It is used to find out the version of DOS you are using, in case you don't know or forget. Try it:

Type   **ver**
Press   **Enter**

Lesson 17: Displaying and Changing the Date and Time

If no AUTOEXEC.BAT file is present in the root directory of the startup disk, DOS will prompt you to enter the new date and time whenever you boot up or reboot the computer. If an AUTOEXEC.BAT file is present, DOS will not prompt you for the date and time unless the commands DATE and TIME are in AUTO-EXEC.BAT. DATE and TIME are internal commands that let you see and change the current date and time kept by the computer's real-time clock. Most micro-computers sold today have a battery that keeps the real-time clock operating even when the computer is off, so you don't need to execute DATE and TIME every time you boot up. Nevertheless, you can still use DATE and TIME to see the current date and time. In addition, DATE and TIME are sometimes needed to correct the internal clock, such as when changing to or from daylight saving time. It is important to set your computer to the correct date and time so that you know when files were created or last changed.

Step 1: Execute the DATE Command

To see the current date kept by your computer, without changing it, execute this command:

Type   **date**
Press   **Enter** (2 times)

Step 2: Change the Date

One way to change the current date is to execute the DATE command without any parameters. DOS will prompt you to enter the new date. Another way to change the date is to specify the new date after the DATE command before you press Enter. For example, execute this command:

> Type   **date 1-1-90**
> Press   **Enter**

Now, use the DATE command without any parameters to see the date you set. Notice how DOS automatically figures out the correct day of the week.

When you specify a new date, you must use only numbers: 1–12 for the month, 1–31 for the day, and 80–79 or 1980–2079 for the year. The month, day, and year entries may be separated with hyphens (-) or slashes (/).

Step 3: Execute the TIME Command

To see the current time kept by your computer, without changing it, execute this command:

> Type   **time**
> Press   **Enter** (2 times)

Step 4: Change the Time

One way to change the current time is to execute the TIME command without any parameters. DOS will prompt you to enter the new date. Another way to change the time is to specify the new time after the TIME command before you press Enter. For example, execute this command:

> Type   **time 14:22:13.45**
> Press   **Enter**

Now, use the TIME command without any parameters to see the time you set (see Figure 23). Notice that the new time starts ticking as soon as you enter it.

When you specify a new time, you must use the 24-hour format. If you like, you can specify a new time accurate to hundredths of seconds. The command you just executed sets the time to 22 minutes, 13.45 seconds past 14 hundred hours (2 P.M.). You don't have to enter the seconds or hundredths of seconds. If the time is exactly on the hour, you don't have to enter the minutes. Any portion of the time you omit will be set to zero.

Practice

1. Use the DATE command to reset the correct date.
2. Use the TIME command to reset the correct time.
3. Check the current date and time again.

Lesson 18: Displaying a Memory Report

Starting with version 4.0, DOS includes MEM, an external command that presents a memory report. This report displays the amount of memory used and free. It can also specify the location, size, and name of each program or data area

```
C:\>date
Current date is Sun 07-16-1989
Enter new date (mm-dd-yy):

C:\>date 1-1-90

C:\>date
Current date is Mon 01-01-1990
Enter new date (mm-dd-yy):

C:\>time
Current time is 10:41:11.84a
Enter new time:

C:\>time 14:22:13.45

C:\>time
Current time is  2:22:15.09p
Enter new time:

C:\>_
```

currently loaded into memory. MEM can provide more detailed and technical information about memory usage than CHKDSK.

Step 1: Execute the MEM Command

If you don't have DOS 4.00 or newer, you cannot use MEM. Otherwise, execute this command:

Type   **mem**
Press   **Enter**

Figure 24 shows the result, although your report may have different numbers, depending on the amount of RAM installed and the programs that have been loaded in your computer.


```
C:\>mem

    655360 bytes total memory
    655360 bytes available
    521248 largest executable program size

C:\>_
```

Step 2: Use the /PROGRAM Parameter

The MEM command has an optional parameter that will also display the programs loaded into memory. Execute this command:

Type   **mem /program**
Press   **Enter**

The resulting report will be longer and contain technical details concerning the location, name, and size of each program and data area in memory.

MEM has one other optional parameter, /DEBUG, that provides even more detailed information than the /PROGRAM parameter. The /DEBUG parameter presents technical facts of interest mainly to assembly language programmers, but you can still try it. Execute this command:

Type   **mem /debug**
Press   **Enter**

The /PROGRAM and /DEBUG parameters cannot be used at the same time.

Lesson 19: Reassigning, Joining, and Substituting Drives

DOS has three external commands that influence the use of disk drives and subdirectories, namely ASSIGN, JOIN, and SUBST. These commands can be handy when working with programs that require certain disks to be in certain drives, when programs don't allow you to specify paths, or when paths get too long. JOIN and SUBST do not work when running DOS from a network.

Step 1: Execute the ASSIGN Command

The ASSIGN command lets you change the drive letter associated with a disk drive. It is sometimes used with application programs developed before hard disks were common. A program, for example, may only work with diskette drives A and B. With ASSIGN, however, you may be able to trick the program into thinking that your hard disk is drive A. Make sure you are at the root directory of your hard disk and then execute this command:

Type   **assign a = c**
Press   **Enter**

To see the result, execute this command:

Type   **dir a:**
Press   **Enter**

DOS will present the directory of the hard disk, not the diskette in drive A. It "thinks" the hard disk is drive A, even though the DOS prompt still reports your current drive and directory as C:\ (see Figure 25).

To change all drives back to their original assignments, execute this command:

Type   **assign**
Press   **Enter**

*Figure 25 Using ASSIGN to
Change a Drive's Letter*

```
C:\>assign a = c

C:\>dir a:

 Volume in drive A is HARD DISK
 Volume Serial Number is 3324-07CC
 Directory of  A:\

CONFIG   SYS       146 07-09-89   1:22p
COMMAND  COM     37557 12-19-88  12:00a
DOS          <DIR>      07-09-89   1:23p
LESSONS      <DIR>      07-12-89   4:01p
AUTOEXEC BAT       256 01-01-80  12:03a
        5 File(s)   19652608 bytes free

C:\>_
```

In practice, you should avoid using ASSIGN if at all possible because it disguises the true type of the disk drive. Microsoft suggests that you use an equivalent SUBST command instead, which we will discuss shortly, because ASSIGN may not be compatible with future versions of DOS.

Step 2: Execute the JOIN Command

The JOIN command lets you treat an entire disk as if it were a subdirectory on another disk. You can then work with files on multiple disks as if they were part of one subdirectory on one disk. Let's try an example. Make sure you are at the root directory of your hard disk. Create a new subdirectory by executing this command:

> Type   **md diska**
> Press   **Enter**

Put a formatted diskette in drive A. Then execute this command:

> Type   **join a: diska**
> Press   **Enter**

To see the result, execute these commands:

> Type   **join**
> Press   **Enter**
> Type   **dir diska**
> Press   **Enter**

Figure 26 shows the result. When the JOIN command is entered without any parameters, it displays the current drives and subdirectories that are joined. The DIR command presents the files on the floppy disk, in this case just COMMAND.COM, as if they were in the DISKA subdirectory on the hard disk.

You use the /D parameter to undo a previous JOIN command. Execute the following commands to disconnect the join and remove the DISKA subdirectory:

> Type   **join a: /d**
> Press   **Enter**

Figure 26 Using JOIN to Treat a Disk as a Subdirectory

```
C:\>md diska

C:\>join a: diska

C:\>join
A: => C:\DISKA

C:\>dir diska

 Volume in drive C is HARD DISK
 Volume Serial Number is 3324-07CC
 Directory of  C:\DISKA

COMMAND  COM     37557 12-19-88  12:00a
        1 File(s)   19650560 bytes free

C:\>_
```

Type   **rd diska**
Press   **Enter**

Step 3: Execute the SUBST Command

SUBST is the opposite of the JOIN command; it lets you treat a subdirectory as if it were a disk in a separate drive. For example, let's substitute the imaginary drive letter D for your LESSONS subdirectory. If you have a real disk drive D in your computer, choose a different letter. Make sure you are at the root directory of your hard disk and execute these commands:

Type   **subst d: lessons**
Press   **Enter**
Type   **subst**
Press   **Enter**
Type   **dir d:**
Press   **Enter**

SUBST entered without any parameters reports the substitutions that have been made. As Figure 27 shows, the subdirectory C:\LESSONS can now be referred to as simply D:.

You use the /D parameter to cancel a previous substitution. For example, execute the following command:

Type   **subst d: /d**
Press   **Enter**

Note that the following DOS commands do not work on drives used in the JOIN or SUBST commands: BACKUP, CHKDSK, DISKCOMP, DISKCOPY, FDISK, FORMAT, LABEL, RECOVER, RESTORE, and SYS.

Practice

The MS-DOS 4.01 *User's Reference* manual suggests that you use the SUBST command instead of ASSIGN. Repeat Step 1 of this lesson, except execute the following command instead of the ASSIGN command:

Type   **subst a: c:**
Press   **Enter**

Figure 27 Using SUBST to Treat a Subdirectory as a Disk

```
C:\>subst d: lessons

C:\>subst
D: => C:\LESSONS

C:\>dir d:

 Volume in drive D is HARD DISK
 Volume Serial Number is 3324-07CC
 Directory of  D:\

 .             <DIR>      07-15-89  11:06a
 ..            <DIR>      07-15-89  11:06a
 PART1    TXT       35 07-15-89  11:45a
 PART2    TXT      113 07-15-89  11:08a
 EXAMPLE  TXT      149 07-15-89  11:48a
 COMMAND  BAK    37557 12-19-88  12:00a
 PARTX    TXT       35 07-15-89   2:49p
        7 File(s)   19652608 bytes free

C:\>_
```

When you are finished examining the directory, use the SUBST command with the /D parameter to restore the original drive assignments.

Lesson 20: Learning More About the PRINT Command

PRINT is a sophisticated command that can print one or more files in the background while you continue your work with DOS. This limited multitasking ability is called **spooling.** Several PRINT parameters allow you to fine-tune this spooling capability on your computer.

Step 1: Examine the First Time PRINT Parameters

Several of the PRINT parameters may be used only the first time you execute the PRINT command after booting up. These parameters set the stage for the way PRINT will work for the rest of your DOS session. You have already used the PRINT command since you booted up, so don't try the following parameters. Just read and try to understand the explanations.

Parameter	*Action*
/D:*device*	Specifies the device name of the printer to be used by PRINT. The default is PRN or LPT1, the printer connected to the first parallel port on your computer. LPT2, LPT3, and COM1 through COM4 are device names of other parallel ports and serial ports to which a printer might be connected. If you don't specify the /D parameter, DOS will prompt you for the device name the first time you use the PRINT command.
/B:*size*	Sets the size in bytes of the memory buffer to be used for data to be printed. The minimum and default value is 512. The maximum value is 1634. Larger values enable PRINT to work faster, but use more memory.

/U:*ticks*	Specifies how long in clock ticks PRINT should wait before giving up for a printer that is still busy. The minimum and default value is 1. The maximum value is 255.
/M:*ticks*	Specifies the number of clock ticks it can take to print a character. The value can range from 1 to 255. The default value is 2.
/S:*time*	Specifies the time interval PRINT must wait before getting the attention of the CPU. The value can range from 1 to 255. The default value is 8.
/Q:*number*	Specifies the number of files that can be held in the **print queue,** the list of files to be printed in the background. The number can range from 4 to 32. The default number is 10.

Step 2: Print Several Files

The remaining parameters to the PRINT command can be used any time, not just the first time PRINT is executed for a given DOS session. Change to your LESSONS subdirectory on the hard disk. If you have a printer, turn it on, but take it off line. In other words, press the On Line button so that the On Line light turns off. This will simulate a busy printer. Execute the following commands:

> Type **print part1.txt**
> Press **Enter**
> Type **print part2.txt**
> Press **Enter**
> Type **print example.txt**
> Press **Enter**

Figure 28 shows the result. Each time you execute a PRINT command, the file is placed in the queue and the DOS prompt returns.

Figure 28 Placing Files in the Print Queue

```
C:\LESSONS>print part1.txt


  C:\LESSONS\PART1.TXT is currently being printed

C:\LESSONS>print part2.txt


  C:\LESSONS\PART1.TXT is currently being printed
  C:\LESSONS\PART2.TXT is in queue

C:\LESSONS>print example.txt
Errors on list device indicate that it
may be off-line. Please check it.


  C:\LESSONS\PART1.TXT is currently being printed
  C:\LESSONS\PART2.TXT is in queue
  C:\LESSONS\EXAMPLE.TXT is in queue

C:\LESSONS>_
```

Step 3: Use the /C Parameter

The /C parameter removes a file from the print queue. Execute this command:

> Type   **print part2.txt /c**
> Press   **Enter**

PART2.TXT will not be printed.

Step 4: Use the /T Parameter

To remove all the files from the print queue, use the /T parameter like this:

> Type   **print /t**
> Press   **Enter**

Step 5: Use the /P Parameter

Press your printer's On Line button. The final PRINT parameter /P adds a file to the print queue. This default option is assumed if you don't specify any parameters. For example, try this command:

> Type   **print example.txt /p**
> Press   **Enter**

Executing the above command is the same as executing this command:

> Type   **print example.txt**
> Press   **Enter**

In either case, the file EXAMPLE.TXT will be printed.

Summary

- *Using the DOS editing and function keys*. Delete, Insert, Escape, and F1 through F6 perform various editing functions on the DOS command line.

- *Setting the BREAK option*. The BREAK command changes the status of the BREAK option, OFF or ON, which controls when Ctrl-Break will cancel a program.

- *Working with subdirectories*. MD or MKDIR creates a new subdirectory, CD or CHDIR moves into a subdirectory, TREE displays the structure of a disk, and RD or RMDIR removes an empty subdirectory.

- *Using the PATH and APPEND commands*. PATH sets up a directory search path for BAT, COM, and EXE files. APPEND sets up a directory search path for all other files.

- *Changing the DOS prompt*. PROMPT followed by one or prompt codes, such as pg, changes the DOS prompt.

- *Backing up and restoring disks and files*. BACKUP backs up all or part of a hard disk onto floppy diskettes. RESTORE copies files from backup diskettes onto a hard disk.

- *Recovering files from damaged disks*. RECOVER attempts to salvage data from a damaged disk.

- *Using the prompt option when erasing files.* The ERASE (or DEL) command's /P parameter causes DOS to ask for confirmation before erasing each file.

- *Appending files and copying files to devices.* The COPY command can be used to append two or more files together. It can also be used to copy data directly to devices such as displays and printers.

- *Setting the VERIFY option.* The VERIFY command changes the status of the VERIFY option OFF or ON, which controls error checking whenever writing data to a disk.

- *Changing file attributes.* The ATTRIB command can change the status of a file's read-only and archive attributes.

- *Copying groups of files.* XCOPY is often faster and more flexible than COPY for duplicating files, subdirectories, and disks.

- *Updating sets of files.* REPLACE is used to update existing files or add new files from one disk to another.

- *Transferring the DOS system files.* If a disk has been formatted with the /B parameter, SYS can transfer the hidden DOS system files to that disk.

- *Comparing files and disks.* COMP checks two files to see if they are identical. DISKCOMP checks two diskettes to see if they are identical.

- *Changing volume labels.* LABEL can display or change the name of a disk.

- *Changing the current date and time.* DATE and TIME can display or change the current date and time kept by the computer.

- *Displaying a memory report.* MEM can present a more detailed and technical memory report than CHKDSK.

- *Reassigning, joining, and substituting drives.* ASSIGN can change the drive letter associated with a disk drive. JOIN can tell DOS to treat an entire disk as if it were a subdirectory on another disk. SUBST can tell DOS to treat a subdirectory as if it were a disk in a separate drive.

- *Printing multiple files.* PRINT can print one or more files in the background. The /P, /C, and /T parameters add or remove files from the print queue.

Key Terms

As an extra review of this chapter, try defining the following terms.

archive attribute	path
ASCII file	print queue
binary file	read-only attribute
file attribute	root directory
hierarchical	spooling
incremental backup	volume label

Multiple Choice

Choose the best selection to complete each statement.

1. Which keys would you press to repeat the previous DOS command?
   - (a) F1 and then Enter
   - (b) F2 and then Enter
   - (c) F3 and then Enter
   - (d) Escape and then Enter

2. Which key would you press to skip over a character from the previous DOS command?
   - (a) Insert
   - (b) Delete
   - (c) Escape
   - (d) F1

3. What keypresses are influenced by the BREAK command?
   - (a) Alt-Break
   - (b) Ctrl-Break
   - (c) Alt-Num Lock
   - (d) Ctrl-Num Lock

4. Which item cannot be contained in a subdirectory?
   - (a) file
   - (b) subdirectory
   - (c) DOS external command
   - (d) disk

5. Every disk has a single main directory known as the
   - (a) root directory
   - (b) prime directory
   - (c) subdirectory
   - (d) master directory

6. Which expression is a valid path?
   - (a) c: hard disk lessons
   - (b) a:\lessons/c:
   - (c) c:\lessons\part1
   - (d) c:/lessons/part1

7. Which DOS command is used to create a new subdirectory?
   - (a) MD
   - (b) CD
   - (c) RD
   - (d) TREE

8. Which DOS command displays the subdirectory structure of a disk?
   - (a) MD
   - (b) CD
   - (c) RD
   - (d) TREE

9. What must be done before you can remove a subdirectory?
   - (a) execute DIR
   - (b) execute TREE
   - (c) delete all files in the subdirectory
   - (d) delete all files in the root directory

10. Which command is used to establish a subdirectory search path for BAT, COM, and EXE files?
    - (a) APPEND
    - (b) PATH
    - (c) TREE
    - (d) SEARCH

11. Which prompt codes would you use with the PROMPT command to have the DOS prompt always display the current path?
    - (a) Hello
    - (b) pg
    - (c) dg
    - (d) vq

12. Which command would back up the entire contents of the hard disk to diskettes in drive A?
    - (a) backup c: a: /s
    - (b) backup c:\lessons*.* a: /s
    - (c) backup a: c: /s
    - (d) backup hard disk a:

13. Which command is used to salvage files from damaged diskettes?

    (a) RESTORE
    (b) RECOVER
    (c) COPY
    (d) SYS

14. Of the following commands, which is the safest to use?

    (a) del *.*
    (b) erase *.*
    (c) erase ????????.*
    (d) erase *.* /p

15. Which device name stands for the keyboard or display screen?

    (a) CON
    (b) PRN
    (c) LPT1
    (d) COM1

16. Which command appends two files to form a third?

    (a) append file1 + file2 file3
    (b) copy file1 + file2 file3
    (c) xcopy file1 + file2 file3
    (d) diskcopy file1 + file2 file3

17. Which command makes it impossible to delete the file SAMPLE.TXT?

    (a) attrib + r sample.txt
    (b) attrib + a sample.txt
    (c) attrib − r sample.txt
    (d) attrib − a sample.txt

18. Which command will read as many files as it can into memory first, before copying them?

    (a) copy a:*.* c:
    (b) xcopy a:*.* c:
    (c) copy a:*.* c: /all
    (d) mem a:*.* c:

19. Which command will copy only those files from the disk in drive A that don't already exist on the disk in drive C?

    (a) copy a:*.* c: /a
    (b) xcopy a:*.* c: /a
    (c) append a:*.* c: /a
    (d) replace a:*.* c: /a

20. What command must have been used on a diskette before you can use the SYS command to copy the DOS system files to it?

    (a) TREE
    (b) APPEND
    (c) FORMAT /S or FORMAT /B
    (d) FORMAT /V

Fill-In

1. The simplest path is _______, which represents the root directory of the default drive.

2. You can copy files into a _______ just as if it were a separate disk.

3. The _______ command tells DOS the directories to be searched for files that have extensions other than BAT, COM, or EXE.

4. The _______ command lets you change the DOS prompt.

5. Unlike COPY, the _______ command can automatically use as many diskettes as needed to save the files from a hard disk.

6. The _______ command reinstates files that have been saved with the BACKUP command.

7. The _______ parameter of the ERASE (or DEL) command tells DOS to ask for confirmation before erasing each file.

8. You can use _______ names such as CON and PRN as if they were file names in commands such as COPY.

9. The ________ parameter of the COPY command tells DOS to verify that the copy has been made successfully with no errors.

10. Another term for text file is ________ file.

11. A ________ file is a file that contains programs or data that are not encoded as ASCII characters.

12. The ________ attribute indicates whether a file has been changed since it was last saved with the BACKUP command.

13. Unlike the COPY command, ________ can be instructed to copy files from all the subdirectories in the source disk or directory.

14. The ________ command is used to update previous versions of files.

15. The ________ command is used to compare the contents of two diskettes.

16. The ________ command lets you change the name of a disk.

17. Starting with version 4.0, DOS included ________, an external command that can present a memory report more detailed than CHKDSK.

18. The ASSIGN command lets you change the drive ________ associated with a disk drive.

19. The ________ command, which is the opposite of the JOIN command, lets you treat a subdirectory as if it were a disk in a separate drive.

20. The /T parameter of the PRINT command removes all files from the print ________.

Short Problems

1. Change to your LESSONS subdirectory on the hard disk if you are not already there. Use the ATTRIB command to turn on the read-only attribute for every file in the subdirectory. Hint: you can use the global file name character * to do this with a single command. Now try to erase every file in the LESSONS subdirectory. When you are finished, turn off the read-only attributes of all the files in the LESSONS subdirectory.

2. Put a formatted floppy disk in drive A. Back up the contents of the LESSONS subdirectory using the /L parameter to create a log file. Don't specify a file name after the /L. When the BACKUP command is finished, a file named BACKUP.LOG will exist in the root directory of your hard disk. Examine this file with the TYPE command. As you can see, BACKUP.LOG lists the date and time of the backup, as well as the backup disk number and full path and name of each backed-up file.

3. You can create many interesting and useful DOS prompts with the PROMPT command. For example, try the following command:

```
Type   prompt Date = $d Time = $t$_$p$g
Press  Enter
```

Press **Enter** a few times to see the result. When you are finished, change the DOS prompt back to the way it was.

4. Insert a formatted floppy disk into drive A. If the LESSONS subdirectory isn't your current directory, change to it. Now, use the DIR command to see a directory listing of the LESSONS subdirectory. Notice that . and .. appear as the first two entries in the listing. These are special DOS designations for your current directory and the parent of your current directory. For example,

execute the following command to see a listing of the directory immediately above your current directory, which, in this case, happens to be the root directory of hard disk C:

> Type **dir ..**
> Press **Enter**

The . designation is equivalent to *.*, meaning your entire directory. Execute this command to see how it works:

> Type **xcopy . a:**
> Press **Enter**

This command will copy all of the files in your current directory, which happens to be LESSONS, to the disk in drive A.

5. Use the COPY command to copy all the files in your DOS subdirectory to a diskette in drive A. It doesn't matter if they all won't fit. Try to time, either with a watch or by counting, approximately how long this takes. Now, turn on the VERIFY option and then repeat the same COPY operation, timing the procedure in the same way. Does turning verification on cause the COPY command to take longer? Turn off the VERIFY option when you are finished.

6. Use the DATE command to find out what day of the week July 4, 2026 will fall on.

7. Create a new subdirectory named TEXT inside your LESSONS subdirectory. Copy all files with an extension of TXT from your LESSONS subdirectory to the LESSONS\TEXT subdirectory. Use the TREE command to display the structure of the LESSONS subdirectory. Then change to the LESSONS\TEXT subdirectory.

8. Make sure you are inside the LESSONS\TEXT subdirectory. You should have the files PART1.TXT, PART2.TXT, PARTX.TXT, and EXAMPLE.TXT inside the subdirectory. Create a new EXAMPLE.TXT file with the COPY command by appending PART2.TXT to PARTX.TXT. Use the TYPE command to examine the new EXAMPLE.TXT file.

9. Erase every file inside the LESSONS\TEXT subdirectory. Use the /P parameter to have DOS prompt you before erasing each file. Answer **y** for yes each time.

10. Use DIR to confirm that the LESSONS\TEXT subdirectory is empty. Move back to its parent subdirectory, LESSONS, by using the .. designation with the CD command. Remove the LESSONS\TEXT subdirectory, but leave the LESSONS subdirectory intact. Use DIR to confirm what you have done.

BEGINNING WORDPERFECT

In This Chapter

Preview

A word processor is a computer system that helps you type, edit, store, and print documents. Memos, letters, term papers, reports, contracts, articles, and book chapters are all examples of documents that can be produced with a word processing package. The typical word processor consists of a microcomputer, printer, and word processing software package. Systems of this type are common today and are helping all kinds of people with their daily writing chores. Students, educators, authors, scientists, business people, professionals, and office workers are some of the people who use word processing systems. Word processing packages, also called word processors, are perhaps the most popular type of software used on microcomputers. And WordPerfect is the most popular word processing package, with versions sold for most major microcomputers, including IBMs and IBM-compatibles, Apple IIs and Apple Macintoshes, Commodore Amigas, and Atari STs. In this chapter and the next two chapters, you will learn to use WordPerfect 5.0 for IBM and IBM-compatible microcomputers.

After studying this chapter, you will know how to

- start WordPerfect.
- use the editing screen.
- execute commands and get help.
- enter text into a document.
- move the cursor.
- insert new text.
- overwrite mistakes.
- delete mistakes.
- search for and replace text.
- save a document in a disk file.
- check spelling.
- mark, move, copy, and delete blocks of text.
- cancel commands and restore deletions.
- underline, boldface, and otherwise format characters.
- set margins, tab stops, justification, line spacing, and line height.
- center text.
- format pages.
- print a document.
- edit an existing document.
- exit WordPerfect.

Getting Started

Although WordPerfect is a large and sophisticated software package, it is not difficult to learn to use it for basic word processing tasks. WordPerfect might be set up at your particular computer installation several different ways. You're most likely to use the package in one of three possible arrangements:

1. on a microcomputer with two floppy drives and WordPerfect installed on several diskettes.

2. on a microcomputer with a hard disk and WordPerfect installed in a subdirectory named WP50 or WP.

3. on a microcomputer connected to a local area network with WordPerfect installed on the network file server.

Insight

What is the Secret to WordPerfect's Success?

Even though you've read and re-read the manual, pressed every key combination you can think of, and asked all your friends, your new word processing software is laughing at you. You haven't even managed to set it up, much less write your term paper. What do you do now?

WordPerfect Corporation, maker of WordPerfect word processing software, has an answer: lifetime, toll-free support for everyone who buys its products. The company has a fleet of support operators on the payroll who answer phoned-in questions Monday through Friday from 7 a.m. to 6 p.m and Saturday from 8 a.m to noon, Mountain Standard Time. The monthly telephone tab for this service tops $300,000.

"It's truly unlimited support," says Stan Mackay, head of Word-Perfect's support group. "We don't even ask for user numbers. We want to help them, unhassled."

Each support worker specializes in either installation; features; printers; the company's other software, including DataPerfect, Library, and PlanPerfect; the Amiga and Atari versions; the Apple Macintosh version; or general questions. Callers hear three levels of recordings, and the goal is to answer the phone in two minutes and never to let anyone languish on hold for more than 45 minutes. That's not exactly lightning fast, but apparently OK to the people who make the 80,000 calls that come in every month.

Of course, no system is perfect. When WordPerfect 5.0 and Word-Perfect for the Macintosh were released within days of one another, so many people called in that all toll-free lines into Utah were knocked out, disabling the telemarketing centers for American Express, Delta Air Lines, and others.

This extensive customer support is a major reason for the astonishing success of the Orem, Utah-based company. Other reasons are its marketing savvy and, as is often the case with software stars, a measure of good timing.

Sources: Christine Strehlo, "What's So Special About WordPerfect?" *Personal Computing,* March 1988, pp. 100–116. Daniel J. Rosenbaum, "Evolutionary Strategy Pays Off for WordPerfect," *PC World,* December 1988, pp. 82–86.

You may need some additional direction from your instructor on how to start WordPerfect, but once you get situated you should be able to do the following lessons.

 Lesson 1: Running WordPerfect

You're all ready to start word processing, but first you must boot up your computer and run WordPerfect.

Step 1: Boot Up the Computer

Start up your computer as you learned in Lesson 1 of Chapter 2.

Step 2: Prepare Diskette or Subdirectory for Documents

The WordPerfect program is stored on its own diskettes or in its own subdirectory on a hard disk or network. It is best to prepare a separate diskette or subdirectory for the document files you will create in the following lessons. If your computer has only floppy drives, obtain a formatted diskette with room for your files. If your computer has a hard disk, create a subdirectory called LESSONS, if you don't already have one, that you can use to store your files. If you are running on a network, your instructor may have other directions for you to follow.

Step 3: Insert the WordPerfect 1 Disk or Switch to the WordPerfect Subdirectory

If you have a system with only floppy drives, remove the DOS startup diskette from drive A and replace it with the diskette labeled "WordPerfect 1."

If you have a microcomputer with a hard disk, WordPerfect should already be installed in its own subdirectory named WP50 or WP (see Appendix B, Software Installation). Switch to the WordPerfect subdirectory by executing the appropriate DOS command:

> Type   **cd c: \wp50**
> Press   **Enter**

If your computer is connected to a local area network, you may have to follow some other directions from your instructor before actually starting the Word-Perfect program.

Step 4: Invoke WordPerfect

Once you get situated in the proper disk drive directory, running WordPerfect is easy.

> Type   **wp**
> Press   **Enter**

It will take a few seconds for WordPerfect to be loaded from the disk into memory. Then your screen will look like Figure 1, which displays the copyright information for WordPerfect. If you are running the program from the WordPerfect 1 diskette in drive A, this message will also appear:

```
Insert diskette labeled "WordPerfect 2" and press any key
```

Figure 1 The WordPerfect Copyright Screen

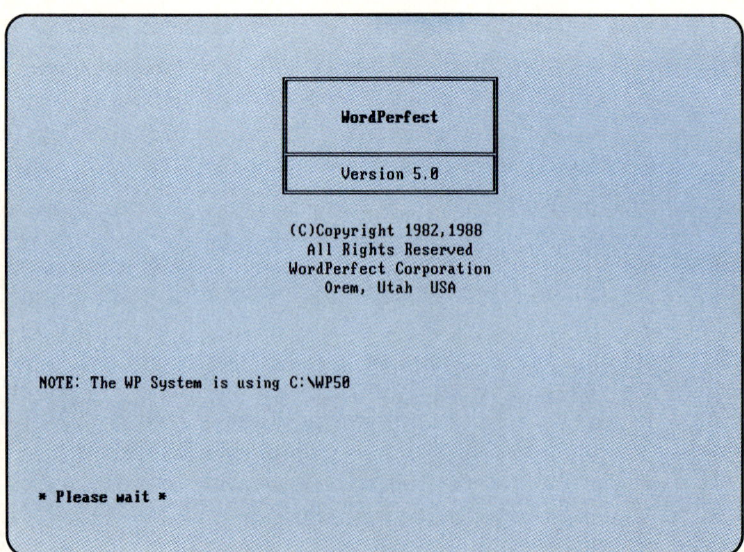

Follow the directions. It will take a few more seconds for the rest of WordPerfect to be loaded from the disk into memory.

 **Practice**   Reboot your computer:

> Press   **Ctrl-Alt-Del**

Follow the steps of this lesson to start up WordPerfect again.

Lesson 2: The Editing Screen

The copyright notice will disappear after a few moments, and WordPerfect will display the almost empty screen shown in Figure 2. This is WordPerfect's editing screen, where you enter, view, and modify text.

Step 1: Examine the Cursor

Look at the upper left corner of the screen. You should see the blinking under-score, known as the **cursor,** which marks your current position within the document. The cursor indicates where text will be inserted, deleted, or changed in some way.

Step 2: Examine the Status Line

The **status line,** shown at the bottom of the screen, displays messages and warnings from WordPerfect. Right now, the status line indicates that you are working on document one (of a possible two) and that your position within the document is 1 inch from the left edge and 1 inch from the top edge of page 1. WordPerfect already has default margins, tab stops, and line spacing set up. To create a document, all you have to do is begin typing.

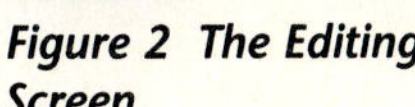

Figure 2 The Editing Screen

Step 3: Examine the Text Area

The rest of the screen, from the cursor down to the status line, is the **text area.** This is the space in which you will enter text and edit your document.

Follow these instructions and notice how the status line changes:

Type   **Hello**
Press   **Backspace** (5 times)

Lesson 3: Executing Commands and Getting Help

Most WordPerfect commands and menus are executed either by pressing a function key alone or by pressing the Shift, Control, or Alternate key with a function key.

Step 1: Invoke the Help Command

As an example, let's execute the Help command. WordPerfect has an on-line help facility that you can use to answer many questions about the package without having to refer to the manual. To invoke the Help command, do this:

Press   **F3**

WordPerfect will present the screen shown in Figure 3. Simply type a letter of the alphabet (A–Z) to see a list of all the features that begin with that letter. For example, to view the WordPerfect features that begin with the letter B, do this:

Type   **b**

Figure 4 shows the result. When you are finished with the help facility, you can press either the Enter key or the Space Bar to return to the editing screen.

Press   **Enter**

Figure 3 The Help Screen

Help   WP 5.0   11/15/88

Press any letter to get an alphabetical list of features.

    The list will include the features that start with that letter, along with the name of the key where the feature is found. You can then press that key to get a description of how the feature works.

Press any function key to get information about the use of the key.

    Some keys may let you choose from a menu to get more information about various options. Press HELP again to display the template.

Press Enter or Space bar to exit Help.

Figure 4 List of Word-Perfect Features Beginning with B

```
Key           Feature                                Key Name

Backspace     Backspace (Delete)                     Backspace
Shft-F1       Backup Files, Automatic                Setup,1
Shft-F1       Backup Directory Location              Setup,7
Shft-F2       Backward Search                        <-Search
Ctrl-F8       Base Font                              Font
Shft-F1       Beep Options                           Setup,5
Shft-F7       Binding Width                          Print
Shft-F1       Black and White, View Doc. in          Setup,3
Alt-F4        Block                                  Block
Ctrl-F4       Block, Append (Block On)               Move
Shft-F6       Block, Center (Block On)               Center
Ctrl-F5       Block, Comment (Block On)              Text In/Out
Del           Block, Delete (Block On)               Del
Ctrl-F4       Block, Move (Block On)                 Move
Shft-F7       Block, Print (Block On)                Print
Shft-F8       Block Protect (Block On)               Page Format
Ctrl-F8; F6   Bold                                   Font,2; Bold
Alt-F9        Box (Figure, Table, Text, Users)       Graphics
```

Step 2: Display the Keyboard Template

When you purchase WordPerfect, you get a **keyboard template** that lists the most common commands. This plastic guide fits over or near the function keys on the keyboard and is invaluable for beginning users. (A cardboard keyboard template is included inside the back cover of this book.) If you don't have the keyboard template, however, you can see an on-screen version by doing this:

Press   **F3** (2 times)

Figure 5 shows the result. While the help facility is active, you can get additional information about any function key simply by pressing the key. For example, do this:

Press   **F7**

Figure 5 On-Screen Keyboard Template

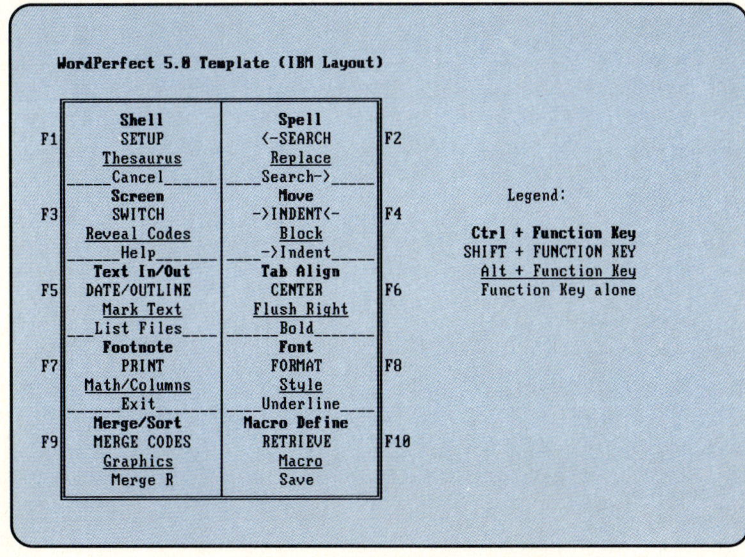

Figure 6 shows the help screen presented when you press the F7 key, referred to by WordPerfect as the Exit key. This is the command you use to exit WordPerfect and return to DOS. When you are finished with the help facility, return to the editing screen by doing this:

Press **Enter**

Practice

1. Invoke the Help facility and display the commands that begin with the letter F. When you are finished reading the list, return to the editing screen.
2. Invoke the Help facility and display the on-screen keyboard template. When you are finished reading the list, return to the editing screen.
3. Execute the Exit command. Answer No to the two prompts that follow, which ask whether you want to save the document and whether you want to exit WordPerfect.

Lesson 4: Entering Text

The process of entering the text with a word processor is similar to typing on a typewriter. There are, however, a few important differences that make using a word processor much easier. To illustrate how to use WordPerfect, let's create a memo. This memo, from the personnel department of a company to its employees, will explain company policy on employee sick leave.

Step 1: Type the Heading

As we said before, WordPerfect initially places the cursor in the first column of the first line of the first page. To create a new document, simply type the words and punctuation. Don't be concerned if you make some typing errors. You will learn how to fix mistakes later. To start out, follow these instructions:

```
Type   To: All Employees
Press  Enter
Type   From: Personnel Department
Press  Enter
Type   Re: Sick Leave
Press  Enter
```

At this point, your screen should look like Figure 7.

Step 2: Type the Body of the Memo

If you had to press Enter at the end of every line typed with a word processor, it wouldn't be all that much better than typing text with an electric typewriter. All word processing programs, however, have a feature called **word wrap** that eliminates having to press Enter most of the time. The word processing program detects when you are approaching the right margin. If you type a word that extends beyond the right margin, that word is automatically shifted, or wrapped around, to the beginning of the next line. In other words, the word processing program inserts a **soft return** just before the wrapped word. You can then continue typing on the new line without having to press the Enter key. Word wrap significantly speeds up typing because it eliminates having to constantly check the screen to make sure you don't overrun the right margin. You need only press

Figure 6 Help Screen for F7

```
Exit

        Gives you the option to save your document and then allows you to either
        exit WordPerfect or clear the screen.

        It is also used to exit from editing headers, styles, footnotes, etc.

        When you are in screens other than editing screens, it is used to leave
        menus and will normally take you back to the editing screen.
```

the Enter key when you want to insert a **hard return,** which forces a new line or begins a new paragraph. For example, insert a hard return to space down a line by doing this:

> Press   **Enter**

Now, to see how word wrap works, type the rest of the memo without pressing the Enter key:

```
Full-time employees are entitled to twelve working days
of sick leave each year. Time taken off is charged
against these twelve days and at the end of the year the
unused balance is carried forward. Sick leave should
only be used for an employee's illness or doctor's
appointments. It is essential that accurate records are
```

Figure 7 Memo Heading

```
To:   All Employees
From:  Personnel Department
Re:   Sick Leave
_




                                              Doc 1 Pg 1 Ln 1.5" Pos 1"
```

```
kept because employees are entitled to payment for one-
half of their unused sick days when they resign or
retire.
```

When you are finished, your screen should look like Figure 8.

 Use the Backspace key to erase the last sentence of the memo. Notice how the cursor automatically moves up to the end of the previous line when necessary. Retype the last sentence, watching the screen to see what happens when a word wrap occurs. Remember: do not press the Enter key. The words will wrap automatically.

Lesson 5: Moving the Cursor

You must be able to move the cursor to change existing text and to see different parts of a long document. Fortunately, there are many ways to move the cursor, the most common of which are quick, direct, and easy.

Step 1: Use the Arrow Keys

All IBM and IBM-compatible keyboards have at least one set of arrow keys. In many programs, including WordPerfect, the simplest way to move the cursor is to press an arrow key. For example, try the following actions:

Press **Up Arrow** (to move up one line)
Press **Down Arrow** (to move down one line)
Press **Left Arrow** (to move back one space)
Press **Right Arrow** (to move forward one space)

To move the cursor rapidly, you can simply hold down an arrow key for more than a second without releasing it. The computer will simulate repeating the key press ten times per second. Try these actions:

Press **Left Arrow** (and hold for 5 seconds)
Press **Right Arrow** (and hold for 5 seconds)

You can also hold down the Control key and press Left Arrow or Right Arrow to move the cursor a word at a time. Try these key presses to move the cursor to the beginning of the word to the left, and then to the beginning of the word to the right:

Press **Ctrl-Left Arrow**
Press **Ctrl-Right Arrow**

Step 2: Use Scrolling and Paging

Your document is quite short, but many documents are too long to fit entirely on the screen. Scrolling and paging commands let you change the part of your document displayed on the screen. One simple way to scroll the screen is to press the Up Arrow or Down Arrow key even after the cursor reaches the top or bottom edge of the text area. This won't work on your document because all of it fits on a single screen. If there were more lines above or below, however, pressing Up Arrow or Down Arrow after reaching the edge would scroll the screen and move the cursor to the next line.

*Figure 8 Word Wrap
Automatically Begins New
Lines*

```
To:  All Employees
From:  Personnel Department
Re:  Sick Leave

Full-time employees are entitled to twelve working days of sick
leave each year.  Time taken off is charged against these twelve
days and at the end of the year the unused balance is carried
forward.  Sick leave should only be used for an employee's illness
or doctor's appointments.  It is essential that accurate records
are kept because employees are entitled to payment for one-half of
their unused sick days when they resign or retire._




                                          Doc 1 Pg 1 Ln 2.67" Pos 6"
```

The Grey Plus (+) and Grey Minus (−) keys on the numeric keypad are used to move the cursor an entire screen at a time. Try this:

Press   **Grey Plus**

Grey Plus moves the cursor down to the last line of the current screen. If your document were too long to entirely fit on the screen, pressing the Grey Plus key again would move the cursor down through the next screen. Now try this:

Press   **Grey Minus**

Grey Minus moves the cursor up to the first line of the current screen. If you had more text above your current screen, pressing the Grey Minus key again would move the cursor up through the previous screen.

Paging is like scrolling an entire page at a time. The Page Down and Page Up keys are used to move between pages. Try this:

Press   **Page Down**

The cursor will move to the first line of the next page. Since your document has only one page, pressing Page Down merely moves the cursor to the end of the document. Now try this:

Press   **Page Up**

The Page Up key moves the cursor to the first line of the previous page. Again, since your document has only one page, pressing Page Up simply moves the cursor to the beginning of the document.

Step 3: Use the End and Home Keys

End and Home are the two other cursor movement keys on all IBM-compatible keyboards. Try this:

Press   **End**

The End key moves the cursor to the end of the current line.

In WordPerfect, the Home key is used with other keys to perform various cursor movements. For example, follow these directions:

> Press   **Home**
> Press   **Left Arrow**

Home followed by Left Arrow moves the cursor to the left edge of the current screen—in other words, the beginning of the current line. Now try this:

> Press   **Home**
> Press   **Right Arrow**

Home followed by Right Arrow moves the cursor to the right edge of the current screen. You can also use the Home key and the Down Arrow or Up Arrow key to move the cursor to the end or beginning of your document. Follow these directions:

> Press   **Home** (2 times)
> Press   **Down Arrow**
> Press   **Home** (2 times)
> Press   **Up Arrow**

Pressing Home twice followed by the Down Arrow key moves the cursor to the end of the document. Pressing Home twice followed by the Up Arrow key moves the cursor to the beginning of the document.

Step 4: Use the Go To Command

Another sequence of keypresses lets you move to a particular page number in a WordPerfect document. Since your current document fits entirely on a single page, the Go To command would be of little use. Nevertheless, you can still try it:

> Press   **Ctrl-Home**

WordPerfect will display the prompt "Go to" on the status line. Then you enter the page number to which you want to go:

> Type   **1**
> Press   **Enter**

WordPerfect will move the cursor to the top of that page.

Practice   Try the following keypresses and explain what each one does:

Up Arrow	**Down Arrow**
Left Arrow	**Right Arrow**
Ctrl-Left Arrow	**Ctrl-Right Arrow**
Grey Plus	**Grey Minus**
Page Up	**Page Down**
Home, Left Arrow	**Home, Right Arrow**
Home, Home, Up Arrow	**Home, Home, Down Arrow**
Ctrl-Home	**End**

Lesson 6: Inserting Text

WordPerfect, like most word processing software, has two basic typing modes: insert and typeover. By default, WordPerfect has insert mode turned on when you open a document. This means that to insert new material into a document, you just move the cursor to the location where you want the insertion to occur and begin typing. The new characters you type push any existing characters to the right. As an example, let's insert some new text into the memo you've typed.

Step 1: Move the Cursor

Suppose you want to insert the word "cumulative" between the words "twelve" and "working" in the first line of the memo. Use any of the cursor movement keys described in Lesson 5 to put the cursor beneath the "w" in the word "working."

Step 2: Type the New Text

Since WordPerfect uses insert mode by default, all you have to do is type the new text to be inserted.

Type   **cumulative**
Press   **Space Bar**
Press   **Up Arrow**

Notice how WordPerfect automatically reforms the paragraph and wraps words to fit within the margins when you move the cursor. Your screen should now look like Figure 9.

Practice   Insert the word "mistake" anywhere in the document. Then use the Backspace key to remove it.

Figure 9 Text Inserted in a Document

```
To:  All Employees
From:  Personnel Department
Re:  Sick Leave

Full-time employees are entitled to twelve cumulative working days
of sick leave each year.  Time taken off is charged against these
twelve days and at the end of the year the unused balance is
carried forward.  Sick leave should only be used for an employee's
illness or doctor's appointments.  It is essential that accurate
records are kept because employees are entitled to payment for one-
half of their unused sick days when they resign or retire.




                                        Doc 1 Pg 1 Ln 1.5" Pos 1"
```

Lesson 7: Overwriting Mistakes

One of the benefits of using a word processor is the ease with which you can make corrections. Since no one is perfect, typing errors are bound to occur—as you may have already discovered. In addition, you may have to go back and change a word or phrase that you already entered. One way to make corrections is by typing over existing text.

Step 1: Move the Cursor

Suppose that employees are only entitled to eleven days of sick leave. You must change the word "twelve" to "eleven" in the memo. Using the cursor movement keys described in Lesson 5, put the cursor beneath the "t" in the first "twelve."

Step 2: Change to Typeover Mode

Insert mode is on by default. To switch, or toggle, between insert and typeover mode, you use the Insert key.

Press   **Insert**

When you change to typeover mode, WordPerfect displays the word "Typeover" in the status line. Now, any characters you type will replace the existing characters in the same positions.

Step 3: Make the Correction

With the cursor at the beginning of the word "twelve," do this:

Type   **eleven**

Your screen should now look like Figure 10.

Figure 10 Word Corrected in Typeover Mode

```
To:  All Employees
From:  Personnel Department
Re:  Sick Leave

Full-time employees are entitled to eleven_cumulative working days
of sick leave each year.  Time taken off is charged against these
twelve days and at the end of the year the unused balance is
carried forward.  Sick leave should only be used for an employee's
illness or doctor's appointments.  It is essential that accurate
records are kept because employees are entitled to payment for one-
half of their unused sick days when they resign or retire.




Typeover                                        Doc 1 Pg 1 Ln 1.67" Pos 5.2"
```

Change from typeover mode to insert mode. Change back to typeover mode.

Lesson 8: Deleting Mistakes

Another common way to make corrections and modifications is to delete text.

Step 1: Move the Cursor

Before text can be deleted, the cursor must be moved to the first character to be erased. Let's change the eleven sick days to ten. The first three letters of "eleven" can simply be overwritten with "ten." Move the cursor to the first "e" in "eleven" and do this:

Type   **ten**

The cursor should now be at the "v." Change to insert mode by doing this:

Press   **Insert**

Step 2: Use the Delete Key

The Delete (Del) key removes the character at the cursor and shifts all characters to the right of the cursor to the left one space. To remove the characters "ven," do this:

Press   **Delete** (3 times)

Your screen should now look like Figure 11.

Figure 11 Characters
Erased with the Delete Key

```
To:  All Employees
From:  Personnel Department
Re:  Sick Leave

Full-time employees are entitled to ten_cumulative working days
of sick leave each year.  Time taken off is charged against these
twelve days and at the end of the year the unused balance is
carried forward.  Sick leave should only be used for an employee's
illness or doctor's appointments.  It is essential that accurate
records are kept because employees are entitled to payment for one-
half of their unused sick days when they resign or retire.




                                    Doc 1 Pg 1 Ln 1.67" Pos 4.9"
```

Step 3: Use the Backspace Key

The Delete key removes the character at the current cursor location. Another way to erase text is to use the Backspace key. This key removes the character to the immediate left of the cursor. For example, erase the "ten" like this:

Press   **Backspace** (3 times)

Make sure insert mode is turned on and restore the memo to its original state:

Type   `twelve`

Step 4: Delete an Entire Word

WordPerfect also makes it easy to erase an entire word. Position the cursor on the first character of the word "twelve." To delete the entire word and the following space, do this:

Press   **Ctrl-Backspace**

Now, make sure insert mode is turned on and put the word back again:

Type   `twelve`
Press   **Space Bar**

Step 5: Delete an Entire Line

WordPerfect has an even more drastic command that lets you erase an entire line all at once. Move the cursor up to the beginning of the third line in the memo, the one that reads "Re: Sick Leave."

Press   **Ctrl-End**
Press   **Delete**

All the text from the current cursor location to the end of the line will be deleted. Pressing the Delete key erases the hard return and causes the lines of text below to move up to fill in the empty space, as shown in Figure 12.

Needless to say, Ctrl-End should be used carefully. Unfortunately, you need the deleted line for the remaining lessons, so do this:

Type   `Re: Sick Leave`
Press   **Enter**

Although WordPerfect has several other commands for deleting text, Delete, Backspace, Ctrl-Backspace, and Ctrl-End are the most frequently used.

Practice   Use each of the following keys to remove text from the memo: Delete, Backspace, Ctrl-Backspace, and Ctrl-End. Then restore the memo to its original state.

Lesson 9: Searching and Replacing

The memo you've typed is fairly short, so making corrections throughout the entire document isn't too difficult. But you may have to modify much longer documents. In some cases, the same mistake is made in several places in the document. Most word processors have features that help you locate specific portions of text and change them if necessary.

Figure 12 An Entire Line Deleted

```
To:  All Employees
From:  Personnel Department

Full-time employees are entitled to twelve cumulative working days
of sick leave each year.  Time taken off is charged against these
twelve days and at the end of the year the unused balance is
carried forward.  Sick leave should only be used for an employee's
illness or doctor's appointments.  It is essential that accurate
records are kept because employees are entitled to payment for one-
half of their unused sick days when they resign or retire.




                                              Doc 1 Pg 1 Ln 1.33" Pos 1"
```

Step 1: Find Text

You may have noticed that the word "twelve" is used twice in the memo. If you found out that employees are really entitled to only eleven days of sick leave, you would have to change both instances of "twelve" to "eleven." In this case, you could simply look through the memo to make sure there are no more occurrences of "twelve" to change. If the document were much longer, however, you would have to scan through many pages of text, and you might miss a "twelve" or two. Fortunately, WordPerfect has a search command that can find text quickly and accurately. This feature can be used to make corrections or merely to locate every place in a document where a certain word or phrase is mentioned.

Execute the following commands to move the cursor to the beginning of the document and then search for the word "twelve":

Press   **Home** (2 times)
Press   **Up Arrow**
Press   **F2**
Type   **twelve**
Press   **F2**

The Search command will advance the cursor just past the next location of the word "twelve." If it cannot find the word you tell it to search for, WordPerfect will display "* Not Found *" on the status line.

Step 2: Modify the Text

In many cases, you search for a piece of text because you want to change it or some text around it. Now that you've found "twelve," change it to "eleven" like this:

Press   **Backspace** (6 times)
Type   **eleven**

Step 3: Repeat the Search

Particular words or phrases are often repeated, especially in a long document. You can tell WordPerfect to find the next occurrence of the word or phrase without having to redo the entire Search command.

   Press   **F2** (2 times)

This action repeats the previous search operation, advancing the cursor to the next location of the word "twelve." Change this "twelve" to "eleven" too.

   Press   **Backspace** (6 times)
   Type   **eleven**

Step 4: Find and Replace Text

Since it is often necessary to find and then change a word or phrase, WordPerfect can do both at once. Execute the following commands to find each "eleven" and change it back to "twelve":

   Press   **Home** (2 times)
   Press   **Up Arrow**
   Press   **Alt-F2**
   Press   **Enter**
   Type   **eleven**
   Press   **F2**
   Type   **twelve**
   Press   **F2**

Pressing Alt-F2 executes the Replace command, which displays the message shown in Figure 13. Here WordPerfect is asking if you want to confirm or cancel each replacement. If you answer yes, WordPerfect will prompt you before replacing each occurrence of the text. If you answer no, or just press Enter, WordPerfect will automatically replace every occurrence of the text without confirmation. This is known as a **global search and replace.** Since you indicated a global search and replace, WordPerfect changed every "eleven" to "twelve" throughout the entire document, without stopping for confirmation.

Practice

1. Move the cursor to the beginning of the document. Use the Search command to locate each occurrence of the word "sick."

2. Move the cursor to the beginning of the document. Use the Replace command with confirmation to change each occurrence of the word "sick" to "ill." Now, use the Replace command without confirmation to change each "ill" back to "sick." Notice how WordPerfect is clever enough to preserve capitalization.

Lesson 10: Saving the Document

Word processing programs are useful not only because they make it easier to enter and edit text, but also because they let you save documents on disks. While you are editing a document, it is kept in the computer's primary memory, which gives the software quick access. The contents of primary memory are lost when the computer is turned off, so you should periodically save a document to disk

Figure 13 Prompt to Confirm Each Replacement

```
To:  All Employees
From:  Personnel Department
Re:  Sick Leave

Full-time employees are entitled to eleven cumulative working days
of sick leave each year.  Time taken off is charged against these
twelve days and at the end of the year the unused balance is
carried forward.  Sick leave should only be used for an employee's
illness or doctor's appointments.  It is essential that accurate
records are kept because employees are entitled to payment for one-
half of their unused sick days when they resign or retire.




w/Confirm? (Y/N) No
```

as you work on it, even if it is not finished yet. This guards against losing all of your work if the power should fail or if you make a drastic mistake. Saving a document in a disk file gives you a more permanent copy of your work that can be stored for future reference, printed out later, or retrieved and modified. A long document, such as an article or a book chapter, can be created and edited a little at a time. Corrections, updates, and new versions can be made without having to retype everything. A document stored on a disk is much more compact and useful than the same document printed on paper. So, before we go on, let's save the memo in a disk file.

Step 1: Invoke the Save Command

Execute WordPerfect's Save command:

    Press **F10**

This command allows you to copy the memo to a disk file, yet continue working on it. If you are using a computer with two floppy drives and no hard disk, you may want to put your document file on a separate diskette. If so, insert a formatted floppy disk into drive B.

Step 2: Enter the File Name

WordPerfect will prompt you for the name of the document to be saved, as shown in Figure 14. You can enter any valid DOS file name. If you are working from a hard disk and want to save the memo in your LESSONS subdirectory, do this:

    Type `\lessons\memo.doc`
    Press **Enter**

If you are using a computer with two floppy drives and want to save your document in a file on the diskette in drive B, do this instead:

    Type `b:memo.doc`
    Press **Enter**

Figure 14 Name the Document to be Saved

```
To:  All Employees
From:  Personnel Department
Re:  Sick Leave

Full-time employees are entitled to twelve cumulative working days
of sick leave each year.  Time taken off is charged against these
twelve days and at the end of the year the unused balance is
carried forward.  Sick leave should only be used for an employee's
sickness or doctor's appointments.  It is essential that accurate
records are kept because employees are entitled to payment for one-
half of their unused sick days when they resign or retire.




Document to be saved: _
```

The document will then be copied to the disk under the name MEMO.DOC and WordPerfect will return to the editing screen. Notice that the left side of the status line now displays the path and name of your document file.

Practice   You can save a document as many times as you like while you are working on it, even if you are not finished creating it. Each time you save a document, the version on the screen and in memory will replace the version on the disk. Execute the Save command again:

> Press   **F10**
> Press   **Enter**
> Type   **y**

Notice how WordPerfect suggests the file name you used last time, so you don't have to retype the name every time you save the document. For safety, the program also prompts you before replacing the old version.

Lesson 11: Checking Spelling

One of WordPerfect's most useful features is its spelling checker. Let's put a misspelled word in the memo to use as an example. Go to the second line and remove an "n" from the word "Personnel."

Step 1: Invoke the Spelling Checker

If you are using WordPerfect on a microcomputer with no hard disk, then you must now put the diskette labeled "Speller" in drive B. If your computer has a hard disk, the spelling checker is probably already installed on it.

Execute this command to invoke the spelling checker:

> Press   **Ctrl-F2**

WordPerfect will present the Check menu shown in Figure 15. To check the entire memo, select the Document option:

>　Type　**d**

Note that you can select an option from a WordPerfect menu either by typing its number or an easy-to-remember letter, usually the first letter of the option, shown in boldface.

After the dictionary has been loaded from the disk into memory, the spelling checker begins to examine each word in your document to see if it is in the dictionary.

Step 2: Correct Spelling Mistakes

When WordPerfect finds a word it doesn't recognize, it highlights the word, suggests possible replacements, and displays the Not Found menu at the bottom of the screen, as shown in Figure 16. To automatically replace "personel" with the second suggested correction, "personnel," do this:

>　Type　**b**

WordPerfect will then check the rest of the memo, find it to be correct, and give you a word count. Press any key to return to the editing screen.

In most longer documents, WordPerfect would likely encounter several more words not in its dictionary. Not all of these would necessarily be misspellings. The spelling checker, for example, cannot recognize many proper names, technical terms, and slang. Nor can it recognize some forms of correctly spelled words. In these cases, you can choose the Skip Once option or the Skip option from the Not Found menu. If you choose Skip Once, WordPerfect will leave the word intact and go on, but it will stop at the next occurrence of the word. If you choose Skip, the program will ignore all occurrences of the word for the rest of the document.

If the spelling checker cannot suggest a correction for a misspelled word, you can choose the Edit option from the Not Found menu and correct the word yourself.

Figure 15 The Spelling Check Menu

```
To:  All Employees
From:  Personel Department
Re:  Sick Leave

Full-time employees are entitled to twelve cumulative working days
of sick leave each year.  Time taken off is charged against these
twelve days and at the end of the year the unused balance is
carried forward.  Sick leave should only be used for an employee's
sickness or doctor's appointments.  It is essential that accurate
records are kept because employees are entitled to payment for one-
half of their unused sick days when they resign or retire.




Check: 1 Word; 2 Page; 3 Document; 4 New Sup. Dictionary; 5 Look Up; 6 Count: 0
```

Figure 16 The Not Found Menu

```
To:  All Employees
From: Personel Department
Re:  Sick Leave

Full-time employees are entitled to twelve cumulative working days
of sick leave each year.  Time taken off is charged against these
twelve days and at the end of the year the unused balance is
carried forward.  Sick leave should only be used for an employee's
sickness or doctor's appointments.  It is essential that accurate
records are kept because employees are entitled to payment for one-
half of their unused sick days when they resign or retire.

==============================================================================

  A. personal              B. personnel




Not Found: 1 Skip Once; 2 Skip; 3 Add; 4 Edit; 5 Look Up; 6 Ignore Numbers: 0
```

Practice

1. A spelling checker cannot find in its dictionary every correctly spelled word, especially names. Insert your last name somewhere in the document. Then execute a spelling check. Select the Skip option from the Not Found menu. Delete your name after you are finished.

2. The spelling checker can be used to check an individual word in your document. Move the cursor to the word "Department." Invoke the spelling checker, but this time select the Word option from the Check menu. If the word is spelled correctly, WordPerfect will simply advance the cursor to the next word. You can continue to check the words one by one. Exit the spelling checker and return to the editing screen:

   Press   **F7**

3. You can also use the spelling checker to look up a word that is not in the document. Invoke the spelling checker, but this time select the Look Up option. Enter a purposely misspelled word and see if WordPerfect can suggest the appropriate correction. Try another misspelled word if you like. When you are finished, exit the spelling checker and return to the editing screen:

   Press   **F7**

Lesson 12: Working with Blocks of Text

In addition to individual characters, words, and lines, most word processing packages let you specify and manipulate blocks of text. In WordPerfect, a **block** is a section of text that can be of any size—from a single character to an entire document. Once a block is designated, or marked, it can be moved, copied, or deleted.

Step 1: Mark a Block

You're going to need more text in your document to better illustrate WordPerfect's block commands. Move the cursor to the end of the document and insert a blank line:

    Press   **Home** (2 times)
    Press   **Down Arrow**
    Press   **Enter** (2 times)

Now, type this paragraph without pressing Enter:

```
Full-time employees earn twenty-four working days of
vacation per year. These are in addition to official
company holidays and must be used by the end of each
year. Accurate records of vacation leave taken must be
kept because employees will be paid for their unused
days when they resign or retire.
```

Leave a blank line at the end of the document:

    Press   **Enter** (2 times)

The paragraph you just typed is the block you're going to work with. To mark the block, move the cursor to the first character in the paragraph and execute the Block command:

    Press   **Up Arrow** (6 times)
    Press   **Alt-F4**

The message "Block on" will flash on and off in the status line. Move the cursor to the last character to be included in the block, in this case, the end of the document:

    Press   **Home** (2 times)
    Press   **Down Arrow**

As the cursor moves, the text in the block will change to reverse video (dark characters against a light background) as shown in Figure 17. You can increase or reduce the size of the marked block by simply moving the cursor.

Step 2: Move a Block

Once a block has been marked, it's easy to move it to another position in the document. Suppose you want to put the vacation leave paragraph before the sick leave paragraph. First, activate the Move menu, shown in Figure 18:

    Press   **Ctrl-F4**

To move the marked block, select the Block option:

    Type   **b**

Another menu appears, as shown in Figure 19. Choose the Move option, move the cursor to the first character in the sick leave paragraph, and press Enter:

    Type   **m**
    Press   **Up Arrow** (8 times)
    Press   **Enter**

Figure 17 A Marked Block

```
To:  All Employees
From:  Personnel Department
Re:  Sick Leave

Full-time employees are entitled to twelve cumulative working days
of sick leave each year.  Time taken off is charged against these
twelve days and at the end of the year the unused balance is
carried forward.  Sick leave should only be used for an employee's
sickness or doctor's appointments.  It is essential that accurate
records are kept because employees are entitled to payment for one-
half of their unused sick days when they resign or retire.

Full-time employees earn twenty-four working days of vacation per
year.  These are in addition to official company holidays and must
be used by the end of each year.  Accurate records of vacation
leave taken must be kept because employees will be paid for their
unused days when they resign or retire.



Block on                                    Doc 1 Pg 1 Ln 4" Pos
```

The marked block will be removed from its original position and inserted in the new location.

Step 3: Copy a Block

Sometimes it's useful to copy text from one location to another. You might need an exact duplicate or a version that's only slightly different. Instead of retyping the text in the new location, you can mark a block, copy the text, then make any necessary modifications. This can save time when you are working on documents that contain repeated sections of text.

Just for practice, let's make a copy of the vacation leave paragraph and put it at the end of the memo. Although the duplicate paragraphs won't make sense in your particular document, the exercise will demonstrate how to copy a block.

Figure 18 The Move Menu

```
To:  All Employees
From:  Personnel Department
Re:  Sick Leave

Full-time employees are entitled to twelve cumulative working days
of sick leave each year.  Time taken off is charged against these
twelve days and at the end of the year the unused balance is
carried forward.  Sick leave should only be used for an employee's
sickness or doctor's appointments.  It is essential that accurate
records are kept because employees are entitled to payment for one-
half of their unused sick days when they resign or retire.

Full-time employees earn twenty-four working days of vacation per
year.  These are in addition to official company holidays and must
be used by the end of each year.  Accurate records of vacation
leave taken must be kept because employees will be paid for their
unused days when they resign or retire.



Move: 1 Block; 2 Tabular Column; 3 Rectangle: 0
```

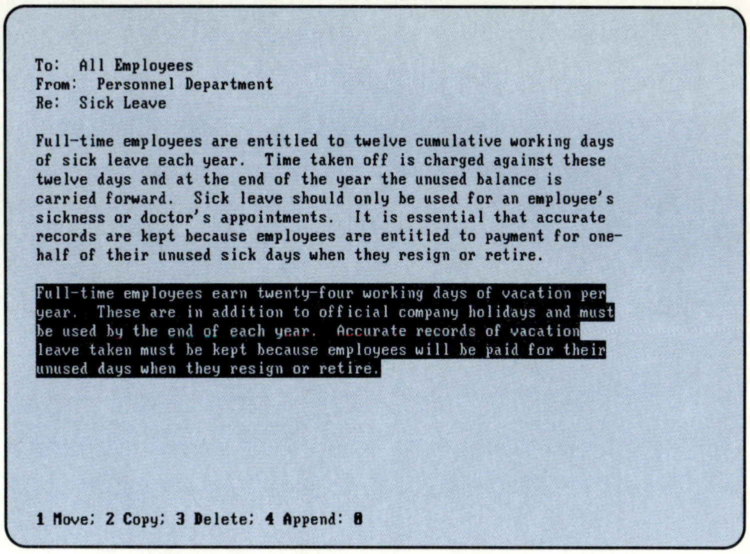

Figure 19 The Move-Block Menu

First, mark the block to be copied, in this case the first paragraph. If the cursor is not already at the first character of the paragraph, move it there. Then do this:

Press   **Alt-F4**
Press   **Down Arrow** (6 times)

Now, activate the Move menu, select the Block option, select the Copy option, move the cursor to the end of the document, and press Enter:

Press   **Ctrl-F4**
Type   **b**
Type   **c**
Press   **Home** (2 times)
Press   **Down Arrow**
Press   **Enter**

WordPerfect will duplicate the vacation leave paragraph at the end of the document, as shown in Figure 20.

Step 4: Delete a Block

You now have two copies of the vacation leave paragraph, but you need only one for this memo. This is a good opportunity to try deleting a block. Instead of deleting every character, word, or line in a paragraph, you can erase the whole thing at once. For example, mark the first vacation leave paragraph and then delete it:

Press   **Home** (2 times)
Press   **Up Arrow**
Press   **Down Arrow** (4 times)
Press   **Alt-F4**
Press   **Down Arrow** (6 times)
Press   **Delete**

Figure 20 First Paragraph Copied at End of Document

```
To:   All Employees
From:  Personnel Department
Re:   Sick Leave

Full-time employees earn twenty-four working days of vacation per
year.  These are in addition to official company holidays and must
be used by the end of each year.  Accurate records of vacation
leave taken must be kept because employees will be paid for their
unused days when they resign or retire.

Full-time employees are entitled to twelve cumulative working days
of sick leave each year.  Time taken off is charged against these
twelve days and at the end of the year the unused balance is
carried forward.  Sick leave should only be used for an employee's
sickness or doctor's appointments.  It is essential that accurate
records are kept because employees are entitled to payment for one-
half of their unused sick days when they resign or retire.

Full-time employees earn twenty-four working days of vacation per
year.  These are in addition to official company holidays and must
be used by the end of each year.  Accurate records of vacation
leave taken must be kept because employees will be paid for their
unused days when they resign or retire.

C:\LESSONS\MEMO.DOC                          Doc 1 Pg 1 Ln 4" Pos 1"
```

WordPerfect will display the prompt

    Delete block? (Y/N) No

Since you are sure that you want to delete the marked block, answer yes:

    Type **y**

Figure 21 shows the result.

Practice

1. Mark the heading of the memo (the first three lines) as a block.
2. Copy the marked block to the end of the memo.
3. Mark the lines you just copied as a block and then delete it.

Figure 21 Paragraph Deleted

```
To:   All Employees
From:  Personnel Department
Re:   Sick Leave

Full-time employees are entitled to twelve cumulative working days
of sick leave each year.  Time taken off is charged against these
twelve days and at the end of the year the unused balance is
carried forward.  Sick leave should only be used for an employee's
sickness or doctor's appointments.  It is essential that accurate
records are kept because employees are entitled to payment for one-
half of their unused sick days when they resign or retire.

Full-time employees earn twenty-four working days of vacation per
year.  These are in addition to official company holidays and must
be used by the end of each year.  Accurate records of vacation
leave taken must be kept because employees will be paid for their
unused days when they resign or retire.

C:\LESSONS\MEMO.DOC                       Doc 1 Pg 1 Ln 1.67" Pos 1"
```

Lesson 13: Canceling Commands

At one time or another, everyone who uses a word processing package makes a mistake deleting text or executing some other command. Fortunately, Word-Perfect has a Cancel command that can restore accidentally erased text or stop an executing command. The Cancel command, which is invoked by pressing the F1 function key, can do the following:

- Return from a WordPerfect menu or cancel your response to a WordPerfect prompt before the response is final
- Turn off, or unmark a marked block
- Restore any of the three most recently deleted text items

Whenever you erase text, whether a single character or an entire block, Word-Perfect temporarily stores that text in a special area of memory. Up to three deletions are saved, allowing you to reverse a delete command. For example, suppose you accidentally delete the last paragraph in the memo.

Step 1: Delete the Paragraph

Mark the last paragraph as a block and delete it by following these instructions:

Press	**Home** (2 times)
Press	**Down Arrow**
Press	**Up Arrow** (6 times)
Press	**Alt-F4**
Press	**Down Arrow** (6 times)
Press	**Delete**
Type	**y**

Step 2: Set the Cursor

Now, suppose you realize your mistake and want the deleted paragraph back. First, you would move the cursor to the place where you want to insert the restored text. In this case, the cursor is already at the correct location, so you don't have to move it.

Step 3: Invoke the Cancel Command

Execute the Cancel command to activate WordPerfect's Undelete menu (see Figure 22) and restore the most recently deleted item at the current cursor location:

Press	**F1**
Type	**r**

The deleted text will be reinstated. To restore a previously deleted item, you would type 2 or P to select Previous Deletion, until the text you want to restore is displayed in reverse video.

Practice

Execute the Cancel command. Select the second option from the Undelete menu to examine the previous deletion. You don't want to insert this text back into your document, so cancel the Cancel command:

Press	**F7**

Figure 22 The Undelete Menu

```
To:  All Employees
From:  Personnel Department
Re:  Sick Leave

Full-time employees are entitled to twelve cumulative working days
of sick leave each year.  Time taken off is charged against these
twelve days and at the end of the year the unused balance is
carried forward.  Sick leave should only be used for an employee's
sickness or doctor's appointments.  It is essential that accurate
records are kept because employees are entitled to payment for one-
half of their unused sick days when they resign or retire.

Full-time employees earn twenty-four working days of vacation per
year.  These are in addition to official company holidays and must
be used by the end of each year.  Accurate records of vacation
leave taken must be kept because employees will be paid for their
unused days when they resign or retire.




Undelete: 1 Restore; 2 Previous Deletion: 0
```

Lesson 14: Formatting Characters

Formatting a document means specifying how it will look when it is printed. True what-you-see-is-what-you-get (WYSIWYG) word processing software has an exact correspondence between the screen and the printed page. WordPerfect is not a WYSIWYG word processing package; some formatting specifications show up on the display screen, but others only become evident when the document is printed. WordPerfect has many features that let you format characters, lines, and entire pages. Let's start with the character formatting options.

Step 1: Underline Text

WordPerfect offers several ways to emphasize characters in a document. Let's add an underlined heading before the sick leave paragraph. First, make sure insert mode is turned on. Then follow these instructions:

Press **Home** (2 times)
Press **Up Arrow**
Press **Down Arrow** (4 times)
Press **F8**
Type **Sick Leave**
Press **F8**
Press **Enter** (2 times)

The F8 key turns underline on and off. On the screen, underlined text may appear underlined, highlighted, or in a different color, depending on the type of monitor you have and the way that WordPerfect has been set up (see Figure 23). When the document is printed, however, the heading "Sick Leave" will be underlined.

Step 2: Boldface Text

WordPerfect makes it just as easy to boldface text. Follow these directions to add a boldfaced heading before the vacation leave paragraph:

Press **Home** (2 times)
Press **Down Arrow**

Figure 23 Underlined Text

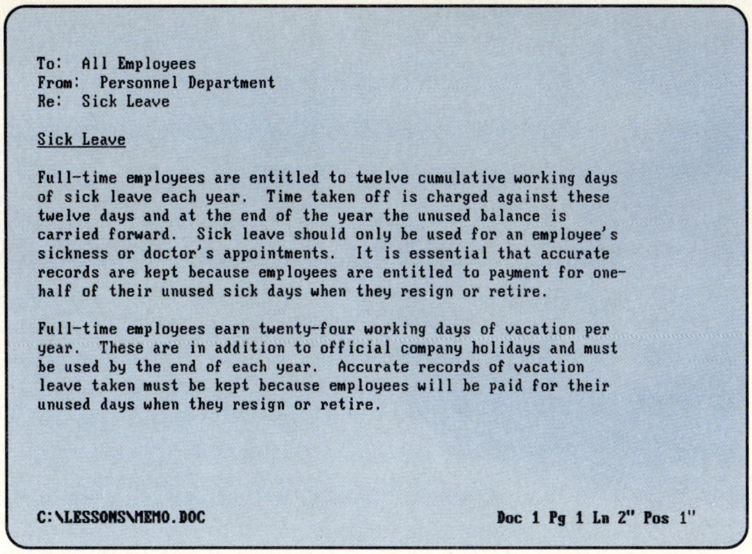

```
To:  All Employees
From:  Personnel Department
Re:  Sick Leave

Sick Leave

Full-time employees are entitled to twelve cumulative working days
of sick leave each year.  Time taken off is charged against these
twelve days and at the end of the year the unused balance is
carried forward.  Sick leave should only be used for an employee's
sickness or doctor's appointments.  It is essential that accurate
records are kept because employees are entitled to payment for one-
half of their unused sick days when they resign or retire.

Full-time employees earn twenty-four working days of vacation per
year.  These are in addition to official company holidays and must
be used by the end of each year.  Accurate records of vacation
leave taken must be kept because employees will be paid for their
unused days when they resign or retire.

C:\LESSONS\MEMO.DOC                        Doc 1 Pg 1 Ln 2" Pos 1"
```

Press	**Up Arrow** (6 times)
Press	**F6**
Type	**Vacation Leave**
Press	**F6**
Press	**Enter** (2 times)

The F6 key turns boldface on and off. On the screen, boldfaced text appears in brighter characters, in a different color, or in reverse video, depending on your monitor and the way in which WordPerfect has been set up (see Figure 24). When the document is printed, however, the "Vacation Leave" heading will be boldfaced.

Figure 24 Boldfaced Text

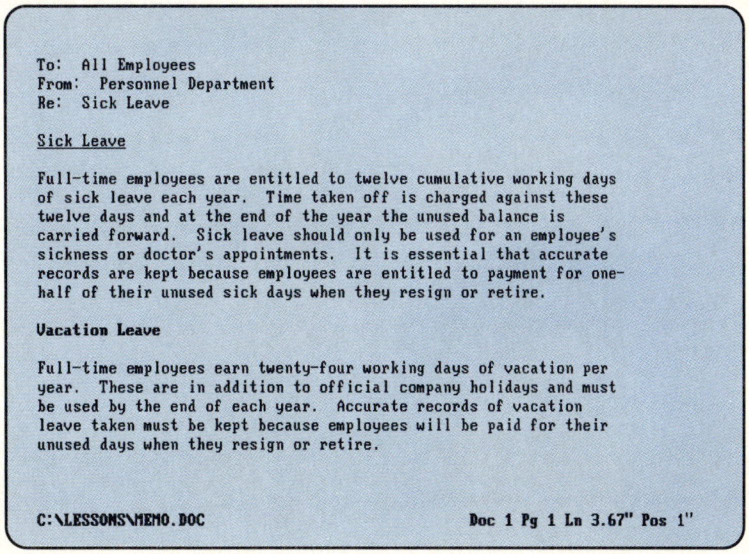

```
To:  All Employees
From:  Personnel Department
Re:  Sick Leave

Sick Leave

Full-time employees are entitled to twelve cumulative working days
of sick leave each year.  Time taken off is charged against these
twelve days and at the end of the year the unused balance is
carried forward.  Sick leave should only be used for an employee's
sickness or doctor's appointments.  It is essential that accurate
records are kept because employees are entitled to payment for one-
half of their unused sick days when they resign or retire.

Vacation Leave

Full-time employees earn twenty-four working days of vacation per
year.  These are in addition to official company holidays and must
be used by the end of each year.  Accurate records of vacation
leave taken must be kept because employees will be paid for their
unused days when they resign or retire.

C:\LESSONS\MEMO.DOC                        Doc 1 Pg 1 Ln 3.67" Pos 1"
```

Step 3: Using other Character Formats

Underline and boldface are the two most commonly used character formats, but WordPerfect also provides other options. Follow these directions to activate the Font menu and select the Appearance option:

Press   **Ctrl-F8**
Type   **a**

The menu shown in Figure 25 will appear on the screen. In addition to boldface and underline, this menu also lists double underline, italics, outline, shadow, small capitals, redline, and strikeout character formats. Exit the menu when you are finished examining it:

Press   **F7**

Practice

1. In Steps 1 and 2, you formatted new characters as you typed them. You can also format existing text. Find the word "essential" in the first paragraph of the memo and move the cursor to the beginning of the word. Mark this word as a block. Now underline the word:

   Press   **F8**

2. Certain combinations of character formats are allowed. For example, text can be underlined and boldfaced. Mark the word "essential" in the first paragraph as a block again. This time, boldface the word:

   Press   **F6**

   The word "essential" should now appear underlined and boldfaced.

3. Choose some other word in the memo and mark it as a block. Activate the Font menu and select the Appearance option:

   Press   **Ctrl-F8**
   Type   **a**

Figure 25 The Font-Appearance Menu

```
To:  All Employees
From:  Personnel Department
Re:  Sick Leave

Sick Leave

Full-time employees are entitled to twelve cumulative working days
of sick leave each year.  Time taken off is charged against these
twelve days and at the end of the year the unused balance is
carried forward.  Sick leave should only be used for an employee's
sickness or doctor's appointments.  It is essential that accurate
records are kept because employees are entitled to payment for one-
half of their unused sick days when they resign or retire.

Vacation Leave

Full-time employees earn twenty-four working days of vacation per
year.  These are in addition to official company holidays and must
be used by the end of each year.  Accurate records of vacation
leave taken must be kept because employees will be paid for their
unused days when they resign or retire.



 1 Bold 2 Undrln 3 Dbl Und 4 Italc 5 Outln 6 Shadw 7 Sm Cap 8 Redln 9 Stkout: 0
```

Select a character format option other than underline or boldface for the marked word. The appearance of the word may or may not change on the screen, depending on the type of monitor you have. It will be printed in the format you selected, however, if your printer is capable of producing it.

4. In WordPerfect, character formatting is indicated by hidden codes stored before and after the formatted text. You turn off character formatting by deleting these codes. Let's turn off the formatting you turned on in the previous Practice exercises. Move the cursor to the space just before the word "essential" in the first paragraph, and do this:

Press   **Right Arrow**
Press   **Delete**

WordPerfect will ask you if you want to delete the underline code.

Type   **y**

Now, turn off the boldface:

Press   **Delete**
Type   **y**

Use what you have learned to turn off the character format you turned on in Practice exercise 3.

Lesson 15: Formatting Lines

Like most word processing packages, WordPerfect has a number of features that control the appearance of lines, paragraphs, and other sections of text. The most common formatting operations allow you to change margins, set tab stops, turn justification on or off, set line spacing, set line height, and center text.

Step 1: Change Margins

WordPerfect initially sets both the left and right margins of a document at one inch from the edge of the paper. Although these margins are usually adequate, you may need to change them for some documents. Let's change the left and right margins of the memo to 1.25 inch. First, move the cursor to the beginning of the document, where you want the new margins to begin:

Press   **Home** (2 times)
Press   **Up Arrow**

Next, activate the Format menu (see Figure 26) and select the first option to display the Line menu (see Figure 27):

Press   **Shift-F8**
Type   **L**

Select the Margins option and enter the new left and right margin measurements:

Type   **m**
Type   **1.25"**
Press   **Enter**
Type   **1.25"**
Press   **Enter**

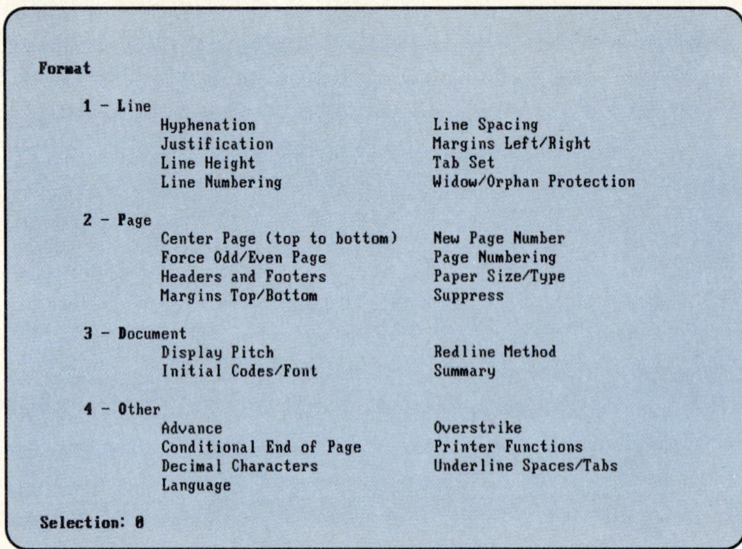

Figure 26 The Format Menu

Execute the Exit command to leave the Line menu and return to the editing screen:

Press   **F7**

The new margins will be established, as shown in Figure 28. They will remain in effect in this document unless you change them later.

Step 2: Set Tab Stops

Like typewriters, computer keyboards have at least one Tab key. When this key is pressed, the cursor advances to some preset location. By default, WordPerfect initially sets tab stops at half-inch intervals. For example, move the cursor to the next tab stop:

Press   **Tab**

Figure 27 The Line Menu

```
Format: Line

     1 - Hyphenation                           Off

     2 - Hyphenation Zone - Left               10%
                           Right               4%

     3 - Justification                         Yes

     4 - Line Height                           Auto

     5 - Line Numbering                        No

     6 - Line Spacing                          1

     7 - Margins - Left                        1"
                   Right                       1"

     8 - Tab Set                               0", every 0.5"

     9 - Widow/Orphan Protection               No


Selection: 0
```

Figure 28 New Margins Have Been Set

```
To:  All Employees
From:  Personnel Department
Re:  Sick Leave

Sick Leave

Full-time employees are entitled to twelve cumulative working days
of sick leave each year.  Time taken off is charged against these
twelve days and at the end of the year the unused balance is
carried forward.  Sick leave should only be used for an employee's
sickness or doctor's appointments.  It is essential that accurate
records are kept because employees are entitled to payment for one-
half of their unused sick days when they resign or retire.

Vacation Leave

Full-time employees earn twenty-four working days of vacation per
year.  These are in addition to official company holidays and must
be used by the end of each year.  Accurate records of vacation
leave taken must be kept because employees will be paid for their
unused days when they resign or retire.


C:\LESSONS\MEMO.DOC                        Doc 1 Pg 1 Ln 1" Pos 1.25"
```

If insert mode is turned on, pressing the Tab key pushes any existing characters to the right; if typeover mode is turned on, the Tab key moves the cursor over existing text. If Insert mode was turned on when you pressed Tab, remove the Tab:

    Press **Backspace**

To view or change the current tab settings, activate the Format menu, select the Line option, and then select the Tab Set option:

    Press **Shift-F8**
    Type **L**
    Type **t**

Figure 29 shows the Tab Set menu. The dotted line near the bottom of the screen is a **ruler line** showing the current tab stops. Each "L" denotes a left-justified tab

Figure 29 The Tab Set Menu

```
To:  All Employees
From:  Personnel Department
Re:  Sick Leave

Sick Leave

Full-time employees are entitled to twelve cumulative working
days of sick leave each year.  Time taken off is charged
against these twelve days and at the end of the year the
unused balance is carried forward.  Sick leave should only be
used for an employee's sickness or doctor's appointments.  It
is essential that accurate records are kept because employees
are entitled to payment for one-half of their unused sick days
when they resign or retire.

Vacation Leave

Full-time employees earn twenty-four working days of vacation
per year.  These are in addition to official company holidays
and must be used by the end of each year.  Accurate records
L....L....L....L....L....L....L....L....L....L....L....L....L....L....L..
!    ^    !    ^    !    ^    !    ^    !    ^    !    ^    !    ^    !
1"       2"       3"       4"       5"       6"       7"       8"
Delete EOL (clear tabs); Enter Number (set tab); Del (clear tab);
Left; Center; Right; Decimal; .= Dot Leader; Press Exit when done.
```

stop. You can use the Left Arrow and Right Arrow keys to move the cursor within the ruler line, and delete existing tab stops with the Delete key. You can add a new tab stop at any position by typing one of the following characters:

L	Inserts a left-justified tab stop, which aligns text along the left side at the tab stop.
C	Inserts a centered tab stop, which centers text at the tab stop.
R	Inserts a right-justified tab stop, which aligns text along the right side at the tab stop.
D	Inserts a decimal tab stop, which aligns numbers by their decimal points at the tab stop.

If you like, you can also delete the existing tab stops in the ruler line by pressing Ctrl-End and insert all new tab stops. For now, just leave the tab stops where they are. Exit the Tab Stop menu and return to the editing screen:

Press   **F7** (2 times)

Step 3: Turn Off Justification

When a document is justified, text is aligned exactly to both the left and right margins. If necessary, **soft spaces** are automatically generated by the word processor and inserted between words to give the text a block look. (**Hard spaces** are inserted only when you press the Space Bar.) By default, WordPerfect's justification feature is turned on, but the on-screen text is not displayed as justified. Justification becomes evident only when the document is printed. Justified text looks best when it is produced by a printer that can do **proportional spacing,** which allots different amounts of space for different characters. The combination of justification and proportional spacing produces text similar to the typeset material in this book.

If your printer cannot do proportional spacing, it is better to turn off justification. The resulting text will have a ragged right margin similar to that of typewritten text. To turn off justification for the memo, follow these directions:

Press	**Home** (2 times)
Press	**Up Arrow**
Press	**Shift-F8**
Type	**L**
Type	**j**
Type	**n**
Press	**F7**

These actions move the cursor to the beginning of the document, activate the Format menu, select the Line option, select the Justification option, turn off justification, and return to the editing screen. Justification will then be turned off from the cursor position to the end of the document, but the appearance of text on the screen will not change.

Step 4: Set Line Spacing

Word processing packages allow you to determine the line spacing for documents. By default, WordPerfect's line spacing is set to 1. In other words, lines are automatically single spaced. This means that no blank lines are left between successive lines of text whenever a word wrap occurs or whenever you press the Enter key. Double spacing leaves one blank line between successive lines of text, triple spacing leaves two blank lines, and so on.

Suppose you want your document to be double spaced. First you move the cursor to where you want double spacing to begin. Then you activate the Format menu, select the Line option, select the Line Spacing option, and specify the line spacing. Follow these directions:

Press **Home** (2 times)
Press **Up Arrow**
Press **Shift-F8**
Type   **L**
Type   **s**
Type   **2**
Press **Enter**
Press **F7**

The memo will be double spaced, as shown in Figure 30. Any new text you type from the current cursor location to the end of the document will also be double spaced.

Since memos are usually single spaced, change the line spacing from 2 back to 1:

Press **Shift-F8**
Type   **L**
Type   **s**
Type   **1**
Press **Enter**
Press **F7**

Step 5: Set Line Height

In WordPerfect, the distance between lines of printed text is called **line height.** This is not the same as line spacing. *Line height* is measured from the bottom of one line to the bottom of the next line below. *Line spacing* is one plus the number of blank lines left between successive lines of text. In practice, line height is

Figure 30 Double-Spaced Memo

```
To:  All Employees

From:  Personnel Department

Re:  Sick Leave


Sick Leave


Full-time employees are entitled to twelve cumulative

working days of sick leave each year.  Time taken off is

charged against these twelve days and at the end of the year

the unused balance is carried forward.  Sick leave should

only be used for an employee's sickness or doctor's

appointments.  It is essential that accurate records are

C:\LESSONS\MEMO.DOC                      Doc 1 Pg 1 Ln 1" Pos 1.25"
```

seldom changed. WordPerfect's default line height yields 6 lines of text per vertical inch, which is the standard line height of most typewriters. To change line height, you activate the Format menu, select the Line option, select the Line Height option, select the Fixed option, and then enter a new line height measurement. Follow these directions:

Press **Shift-F8**
Type   **L**
Type   **h**
Type   **f**

WordPerfect will then display the current line height in inches. Let's just leave it at 0.17", which is 1/6-inch. Return to the editing screen:

Press **F7** (2 times)

Step 6: Center Text

Many documents require certain headings or other text to be centered between the left and right margins. To do this manually is tedious. Fortunately, WordPerfect, like most word processing packages, can automatically center text.

Let's center the headings above the two paragraphs in our memo. Follow these instructions to center the heading "Sick Leave":

Press **Home** (2 times)
Press **Up Arrow**
Press **Down Arrow** (4 times)
Press **Shift-F6**
Press **Left Arrow**

Now, center the "Vacation Leave" heading:

Press **Down Arrow** (11 times)
Press **Shift-F6**
Press **Down Arrow**

Your screen should look like Figure 31.

You can also center a new line of text as you type it. You would simply move the cursor to the left margin of the new line, press Shift-F6 to move the cursor to the center of the line, type the text, and press Enter.

Practice

1. Move the cursor to the beginning of the document. Change the left and right margins to 2 inches. See how the text is automatically reformatted within the new margins. Change them back to 1.25 inches.

2. Triple space your entire document and see how it looks. Then change line spacing back to 1.

3. Type the heading "Unpaid Leave" at the end of the memo, centering it as you type it. When you are finished, delete the heading from the document.

Lesson 16: Formatting Pages

Page formatting features affect entire pages of text. WordPerfect has several commands that let you specify how pages are laid out. Although you don't need to change any of the default page format settings for our simple memo, you may

Figure 31 Centered Headings

```
To:   All Employees
From:  Personnel Department
Re:   Sick Leave

                    Sick Leave

Full-time employees are entitled to twelve cumulative
working days of sick leave each year.  Time taken off is
charged against these twelve days and at the end of the year
the unused balance is carried forward.  Sick leave should
only be used for an employee's sickness or doctor's
appointments.  It is essential that accurate records are
kept because employees are entitled to payment for one-half
of their unused sick days when they resign or retire.

                    Vacation Leave

Full-time employees earn twenty-four working days of
vacation per year.  These are in addition to official
company holidays and must be used by the end of each year.
Accurate records of vacation leave taken must be kept
because employees will be paid for their unused days when
they resign or retire.

C:\LESSONS\MEMO.DOC                    Doc 1 Pg 1 Ln 3.67" Pos 1.25"
```

need to change them for other documents. Let's look at the commands that control paper size and type, top and bottom margins, page breaks, and page numbering.

Step 1: Set the Paper Size and Type

Standard letter-size paper is 8½ inches wide and 11 inches long. Given a standard line height of 6 lines per inch, the number of lines on letter-size paper is 6 times 11, or 66. WordPerfect's default paper size is 8½ by 11 inches, but this can be changed. First, activate the Format menu and then select the Page option:

Press   **Shift-F8**
Type   **p**

WordPerfect will display the Page menu (see Figure 32). Now, select the Paper Size option:

Type   **s**

Here you could select a different paper size (see Figure 33). Let's leave it at 8½ by 11 inches.

Press   **F7**

Next, the Paper Type menu appears, shown in Figure 34. Here you could select a paper type. Let's leave it as Standard. Return to the editing screen:

Press   **F7** (2 times)

Step 2: Set the Top and Bottom Margins

Most documents are printed with some blank space at the top and bottom of every page. By default, WordPerfect leaves one-inch top and bottom margins. You can change these settings from the Page Format menu:

Press   **Shift-F8**
Type   **p**
Type   **m**

Figure 32 The Page Menu

```
Format: Page

     1 - Center Page (top to bottom)     No

     2 - Force Odd/Even Page

     3 - Headers

     4 - Footers

     5 - Margins - Top                    1"
                   Bottom                 1"

     6 - New Page Number                  1
            (example: 3 or iii)

     7 - Page Numbering                   No page numbering

     8 - Paper Size                       8.5" x 11"
                Type                      Standard

     9 - Suppress (this page only)


Selection: 0
```

Here you could enter new top and bottom margin measurements. Let's leave them at one inch. Return to the editing screen:

Press   **F7** (3 times)

Step 3: Start a New Page

The actual number of lines of text printed on a page depends on several factors. For example, WordPerfect's default line height is 1/6 inch. The default page length is 11 inches (66 lines), with a top margin of 1 inch (6 lines) and a bottom margin of 1 inch (6 lines). That leaves 66 minus 12, or 54, as the default number of lines of text printed on a page.

Figure 33 The Paper Size Menu

```
Format: Paper Size

     1 - Standard                 (8.5" x 11")

     2 - Standard Landscape       (11" x 8.5")

     3 - Legal                    (8.5" x 14")

     4 - Legal Landscape          (14" x 8.5")

     5 - Envelope                 (9.5" x 4")

     6 - Half Sheet               (5.5" x 8.5")

     7 - US Government            (8" x 11")

     8 - A4                       (210mm x 297mm)

     9 - A4 Landscape             (297mm x 210mm)

     0 - Other


Selection: 1
```

Figure 34 The Paper Type Menu

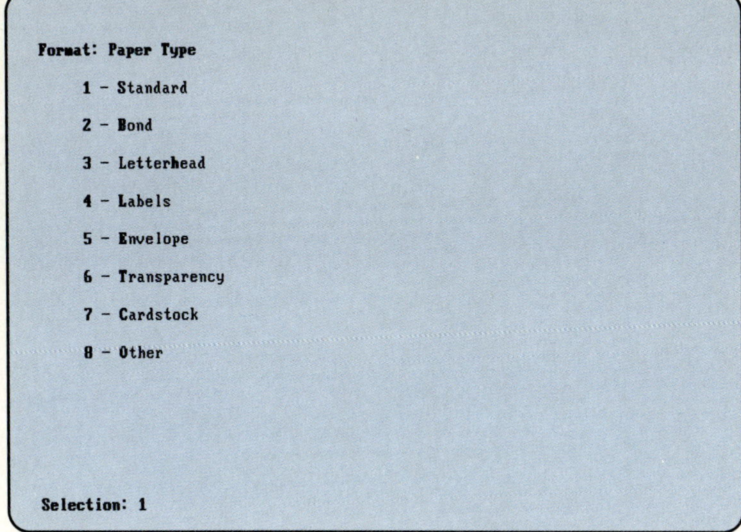

As you type text with WordPerfect, the word wrap feature automatically starts new lines. WordPerfect also automatically starts new pages. Assuming the default page-format settings are in effect, a soft page break is inserted after every 54 lines you type. A **soft page break** is a division between two pages automatically generated by the word processing software. It is symbolized on the screen by a horizontal line of dashes. This line is not actually printed on paper; it simply indicates the place where a new page will begin.

Although WordPerfect's automatic page-break feature is convenient, you may sometimes want to have a page with fewer than 54 lines. A new page can be forced by pressing Ctrl-Enter to insert a **hard page break.** This is a division between two pages that is manually generated by the user. It is symbolized on the screen by a horizontal line of equal signs. You can begin a new page at any point within a document simply by pressing Ctrl-Enter. For example, let's insert a hard page break between the two paragraphs in the memo:

Press **Home** (2 times)
Press **Up Arrow**
Press **Down Arrow** (15 times)
Press **Ctrl-Enter**

Your screen should look like Figure 35. If this document were printed, the text below the line of equal signs would begin on a new page.

A hard page break can be removed from a document with the Delete or Backspace key. Let's remove the hard page break you just inserted. Make sure the cursor is still at the beginning of the line with the "Vacation Leave" heading.

Press **Backspace**

The page break will disappear.

Step 4: Set the Page Numbering

WordPerfect automatically keeps track of page numbers while you work on a document and displays the current page number on the screen in the status line (see Figure 35). But WordPerfect does not print page numbers unless you tell it

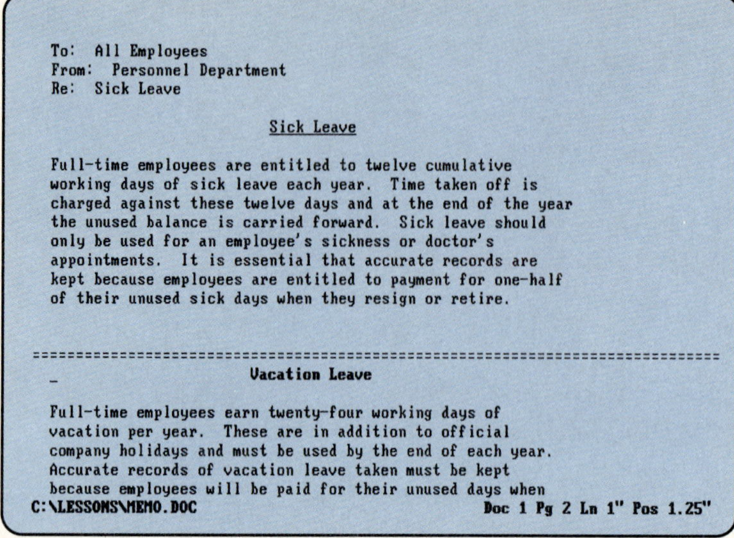

Figure 35 A Hard Page Break

to do so. Although we don't need a page number on our single-page memo, let's see how you would turn on printed page numbering.

Press   **Shift-F8**
Type   **p**
Type   **p**

WordPerfect will display the Page Numbering menu on the screen as shown in Figure 36. Here you would select a page numbering option. For example, if you wanted a page number to appear in the top right corner of every page, you would type 3 and then press F7. Since you don't need page numbering in the memo, return to the editing screen:

Press   **F7**

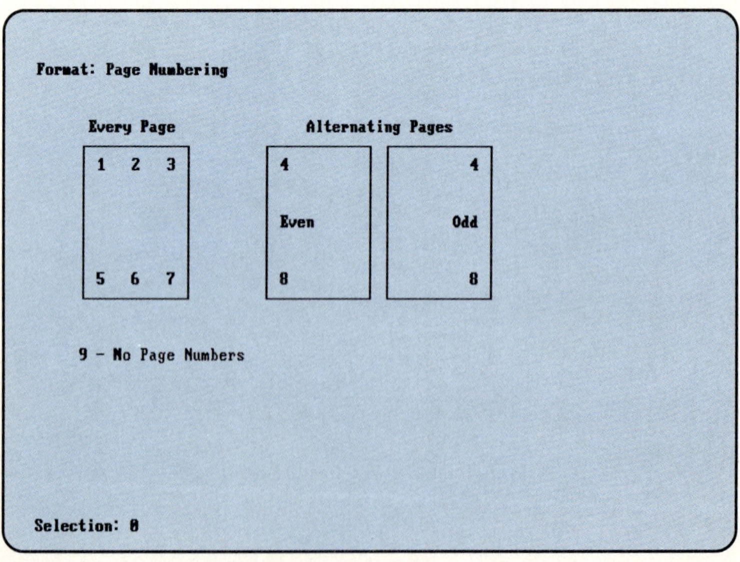

Figure 36 The Page Numbering Menu

Practice

1. Change the paper size to Legal. Then change it back to Standard.
2. Change the top and bottom margins to 2 inches. Then change them back to 1 inch.
3. Insert a page break in the memo before the first paragraph. Now, remove the page break.

Lesson 17: Printing a Document

You've entered, formatted, proofread, and corrected your document. You're satisfied with your work and now it's time to produce the final product. You're ready to print your document on paper.

Step 1: Save the Document

It is a good idea to save your document before printing.

Press   **F10**
Press   **Enter**
Type   **y**

Step 2: Prepare the Printer

Make sure the printer is connected to the computer and turned on. Also, make sure that paper is loaded and aligned to the top of a new page. Finally, make sure that the printer's On Line light is lit. (If it isn't, press the On Line button.)

Step 3: Invoke the Print Command

Activate the Print menu (see Figure 37) and select the Full Document option:

Press   **Shift-F7**
Type   **f**

When WordPerfect is finished printing the document, it will return to the editing screen.

Lesson 18: Returning to DOS

When you are finished working with WordPerfect, you will exit the program and return to DOS.

Step 1: Invoke the Exit Command

Execute the Exit command to tell WordPerfect that you either want to work on a different document or return to DOS:

Press   **F7**

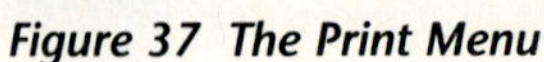

Figure 37 The Print Menu

```
Print

    1 - Full Document
    2 - Page
    3 - Document on Disk
    4 - Control Printer
    5 - Type Through
    6 - View Document
    7 - Initialize Printer

Options

    S - Select Printer          Epson LQ-850/1050
    B - Binding                 0"
    N - Number of Copies        1
    G - Graphics Quality        Medium
    T - Text Quality            High




Selection: 0
```

Step 2: Save the Document

WordPerfect will ask you if you want to save the document. Unless you are just
viewing a document that you don't want to change, you should answer yes. If
you have never saved this document before, you must enter a file name. If you
have saved this document before, as we have done twice in this chapter, WordPerfect
will suggest the current name. You can press Enter to choose this name, or type
a new name if you want to save the document to a different file. If you choose
the same name, WordPerfect will ask if you want to replace the existing document
file with the version on your screen, and you should answer yes.

    Type   **y**
    Press   **Enter**
    Type   **y**

Step 3: Confirm the Exit

WordPerfect will copy the document to the disk and then display the prompt

    Exit WP? (Y/N) No   (Cancel to return to document)

Here the program is asking you if you really want to return to DOS, and it
assumes you do not. If you press F1, the Cancel key, you can return to editing
your document. If you type N or press Enter, you can begin a new document.
Exit WordPerfect:

    Type   **y**

You should see the DOS prompt on your screen.

Practice   Start up WordPerfect. Then exit to DOS.

Lesson 19: Editing an Existing Document

Word processors make it so easy to store documents in disk files that editing an existing document is a common procedure. Any time you want to examine, modify, or update a previously stored document, all you have to do is tell WordPerfect to retrieve the file.

Step 1: Specify the Document When Loading WordPerfect

At this point you should be at the DOS prompt because you exited WordPerfect at the end of the last lesson. Before you can edit an existing document, you must make sure its file is stored on an accessible disk. The location of the document file depends on your default directory or the path and name you chose when you last saved the document. Your document may be on the diskette in drive B, on your hard disk C, or on a network file server disk.

If you know the name and location of the document file you want to edit, you can start WordPerfect and load the document at the same time. If you are using a computer with a hard disk and MEMO.DOC is stored in the LESSONS subdirectory, execute this command:

Type   **wp `\lessons\memo.doc`**
Press   **Enter**

If you are running WordPerfect on a computer with no hard disk and you saved the memo on the diskette in drive B, execute this command instead:

Type   **wp `b:memo.doc`**
Press   **Enter**

Your document will be loaded into memory along with WordPerfect, where you can view or edit it.

Step 2: Use the List Files Menu

Another way to edit an existing document is to retrieve its file from within WordPerfect. Exit WordPerfect and return to DOS. Start WordPerfect again with this command:

Type   **wp**
Press   **Enter**

Now, activate the List Files menu:

Press   **F5**

WordPerfect will suggest your current drive and directory. If your computer has a hard disk and your document is in the LESSONS subdirectory, do this:

Type   **`\lessons\`**
Press   **Enter**

If your document is on the diskette in drive B, do this instead:

Type   **`b:\`**
Press   **Enter**

A screen like the one in Figure 38 will appear. This screen shows the files in the specified directory and presents the List Files menu. Your screen may look somewhat different, depending on the drive or directory you specified.

To load an existing document, use the arrow keys to move the reverse video highlight bar to its file name. Locate MEMO.DOC and highlight it. Then select the Retrieve option:

Type **r**

WordPerfect will load the file into memory and present the memo on the editing screen.

Step 3: Edit the Document

Sometimes you load an existing document file just to read it. Other times you actually want to correct, update, or modify the contents. Let's make a couple of additions to the memo:

Press **Enter**
Press **Up Arrow**
Type **Date:** (today's date)
Press **Down Arrow** (3 times)
Press **Space Bar**
Type **and Vacation Leave**

Except for the date, your screen should look like Figure 39.

Step 4: Exit WordPerfect and Save the File

Execute the Exit command and save the updated memo document:

Press **F7**
Type **y**
Press **Enter**

Figure 38 The List Files Menu

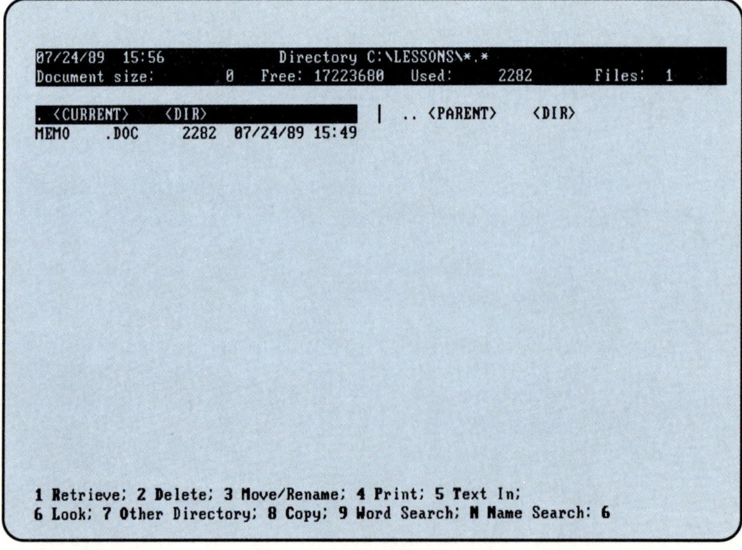

Real World

The Men Behind WordPerfect

Alan Ashton was so happy with his company's profits in 1987 that he took everyone—the whole company—to Hawaii for a week.

Ashton's goal was that his WordPerfect Corporation would make $100 million in profits, double the 1986 figure. On December 22, 1987, the figure stood at $100.3 million in sales. What's more, the company he cofounded has achieved record sales and profits every year since it was created in 1980.

Its success in large part is due to the success of its WordPerfect word processing software. WordPerfect is currently the world's best-selling word processing program. The White House, Congress, and law offices all over the world use it.

Who are the people who took a company to such dizzying heights in just seven years?

Ashton, president and chief executive officer, owns 49.9 percent of the stock in this private company. A former Brigham Young University professor, he is a Mormon who brings strong values and a sense of family to work with him. He is, according to employees, a father figure so down-to-earth that he recently only reluctantly traded in his pickup truck for a Cadillac. But he's a father figure with incredible drive—a tough combination to beat.

Bruce Bastian founded the company along with Ashton and is now an equal partner with him. Also a Mormon and a former college professor, Bastian now serves as chairman of the board and president of WordPerfect's highly successful international division.

The man who holds the tie-breaking 0.2 percent of the company stock is Pete Peterson. Back when the company was called Satellite Software International, Peterson was hired to keep the books. He quit the next day because there were no books.

There were also other problems, including no business license and very sketchy records. But when Ashton and Bastian realized that this man with a psychology degree knew what he was doing, they hired him back. Peterson uses a South American saying to describe the situation: "In the land of the blind, the one-eyed man is king."

Source: Christine Strehlo, "What's So Special About WordPerfect?" *Personal Computing*, March 1988, pp. 100–116.

Figure 39 The Completed Memo

```
Date:  July 24, 1989
To:  All Employees
From:  Personnel Department
Re:  Sick Leave and Vacation Leave_

               Sick Leave

Full-time employees are entitled to twelve cumulative
working days of sick leave each year.  Time taken off is
charged against these twelve days and at the end of the year
the unused balance is carried forward.  Sick leave should
only be used for an employee's sickness or doctor's
appointments.  It is essential that accurate records are
kept because employees are entitled to payment for one-half
of their unused sick days when they resign or retire.

              Vacation Leave

Full-time employees earn twenty-four working days of
vacation per year.  These are in addition to official
company holidays and must be used by the end of each year.
Accurate records of vacation leave taken must be kept
because employees will be paid for their unused days when
they resign or retire.
C:\LESSONS\MEMO.DOC                        Doc 1 Pg 1 Ln 1.5" Pos 4.65"
```

Type   **y**
Type   **y**

You should see the DOS prompt again.

Practice

1. Start WordPerfect and load your MEMO.DOC file. Change the date to tomorrow's date. Exit WordPerfect, saving the updated file.

2. Start WordPerfect without loading MEMO.DOC. Execute the List Files command and examine your WordPerfect subdirectory or diskette. Look at other subdirectories or diskettes from the List Files menu. When you are finished, exit WordPerfect and return to DOS.

Summary

- *Starting WordPerfect.* From DOS, type WP and press Enter.

- *The editing screen.* The cursor marks the place where text will be inserted. The status line indicates the document, page number, and line and column position.

- *Executing commands and getting help.* Most commands are executed by pressing a function key alone or by pressing the Shift, Control, or Alternate key with a function key. Help is obtained by pressing F3.

- *Entering text.* Simply type the text, pressing Enter only to force a new line or start a new paragraph.

- *Moving the cursor.* Arrow keys move up, down, left, and right. Ctrl-Left Arrow and Ctrl-Right Arrow move an entire word at a time. Grey Plus and Grey Minus move an entire screen at a time. Page Up and Page Down move an entire page at a time. End moves to the end of a line. Home, Left Arrow moves to the beginning of a line and Home, Right Arrow moves to the end of a line. Home, Home, Up Arrow moves to the beginning of the document and Home, Home, Down Arrow moves to the end of the document. Ctrl-Home moves to a particular page number.

- *Inserting new text.* Set the cursor, make sure insert mode is on, and type the text.

- *Overwriting mistakes.* Switch to typeover mode by pressing Insert and type over mistakes.

- *Deleting mistakes.* The Delete key removes the character at the cursor. The Backspace key removes the character to the left of the cursor. Ctrl-Backspace deletes an entire word. Ctrl-End deletes an entire line.

- *Searching for and replacing text.* Press F2 to execute the Search command. Press Alt-F2 to execute the Replace command.

- *Saving a document.* Press F10 to save a document to a disk file.

- *Checking spelling.* Press Ctrl-F2 to invoke the spelling checker.

- *Working with blocks of text.* Press Alt-F4 to mark a block. Press Ctrl-F4 to activate the Move menu and then select the Block option to move or copy a marked block. Press Delete to erase a marked block.

- *Canceling commands.* Press F1 to cancel a command in progress or restore a deletion.

- *Formatting characters.* Press F8 to underline text. Press F6 to boldface text. Press Ctrl-F8 to activate the Font menu, then select the Appearance option to choose other character formats.

- *Formatting lines.* Press Shift-F8 to activate the Format menu, then select the Line option to set left and right margins, tab stops, justification, line spacing, and line height. Press Shift-F6 to center text.

- *Formatting pages.* Press Shift-F8 to activate the Format menu, then select the Page option to set paper size and type, top and bottom margins, and page numbering. Press Ctrl-Enter to force a page break.

- *Printing a document.* Press Shift-F7 to activate the Print menu, then select the Full Document option.

- *Editing an existing document.* Type the document name on the command line when starting WordPerfect or press F5 to activate the List Files menu to load an existing document.

- *Exiting WordPerfect.* Press F7 and answer the prompts to return to DOS.

Key Terms

As an extra review of this chapter, try defining the following terms.

block	proportional spacing
cursor	ruler line
global search and replace	soft page break
hard page break	soft return
hard return	soft space
hard space	status line
keyboard template	text area
line height	word wrap

Multiple Choice

Choose the best selection to complete each statement.

1. When you start WordPerfect without loading a document, the only thing on the editing screen, except for the cursor, is the

   (a) Start Up menu. (b) ruler line.

   (c) status line. (d) Help facility.

2. Which keys would you press to see an on-screen version of the WordPerfect function key template?

   (a) F1, F1 (b) F3, F3

   (c) F3, F7 (d) Alt-F3

3. What is inserted into your document when you press the Enter key?

   (a) hard return (b) soft return

   (c) hard page break (d) soft page break

4. What feature eliminates having to press Enter at the end of every line?

(a) justification

(b) proportional spacing

(c) word wrap

(d) auto-hyphenation

5. Which keys would you press to move the cursor to the beginning of the next word to the right?

(a) Right Arrow

(b) Shift-Right Arrow

(c) Ctrl-Right Arrow

(d) Home-Right Arrow

6. You can move the cursor to the beginning of a document by pressing

(a) Ctrl-End.

(b) End, End, Down Arrow.

(c) Ctrl-PgDn.

(d) Home, Home, Up Arrow.

7. Pressing the Insert key toggles the

(a) delete mode.

(b) insert mode.

(c) line spacing.

(d) tab settings.

8. Pressing the Delete key deletes the character

(a) at the current cursor location.

(b) to the immediate right of the cursor.

(c) to the immediate left of the cursor.

(d) farthest from the cursor.

9. Pressing Ctrl-Backspace

(a) deletes the word to the left of the cursor.

(b) deletes the word at the cursor.

(c) moves the cursor to the beginning of the line.

(d) moves the cursor to the end of the line.

10. One operation that WordPerfect cannot do to a marked block is

(a) copy it.

(b) reverse it.

(c) delete it.

(d) move it.

11. Which keys would you press to repeat the previous search operation?

(a) F2, F2

(b) Alt-R

(c) F3, F3

(d) Ctrl-R

12. To force a page break, you must press

(a) Alt-P.

(b) Ctrl-Enter.

(c) Ctrl-PgDn.

(d) Alt-End.

13. Power failures, voltage fluctuations, system crashes, and unknown Word-Perfect bugs are all good reasons to periodically

(a) print your document.

(b) edit your document.

(c) retrieve your document.

(d) save your document.

14. Including a file name after the WP when you start WordPerfect

(a) prints that file.

(b) automatically loads that file.

(c) periodically saves that file.

(d) deletes that file.

15. Which key would you press to restore the most recently deleted word or phrase?

    (a) Ctrl-U   (b) F1

    (c) Ctrl-End   (d) Escape

16. Which two character-formatting options can each be used by pressing a single function key?

    (a) italics and outline   (b) shadow and strikeout

    (c) underline and boldface   (d) double underline and small capitals

17. What are the default WordPerfect settings for left and right margins?

    (a) 1" and 1"   (b) 1.25" and 1"

    (c) 1" and 2"   (d) 0" and 1"

18. How many blank lines are left between double-spaced lines?

    (a) 0   (b) 1

    (c) 2   (d) 3

19. What keys do you press to activate the Print menu?

    (a) Shift-F7   (b) Ctrl-P

    (c) Ctrl-F1   (d) Shift-PrtSc

20. What key do you use to exit WordPerfect and return to DOS?

    (a) F1   (b) F3

    (c) F5   (d) F7

Fill-In

1. To start WordPerfect, you type _______ and press Enter.

2. The line at the bottom of the WordPerfect editing screen is called the _______.

3. Pressing _______ and then _______ moves the cursor to the left edge of the screen.

4. Pressing F3 brings up WordPerfect's _______ facility.

5. _______ is the key you press to move the cursor to the end of the current line.

6. When a document is formatted so that all of the lines line up at the right margin, it is _______.

7. Word processors have a feature called _______ that eliminates having to press Enter at the end of each line.

8. Pressing Enter generates what's known as a _______ return.

9. The _______ keys include the Home, End, Page Up, Page Down, and arrow keys.

10. If insert mode is turned on, pressing the Insert key switches to _______ mode.

11. To overwrite mistakes, you must first turn insert mode _______.

12. Backspace, Delete, Ctrl-Backspace, and Ctrl-End are all examples of commands that _______ text.

13. Existing text can be centered between the left and right margins by pressing
    _______.

14. A _______ is any section of text, from a single character to a whole document,
    that can be marked and treated as a single entity.

15. A global _______ and _______ operation is used to automatically change
    every occurrence of a word or phrase.

16. By default, WordPerfect sets both the top and bottom page margins to _______.

17. When justification is not used, you get a _______ right margin.

18. If the spelling checker stops on a word that is not misspelled, you can use
    the _______ or _______ option to continue.

19. When you _______ a document, WordPerfect copies it from primary memory
    to a disk file.

20. In WordPerfect, page numbering is turned _______ by default.

Short Problems

1. Start up WordPerfect without loading an existing document. Type the following text. Press **Enter** only once, after the last line.

   **The next meeting of the EZ Systems Board of Managers
   will be held at 7:00 P.M on November 19, 1989 in Room
   217 of Champaign Federal Savings. This is an important
   meeting, so please try to attend.**

2. Move the cursor to the top of the document and type the following lines.
   Press **Enter** after each line.

   **To: Board of Managers
   From: David Franklin, Secretary
   Re: Next meeting**

3. Press the **Enter** key again to leave a blank line before the paragraph. Move
   the cursor to the top of the document, and do this:

   Type **M E M O**
   Press **Enter**

   Boldface, underline, and center this title.

4. Move the cursor to the last line of the memo and delete it with a single
   command. Restore the text you've deleted with the Cancel command.

5. Mark "EZ Systems" as a block of text and copy it before the "Board of Managers" after the "To:."

6. Move the cursor to the top of the file. Use the search and replace command
   to change "Managers" to "Directors" throughout the entire document.

7. Move the cursor to the beginning of the document and set the left and right
   margins to 1½ inches.

8. Change the tab stops so that they occur at 1-inch intervals.

9. Turn off justification for this memo.

10. Go back and double space the entire document (use the Line Spacing option
    from the Line Format menu).

11. Save the document in a disk file named MEETING.DOC, but don't exit
    WordPerfect.

12. If your computer is equipped with a printer, make sure it is turned on and on-line, and print this memo.

13. Use WordPerfect's on-line help facility to get a list of all the features that begin with A. Select a different letter and try it again. Now try learning more about the function keys.

Long Problems

1. Use WordPerfect to create a letter to be sent to three different software companies requesting information about the word processor they sell. Use the same basic letter, but tailor it to each company and its product. Save each version in its own disk file and print out all three. If you have no word processors in mind, use these three:

WordPerfect	WordStar	Microsoft Word
WordPerfect Corp.	WordStar International	Microsoft Corp.
1555 No. Technology	Corp.	16011 N.E. 36th Way
Way	33 San Pablo Ave.	Redmond, WA 98073
Orem, UT 84057	San Rafael, CA 94903	

2. Use WordPerfect to write a paper for one of your classes or a report for your company. Be sure to follow any format guidelines specified.

3. Look in a newspaper or placement office listing for a position you might apply for. Prepare a realistic resume and cover letter for this job with WordPerfect. Be sure to use underlining and boldface where appropriate.

4. Investigate three different word processing programs. Use WordPerfect to prepare a report that compares their features.

5. Use WordPerfect to create your academic schedule for this semester. List the days, times, classes, buildings, rooms, and instructors.

6. Create a weekly appointment calendar with WordPerfect. Print out several copies for the next few weeks.

7. Write a letter with WordPerfect to a company praising or criticizing their product or service.

8. Use WordPerfect to write a letter to WordPerfect Corporation detailing some of the things you like or dislike about their word processing package. You can use the address given in Problem 1.

9. Create an address and phone listing of your friends and acquaintances using WordPerfect.

10. Create a quick reference guide to DOS with WordPerfect. In other words, list each DOS command along with a brief description of what it does and how to invoke it.

11. Use WordPerfect to create a quick reference guide to WordPerfect. List the commands and operations that you think are most important to remember.

12. Take a week's worth of notes from a class you are taking and redo them with WordPerfect. Try to do more than just type them as is. Organize, rearrange, and reword the material if you can. Do you think using a word processor can improve your notes?

13. As you redo your notes for Problem 12, keep in mind any questions you might have about the material. Write a letter to your professor in which you

outline your questions. If possible, copy sections or even direct quotes from your notes and include them in your letter.

14. Perhaps you have an item that you would like to sell through a newspaper ad, such as a musical instrument, bicycle, car, couch, television, stereo, or computer. You might be looking for a roommate or have an apartment to sublet. Use WordPerfect to design a classified ad to place in your school or local newspaper.

15. Choose a current event or local news item that interests you and use WordPerfect to write a letter expressing your views on it to the editor of your school or town newspaper.

INTERMEDIATE WORDPERFECT

In This Chapter

 **Preview**

In Chapter 4 you learned the basics of WordPerfect, the most popular microcomputer word processing package. This chapter continues your exploration of WordPerfect with slightly more advanced topics.

After studying this chapter, you will know how to

- manage documents with the List Files menu.
- create longer documents.
- use additional cursor movement commands.
- use additional delete commands.
- work with formatting codes.
- use the built-in thesaurus.
- split the screen into two windows.
- indent paragraphs.
- create tables with tab stops.
- align numbers to tab stops.
- move text flush right.
- insert the current date automatically.
- center text on a page.
- create a document summary.
- retrieve and save text files.
- execute a DOS command within WordPerfect.

Getting Started

You've already learned how to start WordPerfect and use its most common features and commands. This chapter assumes you have completed all of the lessons and exercises in Chapter 4. Furthermore, it assumes that you have a computer with a hard disk and WordPerfect 5.0 installed on it in a subdirectory named WP50. It also assumes you have a subdirectory named LESSONS in which to store your document files.

Lesson 1: Managing Documents

WordPerfect makes it easy to create new documents, retrieve existing documents, save and search for documents, as well as delete, rename, copy, and print documents. You can also change the default directory and examine the contents of a directory or file. All of these features are available either as a function key command or as an option in the List Files menu.

Step 1: Start WordPerfect

If you are not already running WordPerfect, switch to the proper subdirectory and start the program:

Type   **cd c:\wp50**
Press **Enter**
Type   **wp**
Press **Enter**

Step 2: Retrieve a Document By Name

In the previous chapter, you learned how to load an existing document file by specifying the file name on the command line when starting WordPerfect or by selecting the file from the List Files screen and executing the Retrieve option. If you know the location and name of the document file you want, a third method exists to retrieve it. Suppose you want to work on the MEMO.DOC file in the LESSONS subdirectory. Execute the Retrieve command:

Press   **Shift-F10**

WordPerfect will display the prompt

```
Document to be retrieved:
```

Enter the path and name of the document file:

Type   **c:\lessons\memo.doc**
Press   **Enter**

The document will be loaded into memory and displayed on the screen in the text area.

Step 3: Starting a New Document

If you are finished looking at or working on a document, you can clear the screen to start a new document without actually exiting WordPerfect and restarting the program. Suppose you have either already saved the current document or don't want to save it. Execute the Exit command and answer "no" to both prompts:

Press   **F7**
Type   **n**
Type   **n**

WordPerfect will not save the file and will not return to DOS, but will clear the screen so you can start a new document.

Step 4: Execute the List Files Command

The screen and menu presented by the List Files command provide many options for managing your documents. This command lets you see the names of the files stored on a disk or in a subdirectory. It also lets you retrieve, delete, rename, copy, and print files. Execute the List Files command to examine your default directory, which should be the subdirectory C:\WP50:

Press   **F5**
Press   **Enter**

As Figure 1 shows, WordPerfect will display the directory of C:\WP50 and present the List Files menu at the bottom of the screen.

Step 5: Select the Other Directory Option

You can look at any disk or subdirectory from the List Files menu. Select the Other Directory option:

Type   **o**

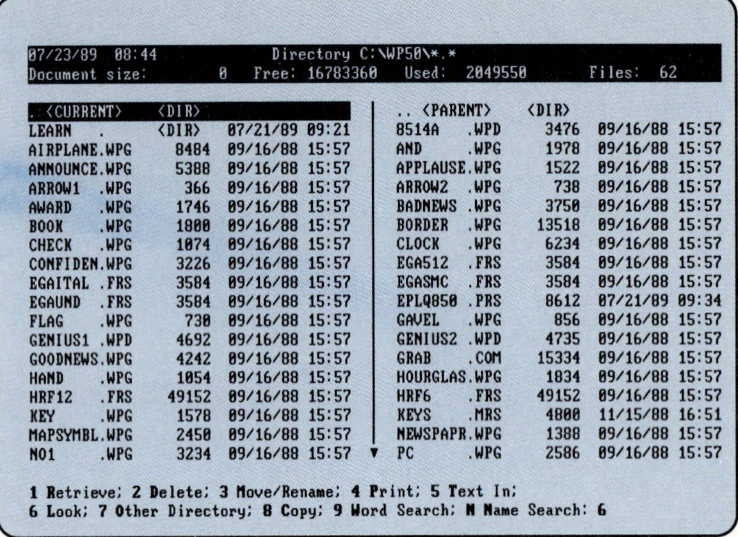

Figure 1 The List Files Menu

WordPerfect will display the prompt

    New directory = C: \WP50

Here the program is presenting the current path and is asking you to enter the path of the other directory you want to examine. Specify the LESSONS subdirectory:

    Type   **c: \lessons**
    Press   **Enter** (2 times)

The list of files will change to reveal the contents of the LESSONS subdirectory.

Step 6: Select the Look Option

Look is the default option of the List Files menu. This option lets you examine the contents of a directory, which you have just done. The Look option also allows you to examine the contents of a file without actually loading that file into the editing screen. Let's look at the file MEMO.DOC. Highlight the file name and select the Look option:

    Press   **Down Arrow**
    Type   **L**

Your screen should look like Figure 2. The file MEMO.DOC is presented, but you can only look at it, not edit it. If the file is too long to fit on a single screen, you can use the cursor movement keys to see the rest of it. When you are finished examining the file, execute the Exit command:

    Press   **F7**

Step 7: Select the Retrieve Option

You have already learned to use the Retrieve option, but let's try it again. The file name MEMO.DOC should already be highlighted, so just select the Retrieve option:

    Type   **r**

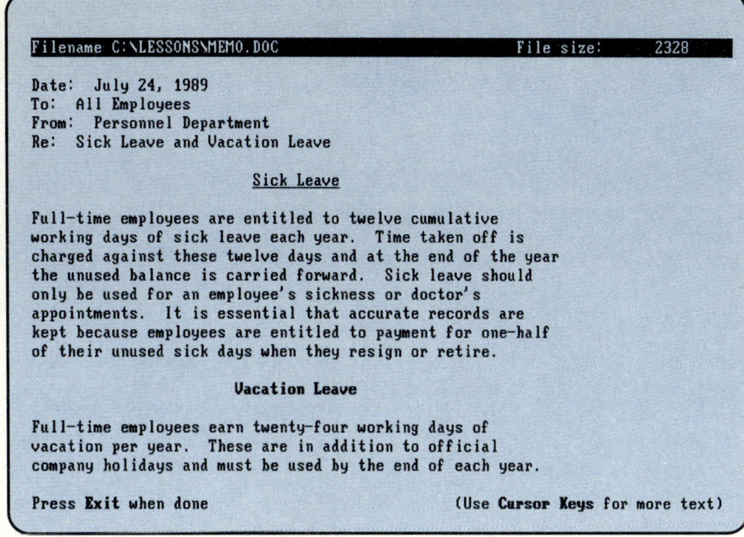

Figure 2 MEMO.DOC Presented with the List Files Look Option

WordPerfect will load the file into memory and present it on the editing screen. Unlike using the Look option, using the Retrieve option lets you edit the document.

Now, clear the screen and execute the List Files command again:

Press   **F7**
Type   **n**
Type   **n**
Press   **F5**
Press   **Enter**

Step 8: Select the Copy Option

You can use the Copy option of the List Files menu to duplicate a file. The duplicate can be created either in the same directory or in a different directory. If it is in the same directory as the original, the duplicate must be given a different name. Let's copy the file MEMO.DOC and name the duplicate MEMO.BAK. First, highlight the file MEMO.DOC and then select the Copy option:

Press   **Down Arrow**
Type   **c**

WordPerfect will display the prompt

```
Copy this file to:
```

Simply enter the name of the duplicate to be created:

Type   **memo.bak**
Press   **Enter**

The file MEMO.BAK will be created in the current directory. Unfortunately, the List Files screen isn't updated, so highlight the current directory and execute the Look option to see what you have done:

Press   **Up Arrow**
Type   **L**
Press   **Enter**

The file MEMO.BAK will now appear in the directory listing shown on the screen.

Step 9: Select the Move/Rename Option

The Move/Rename option of the List Files menu can be used to move a file to a different subdirectory or change the name of a file. Let's rename MEMO.BAK to MEMO.OLD. First, highlight MEMO.BAK. Then select the Move/Rename option:

Type   **m**

WordPerfect will display the prompt

New name: C:\LESSONS\MEMO.BAK

To move the file, you would edit the path. To rename the file, simply enter the new name:

Type   **memo.old**
Press   **Enter**

The file MEMO.BAK will become MEMO.OLD in the LESSONS subdirectory.

Step 10: Select the Print Option

In the previous chapter you learned how to print a document from the editing screen. You can also print a document that is not currently loaded into memory from the List Files menu. Let's print MEMO.OLD. Make sure your printer is turned on, loaded with paper, and on-line. Highlight the file to be printed. Then select the Print option from the List Files menu:

Type   **p**

WordPerfect will display the prompt

Page(s): (All)

Select the default option to print all of the pages:

Press   **Enter**

The document will be sent to the printer.

Step 11: Select the Text In Option

WordPerfect documents are files that contain various formatting codes in addition to the actual text. ASCII files, also known as text files, contain only letters, numbers, punctuation marks, and other symbols you can produce from the keyboard. Batch files, CONFIG.SYS, programming language source code, and certain data files are examples of ASCII files. The Text In option of the List Files menu lets you load and edit ASCII files. Let's use this option to load AUTOEXEC.BAT, the auto-execute batch file in the root directory of the hard disk. First, use the Other Directory option to change to the root directory:

Type   **o**
Type   **c:**
Press   **Enter** (2 times)

Use the arrow keys to highlight the file AUTOEXEC.BAT. Then select the Text In option:

Type   **t**

AUTOEXEC.BAT will be retrieved from the disk and displayed on the editing screen (see Figure 3). There the text can be edited, but without formatting features such as margins, page breaks, underlining, and so on.

Now, clear the screen, execute the List Files command, and change to the WP50 subdirectory:

Press	**F7**
Type	**n**
Type	**n**
Press	**F5**
Type	**c:\wp50**
Press	**Enter**

Step 12: Select the Name Search Option

The Name Search option of the List Files menu allows you to highlight a file name by typing its name instead of using the arrow keys to move through the list. When you type the first letter of the file name, the highlight moves to the first file name that begins with that letter. As you type more letters of the file name, the highlight moves to the next file name that matches what you have typed so far. You can usually highlight the file name you want by typing just a few characters.

The WordPerfect subdirectory displayed on your screen contains many files. Suppose you want to find the file named WP.EXE. Instead of scrolling through the long list with the arrow keys to highlight WP.EXE, use the Name Search option:

Type	**n**
Type	**wp.e**

Each file name character you type moves the highlight to the next matching file name. By the time you type the "e," the file WP.EXE is highlighted (see Figure 4). Return to the List Files menu:

Press	**Enter**

Figure 3 The Text File
AUTOEXEC.BAT Retrieved

```
@ECHO OFF
SET COMSPEC=C:\DOS\COMMAND.COM
VERIFY OFF
PATH C:\DOS
APPEND /E
APPEND C:\DOS
PROMPT $P$G
C:\DOS\GRAPHICS
ASTCLOCK
VER
PRINT /D:LPT1




C:\AUTOEXEC.BAT                              Doc 1 Pg 1 Ln 1" Pos 1"
```

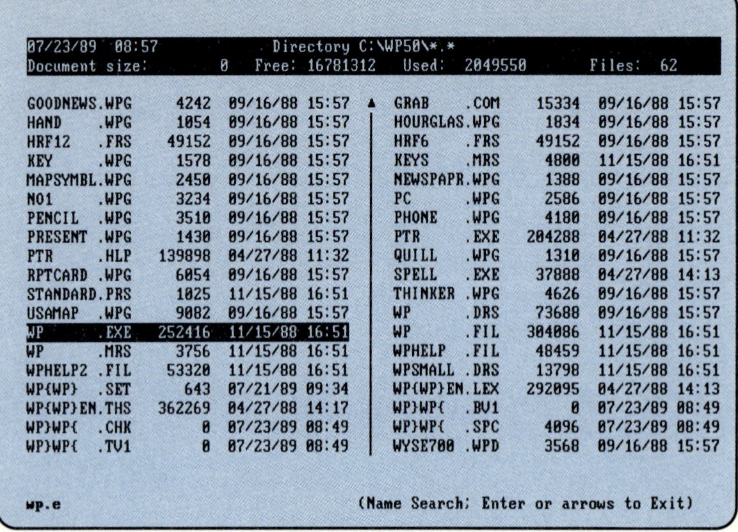

Figure 4 The Name Search Option of the List Files Menu

Now, change to the LESSONS subdirectory:

> Type   **o**
> Type   **c:\lessons**
> Press   **Enter** (2 times)

Step 13: Mark Files

In some cases it is necessary to perform an operation on a group of files. For example, you may want to copy, delete, or print several files at once. WordPerfect allows you to mark each file you want on the List Files screen with an asterisk (*). After the files are marked, you can select Copy, Delete, or Print from the List Files menu. Let's see how to mark and unmark files. First, move the highlight to the file MEMO.OLD. Then mark the file with an asterisk:

> Type   *****

An asterisk will appear in the directory listing just after the file size. Now mark MEMO.DOC too. If you have a printer connected to your computer, select the Print option:

> Type   **p**
> Type   **y**

Both files will be printed.

To unmark a file, simply repeat the process by highlighting the file name and typing another asterisk. The asterisk will disappear from the directory listing. Unmark MEMO.DOC and MEMO.OLD.

Step 14: Select the Word Search Option

Word Search is a powerful List Files option that lets you mark files that meet specific conditions. For example, you can mark all those files that contain the word "vacation." Select the Word Search option:

> Type   **w**

WordPerfect will present a menu that lists four types of searches:

- **1 Doc Summary** This option searches document summaries for the specified word pattern. A *document summary* is a collection of information about a document. You will learn how to create document summaries later in this chapter.
- **2 First Page** This option searches only the first page or the first 4000 characters of documents for the specified word pattern.
- **3 Entire Doc** This option searches entire documents for the specified word pattern.
- **4 Conditions** This option allows you to enter criteria to conduct a more detailed search.

Let's use the Entire Document option:

Type **e**

WordPerfect will display the prompt

```
Word pattern:
```

Now you specify the text you want to search for. You can use a question mark (?) to represent any single character and an asterisk (*) to represent any group of characters. These **wild-card characters** work just like the DOS global file name characters ? and *. In our simple example, however, you don't need wild-card characters because you are just searching for documents that contain the word "vacation." Specify the word pattern:

Type **vacation**
Press **Enter**

WordPerfect will search through all the documents in the current directory and mark with an asterisk those documents that contain the word "vacation." Since MEMO.DOC and MEMO.OLD are duplicates that both contain the word "vacation," both files are marked with asterisks.

Now, unmark both files. You can unmark every file on the List Files screen with a single command:

Press **Home**
Type *****

Step 15: Select the Delete Option

The Delete option in the List Files menu lets you erase files. Let's delete MEMO.OLD. First, highlight MEMO.OLD. Then select the Delete option:

Type **d**

WordPerfect will display the prompt

```
Delete C:\LESSONS\MEMO.OLD? (Y/N) No
```

If you are sure you want to delete the file, answer yes:

Type **y**

The file will be erased from the disk and removed from the List Files screen.
Now, exit the List Files screen and return to the editing screen:

Press **F7**

Practice

1. Execute the List Files command. Put a formatted diskette in drive A. Select the Other Directory option and examine the contents of the diskette in drive A.

2. Use the Other Directory option to switch to the root directory of the hard disk. Use the Text In option to load the file CONFIG.SYS. Use the Exit command to clear the screen without saving the file and without leaving WordPerfect.

3. Execute the List Files command and specify the LESSONS subdirectory. Copy the file MEMO.DOC and name the duplicate NOTE.DOC.

4. Use the Look option to examine the contents of NOTE.DOC.

5. Retrieve NOTE.DOC into the editing screen. Make a change to the file and then save it. Execute the List Files command again.

6. Rename NOTE.DOC to NOTE.OLD.

7. Print NOTE.OLD.

8. Delete NOTE.OLD. Exit the List Files screen and return to the editing screen.

Lesson 2: Creating a Longer Document

To illustrate more of WordPerfect's capabilities, you need a more substantial document. In this lesson, you will create a simple newsletter for a fictional business, Paddle and Portage Canoe Outfitters.

Step 1: Type the Heading

The top of the newsletter will present the centered address and phone number of the business. Follow these instructions:

```
Press   Shift-F6
Type    Paddle and Portage Canoe Outfitters
Press   Enter
Press   Shift-F6
Type    Box 555
Press   Enter
Press   Shift-F6
Type    Grand Marais, MN   55604
Press   Enter
Press   Shift-F6
Type    (218) 555-1234
Press   Enter (2 times)
```

Step 2: Type the Title

The title of the newsletter will also be centered. Follow these instructions:

```
Press   Shift-F6
Type    NEWSLETTER
Press   Enter
Press   Shift-F6
Type    1991
Press   Enter (2 times)
```

Step 3: Type the First Section

Each section of the newsletter will have an underlined heading.

    Press   **F8**
    Type   **New Outfitting Post**
    Press   **F8**
    Press   **Enter**

Type the paragraph without pressing Enter at the end of each line:

    **This winter we completed our new outfitting facility. It
    will house our office, staff kitchen, retail sales, and
    equipment storage area. Located close to the lake for
    easy access, this new building will give us the room we
    need to help serve you better.**

Space down for the next section:

    Press   **Enter** (2 times)

Step 4: Type the Next Section

Follow these directions:

    Press   **F8**
    Type   **Sport Shows**
    Press   **F8**
    Press   **Enter**
    Type   **This year we will be attending the following sport
            shows:**
    Press   **Enter** (2 times)
    Type   **Jan 23-Feb 1**
    Press   **Enter**
    Type   **Chicagoland Show, O'Hare Exposition Center**
    Press   **Enter** (2 times)
    Type   **Feb 14-Feb 22**
    Press   **Enter**
    Type   **Greater Northwest Sport Show, Minneapolis Auditorium**
    Press   **Enter** (2 times)
    Type   **Mar 13-Mar 22**
    Press   **Enter**
    Type   **Milwaukee Sentinel Sport Show, MECCA Building**
    Press   **Enter** (2 times)
    Type   **If you can, stop by and say "Hi." Remember our
            SPECIAL BONUS RATES for sport show reservations.**
    Press   **Enter** (2 times)

Step 5: Save the Document So Far

It is a good idea to periodically save your document on a disk as you are creating
it, even if it is not yet finished. Save the document in the LESSONS subdirectory
and name it NEWS.DOC:

    Press   **F10**
    Type   **c:\lessons\news.doc**
    Press   **Enter**

Step 6: Type the Rest of the Document

Follow these directions to type the rest of the newsletter:

> Press   **F8**
> Type   `New Regulations`
> Press   **F8**
> Press   **Enter**

Type this paragraph:

> `Only Ontario's Quetico Provincial Park has changed regulations for this season. Reservations for Quetico camping permits will be accepted no sooner than January 19. Written reservations may be made 21 days in advance of trip departure. Phone reservations may be made from 21 days prior to and up to the date of departure. As always, we will handle all permit reservations for our guests.`

> Press   **Enter** (2 times)
> Press   **F8**
> Type   `Equipment Improvements`
> Press   **F8**
> Press   **Enter**

Type this paragraph:

> `Our most exciting equipment addition this year is a new Super-Lite Badger canoe. It weighs, believe it or not, slightly over 40 pounds. We feel that this new 17-foot Badger canoe is ideal for wilderness tripping. It's stable, safe, and much easier to paddle and portage.`

> Press   **Enter**
> Press   **Tab**

Type this paragraph:

> `Last year we field tested several nylon packs and found one in particular that offered several advantages. Lighter and dryer than canvas Duluth packs, we will be incorporating these new nylon packs into our equipment line beginning this year. The Super-Lite Badger canoes and nylon packs will be available on a first-come, first-serve basis.`

> Press   **Enter** (2 times)
> Press   **F8**
> Type   `Trail Food Improvements`
> Press   **F8**
> Press   **Enter**

Type this paragraph:

> `We have replaced the Ham and Potatoes with Meatballs and Gravy, the Beef Stromboli with Chicken Stew 'N Dumplings, and the Buttermilk Pancakes with Blueberry Pancakes. These are all taste improvements, not cost savings, so our Trail Food will be even better this year.`

```
Press   Enter (2 times)
Press   F8
Type    Trips
Press   F8
Press   Enter
```

Type this paragraph:

```
This fall we took a trip into the Cherry Lake area for
some lake trout fishing. We had our usual quota of rain,
but did enjoy two beautiful crisp autumn days. Mornings
we awoke to clear, deep blue skies with heavy, white
steam rising from Cherry Lake. It was almost like being
in a shaving commercial. On shore we could look up into
the blue sky, but as we paddled into the steam we
disappeared into white nothingness. It was a trip we'll
long remember.
```

```
Press   Enter
Press   Tab
```

Type this paragraph:

```
We extended our camping into winter this year with
several overnight trips in December. From our house we
have easy access to about 15 kilometers of cross-country
ski trails that lead to Boundary Waters Canoe Area
campsites. After setting up a base camp, we would
typically venture out for exploring and ice fishing.
Nothing like twenty below temperatures to get you moving
in the morning!
```

```
Press   Enter (2 times)
Press   F8
Type    A Final Note...
Press   F8
Press   Enter
```

Type this paragraph:

```
After having our best year ever, we want to thank all of
you for your friendship and patronage and wish you a
happy and prosperous New Year. We look forward to seeing
you this spring, summer, or fall.
```

```
Press   Enter (2 times)
Type    Becky and Bob Johnson, owners/operators
Press   Enter
Type    Paddle and Portage Canoe Outfitters
Press   Enter
```

Step 7: Check Your Work

Read over the document you have created and make sure it contains no errors.
Use what you have learned in the previous chapter to correct any typographical
errors you may have made.

Step 8: Save the Completed Document

Now that the document is finished, you must save it on a disk. Execute the Save command and replace your previous version of NEWS.DOC:

Press   **F10**
Press   **Enter**
Type   **y**

Step 9: Move to the Beginning

Move the cursor up to the beginning of the document:

Press   **Home** (2 times)
Press   **Up Arrow**

Your screen should look like Figure 5.

1. Use the spelling checker to further inspect the newsletter for typographical errors. Tell the spelling checker to skip proper names that are not in the dictionary, such as Marais, Chicagoland, O'Hare, Quetico, Stromboli, and Becky.

2. Move the cursor back to the beginning of the document.

Lesson 3: Learning More Cursor-Movement Commands

In the previous chapter you learned several ways to move the cursor within a WordPerfect document. This lesson covers a few other cursor movement commands.

Step 1: Move to the Bottom and Top of the Screen

Pressing Home once followed by an arrow key moves the cursor to that end of the text on the screen. Home, Left Arrow moves the cursor to the left edge of the screen and Home, Right Arrow moves the cursor to the right edge of the screen. You can also move to the bottom edge and top edge of the current screen. Execute this command:

Press   **Home**
Press   **Down Arrow**

The cursor will jump to the bottom edge of the current screen in the same column, or close to the same column, as its original position. If you repeat the command, the cursor will advance to the bottom of the next screen. Pressing Home, Down Arrow is the same as pressing Grey Plus. Now, execute the opposite command:

Press   **Home**
Press   **Up Arrow**

The cursor will jump to the top of the current screen. Pressing Home, Up Arrow is the same as pressing Grey Minus.

*Figure 5 The Completed
Newsletter*

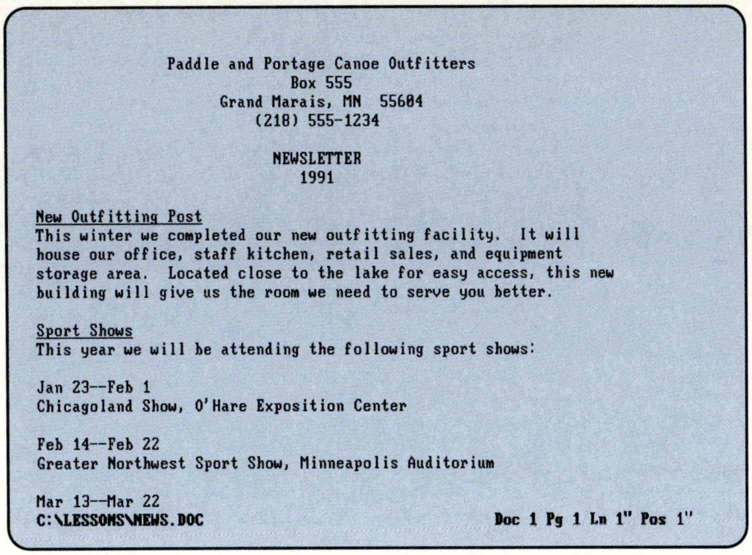

```
                    Paddle and Portage Canoe Outfitters
                                 Box 555
                           Grand Marais, MN  55604
                              (218) 555-1234

                                 NEWSLETTER
                                    1991

New Outfitting Post
This winter we completed our new outfitting facility.  It will
house our office, staff kitchen, retail sales, and equipment
storage area.  Located close to the lake for easy access, this new
building will give us the room we need to serve you better.

Sport Shows
This year we will be attending the following sport shows:

Jan 23--Feb 1
Chicagoland Show, O'Hare Exposition Center

Feb 14--Feb 22
Greater Northwest Sport Show, Minneapolis Auditorium

Mar 13--Mar 22
C:\LESSONS\NEWS.DOC                            Doc 1 Pg 1 Ln 1" Pos 1"
```

Step 2: Move a Specified Number of Lines

WordPerfect lets you move up or down a specified number of lines. Suppose you
want to move the cursor down 12 lines. Follow these instructions:

Press   **Escape**
Type   **12**
Press   **Down Arrow**

The cursor will move down 12 lines, just as if you had pressed Down Arrow 12
times. Now, move up 6 lines with this command:

Press   **Escape**
Type   **6**
Press   **Up Arrow**

Repeat this command to move the cursor up another 6 lines.

Step 3: Move a Specified Number of Characters

In fact, the Escape key can be used in this manner with other cursor movement
keys as well. Suppose you want to move the cursor right 20 characters. Execute
this command:

Press   **Escape**
Type   **20**
Press   **Right Arrow**

The cursor will move to the right 20 characters just as if you had pressed Right
Arrow 20 times. Now, try the opposite command:

Press   **Escape**
Type   **20**
Press   **Left Arrow**

Step 4: Move a Specified Number of Screens or Pages

The Escape key can also be used to rapidly scroll or page. For example, try this command:

Press   **Escape**
Type   **3**
Press   **Grey Plus**

The cursor will move down three screens, just as if you had pressed Grey Plus three times. Now, try a repeated paging command:

Press   **Escape**
Type   **2**
Press   **Page Up**

The cursor will move up two pages, in this case to the top of the document.

Step 5: Move to a Specific Character

A variation of the Go To feature, executed by pressing Ctrl-Home, lets you position the cursor to the immediate right of the first occurrence of a particular character. For example, move the cursor to the beginning of the first line of the newsletter. Suppose you want to advance the cursor just past the "C" in the word "Canoe." Execute this command:

Press   **Ctrl-Home**
Type   **C**

The cursor will be placed on the "a" following the "C" in the word "Canoe."

 1. Move the cursor to the beginning of the document.
2. Advance the cursor 10 characters to the right, then move the cursor 5 characters to the left. (Don't press the arrow keys repeatedly.)
3. Move the cursor down 10 lines without repeatedly pressing Down Arrow.
4. Advance the cursor to the next occurrence of the letter R.
5. Move the cursor down 4 screens, then move the cursor back up 4 screens. Now, move the cursor to the beginning of the line.

Lesson 4: Learning More Delete Commands

WordPerfect provides several commands for deleting text. You have already learned the most common methods in the previous chapter.

Step 1: Delete to Word Boundary

Suppose you want to delete just part of a word. WordPerfect lets you erase characters from the current cursor location to the beginning or end of a word. For example, move the cursor to the letter "f" in the word "Outfitters" in the first line of the newsletter. Delete the first part of the word:

Press   **Home**
Press   **Backspace**

The "Out" part of the word will be deleted. Now, restore what you have deleted:

> Press　**F1**
> Type　**r**

This time, try deleting the latter part of the word:

> Press　**Home**
> Press　**Delete**

The "fitters" part of the word will be deleted. Restore what you have deleted:

> Press　**F1**
> Type　**r**

Step 2: Delete Several Lines

You can use the Escape key to repeat the Delete to End of Line command and erase several lines at once. For example, move the cursor to the beginning of the paragraph beneath the title "New Outfitting Post." Delete four lines by executing this command:

> Press　**Escape**
> Type　**4**
> Press　**Ctrl-End**

The four lines will disappear from the screen. Now, restore the lines you have deleted:

> Press　**F1**
> Type　**r**

Step 3: Delete to End of Page

WordPerfect provides an even more drastic command that lets you delete the text from the current cursor position to the end of the page. Execute this command:

> Press　**Ctrl-PgDn**
> Type　**y**

After you answer yes to the prompt (see Figure 6), WordPerfect will delete the rest of the text on the current page. Now, restore what you have erased:

> Press　**F1**
> Type　**r**

Practice

1. Select a long word in the newsletter. Move the cursor into the middle of the word. Delete the first half of the word. Restore what you have deleted. Then delete the second half of the word. Again, restore what you have deleted.
2. Delete ten lines of text from the newsletter with one command. Restore the lines you have deleted.
3. Delete half of the second page of the newsletter. Restore what you have deleted. Move the cursor to the beginning of the document.

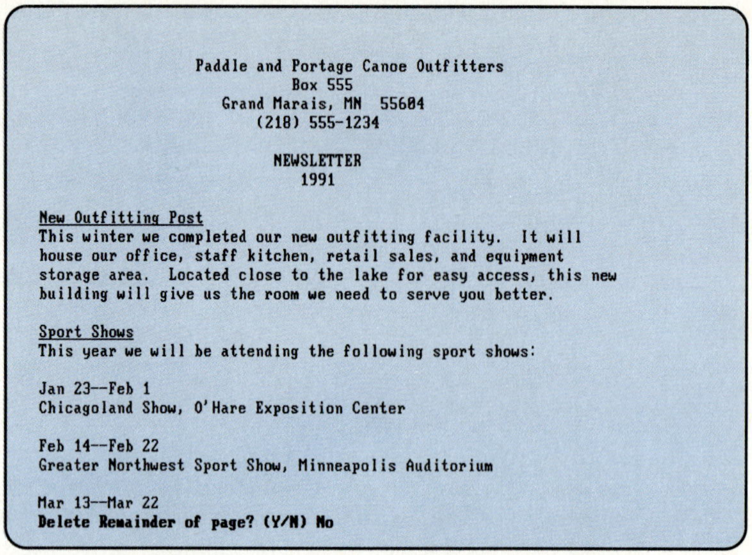

```
              Paddle and Portage Canoe Outfitters
                          Box 555
                  Grand Marais, MN  55604
                       (218) 555-1234

                         NEWSLETTER
                            1991

New Outfitting Post
This winter we completed our new outfitting facility.  It will
house our office, staff kitchen, retail sales, and equipment
storage area.  Located close to the lake for easy access, this new
building will give us the room we need to serve you better.

Sport Shows
This year we will be attending the following sport shows:

Jan 23--Feb 1
Chicagoland Show, O'Hare Exposition Center

Feb 14--Feb 22
Greater Northwest Sport Show, Minneapolis Auditorium

Mar 13--Mar 22
Delete Remainder of page? (Y/N) No
```

Figure 6 The Delete to End of Page Prompt

Lesson 5: Working with Codes

Whenever you press the Enter key, WordPerfect inserts a **code** in your document that tells the display or printer to start a new line. Although this code does not appear on the screen, it is stored in your document like any other character. WordPerfect has many such hidden formatting codes. Codes are inserted whenever you press the Tab key, underline text, center text, change margins, or execute any of a number of commands that change a document's appearance. Codes not only control how the document should look on the screen, they tell the printer how to print the document. Learning about codes helps you understand and control the way in which WordPerfect formats text.

Step 1: Reveal Codes

By default, codes are hidden from view to simplify the editing screen. You can display codes along with the text at any time, however, by executing the Reveal Codes command. Do this now:

Press **Alt-F3**

Your screen should look like Figure 7. The top part of the screen is the normal view of the document with codes hidden. The bar across the middle of the screen is a ruler line that indicates the current left margin (open brace {), the tab stops (triangles), and the right margin (close brace }). The portion of the screen below the ruler line reveals the codes, which are bright characters enclosed in square brackets, and the text in ordinary characters. For example, [Und] is the code that turns underlining on and off. It appears in uppercase [UND] when turned on and lowercase [und] when turned off.

WordPerfect has nearly 120 different formatting codes. The following table lists a few of the most common codes.

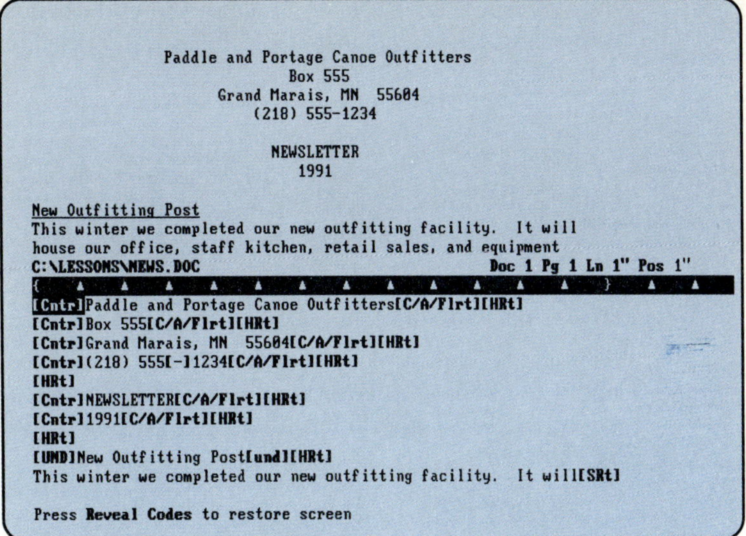

Figure 7 Formatting Codes Revealed

Code	Description
[-]	Hard hyphen inserted by pressing - key
[Bold]	Boldface on or off
[Cntr]	Begin centering text
[C/A/Flrt]	End centering, Align, or Flush Right text
[HPg]	Hard page break inserted by Ctrl-Enter
[HRt]	Hard return inserted by pressing Enter
[SPg]	Soft page break inserted by WordPerfect
[SRt]	Soft return inserted by word wrap
[Tab]	Advance to next tab stop
[Und]	Underline on or off

Step 2: Examine the Document

With Reveal Codes turned on, use the Down Arrow key to examine the document. Notice how the Reveal Codes cursor, a reverse video block, moves as you press the Down Arrow key. Look up the codes you see in the previous table and try to understand what they mean.

Step 3: Delete Codes

Codes are special characters that you can insert and delete. For example, to remove centering or underlining, you simply delete the appropriate codes. Although you don't have to reveal codes to delete them, revealing codes does make it easier to see what is happening. For example, let's uncenter the first line in the newsletter. Move the cursor to the first [Cntr] code in the file and then delete it:

Press   **Delete**

The [C/A/Flrt] code that symbolizes the end of centering will also be removed and the text will shift to the left edge of the screen. Now, restore the code you have deleted:

> Press   **F1**
> Type   **r**

You can also delete codes to remove underlining and remove hard returns [HRt] to join lines or paragraphs.

Step 4: Hide Codes

Revealing codes displays two views of the same document, but you can see only about ten lines at a time. You can leave codes revealed for as long as you like, but most users prefer to turn them on only when needed. When you are finished working with codes, you can hide them again:

> Press   **Alt-F3**

The editing screen will return to full size, the ruler line will disappear, and codes will be hidden again.

1. Reveal codes.
2. Remove the underline from the heading "New Outfitting Post." Restore the underline by marking the heading as a block and then pressing the underline key (F8).
3. Move the cursor down to the end of the first paragraph after the heading "Equipment Improvements." Remove the hard return and the following tab to join the two paragraphs. Restore the hard return and tab. Move the cursor to the beginning of the document.
4. Use the help facility to read more about the Reveal Codes command:

   > Press   **F3**
   > Press   **Alt-F3**

   When you are finished reading the help screen, return to the document:

   > Press   **Enter**

5. Hide codes.

Lesson 6: Using the Thesaurus

Like most modern word processing packages, WordPerfect includes a built-in thesaurus program that can help you select just the right word for a situation. The WordPerfect thesaurus can examine a word already in your document or a word that you enter and display a list of synonyms (words with the same or similar meaning) and antonyms (words with the opposite meaning).

Step 1: Move the Cursor to the Desired Word

The thesaurus feature is very easy to use. For example, suppose you want to see alternatives to the word "house" in the second sentence of the New Outfitting Post paragraph. First, move the cursor anywhere within the word "house."

Step 2: Execute the Thesaurus Command

After you have selected the word you want to look up, simply execute the the-saurus command:

Press **Alt-F1**

Step 3: Examine the Thesaurus Screen

Your screen should look like Figure 8. In this case, "house" is the **headword,** a word that can be looked up in the thesaurus. The words under the headword, called references, are divided into nouns (n), verbs (v), adjectives (a), and antonyms (ant). No adjectives are available for "house." References preceded by a dot are other headwords that can also be looked up in the thesaurus. The references are collected into numbered groups of words with the same meaning. Six groups of references are available for "house." The Reference menu is the column of capital letters preceding the references. The Thesaurus menu is the list of four options across the bottom of the screen. Presently, the Reference menu is on the first column of words: abode, dwelling, home, residence, and so on. You can move the Reference menu from column to column by pressing Right Arrow and Left Arrow. For example, move the Reference menu to the second column of references:

Press **Right Arrow**

The column of capital letters will move over so that the word "accommodate" is A, "lodge" is B, "quarter" is C, and so on.

Step 4: Replace the Word

If you find a word in the list of references that you like, you can tell WordPerfect to replace the word you have looked up. Suppose you want to replace "house" with "accommodate." Select the Replace Word option from the Thesaurus menu and then type the letter of the word you want:

Type   **1**
Type   **a**

Figure 8 The Thesaurus Screen

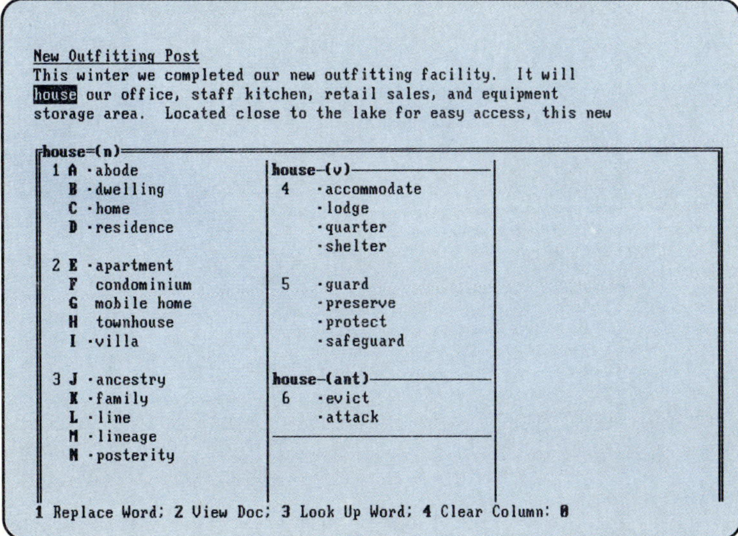

The word "house" will automatically be replaced with "accommodate."

Step 5: Look Up Other Words

Invoke the thesaurus again:

Press **Alt-F1**

This time, "accommodate" is the headword. While the thesaurus is on the screen, you can use three methods to look up other words. The first method is to select the Look Up Word option and enter the word you want. Suppose you want to look up the word "lodge."

Type   **3**
Type   **lodge**
Press **Enter**

WordPerfect will display references for "lodge" in addition to the references for "accommodate" already on the screen (see Figure 9).

Step 6: Specify a Letter

Another way to look up a word while in the thesaurus is to type the letter next to a headword marked with a dot. Suppose you want to look up the word "board," which is preceded by the letter "M."

Type   **m**

WordPerfect will display references for "board" in addition to the references for "lodge" and "accommodate" already on the screen (see Figure 10). You can move down or up within columns to see more references by pressing the Down Arrow or Up Arrow keys.

Figure 9 References for Two Headwords Displayed

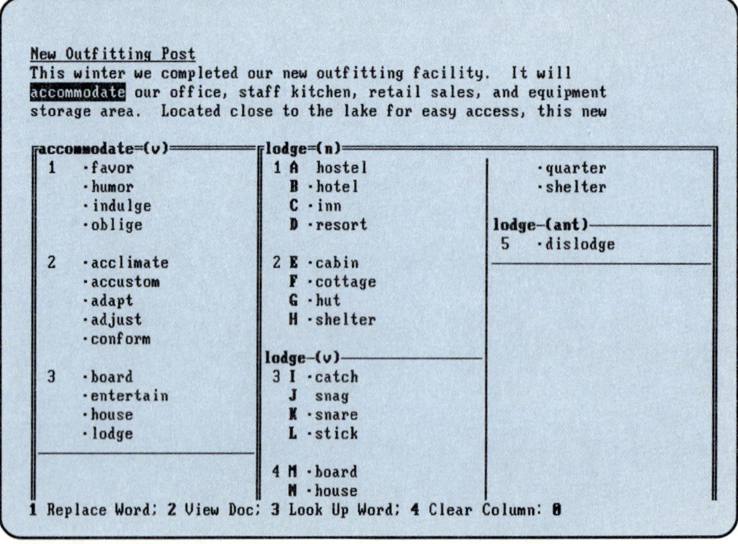

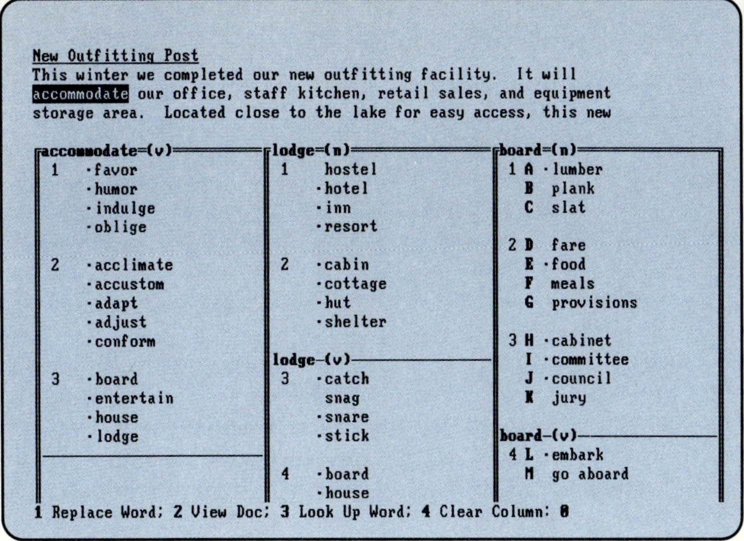

Figure 10 References for Three Headwords Displayed

Step 7: Use the View Doc Option

The third way to look up other words while using the thesaurus is to select the View Doc option, move the cursor to another word in the document, and execute the Thesaurus command.

> Type **2**

The cursor will move to the top of the screen where four lines of the document are displayed. You can now move the cursor within the document while the thesaurus remains on the screen. Move the cursor to the word "office" and then execute the Thesaurus command:

> Press **Alt-F1**

The thesaurus screen will clear to reveal only the references for "office."

Step 8: Clear a Column

One more option is in the Thesaurus menu at the bottom of the screen: Clear Column. This option is handy for clearing the contents of a column to make room for the references of another word.

> Type **4**

The column of references for the headword "office" will clear. You now have three empty columns in the thesaurus screen for looking up other words.

Step 9: Exit the Thesaurus

If you replace a word from the thesaurus, WordPerfect will automatically return to the editing screen. You can also exit the thesaurus without replacing a word.

> Press **F7**

Practice

1. Move the cursor to the word "room" in the New Outfitting Post paragraph and invoke the thesaurus.

2. Tell the thesaurus to replace the word "room" with "space."

3. Invoke the thesaurus again. Use the Look Up Word option to look up any words you like. When you are finished, exit the thesaurus and move the cursor to the beginning of the document. Save the document to preserve any changes you have made.

Lesson 7: Working with Windows

WordPerfect's Window feature allows you to split the display into two separate document editing screens, each with its own status line. You can then show two different areas of the same document or work on two different documents at the same time. The Window feature is especially handy for referring to one part of a document while working on another part or for copying text from one document to another.

Step 1: Split the Screen

Suppose you want to create a new document while looking at an existing document. You can split the screen into two windows. Execute the Screen command, select the Window option, and specify the number of lines to be in the window:

Press   **Ctrl-F3**
Type   **w**
Type   **11**
Press   **Enter**

Figure 11 shows the result. The top window, which is eleven lines, contains the NEWS.DOC document. It has its own status line at the bottom. A ruler line

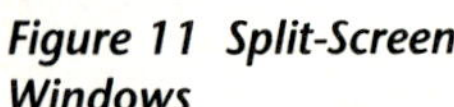

Figure 11 Split-Screen Windows

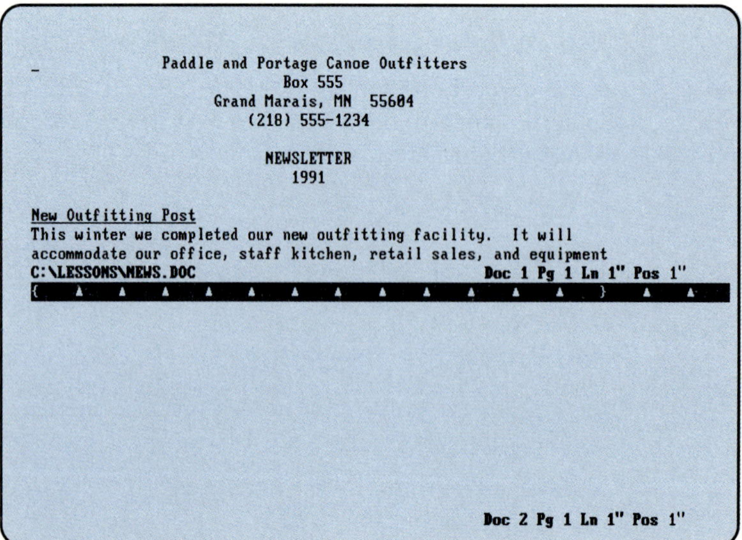

showing the current margin and tab stop settings separates the two windows. The bottom window, also eleven lines, is empty. In it you can create a new document. Notice that the bottom status line indicates that it is for document number 2.

Step 2: Switch Windows

The top window, which contains the cursor, is the active window. The ruler line reflects the settings in this window and the tab stop triangles point up. The commands you execute and the text you enter affect only this window. Before you can work in the bottom window, you must switch to it. Execute the Switch command:

    Press   **Shift-F3**

The cursor will move into the bottom window and the tab stop arrows in the ruler line will point down. Any text you enter or commands you execute will now affect only the bottom window. To go back up to the first window, execute the Switch command again:

    Press   **Shift-F3**

Step 3: Copy the Letterhead

Let's create a new document in the bottom window that will be a letter to a customer who inquired about Paddle and Portage Canoe Outfitters' sport show schedule. Fortunately, some of the text can be copied from the newsletter instead of being retyped.

Mark the letterhead at the top of the newsletter as a block of text:

    Press   **Home** (2 times)
    Press   **Up Arrow**
    Press   **Alt-F4**
    Press   **Down Arrow** (4 times)

Execute the Move Block Copy command:

    Press   **Ctrl-F4**
    Type   **b**
    Type   **c**

Position the cursor in the bottom window where you want to copy the block by executing the Switch command and then pressing Enter:

    Press   **Shift-F3**
    Press   **Enter**

The letterhead will be copied from NEWS.DOC in the top window to the new document in the bottom window (see Figure 12).

Step 4: Type the Letter

Follow these instructions to type the letter in the bottom window:

    Press   **Home** (2 times)
    Press   **Down Arrow**
    Press   **Enter**
    Type   **January 2, 1990**

Figure 12 The Letterhead Copied to the Bottom Window

Press	**Enter** (2 times)
Type	**Mr. Richard Holmes**
Press	**Enter**
Type	**444 Adams Street**
Press	**Enter**
Type	**Green Bay, WI 54301**
Press	**Enter** (2 times)
Type	**Dear Mr. Holmes:**
Press	**Enter** (2 times)
Type	**Here is our sport show schedule for 1991.**
Type	**We hope to see you soon!**
Press	**Enter** (5 times)
Type	**Sincerely,**
Press	**Enter** (4 times)
Type	**Bob Johnson**
Press	**Enter**

Step 5: Copy the Schedule

Notice that the sport show schedule was purposely omitted from the letter. Instead of retyping the sport show schedule, you can copy it from the newsletter. Follow these directions:

Press	**Up Arrow** (8 times)
Press	**Shift-F3**
Press	**Home** (2 times)
Press	**Up Arrow**
Press	**Down Arrow** (17 times)
Press	**Alt-F4**
Press	**Down Arrow** (11 times)
Press	**Ctrl-F4**
Type	**b**
Type	**c**
Press	**Shift-F3**
Press	**Enter**

Figure 13 More Text Copied to the Bottom Window

```
Chicagoland Show, O'Hare Exposition Center

Feb 14--Feb 22
Greater Northwest Sport Show, Minneapolis Auditorium

Mar 13--Mar 22
Milwaukee Sentinel Sport Show, MECCA Building

If you can, stop by and say "Hi."  Remember our SPECIAL BONUS RATES
for sport show reservations.

Move cursor; press Enter to retrieve.          Doc 1 Pg 1 Ln 5.67" Pos 1"
{   ▼   ▼   ▼   ▼   ▼   ▼   ▼   ▼   ▼   }   ▼   ▼
Here is our sport show schedule for 1991.  We hope to see you soon!

Jan 23--Feb 1
Chicagoland Show, O'Hare Exposition Center

Feb 14--Feb 22
Greater Northwest Sport Show, Minneapolis Auditorium

Mar 13--Mar 22
Milwaukee Sentinel Sport Show, MECCA Building

                                           Doc 2 Pg 1 Ln 3.5" Pos 1"
```

The sport show schedule and the two sentences that follow it will be copied to the letter in the bottom window (see Figure 13).

Step 6: Save the Letter

Move the cursor to the top of the letter and examine it for typographical errors. After you are sure that it is correct, save the file on the hard disk in the LESSONS subdirectory and name it HOLMES.DOC.

> Press   **F10**
> Type   **c:\lessons\holmes.doc**
> Press   **Enter**

Step 7: Clear the Bottom Window

After the letter has been saved, you can clear the bottom window and use it to view some other document. Execute the Exit command:

> Press   **F7**
> Type   **n**
> Type   **y**

The bottom window will be cleared and the cursor will be moved into the top window. Move the cursor to the beginning of the document:

> Press   **Home** (2 times)
> Press   **Up Arrow**

Step 8: View the Same Document in the Bottom Window

The Window feature can also be used to view two different parts of the same document. This capability is especially handy for long documents if you have to refer to distant sections at the same time. Follow these directions to switch to the bottom window and retrieve NEWS.DOC:

Press   **Shift-F3**
Press   **Shift-F10**
Type   `c:\lessons\news.doc`
Press   **Enter**

The newsletter will be loaded into the bottom window. Now you can look at two different parts of the same document. Move to the end of the newsletter in the bottom window:

Press   **Home** (2 times)
Press   **Down Arrow**

As Figure 14 shows, the beginning of the newsletter appears in the top window and the end of the newsletter appears in the bottom window.

Step 9: Close a Window

Suppose you are finished working on two different sections of the same document or two different documents and want to close one of the windows. First, switch to the window you want to close, if the cursor is not already there, and execute the Exit command:

Press   **F7**
Type   **y**
Press   **Enter**
Type   **y**
Type   **y**

The document will be saved and disappear from the window, but the screen will still be split. The cursor will move to the window containing text. To remove the empty window, expand the other window to 24 lines so that it fills the entire screen:

Press   **Ctrl-F3**
Type   **w**
Type   **24**
Press   **Enter**

A single window will expand to fill the entire screen.

Practice

1. Split the screen into two windows of equal size.
2. Retrieve the document MEMO.DOC into the bottom window.
3. Switch back and forth between the windows, examining their contents.
4. Exit and close the second window. The document NEWS.DOC should be on your screen. Move the cursor to the beginning of the newsletter.

Lesson 8: Indenting Paragraphs

Indenting refers to moving text away from the margin toward the center of the page. Several types of paragraph indentation are commonly used in documents. WordPerfect lets you use the first line indent, left indent, left and right indent, and hanging indent.

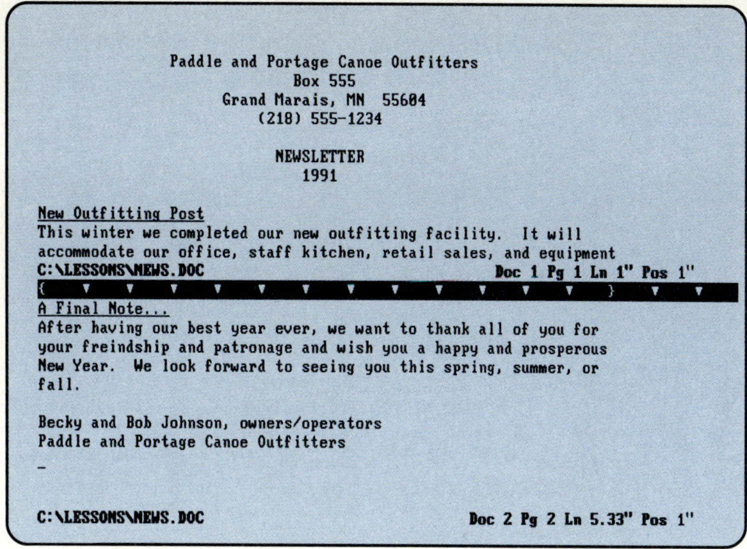

Figure 14 The Same Document In Two Windows

Step 1: Start a New Document

To illustrate paragraph indentation with WordPerfect, exit NEWS.DOC and create a new document:

Press　**F7**
Type　**n**
Type　**n**

Your editing screen should now be empty.

Step 2: Indent the First Line of a Paragraph

The **first line indent** moves only the first line of the paragraph in from the left margin. This is done by pressing the Tab key before typing the paragraph.

Press　**Tab**

Now type the text:

> **This paragraph illustrates the first line indent. Only the first line of the paragraph is moved from the left margin toward the center of the page.**

Press　**Enter** (2 times)

Step 3: Indent Paragraphs from the Left Margin

The **left indent** moves all lines of the paragraph in from the left margin. This is done by executing the Left Indent command.

Press　**F4**

Now type the text:

> **This paragraph illustrates the left indent, in which all lines are moved from the left margin toward the center**

> **of the page. Pressing F4 creates a temporary left margin**
> **one tab stop in from the permanent left margin. Words**
> **will automatically wrap to the indented left margin.**

Press   **Enter** (2 times)
Press   **F4** (2 times)

Type this text:

> **Each time you press F4, the temporary left margin moves**
> **in another tab stop toward the center of the page.**

Press   **Enter** (2 times)

Step 4: Indent Paragraphs from Both Margins

A paragraph can be indented from both the left and right margins. This is done by executing the Left and Right Indent command.

Press   **Shift-F4**

Now type the text:

> **This paragraph is indented from both the left and right**
> **margins. All lines are moved in from both margins toward**
> **the center of the page.**

Press   **Enter** (2 times)
Press   **Shift-F4** (2 times)

Type this text:

> **Each time you press Shift-F4, the temporary left and**
> **right margins move in another tab stop toward the center**
> **of the page.**

Press   **Enter** (2 times)

Step 5: Create a Hanging Indent

A **hanging indent** occurs when all lines of a paragraph except for the first are indented from the left margin. It is created by executing both the Left Indent and Margin Release commands.

Press   **F4**
Press   **Shift-Tab**

Now type the text:

> **This paragraph illustrates the hanging indent. The first**
> **line of the paragraph stays at the left margin, while**
> **all of the remaining lines are moved toward the center**
> **of the page.**

Your screen should look like Figure 15.

Step 6: Save the Document

Save the new document you have created in a file named INDENT.DOC in the LESSONS subdirectory.

Figure 15 Paragraph Indentation

```
        This paragraph illustrates the first line indent.  Only the
first line of the paragraph is moved from the left margin toward
the center of the page.

        This paragraph illustrates the left indent, in which all lines
        are moved from the left margin toward the center of the page.
        Pressing F4 creates a temporary left margin one tab stop in
        from the permanent left margin.  Words will automatically wrap
        to the indented left margin.

                Each time you press F4, the temporary left margin moves
                in another tab stop toward the center of the page.

        This paragraph is indented from both the left and right
        margins.  All lines are moved in from both margins toward
        the center of the page.

                Each time you press Shift-F4, the temporary
                left and right margins move in another tab stop
                toward the center of the page.

This paragraph illustrates the hanging indent.  The first line of
        the paragraph stays at the left margin, while all of the
        remaining lines are moved toward the center of the page._
                                          Doc 1 Pg 1 Ln 4.83" Pos 7.1"
```

Press   **F10**
Type   **c:\lessons\indent.doc**
Press   **Enter**

Practice　　1. Move the cursor to the beginning of the INDENT.DOC document. Then execute the Reveal Codes command:

Press   **Alt-F3**

Scroll through the document and examine the indentation codes. You should be able to understand what they mean. Try deleting one of the indentation codes and see what happens. Then restore the deleted code. Execute the Reveal Codes command again to return to the regular editing screen.

2. Use the help facility to read about the Left Indent command:

Press   **F3**
Press   **F4**

Then use the help facility to read about the Left and Right Indent (Shift-F4) and the Margin Release (Shift-Tab) commands.

Lesson 9: Using Tab Stops to Create Tables

Tab stops allow you to position text precisely within a line. They are often used for aligning text or numbers in a table. Tab stops should always be used instead of pressing the Space Bar to vertically align items in a table because the size of a space varies from font to font. To align items in a table, you press the Tab key to insert a tab code and move the cursor to the next tab stop.

Initially, WordPerfect has a tab stop set at every half-inch position. But you can change these tab stop settings by executing the Format command, selecting the Line option, and then selecting the Tab Set option.

To illustrate the use of tab stops, let's add a short table to NEWS.DOC that presents the current outfitting rates.

Step 1: Retrieve NEWS.DOC

Clear the editing screen and retrieve the newsletter document by executing these commands:

Press	**F7**
Type	**n**
Type	**n**
Press	**Shift-F10**
Type	`c:\lessons\news.doc`
Press	**Enter**

Step 2: Move the Cursor

Let's insert the new table between the Trail Food Improvements paragraph and the Trips paragraph. A quick way to move the cursor is to use the Search command:

Press	**F2**
Type	**Trips**
Press	**F2**
Press	**Up Arrow**

The cursor should now be on the blank line just before the Trips paragraph.

Step 3: Insert the Heading

The table will be entitled "Current Outfitting Rates," so insert this underlined heading:

Press	**Enter**
Press	**F8**
Type	`Current Outfitting Rates`
Press	**F8**
Press	**Enter**

Step 4: Change the Tab Stop Settings

A left-aligned tab stop lines up the left edge of text to the tab stop. This is the default and most commonly used type of tab stop. Let's insert left-aligned tab stops at the 2-inch and 4-inch positions. These tab stops will then affect all text at and below the cursor. Follow these directions:

Press	**Shift-F8**
Type	**L**
Type	**t**
Press	**Ctrl-End**
Type	**2"**
Press	**Enter**
Type	**L**
Type	**4"**
Press	**Enter**
Type	**L**

At this point, your screen should look like Figure 16. Pressing Ctrl-End deletes all of the default tab stops. Left-aligned tab stops are inserted by entering the desired line position and typing L. You can also press Right Arrow or Left Arrow

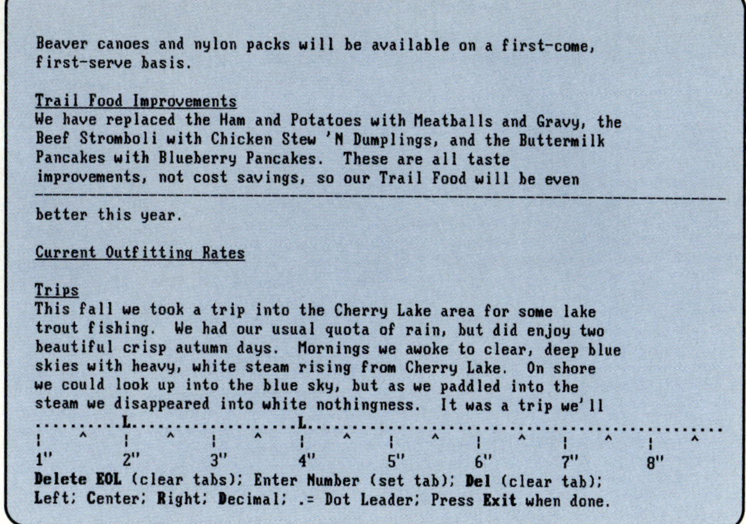

Figure 16 The New Tab Stop Settings

to move the cursor within the ruler line to select the desired tab stop position. Now execute the Exit command twice to finalize your new tab stops and return to the editing screen:

Press   **F7** (2 times)

Step 5: Enter the Table

Follow these directions to enter the Current Outfitting Rates table:

Press   **Tab**
Type   **Number In Party**
Press   **Tab**
Type   **Rate Per Person Per Day**
Press   **Enter**
Press   **Tab**
Type   **1 to 3 persons**
Press   **Tab**
Type   **$31.00**
Press   **Enter**
Press   **Tab**
Type   **4 to 6 persons**
Press   **Tab**
Type   **$29.25**
Press   **Enter**
Press   **Tab**
Type   **7 to 9 persons**
Press   **Tab**
Type   **$28.50**
Press   **Enter**

Your screen should look like Figure 17.

Figure 17 The Current Outfitting Rates Table

Beaver canoes and nylon packs will be available on a first-come,
first-serve basis.

Trail Food Improvements
We have replaced the Ham and Potatoes with Meatballs and Gravy, the
Beef Stromboli with Chicken Stew 'N Dumplings, and the Buttermilk
Pancakes with Blueberry Pancakes. These are all taste
improvements, not cost savings, so our Trail Food will be even
____

better this year.

Current Outfitting Rates
            Number In Party   Rate Per Person Per Day
            1 to 3 persons $31.00
            4 to 6 persons $29.25
            7 to 9 persons $28.50

Trips
This fall we took a trip into the Cherry Lake area for some lake
trout fishing. We had our usual quota of rain, but did enjoy two
beautiful crisp autumn days. Mornings we awoke to clear, deep blue
skies with heavy, white steam rising from Cherry Lake. On shore
we could look up into the blue sky, but as we paddled into the
steam we disappeared into white nothingness. It was a trip we'll
C:\LESSONS\NEWS.DOC   Doc 1 Pg 2 Ln 2.17" Pos 1"

Step 6: Reset Default Tab Stops Below the Table

Changing tab stops affects all text at and below the current cursor location. But you don't want the rest of the document to have the same tab stops as the table. So, you must reset the default tab stops below the table. Follow these directions:

Press   **Shift-F8**
Type   **L**
Type   **t**
Type   **0,0.5**
Press   **Enter**
Press   **F7** (2 times)

This will set a tab stop at every half inch position beginning at position 0, the left edge of the page.

Step 7: Save the Document

Save the document to the disk to preserve the changes you have made:

Press   **F10**
Press   **Enter**
Type   **y**

Practice

1. Use the Reveal Codes command to examine the Tab Set codes that appear before and after the Current Outfitting Rates table. When you are finished, execute the Reveal Codes command again to return to the full editing screen.

2. Using tabs is better than using spaces to align text and numbers in columns. One reason is that different characters are different widths in some fonts, so columns may not line up when the document is printed if you have used the Space Bar to align text on the screen. Another reason to use tabs is that they make it easy to change the position of columns later. For example, move the

cursor to the beginning of the line just below the heading "Current Outfitting Rates." Activate the Tab Set menu:

Press   **Shift-F8**
Type   **L**
Type   **t**

Delete the tab stop at the 2-inch position by moving the cursor there and pressing the Delete key. Insert a new tab stop at the 2.5-inch position. Delete the tab stop at the 4-inch position and insert a new one at the 4.5-inch position. Exit the Tab Set menu and return to the editing screen. The entire table will be shifted a half inch to the right.

3. Execute the Reveal Codes command again. Note that WordPerfect simply inserted a new Tab Set code for the new tab stop settings you created in the previous exercise. You can remove that Tab Set code and revert to the previous tab stop settings:

Press   **Left Arrow**
Press   **Delete**

The table will shift back to the left a half inch. Execute the Reveal Codes command again to return to the full editing screen. Move the cursor to the beginning of the document.

Lesson 10: Using the Tab Align Command

The numbers in the Current Outfitting Rates table line up nicely, but only because they all have the same number of characters. Numbers with fewer or more digits would not line up on the decimal points. In such cases, you can use a decimal tab stop instead of a left-aligned tab stop. Another alternative is to use the Tab Align command. To illustrate this command, let's insert another table that lists the Paddle and Portage 1990 fishing records.

Step 1: Move the Cursor

Let's insert the new table after the Current Outfitting Rates table. Move the cursor to the end of the last line of the table. By inserting the new table here, you use the same tab stop settings as the Current Outfitting Rates table.

Step 2: Insert the Heading

The table will be entitled "1990 Fishing Records," so do this:

Press   **Enter** (2 times)
Press   **F8**
Type   **1990 Fishing Records**
Press   **F8**
Press   **Enter**

Step 3: Enter the Table

Now, enter the table as follows:

Press   **Tab**
Type   **Bluegill**

Figure 18 The Numbers Aligned with the Tab Align Command

```
improvements, not cost savings, so our Trail Food will be even
---------------------------------------------------------------
better this year.

Current Outfitting Rates
         Number In Party      Rate Per Person Per Day
         1 to 3 persons       $31.00
         4 to 6 persons       $29.25
         7 to 9 persons       $28.50

1990 Fishing Records
         Bluegill              3.00 lbs.
         Large Mouth Bass     20.25 lbs.
         Northern Pike        42.33 lbs.
         Sunfish               2.20 lbs.
         Walleye              25.00 lbs._

Trips
This fall we took a trip into the Cherry Lake area for some lake
trout fishing.  We had our usual quota of rain, but did enjoy two
beautiful crisp autumn days.  Mornings we awoke to clear, deep blue
skies with heavy, white steam rising from Cherry Lake.  On shore
we could look up into the blue sky, but as we paddled into the
steam we disappeared into white nothingness.  It was a trip we'll
C:\LESSONS\NEWS.DOC                          Doc 1 Pg 2 Ln 3.17" Pos 4.8"
```

Press   **Ctrl-F6**
Type   **3.00 lbs.**
Press   **Enter**
Press   **Tab**
Type   **Large Mouth Bass**
Press   **Ctrl-F6**
Type   **20.25 lbs.**
Press   **Enter**
Press   **Tab**
Type   **Northern Pike**
Press   **Ctrl-F6**
Type   **42.33 lbs.**
Press   **Enter**
Press   **Tab**
Type   **Sunfish**
Press   **Ctrl-F6**
Type   **2.20 lbs.**
Press   **Enter**
Press   **Tab**
Type   **Walleye**
Press   **Ctrl-F6**
Type   **25.00 lbs.**

Your screen should look like Figure 18. In each line of the table, you pressed Ctrl-F6 instead of Tab before typing the number. This keypress executes the Tab Align command, which lines up text or numbers on an alignment character. The default alignment character is the period or decimal point. When you press Ctrl-F6, the cursor moves to the next tab stop and WordPerfect displays the prompt

```
Align char=.
```

This prompt tells you the default alignment character and lets you change it. For entering numbers, you want the period to be the alignment character so you can ignore the prompt. Characters you type at the tab stop move left until the alignment character is typed, or until Ctrl-F6, Tab, or Enter are pressed. Characters typed after the alignment character move to the right, as they normally do. The result is that all numbers line up on their decimal points at the tab stop.

Step 4: Save the Document

Save the document to the disk to preserve the changes you have made:

Press   **F10**
Press   **Enter**
Type   **y**

Practice

1. Execute the Reveal Codes command and examine the table you have just entered. The [Align] code indicates the execution of a Tab Align command and the [C/A/Flrt] code indicates the end of a Tab Align command. Return to the normal editing screen.

2. Invoke the help facility and read about the Tab Align command:

   Press   **F3**
   Press   **Ctrl-F6**

   When you are finished, return to the editing screen:

   Press   **Space Bar**

3. Insert another line in the 1990 Fishing Records table:

   Lake Trout 50.00 lbs.

   Save the document to the disk. Move the cursor to the beginning of the document.

Lesson 11: Using the Flush Right Command

The Flush Right command lets you easily align text to the right margin. This feature is especially handy for typing the return address and date in a letter. Let's see how this feature works in the HOLMES.DOC letter you created in Lesson 7.

Step 1: Clear the Screen

Exit NEWS.DOC and clear the screen:

Press   **F7**
Type   **n**
Type   **n**

Step 2: Retrieve the Letter

Execute the Retrieve command to load the document HOLMES.DOC and display it on the editing screen:

Press   **Shift-F10**
Type   **c:\lessons\holmes.doc**
Press   **Enter**

Step 3: Type a New Line Flush Right

The letterhead at the top of the document HOLMES.DOC is centered. Let's delete the first line and retype it flush right. The cursor should already be at the beginning of the first line of HOLMES.DOC. Delete to the end of the line:

Press   **Ctrl-End**

Now, execute the Flush Right command and retype the line:

Press   **Alt-F6**
Type   `Paddle and Portage Canoe Outfitters`

Notice how the cursor moves to the right margin when you press Alt-F6 and how the text you type moves to the left. Since a hard return already exists at the end of the line, move to the beginning of the next line without pressing Enter:

Press   **Right Arrow** (2 times)

You have to press Right Arrow twice to skip over the end flush right code and the hard return code.

Step 4: Move an Existing Line Flush Right

The Flush Right command can also move an existing line of text to the right margin. Let's move the second line of the letterhead flush right. First, uncenter the line by deleting the Center code:

Press   **Delete**

Now, move the line flush right:

Press   **Alt-F6**
Press   **Down Arrow**

The end of the second line will be aligned to the right margin.

Step 5: Move a Block Flush Right

You can move several lines of text flush right by first marking them as a block. Execute the following commands:

Press   **Home**
Press   **Left Arrow**
Press   **Alt-F4**
Press   **Down Arrow** (4 times)
Press   **Alt-F6**
Type   **y**

The rest of the letterhead and date will move flush right as shown in Figure 19.

Step 6: Save the Document

Save the document to the disk to preserve the changes you have made:

Press   **F10**
Press   **Enter**
Type   **y**

Figure 19 Letterhead and Date Moved Flush Right

```
                              Paddle and Portage Canoe Outfitters
                                            Box 555
                                     Grand Marais, MN  55604
                                        (218) 555-1234

                                        January 2, 1990

Mr. Richard Holmes
444 Adams Street
Green Bay, WI  54301

Dear Mr. Holmes:

Here is our sport show schedule for 1991.  We hope to see you soon!

Jan 23--Feb 1
Chicagoland Show, O'Hare Exposition Center

Feb 14--Feb 22
Greater Northwest Sport Show, Minneapolis Auditorium

Mar 13--Mar 22
Milwaukee Sentinel Sport Show, MECCA Building

C:\LESSONS\HOLMES.DOC                             Doc 1 Pg 1 Ln 2" Pos 1"
```

Practice

1. Execute the Reveal Codes command and examine the text you have just moved. The [Flsh Rt] code indicates the start of a flush right line and the [C/A/Flrt] indicates the end.

2. Move the cursor to the [Flsh Rt] code before the date and delete it. See how the date moves back to the left margin. Move the date flush right again:

   Press **Alt-F6**
   Press **Down Arrow**

   Execute the Reveal Codes command to return to the normal editing screen.

3. Execute the Help command and read about the Flush Right command:

   Press **F3**
   Press **Alt-F6**

   When you are finished reading the description, return to the editing screen:

   Press **Space Bar**

Lesson 12: Using the Date Command

WordPerfect's Date command lets you insert the current date into your document as text or as a code that is automatically updated and converted to text whenever the document is retrieved or printed. This feature is handy for letters, memos, and other documents that must display the current date. As an example, let's use the Date command to insert the date into the HOLMES.DOC letter. Note that in order for the Date command to work, your computer's clock must be set to the correct date. If the current date is not maintained by a built-in battery, you must use the DOS DATE command to specify the correct date when you boot up.

Step 1: Delete the Existing Date

First, delete the date that you have already typed into the document. Move the cursor to the line that contains the date and delete to the end of the line:

Press   **Ctrl-End**

Step 2: Execute the Flush Right Command

The Flush Right codes were deleted in the previous step, so execute the Flush Right command before inserting the date:

Press   **Alt-F6**

Step 3: Select the Date Text Option

Activate the Date/Outline menu:

Press   **Shift-F5**

Your screen should look like Figure 20. To insert the current date as text, just as you would type it yourself, select the Date Text option:

Type   **t**
Press   **Down Arrow**

The current date will be inserted into the document, flush against the right margin.

Step 4: Select the Date Code Option

The date you inserted in the previous step is ordinary text. It will not change to reflect the current date if you retrieve or print the letter tomorrow. If you want the date in the letter to be current whenever it is retrieved or printed, you must

Figure 20 The Date/ Outline Menu

```
                              Paddle and Portage Canoe Outfitters
                                                         Box 555
                                          Grand Marais, MN  55604
                                                  (218) 555-1234


    Mr. Richard Holmes
    444 Adams Street
    Green Bay, WI  54301

    Dear Mr. Holmes:

    Here is our sport show schedule for 1991.  We hope to see you soon!

    Jan 23--Feb 1
    Chicagoland Show, O'Hare Exposition Center

    Feb 14--Feb 22
    Greater Northwest Sport Show, Minneapolis Auditorium

    Mar 13--Mar 22
    Milwaukee Sentinel Sport Show, MECCA Building

    1 Date Text; 2 Date Code; 3 Date Format; 4 Outline; 5 Para Num; 6 Define: 0
```

use the Date Code option from the Date/Outline menu. Follow these directions to delete the date text and insert the date code instead:

Press **Up Arrow**
Press **Ctrl-End**
Press **Alt-F6**
Press **Shift-F5**
Type **c**
Press **Down Arrow**

The result looks the same as in the previous step, but the date you see will change if you retrieve or print the letter in the future.

Step 5: Select the Format Option

The Format option in the Date/Outline menu lets you change the way the date is displayed. Activate the Date/Outline menu and select the Format option:

Press **Shift-F5**
Type **f**

The Date Format menu will appear on the screen (see Figure 21). The default date format is presented at the bottom of the screen. The format code 3 1, 4 means the month (word) followed by the day of the month, a comma, and all four digits of the year. The date format menu gives you a great deal of flexibility in specifying how the date is to appear when you execute the Date command. Return to the editing screen without changing the date format:

Press **F7** (2 times)

Step 6: Save the Document

Save the document to the disk to preserve the changes you have made:

Press **F10**
Press **Enter**
Type **y**

Figure 21 The Date Format Menu

```
Date Format

    Character    Meaning
        1        Day of the Month
        2        Month (number)
        3        Month (word)
        4        Year (all four digits)
        5        Year (last two digits)
        6        Day of the Week (word)
        7        Hour (24-hour clock)
        8        Hour (12-hour clock)
        9        Minute
        0        am / pm
        %        Used before a number, will:
                     Pad numbers less than 10 with a leading zero
                     Output only 3 letters for the month or day of the week


    Examples:  3 1, 4       = December 25, 1984
               %6 %3 1, 4   = Tue Dec 25, 1984
               %2/%1/5 (6)  = 01/01/85 (Tuesday)
               8:90         = 10:55am


Date format: 3 1, 4
```

Practice

1. Execute the Reveal Codes command to examine the date code. Note that no text is actually stored in the document, just the code [Date:3 1, 4], which specifies the format in which to present the current date. Return to the full editing screen.

2. Try moving the cursor within the date. You will find that WordPerfect treats the date as a single character because it is really a date code. You can delete it, but not change it.

3. Delete the date code in the letter. Execute the Date/Outline command and select the Format option. Change the date format and insert a new date code:

   Type   **2/1/5**
   Press   **Enter**
   Type   **c**

   Observe the new date format. Now delete the date code, change the date format back to the way it was, and insert a new date code.

Lesson 13: Centering Text on a Page

Short letters and memos often look better when they are centered from top to bottom on a page. Centering from top to bottom is also used for title pages. The Center Page feature makes it easy to center text on a page when it is printed.

Step 1: Move Cursor Before All Codes

To center text on a page, you must move to the very beginning of the document, before any codes that may be hidden. Pressing the Home key three times followed by an Up Arrow or Left Arrow key moves the cursor ahead of any codes at the beginning of a document or line. Execute this command:

   Press   **Home** (3 times)
   Press   **Up Arrow**

Step 2: Select the Center Page Option

Execute the Format command, select the Page option, select the Center Page option, and then execute the Exit command:

   Press   **Shift-F8**
   Type   **p**
   Type   **c**
   Press   **F7**

The document will not look any different on the screen, but it will be centered vertically on the page when it is printed.

Step 3: Print the Document

To see the result of using the Center Page option, print the letter:

   Press   **Shift-F7**
   Type   **f**

Practice

1. Execute the Reveal Codes command. The first code in the document is [Center Pg], which tells WordPerfect to center the text vertically on the page when printed. Return to the full editing screen.

2. Turn off the Center Page option for this document. You can either delete the Center Page code or select the Center Page option from the Page menu of the Format command.

3. Execute the Help command and read about the Center Page option:

   Press　**F3**
   Press　**Shift-F8**
   Type　**p**
   Type　**c**

   When you are finished reading the description, return to the editing screen:

   Press　**Space Bar**

Lesson 14: Adding a Document Summary

DOS file names, such as HOLMES.DOC, are limited to eight characters plus a three-character extension. Even if you try to use mnemonic file names, remembering important details about your documents can become difficult, especially if you collect a large number of documents over a long period of time. Fortunately, WordPerfect lets you create a summary for each document that contains a descriptive file name, the subject, the author, the typist, and comments. Although a document summary is never printed, you can look at it on the screen. Document summaries may also be searched by the Word Search option of the List Files menu. As an example, let's add a document summary to HOLMES.DOC.

Step 1: Select the Summary Option

A document summary can be created or edited from any place in a document. Simply execute the Format command, select the Document option, and then select the Summary option:

   Press　**Shift-F8**
   Type　**d**
   Type　**s**

WordPerfect will display the Document Summary screen, as shown in Figure 22.

Step 2: Enter the Descriptive Filename

The System Filename and Date of Creation have already been entered for you by WordPerfect. In addition, the first 400 characters of the document are automatically inserted in the Comments box. To enter the Descriptive Filename, select the first option and type the name:

   Type　**d**
   Type　**Letter to Richard Holmes**
   Press　**Enter**

You are limited to 40 characters for each item in the document summary except comments, which can contain up to 780 characters.

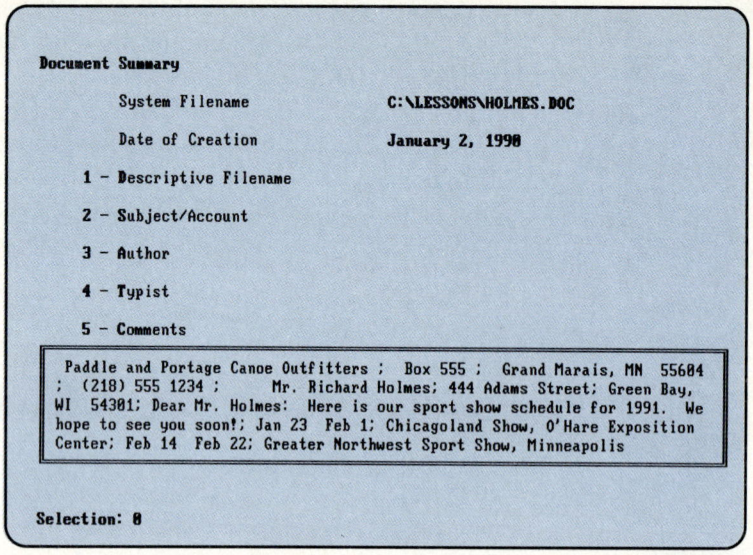

Figure 22 The Initial Document Summary Screen

Step 3: Enter the Subject

To enter the subject of the document, select the second option and enter the information:

Type   **s**
Type   **Sport Show Schedule**
Press   **Enter**

Step 4: Enter the Author

To enter the author's name, select the third option:

Type   **a**
Type   **Bob Johnson**
Press   **Enter**

In this case, you are pretending to be Bob Johnson. There is no other typist, so you can leave the Typist section blank. You can also leave the Comments box unchanged. Your screen should look like Figure 23.

Step 5: Exit the Document Summary Screen

To save the document summary and return to the editing screen, execute the exit command:

Press   **F7**

Step 6: Save the Document

Save the document, along with its summary, to the disk to preserve the changes you have made:

Press   **F10**
Press   **Enter**
Type   **y**

*Figure 23 The Completed
Document Summary
Screen*

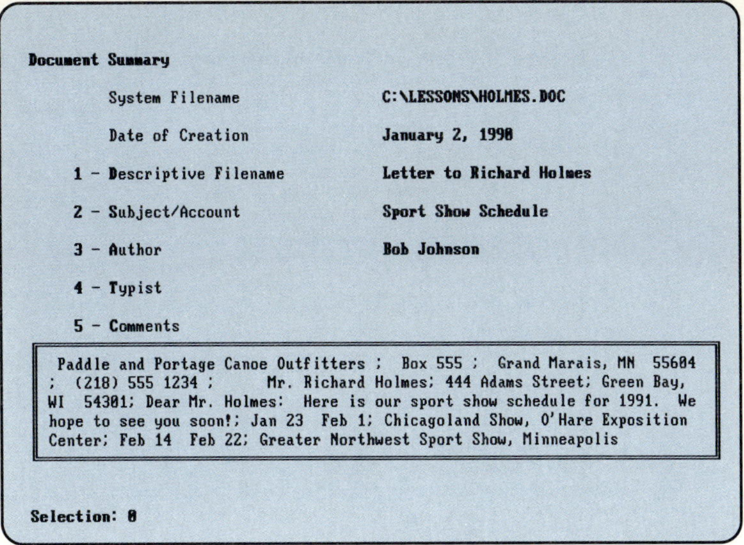

Practice

1. Display the document summary for HOLMES.DOC on your screen. Then return to the editing screen.

2. Execute the List Files command and specify the subdirectory C:\LESSONS. Select the Word Search option from the List Files menu and then select the Doc Summary option. Specify the following word pattern:

   Type   **Schedule**
   Press **Enter**

   WordPerfect should highlight the file HOLMES.DOC and mark it with an asterisk. Unmark the file and exit the List Files screen.

Lesson 15: Use the Text In/Out Command

A text file or ASCII file is a file that contains no special formatting codes—only letters, numbers, punctuation marks, spaces, tabs, and carriage returns. Text files are used for DOS batch files, the CONFIG.SYS file, programming language source code files, and some types of data files. In addition, text files are sometimes used to store documents in a format that can be read by other programs and word processing packages. The Text In/Out command lets you work with text files in WordPerfect. More specifically, it can perform the following procedures:

- Save the current document as a text file.
- Retrieve a text file to be edited with WordPerfect.
- Save the current document in a generic word processing format.
- Save the current document as a WordPerfect version 4.2 file.

Let's examine the Text In/Out command more closely.

Step 1: Clear the Editing Screen

Exit your current document and clear the editing screen:

Press   **F7**
Type   **n**
Type   **n**

Step 2: Retrieve a Text File

Suppose you want to change the AUTOEXEC.BAT file in the root directory of the hard disk. In Lesson 1, you learned that you can retrieve a text file with the Text In option of the List Files menu. You can also retrieve a text file with the Text In/Out command.

Press   **Ctrl-F5**

WordPerfect will display the Text In/Out menu (see Figure 24). To load a text file, select the first option:

Type   **t**

Another menu will be presented with three options. The first option is for saving a text file. The second option will retrieve a text file and convert carriage return and line feed pairs into hard returns. The third option retrieves a text file and converts carriage return/line feeds into soft returns. You use the second option for editing text files that will not be converted into WordPerfect documents. Select the Retrieve option and specify the file:

Press   **r**
Type   **c:\autoexec.bat**
Press   **Enter**

The file AUTOEXEC.BAT will be loaded into the editing screen.

Figure 24 The Text In/Out Menu

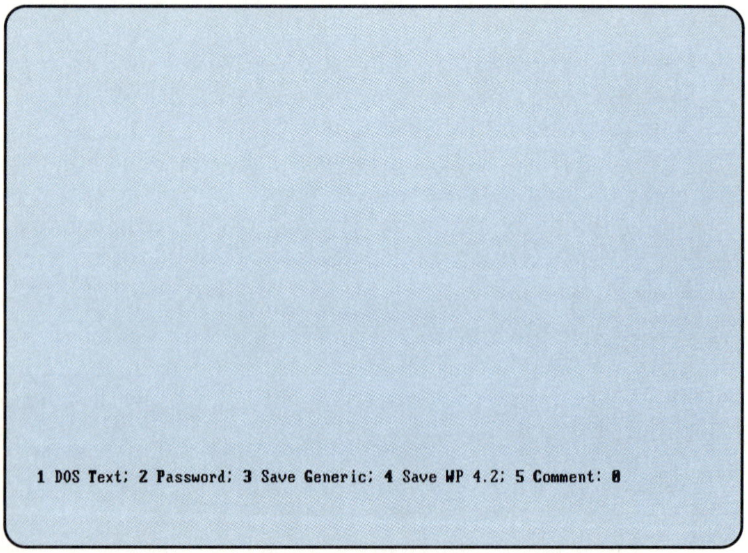

Step 3: Save a Text File

You can now edit the file AUTOEXEC.BAT with WordPerfect. Since it is not a document, you should not use formatting features such as margins, underlining, flush right, and so on. You can, however, insert, typeover, and delete text. Suppose you are finished editing the file. You save it to the disk with the Text In/Out command.

Press	**Ctrl-F5**
Type	**t**
Type	**s**
Press	**Enter**
Type	**y**

Step 4: Examine the Other Text In/Out Options

Execute the Text In/Out command again to display the menu:

Press   **Ctrl-F5**

The Password option allows you to protect a document so that no one will be able to retrieve or print it without knowing the password. This option works with WordPerfect document files, not text files. It seems out of place in the Text In/Out menu.

The Save Generic option lets you save a document so that the general format is preserved without WordPerfect-specific codes. For example, spaces would be used to center, indent, and flush right text instead of WordPerfect formatting codes. This option might be used to save a WordPerfect document in a file to be read by some other word processing package.

The Save WP 4.2 option lets you save a document in a file that can be read by WordPerfect version 4.2.

Finally, the Comment option is used to insert or edit comments in a document. Comments can be displayed on the screen, but are never printed with a document. They can be used for reminders, notes, and suggestions that are not actually part of the document. Like the Password option, the Comment option has nothing to do with text files. Who knows why it is in the Text In/Out menu?

Practice

1. Execute the Help command and read about the Text In/Out command and all of its options.

2. Clear the editing screen. Use the Text In/Out command to retrieve the text file CONFIG.SYS from the root directory of the hard disk. Without changing the file, save it to the disk with the Text In/Out command.

Lesson 16: Execute a DOS Command within WordPerfect

Like many of today's application packages, WordPerfect lets you execute one or more DOS commands without actually exiting the program. The Shell command keeps WordPerfect in memory while control is passed to a secondary DOS command processor. When you are finished performing DOS commands, you execute the DOS EXIT command and return to WordPerfect, which is still in memory. This handy feature, for example, can be used to check a disk, format a diskette, or copy files without exiting WordPerfect.

Step 1: Execute the SHELL Command

Suppose you want to execute CHKDSK or some other DOS command without exiting WordPerfect. Execute the WordPerfect Shell command:

Press   **Ctrl-F1**
Type   **g**

WordPerfect will load a secondary DOS command processor and display a message telling you how to get back to the program (see Figure 25).

Step 2: Execute the DOS Commands

You are now at the DOS prompt and can execute any DOS commands, but WordPerfect is still dormant in memory. Execute the following DOS commands:

Type   **chkdsk**
Press   **Enter**
Type   **dir**
Press   **Enter**

Step 3: Execute the EXIT Command

When you are finished with DOS, you execute the EXIT command to return to WordPerfect:

Type   **exit**
Press   **Enter**

The computer will immediately return to the editing screen, just where you left off when you executed the Shell command.

Practice   1. Execute the Shell command and return to DOS. Theoretically, you can now execute any DOS command and even start an application package. In reality,

Figure 25 The Secondary DOS Command Processor Prompt

```
Microsoft(R) MS-DOS(R) Version 4.01
          (C)Copyright Microsoft Corp 1981-1988

Enter 'EXIT' to return to WordPerfect
C:\WP50>_
```

you are limited by the amount of memory installed in your computer. Try running WordPerfect from the secondary command processor. You will probably get the DOS error message:

```
Program too big to fit in memory
```

The reason is that you already have WordPerfect in memory along with a secondary DOS command processor.

2. If you are running DOS version 4 or newer, execute this command:

Type **mem /program**
Press **Enter**

You should see WP, which stands for WordPerfect, in the list of programs in memory.

3. Execute the DOS EXIT command to return to WordPerfect. This will discard the secondary DOS command processor. Exit WordPerfect the usual way and return to the primary DOS command processor.

Summary

- *Managing documents with the List Files menu.* Press F5 to activate the List Files menu. Then select an option to change the directory, look at a file, retrieve a file, copy a file, move or rename a file, print a file, load a text file, select a file name, search for files, or delete a file.

- *Using additional cursor movement commands.* Pressing Home, Down Arrow moves the cursor to the bottom edge of the screen. Home, Up Arrow moves to the top edge. Pressing Escape, typing a number, and then pressing a cursor movement key repeats that key the specified number of times. Pressing Ctrl-Home and then typing a character advances the cursor just past the next occurrence of that character.

- *Using additional delete commands.* Pressing Home, Backspace deletes to the beginning of a word. Home, Delete erases to the end of a word. Pressing Escape, typing a number, and pressing Ctrl-End deletes the specified number of lines. Ctrl-PgDn deletes to the end of the page.

- *Working with formatting codes.* Press Alt-F3 to reveal or hide formatting codes. Press the Delete key to remove a code.

- *Using the built-in thesaurus.* Move the cursor to the word to be looked up and press Alt-F1 to invoke the thesaurus.

- *Splitting the screen into two windows.* Press Ctrl-F3, select the Window option, and specify the number of lines to split the screen into two windows. Press Shift-F3 to move the cursor into the other window.

- *Indenting paragraphs.* Press Tab for a first-line indent, press F4 for a left indent, press Shift-F4 for a left and right indent, and press F4 followed by Shift-Tab for a hanging indent.

- *Creating tables with tab stops.* Press Shift-F8 to execute the Format command, select the Line option, and then select the Tab Set option to change the default tab stops.

- *Aligning numbers to tab stops.* Press Ctrl-F6 to execute the Tab Align command, which advances to the next tab stop and aligns text or numbers on an alignment character, usually the period.

- *Moving text flush right.* Press Alt-F6 to execute the Flush Right command, which lets you type new text or move existing text flush against the right margin.

- *Inserting the current date automatically.* Press Shift-F5 to activate the Date/Outline menu and then select the Date Text or Date Code option.

- *Centering text on a page.* Move the cursor before all codes, press Shift-F8 to activate the Format menu, select the Page option, and then select the Center Page option to center text vertically on a page.

- *Creating a document summary.* Press Shift-F8 to activate the Format menu, select the Document option, and then select the Summary option to enter or edit document summary information.

- *Retrieving and saving text files.* Press Ctrl-F5 to activate the Text In/Out menu, select the DOS Text option, and then select the Retrieve or Save option.

- *Executing a DOS command within WordPerfect.* Press Ctrl-F1 to execute the Shell command. Then execute one or more DOS commands. Use the EXIT command to return to WordPerfect.

Key Terms

As an extra review of this chapter, try defining the following terms.

code	indenting
first line indent	left indent
hanging indent	wild-card characters
headword	

Multiple Choice

Choose the best selection to complete each statement.

1. Which command do you execute to clear the screen to start work on a new document?

    (a) Retrieve   (b) Save

    (c) Cancel   (d) Exit

2. Which command would you execute to examine the files in a subdirectory, retrieve a file, copy a file, or delete a file?

    (a) Switch   (b) Search

    (c) List Files   (d) Format

3. ASCII files, also known as text files, differ from document files in that they contain no

    (a) carriage returns.   (b) special formatting codes.

    (c) punctuation marks. (d) numbers.

4. Which key or character do you type to mark a file on the List Files screen?

    (a) asterisk (*)

    (b) F1

    (c) F10

    (d) ampersand (&)

5. Which sequence of keypresses will move the cursor to the top edge of the current screen?

    (a) Ctrl-Home

    (b) Ctrl-Up Arrow

    (c) Home, Up Arrow

    (d) Home, Left Arrow

6. Which sequence of keystrokes will move the cursor down five lines?

    (a) Down Arrow, 5

    (b) Escape, 5, Down Arrow

    (c) F1, 5, Down Arrow

    (d) Home, Home, Home, Home, Home, Down Arrow

7. Which sequence of keystrokes will advance the cursor just past the next occurrence of the letter *x*?

    (a) Ctrl-Home, x

    (b) Home, Home, x

    (c) Right Arrow, x

    (d) F3, x

8. Which sequence of keypresses will delete characters from the cursor to the end of the word?

    (a) Home, Backspace

    (b) Home, Delete

    (c) Home, Right Arrow

    (d) Delete-Right Arrow

9. What do you press to reveal or hide formatting codes?

    (a) Alt-C

    (b) Alt-PgDn

    (c) Alt-F3

    (d) Ctrl-F3

10. To use the thesaurus, move the cursor to the word you want to look up and then press

    (a) Alt-F1.

    (b) Alt-T.

    (c) F1.

    (d) F3.

11. Which command do you execute to display two windows?

    (a) Format

    (b) Help

    (c) Screen

    (d) Exit

12. Which type of paragraph indentation moves all lines toward the center of the page except for the first line?

    (a) first line indent

    (b) left indent

    (c) left and right indent

    (d) hanging indent

13. By default, WordPerfect has a tab stop set every

    (a) half inch.

    (b) inch.

    (c) inch and a half.

    (d) two inches.

14. Which command is an alternative to using decimal tab stops?

    (a) Tab

    (b) Tab Align

    (c) Indent

    (d) Flush Right

15. Which command is used to type text aligned to the right margin?

    (a) Tab

    (b) Tab Align

    (c) Indent

    (d) Flush Right

16. Which code indicates the end of a Center, Tab Align, or Flush Right command?

    (a) [HRt]   (b) [SRt]

    (c) [C/A/Flrt]   (d) [Und]

17. Which option from the Date/Outline menu do you select to insert a date that will always show the current date whenever the document is retrieved or printed?

    (a) Date Text   (b) Date Code

    (c) Format   (d) Outline

18. Which command do you execute first to create a document summary?

    (a) Screen   (b) Shell

    (c) Format   (d) List Files

19. Which command do you execute to retrieve an ASCII file, such as AUTO-EXEC.BAT or CONFIG.SYS?

    (a) Retrieve   (b) Search

    (c) Switch   (d) Text In/Out

20. Which command do you execute to temporarily return to DOS while keeping WordPerfect loaded in memory?

    (a) Exit   (b) Text In/Out

    (c) Shell   (d) Cancel

Fill-In

1. The ________ option of the List Files menu lets you examine the contents of a file or subdirectory.

2. The Word Search option of the List Files menu lets you ________ files that meet specific conditions.

3. The ________ key lets you repeat a cursor-movement command a number of times.

4. A WordPerfect document contains special ________ that specify how the document is to be formatted.

5. The built-in ________ can examine a word in your document or a word that you enter, and display a list of synonyms and antonyms.

6. The ________ option of the Screen command lets you split the display into two separate document-editing screens, each with its own status line.

7. The ________ command, executed by pressing Shift-F3, allows you to move the cursor from one window to the other.

8. ________ refers to moving text away from the margin toward the center of the page.

9. A hanging indent is created by executing both the Left Indent and ________ commands.

10. The default and most commonly used type of tab stop is the ________ tab stop.

11. The Tab Align command, executed by pressing Ctrl-F6, lines up text or numbers on an ________ character, usually the period.

12. The ________ command is especially handy for typing the return address and date against the right margin in a letter.

13. You can move several lines of text against the right margin at once by pressing Alt-F4 if you first mark the lines as a _______.

14. If you want the date in a document to be updated whenever it is retrieved or printed, you must use the Date _______ option from the Date/Outline menu.

15. The _______ option in the Date/Outline menu lets you change the way the date is displayed.

16. Press the _______ key three times and then press Up Arrow to move the cursor ahead of any codes at the beginning of a document.

17. Adding a Document _______ lets you maintain detailed information about a document, including a descriptive file name, the subject, the author, the typist, and other comments.

18. The _______ command lets you save a document in a generic format that can be used by word processors other than WordPerfect.

19. Press Ctrl-F1 to execute the _______ command, which lets you temporarily return to the DOS prompt.

20. The DOS _______ command is used to return to WordPerfect from a secondary command processor.

Short Problems

1. Start WordPerfect if you are not already running the program.

    The Escape key can be used to repeat a character or some WordPerfect features a specified number of times. The default number is 8, but you can change this value. You have already learned to use the Escape key to repeat certain cursor movements. Now use the Escape key to type the letter A twenty times:

    Press   **Escape**
    Type   **20**
    Type   **a**

    The Escape key can also be used with the Delete key. Move the cursor to the beginning of the line and use the Escape key with Delete to remove the first ten letters.

2. Normally, WordPerfect displays only the status line below the text area on the editing screen. Some people like to have a ruler line also displayed on the screen to see the current margins and tab stop settings. You can use the Window option of the Screen command to present a ruler line at the bottom of the screen.

    Press   **Ctrl-F3**
    Type   **w**
    Type   **23**
    Press   **Enter**

    Setting the window size to 23 lines displays the ruler line below the status line at the bottom of the screen. Note that you have really opened two windows, but only one window fits on the screen at a time. You can move to the other window with the Switch command (Shift-F3), and edit a different document or view a different part of the same document.

3. The Date command can insert the current time as well as the date into your document. Execute the Date/Outline command and select the Format option. Examine the Date Format menu and change the format to

   ```
   3 1, 4 8:90
   ```

   Select the Date Text or Date Code option and observe the result.

4. WordPerfect has four styles of tabs you can set: left, center, right, and decimal. In addition, the program has a dot leader feature that can fill in the blank space preceding a tab stop with periods. Execute the Format command, select the Line option, and then select the Tab Set option to display the Tab Set menu on your screen. Clear the default tab settings by deleting to the end of the line. Set a left tab stop at 2 inches and a right tab stop at 7 inches. With the cursor still at the 7-inch position, type a period to specify a dot leader for the right tab stop. Return to the editing screen. Enter these lines:

Press	**Tab**
Type	**John Anderson**
Press	**Tab**
Type	**555-1234**
Press	**Enter**
Press	**Tab**
Type	**Melissa Smith**
Press	**Tab**
Type	**555-2468**
Press	**Enter**

5. Now try the center and decimal tab styles. Activate the Tab Set menu and clear the current tab stops. Set a center tab stop at 4 inches and a decimal tab stop at 6 inches. Enter these lines:

Press	**Tab**
Type	**Advertising**
Press	**Tab**
Type	**$1,236.22**
Press	**Enter**
Press	**Tab**
Type	**Office Supplies**
Press	**Tab**
Type	**$287.15**
Press	**Enter**

6. Execute the Thesaurus command and select the Look Up Word option. (If the cursor is at the beginning of a new line, the Look Up Word option will be selected automatically.) Look up the word "wonderful." Select the Look Up Word option again and try these words: "powerful" and "unusual."

7. Obtain a new diskette or one that can be reformatted. Execute the Shell command to temporarily return to DOS without exiting WordPerfect. Put the diskette in drive A. Execute the FORMAT A: command to format the diskette. Copy the file NEWS.DOC from the LESSONS subdirectory to the diskette. Execute the EXIT command to return to WordPerfect.

8. Clear the screen and retrieve MEMO.DOC. Center the document vertically on the page. Print MEMO.DOC by executing the Print command and selecting the Full Document option.

9. Use the Print option from the List Files menu to print the document INDENT.DOC.

10. You have already created a document summary for HOLMES.DOC. Now create document summaries for the files MEMO.DOC, INDENT.DOC, and NEWS.DOC. Note that you have to retrieve a document into the editing screen before you can add a document summary.

Long Problems

1. Use what you have learned about the Date and Right Flush commands to create a letter of complaint to a company about inadequate service you may have received or an inferior product you may have purchased.

2. Create a table of contents for this chapter, using a right tab stop with a dot leader to align all the page numbers at the right margin.

3. Reproduce a page from the Glossary in this book, using ½-inch hanging indents. Each term along with its definition should be a single paragraph. Remember to boldface the terms.

4. Reproduce the following table of information about the United States. Use tab stops, not spaces, to align the columns. Use left tab stops for the State and Capital columns, a center tab stop for the Admitted column, and a right tab stop for the Size Rank column.

State	Capital	Admitted	Size Rank
Alabama	Montgomery	1819	29
Alaska	Juneau	1959	1
Arizona	Phoenix	1912	6
Arkansas	Little Rock	1836	27
California	Sacramento	1850	3
Colorado	Denver	1876	8
Connecticut	Hartford	1788	48
Delaware	Dover	1787	49
District of Columbia	Washington	—	51
Florida	Tallahassee	1845	22
Georgia	Atlanta	1788	21
Hawaii	Honolulu	1959	47
Idaho	Boise	1890	13
Illinois	Springfield	1818	24
Indiana	Indianapolis	1816	38
Iowa	Des Moines	1846	25
Kansas	Topeka	1861	14
Kentucky	Frankfort	1792	37
Louisiana	Baton Rouge	1812	31
Maine	Augusta	1820	39
Maryland	Annapolis	1788	42
Massachusetts	Boston	1788	45
Michigan	Lansing	1837	23
Minnesota	St. Paul	1858	12
Mississippi	Jackson	1817	32
Missouri	Jefferson City	1821	19
Montana	Helena	1889	4
Nebraska	Lincoln	1867	15

State	Capital	Admitted	Size Rank
Nevada	Carson City	1864	7
New Hampshire	Concord	1788	44
New Jersey	Trenton	1787	46
New Mexico	Santa Fe	1912	5
New York	Albany	1788	30
North Carolina	Raleigh	1789	28
North Dakota	Bismarck	1889	17
Ohio	Columbus	1803	35
Oklahoma	Oklahoma City	1907	18
Oregon	Salem	1859	10
Pennsylvania	Harrisburg	1787	33
Rhode Island	Providence	1790	50
South Carolina	Columbia	1788	40
South Dakota	Pierre	1889	16
Tennessee	Nashville	1796	34
Texas	Austin	1845	2
Utah	Salt Lake City	1896	11
Vermont	Montpelier	1791	43
Virginia	Richmond	1788	36
Washington	Olympia	1889	20
West Virginia	Charleston	1863	41
Wisconsin	Madison	1848	26
Wyoming	Cheyenne	1890	9

5. Use the Text In/Out command to create the following DOS batch file for starting WordPerfect. Name the file W.BAT when you save it.

```
cd c:\wp50
wp
cd c:\
```

6. Create an inventory of your personal property. Use tab stops to arrange the data into columns. Use a decimal tab stop for the column listing the cost of each item.

7. Use successively nested left and right indentation to reproduce the following paragraphs. Turn on justification for this document and print it when you are finished.

Supercomputers are extremely fast mainframes that execute billions of instructions per second and can serve hundreds of users simultaneously. They cost between $5 million and $20 million each. Only a few hundred supercomputers are operating in the world today.

> Mainframes are big, powerful, fast, expensive computers. They execute many millions of instructions per second, can serve hundreds of users at the same time, and cost between $100,000 and $20 million. A mainframe computer may be as small as one or two file cabinets or large enough to fill an entire room.

>> Minicomputers are medium-sized computers that serve several users simultaneously or control complex equipment. The smallest minicomputers are about the same size as floor-standing microcomputers; the largest may be as big as one or two file cabinets. Minicomputers cost between $15,000 and $500,000.

Workstations are small, powerful computers generally used by only one person at a time. They are superior to microcomputers in their ability to perform complex calculations, display sharp and colorful graphics, and communicate with other computers. Workstations range in price from $4000 to $100,000.

Microcomputers are small enough to fit on a desk and are almost always used by one person at a time. The CPU usually consists of a single micro-processor chip. Prices range from $100 to $15,000.

8. Create a list of all the college courses you have taken, when you took them, the instructor (if you remember), and the grade you received. Use tab stops to align the columns.

9. Create a list of the LP records, cassette tapes, and compact discs you own. Include the title, artist, and type of media. Use tab stops to align the columns.

10. Create a document that lists the 10 or 12 function keys on your computer and the WordPerfect commands that correspond to these keys. Include columns for the key pressed alone, and the key pressed with Shift, Alternate, and Control. Use tab stops to align the columns.

ADVANCED WORDPERFECT

In This Chapter

Preview

Chapters 4 and 5 taught you most of what the average user needs to know about WordPerfect. This chapter proceeds to more advanced word processing topics. You may not need all of the commands and features presented in this chapter, but many of them can make your work easier, quicker, and less tedious. Learning more about WordPerfect can help you create more complex and attractive documents.

After studying this chapter, you will know how to

- use the Print menu.
- hyphenate words.
- avoid orphans and widows.
- avoid splitting paragraphs between pages.
- use the Font menu.
- add headers and footers.
- create text columns.
- add footnotes and endnotes.
- sort text.
- perform math.
- outline a document.
- generate a table of contents.
- generate an index.
- add graphics.
- use macros.
- create form letters.
- use styles.
- customize WordPerfect.

Getting Started

You've already learned how to start WordPerfect and use its most common features and commands. This chapter assumes you have completed all of the lessons and exercises in Chapters 4 and 5. Furthermore, it assumes that you have a computer with a hard disk and WordPerfect 5.0 installed on it in a subdirectory named WP50 and you have a subdirectory named LESSONS that contains your document files. To work the following lessons, boot up your computer, change to the WP50 subdirectory, and start WordPerfect.

Lesson 1: Using the Print Menu

In the two previous chapters you used the Full Document option of the Print menu to print your documents. Full Document is the most commonly used option, but the Print menu's other options can be handy in some circumstances.

Step 1: Retrieve NEWS.DOC

Retrieve the newsletter document:

    Press **Shift-F10**
    Type   **c:\lessons\news.doc**
    Press **Enter**

Step 2: Execute the Print Command

Activate the Print menu:

>   Press   **Shift-F7**

Your screen should look like Figure 1.

Step 3: Prepare the Printer

Make sure the printer is connected to the computer and turned on. Also, make sure that paper is loaded and aligned to the top of a new page. Finally, make sure that the printer's On Line light is lit. (If it isn't, press the On Line button.)

Step 4: Select the Page Option

You already know how to use Full Document, the first option in the Print menu. The second option, Page, lets you print the single page in which the cursor is located. At this point, the cursor should be in the first page of NEWS.DOC. Print the current page:

>   Type   **p**

Only the first page will be printed. WordPerfect will then return to the editing screen.

Step 5: Select the Document on Disk Option

When you choose the Full Document or Page option, the document currently on the editing screen is printed. The Document on Disk option lets you print a document other than the one you are editing. Suppose you want to print MEMO.DOC without retrieving it. Activate the Print menu, select the Document on Disk option, and enter the name of the document to be printed:

>   Press   **Shift-F7**
>   Type   **d**

Figure 1 The Print Menu

```
Print

    1 - Full Document
    2 - Page
    3 - Document on Disk
    4 - Control Printer
    5 - Type Through
    6 - View Document
    7 - Initialize Printer

Options

    S - Select Printer          Epson LQ-850/1050
    B - Binding                 0"
    N - Number of Copies        1
    G - Graphics Quality        Medium
    T - Text Quality            High




Selection: 0
```

Type   `c:\lessons\memo.doc`
Press   **Enter**

WordPerfect displays the prompt

`Page(s):  (All)`

You can enter a page number or range of pages, or simply press the Enter key to print the entire document.

Press   **Enter**

The document MEMO.DOC will be printed and the Print menu will remain on the screen.

Step 6: Select the Control Printer Option

If you use the Full Document option, WordPerfect returns to the editing screen and lets you work while the document is printing. You can also return to the editing screen from the Print menu after selecting the Document on Disk option. In fact, you can choose Document on Disk several times and specify several documents to be printed. WordPerfect stores the names of the documents you have sent to the printer in a **print queue,** or waiting line of print jobs. The Printer Control option of the Print menu lets you manage these print jobs. Let's see how it works.

Press your printer's On Line button to take it off line (the On Line light should be off). This will prevent the printer from printing while you examine the print queue. The Print menu should be displayed on your screen. Follow these instructions to load two files into the print queue and then select the Control Printer option:

Type   **d**
Type   `c:\lessons\memo.doc`
Press   **Enter** (2 times)
Type   **d**
Type   `c:\lessons\news.doc`
Press   **Enter** (2 times)
Type   **c**

Information about your print jobs and the Printer Control menu will appear on the screen (see Figure 2). The messages displayed on the screen can diagnose most printing problems and help you solve them. The menu provides options for controlling your print jobs. The Cancel option lets you terminate one or more print jobs. The Rush Job option changes the priority of a document in the print queue. The Display Jobs option presents all of the print jobs if they are not already shown on the screen. The Go (start printer) option restarts the printer after it has been halted to change a cartridge or after using the Stop option. The Stop option halts the printer, without canceling any print jobs, to let you handle a paper jam, ribbon change, or some other problem.

Cancel all of the print jobs and return to the editing screen:

Type   **c**
Type   *****
Type   **y**
Press   **F7**

Figure 2 The Printer Control Menu

```
Print: Control Printer

Current Job

Job Number: 5                                   Page Number:  1
Status:      End of job                         Current Copy: 1 of 1
Message:     Printer not accepting characters
Paper:       Standard 8.5" x 11"
Location:    Continuous feed
Action:      Check cable, make sure printer is turned ON


Job List

Job  Document               Destination         Print Options
  5  C:\LESSONS\MEMO.DOC    LPT 1
  6  C:\LESSONS\NEWS.DOC    LPT 1


Additional Jobs Not Shown: 0



 1 Cancel Job(s); 2 Rush Job; 3 Display Jobs; 4 Go (start printer); 5 Stop: 0
```

Press your printer's On Line button again. Part of the first document may still be printed, because many printers have their own internal memory buffer. WordPerfect cannot control text that has already been sent to a printer's buffer. You can, however, shut off the printer while it is still off-line to clear the buffer, wait a few seconds, and then turn it on again.

Step 7: Select the Type Through Option

The Type Through option of the Print menu allows you to use your computer and printer as if they were a typewriter. Each character or line you type is sent immediately to the printer. This feature is sometimes used for creating short memos or filling in a pre-printed form. Execute the Print command and select the Type Through option:

Press   **Shift-F7**
Type   **y**

Two Type Through options are available: Line and Character. The Line option lets you correct mistakes on a line with the Backspace and Delete keys. The line you type is not sent to the printer until you press Enter. The Character option sends each character you type immediately to the printer, just like a typewriter. Some printers, however, will not work with the Character option. Make sure your printer is on line and select the Line option:

Type   **L**
Type   **Hello there!**
Press   **Enter**

The message you typed will then be printed. When you are finished with the Type Through option, execute the Exit command to return to the Print Menu:

Press   **F7**

Step 8: Select the View Document Option

The View Document option lets you see how your document will look when it is printed, without actually printing it. This option works best on a computer with a graphics adapter and display. A graphics screen can show as closely as possible the appearance of the printed page, including the position of text on the page, margins, page numbers, and character formats such as underline and boldface. View Document can be useful in the preparation of documents that include some of the advanced features we will discuss later in this chapter, including headers and footers, footnotes and endnotes, columns, and graphics.

The Print menu should be on your screen. Select the View Document option:

Type   **v**

If your computer has graphics capability, WordPerfect will present a full-page view of the first page of the current document (see Figure 3). Although it is difficult to read the tiny text, called **greeking,** you can easily see the layout of the page. Use the Page Down key to see the next page in the document:

Press   **Page Down**

Now, return to the first page:

Press   **Page Up**

The View Document menu at the bottom of the screen presents several options for showing a page. The default option, Full Page, shows an entire page of the document on the screen, using greeking to represent text. Try the 100% option, which presents the page in the actual size it would be if it were printed:

Type   **1**

Figure 4 shows the result. The entire page does not fit on the screen, but you can use the arrow keys to see other parts of the page:

Press   **Right Arrow**
Press   **Down Arrow** (4 times)

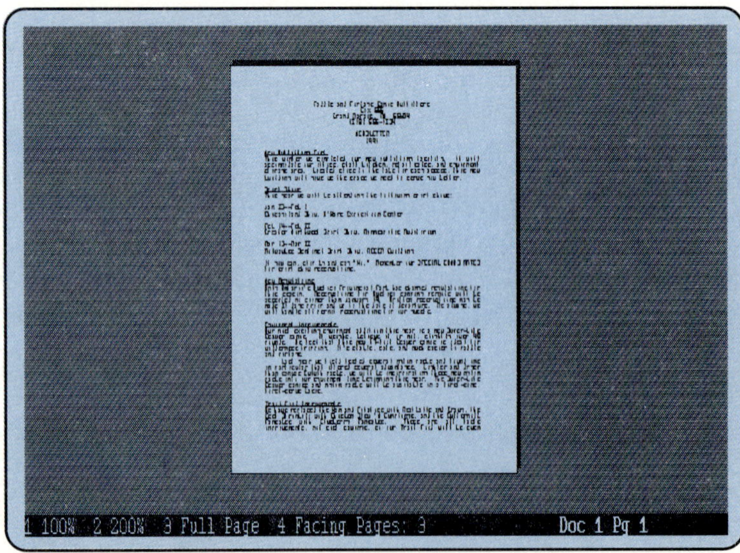

Figure 3 View Document Showing the Full Page

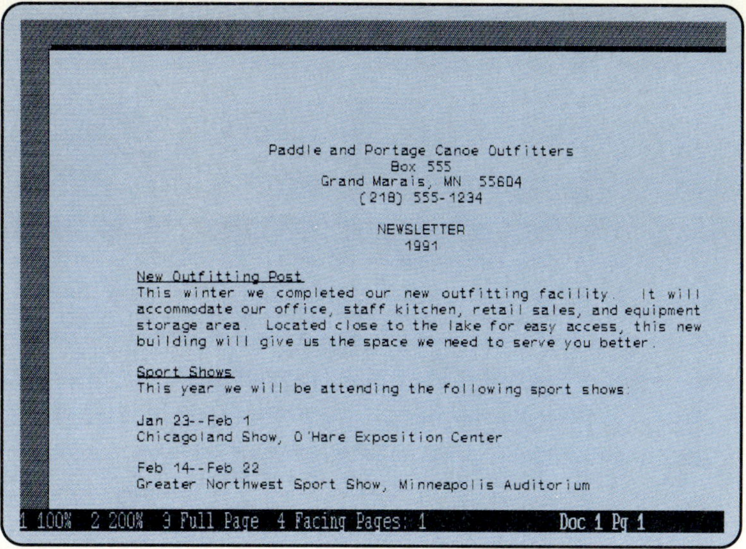

Figure 4 View Document Showing the Actual Size Page

Now, return to the top of the document:

Press   **Home** (2 times)
Press   **Up Arrow**

The 200% option presents a page twice its actual size.

Type   **2**
Press   **Right Arrow** (5 times)

Your screen should look like Figure 5. The last option in the View Document menu, Facing Pages, is used to display odd-numbered pages on the right and even-numbered pages on the left. Note that you cannot edit text in the View

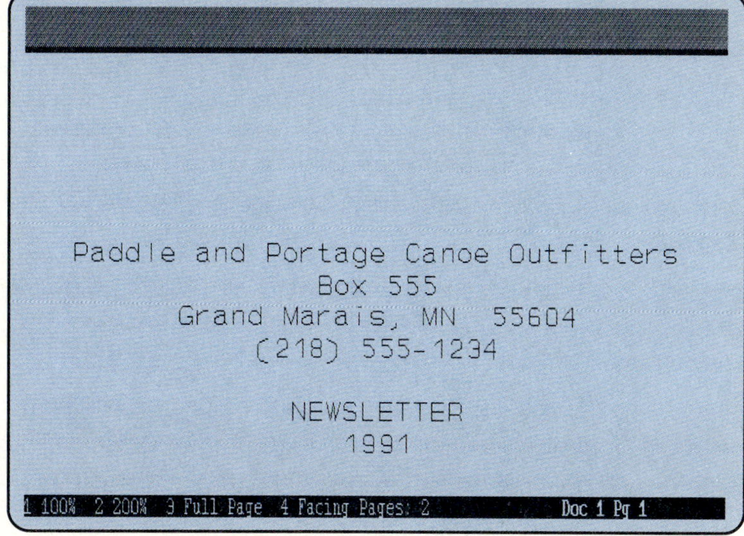

Figure 5 View Document Showing the Page Twice Actual Size

Document screen, only examine it. Use the Exit command to return to document editing screen:

Press   **F7**

Step 9: Examine the Other Print Options

Execute the Print command again:

Press   **Shift-F7**

Several other options are available in the Print menu. Option number 7, Initialize Printer, is normally used only with certain laser printers to load software fonts. The Select Printer option is used to connect a new printer to your computer or choose another connected printer. The Binding option lets you leave space along the edges of pages that are to be bound into a book. You can print several copies of the same document with the Number of Copies option. The last two options, Graphics Quality and Text Quality, allow you to control the resolution and speed of printing. High quality looks the best, but it also takes the longest to print. In addition to High and Medium quality settings, WordPerfect also has Draft, which prints a fast, rough copy. The Do Not Print option is also available for printing text and graphics separately.

1. With NEWS.DOC on your editing screen, print HOLMES.DOC from the LESSONS subdirectory.

2. Use the Type Through option to print the following message:

   `A computer is a rather expensive typewriter.`

3. Use the View Document option to examine the bottom half of the second page of NEWS.DOC. Use the 200% option to magnify the page.

4. Change the Number of Copies option to print two copies of MEMO.DOC with the Document on Disk option.

Lesson 2: Hyphenating Words

By default, word wrap moves an entire word to the next line whenever that word extends past the right margin. WordPerfect will not split words between lines unless you turn on the hyphenation feature. **Hyphenation** is the division of certain words at the ends of lines to improve the appearance of text. Hyphenation is most useful when text is justified. If hyphenation is turned off for justified text, large gaps may appear between the words on some lines. These gaps occur when a long word at the end of a line is wrapped to the next line. Hyphenation can make justified text more attractive by splitting long words at the ends of lines, which reduces large gaps between words. It can also improve the appearance of unjustified text by reducing the raggedness of the right margin.

Step 1: Move the Cursor

Before turning on hyphenation, you must move the cursor to the place where you want hyphenation to begin. In most cases, this place will be the beginning of the document.

Press   **Home** (2 times)
Press   **Up Arrow**

Step 2: Turn On Justification

You can use hyphenation with justification turned off, but hyphenation is most often used with justification turned on. Turn on justification for the newsletter:

Press	**Shift-F8**
Type	**L**
Type	**j**
Type	**y**
Press	**F7**

The appearance of text on the screen will not change, but the text will be justified when it is printed or examined with View Document.

Step 3: Turn On Manual Hyphenation

WordPerfect offers two types of hyphenation: Manual and Automatic. **Manual hyphenation** requires you to confirm the splitting of each word as you scroll through the document. **Automatic hyphenation** uses a set of built-in rules to attempt splitting words without confirmation. If the rules cannot be applied to a particular word, WordPerfect reverts to manual hyphenation for that word only. Let's try manual hyphenation first. Execute the Format command, select the Line option, select the Hyphenation option, and then select the Manual option:

Press	**Shift-F8**
Type	**L**
Type	**y**
Type	**m**
Press	**F7**

Step 4: Scroll Through the Document

In order to hyphenate an existing document, you must scroll through it. WordPerfect will beep and display a prompt when it finds a word that should be hyphenated. Use the Down Arrow key to move the cursor through the document:

> Press   **Down Arrow** (until WordPerfect beeps)

The first hyphenation will occur in the Trail Food Improvements paragraph. WordPerfect will beep and display the prompt shown in Figure 6. It presents the word "improvements" and suggests where to insert the hyphen. You can press the Left Arrow or Right Arrow key to change the position of the hyphen. When the hyphen is where you want it, you press the Escape key. In this case, the hyphen is fine.

> Press   **Escape**

The word will be hyphenated in the text. In this manner, you could scroll through the rest of the document and confirm each of WordPerfect's hyphenation suggestions.

Step 5: Turn On Automatic Hyphenation

Now, let's try automatic hyphenation.

Press	**Shift-F8**
Type	**L**
Type	**y**

Figure 6 The Manual
Hyphenation Prompt

New Regulations
Only Ontario's Quetico Provincial Park has changed regulations for
this season. Reservations for Quetico camping permits will be
accepted no sooner than January 19. Written reservations may be
made 21 days prior and up to the date of departure. As always, we
will handle all permit reservations for our guests.

Equipment Improvements
Our most exciting equipment addition this year is a new Super-Lite
Beaver canoe. It weighs, believe it or not, slightly over 40
pounds. We feel that this new 17-foot Beaver canoe is ideal for
wilderness tripping. It's stable, safe, and much easier to paddle
and portage.
     Last year we field tested several nylon packs and found one
in particular that offered several advantages. Lighter and dryer
than canvas Duluth packs, we will be incorporating these new nylon
packs into our equipment line beginning this year. The Super-Lite
Beaver canoes and nylon packs will be available on a first-come,
first-serve basis.

Trail Food Improvements
We have replaced the Ham and Potatoes with Meatballs and Gravy, the
Beef Stromboli with Chicken Stew 'N Dumplings, and the Buttermilk
Pancakes with Blueberry Pancakes. These are all taste
Position hyphen: Press ESC improve-ments,

> Type   **a**
> Press   **F7**

Hyphenation also works while you are entering new text. To see it in action, delete the word "improvements":

> Press   **Ctrl-Backspace**

Retype the word and see how it is automatically hyphenated:

> Type   **improvements,**
> Press   **Space Bar**

Step 6: View the Document

The best way to see the full result of hyphenation and justification is to print the document or use the View Document feature.

> Press   **Shift-F7**
> Type   **v**
> Type   **1**

You may have to use the arrow keys to bring the Trail Food Improvements paragraph into view. Your screen should look like Figure 7. When you are finished examining the page, return to the editing screen:

> Press   **F7**

Step 7: Turn Off Hyphenation

You turn off hyphenation by selecting the first option in the Hyphenation menu. Move the cursor to the beginning of the document and turn off hyphenation:

> Press   **Home** (2 times)
> Press   **Up Arrow**
> Press   **Shift-F8**

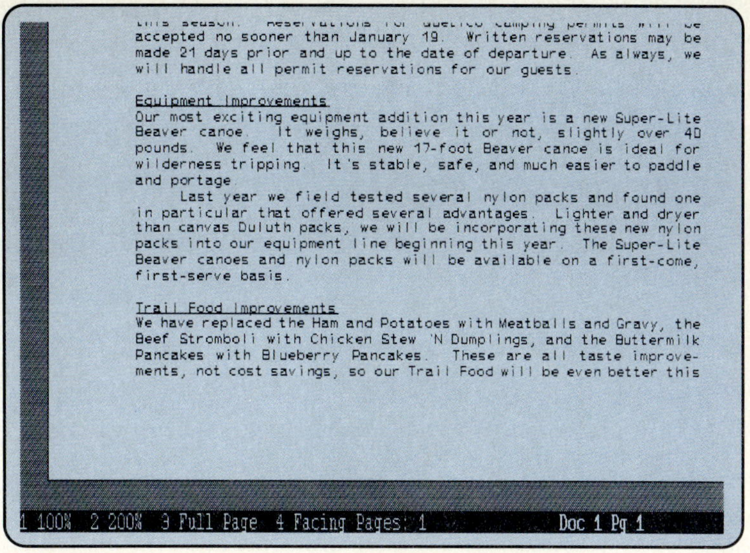

Figure 7 Hyphenation and Justification

Type   **L**
Type   **y**
Type   **f**
Press   **F7**

Practice

1. Move the cursor to the beginning of the document and turn on automatic hyphenation.

2. Use the Down Arrow key to scroll through the entire document.

3. Use the View Document feature to examine the document. Return to the editing screen, move the cursor to the beginning of the document, and leave automatic hyphenation turned on.

Lesson 3: Avoiding Orphans and Widows

The page formatting settings determine how many lines of text will appear on a page. WordPerfect simply counts the number of lines and inserts a soft page break wherever necessary. Some paragraphs, however, may be divided inappropriately between pages. An **orphan** is the last line of a paragraph that appears at the top of a page. A **widow** is the first line of a paragraph that appears at the bottom of a page. Both orphans and widows are considered poor form because they can confuse the reader. It is better to have two lines from a paragraph at the top or bottom of a page. Fortunately, WordPerfect can automatically eliminate orphans and widows.

Step 1: Examine the Document

The document NEWS.DOC contains a good example of an orphan. A single-word line from the end of a paragraph appears at the top of the second page. To see it on the screen, follow these directions:

Press   **Home** (2 times)
Press   **Up Arrow**

Figure 8 An Orphan at the Top of the Second Page

Press   **Page Down**
Press   **Up Arrow**

The word "year" is all by itself at the top of the page (see Figure 8). This is the worst kind of orphan and it should not appear in the final document.

Step 2: Move the Cursor

Before eliminating orphans and widows from an entire document, you must move the cursor to the beginning.

Press   **Home** (2 times)
Press   **Up Arrow**

Step 3: Turn On Widow and Orphan Protection

To avoid orphans and widows, execute the Format command, select the Line option, and then select the Widow/Orphan Protection option:

Press   **Shift-F8**
Type   **L**
Type   **w**
Type   **y**
Press   **F7**

Step 4: Examine the Document

Examine the document again to see if the orphan has been eliminated.

Press   **Page Down**
Press   **Up Arrow**

As you can see from Figure 9, the page break has been inserted one line earlier so that two lines from the end of the paragraph appear at the top of the second page.

Figure 9 The Orphan Has Been Eliminated

```
Pancakes with Blueberry Pancakes.  These are all taste improve-
----------------------------------------------------------------
ments, not cost savings, so our Trail Food will be even better this
year.

Current Outfitting Rates
            Number In Party      Rate Per Person Per Day
            1 to 3 persons       $31.00
            4 to 6 persons       $29.25
            7 to 9 persons       $28.50

1990 Fishing Records
            Bluegill              3.00 lbs.
            Large Mouth Bass     20.25 lbs.
            Northern Pike        42.33 lbs.
            Sunfish               2.20 lbs.
            Walleye              25.00 lbs.
            Lake Trout           50.00 lbs.

Trips
This fall we took a trip into the Cherry Lake area for some lake
trout fishing.  We had our usual quota of rain, but did enjoy two
beautiful crisp autumn days.  Mornings we awoke to clear, deep blue
skies with heavy, white steam rising from Cherry Lake.  On shore
C:\LESSONS\NEWS.DOC                        Doc 1 Pg 1 Ln 9.67" Pos 1"
```

Step 5: Save the Document

Save the document to the disk to preserve the changes you have made:

Press   **F10**
Press   **Enter**
Type   **y**

Practice

1. Move the cursor to the beginning of NEWS.DOC and execute the Reveal Codes command. Note the [Hyph On] code, which indicates that hyphenation is turned on, and the [W/O On] code, which indicates that widow and orphan protection is turned on. Return to the full editing screen.

2. Execute the Help command and read about widow and orphan protection:

Press   **F3**
Press   **Shift-F8**
Type   **L**
Type   **w**

When you are finished reading, return to the editing screen:

Press   **Space Bar**

Lesson 4: Using the Conditional End of Page Feature

Widow and orphan protection keeps the two lines at the beginning or end of a paragraph from being split between pages. The Conditional End of Page feature is another way to protect text from being split between pages. This feature is handy for keeping titles or headings together with their first paragraphs or for preventing tables from being split between pages.

Step 1: Move the Cursor to the Line Above

Suppose you want to keep the three lines at the end of the paragraph from being split between pages. The first step is to move the cursor to the line before the lines you want to keep together.

Press   **Home** (2 times)
Press   **Up Arrow**
Press   **Page Down**
Press   **Up Arrow** (2 times)

Step 2: Select the Conditional End of Page Option

Execute the Format command, select the Other option, and then select the Conditional End of Page option:

Press   **Shift-F8**
Type   **o**
Type   **c**

Step 3: Enter the Number of Lines

WordPerfect will prompt you for the number of lines to keep together (see Figure 10). Enter the number and exit the menu:

Type   **3**
Press   **Enter**
Press   **F7**

Step 4: Move the Cursor

The page break will not actually change position until you move the cursor.

Press   **Down Arrow** (2 times)

Figure 10 Conditional End of Page Prompt

```
Format: Other

     1 - Advance

     2 - Conditional End of Page

     3 - Decimal/Align Character          .
         Thousands' Separator             ,

     4 - Language                         US

     5 - Overstrike

     6 - Printer Functions

     7 - Underline - Spaces               Yes
                     Tabs                 No




Number of Lines to Keep Together:_
```

The last three lines of the paragraph will be kept together after the page break (see Figure 11).

Practice

1. Execute the Reveal Codes command. Note the code [Cndl EOP:3], which indicates the Conditional End of Page option has been set for the three lines below the current line. Delete this code to turn the option off. Return to the full editing screen and move the cursor to the beginning of the document.

2. Execute the Help command and read about the Conditional End of Page option. When you are finished, return to the editing screen.

Lesson 5: Using the Font Menu

WordPerfect has the ability to use different fonts and change the size, appearance, and color of text. Whether or not you can actually use these features depends on your computer and printer. Nevertheless, let's examine the options of the Font menu.

Step 1: Clear the Editing Screen

Exit NEWS.DOC and start a new document to illustrate the capabilities of the Font menu:

Press   **F7**
Type   **n**
Type   **n**

Step 2: Activate the Font Menu

Execute the Font command:

Press   **Ctrl-F8**

Figure 11 Last Three Lines of the Paragraph Kept Together

```
   e have replaced the Ham and Potatoes with Meatballs and Gravy, the
 Beef Stromboli with Chicken Stew 'N Dumplings, and the Buttermilk
-------------------------------------------------------------------
 Pancakes with Blueberry Pancakes.  These are all taste improve-
 ments, not cost savings, so our Trail Food will be even better this
 year.

 Current Outfitting Rates
         Number In Party     Rate Per Person Per Day
         1 to 3 persons      $31.00
         4 to 6 persons      $29.25
         7 to 9 persons      $28.50

 1990 Fishing Records
         Bluegill            3.00 lbs.
         Large Mouth Bass   20.25 lbs.
         Northern Pike      42.33 lbs.
         Sunfish             2.20 lbs.
         Walleye            25.00 lbs.
         Lake Trout         50.00 lbs.

 Trips
 This fall we took a trip into the Cherry Lake area for some lake
 trout fishing.  We had our usual quota of rain, but did enjoy two
 C:\LESSONS\NEWS.DOC                          Doc 1 Pg 2 Ln 1" Pos 1"
```

Five options will be listed in a menu across the bottom of the screen: Size, Appearance, Normal, Base Font, and Print Color.

Step 3: Select the Size Option

The Size option of the Font menu deals with the height of characters or their relative position in a line. Select the Size option:

Type **s**

Seven options will be listed in a new menu across the bottom of the screen: Superscript, Subscript, Fine, Small, Large, Very Large, and Extra Large. While these options do not change the appearance of text on the screen, they do allow you to change the size of text in the printed document. The Superscript and Subscript options also change the position of text. Superscript characters are small and raised, like [this], and subscript characters are small and lowered, like [this]. Follow these directions to try all of the Size options:

Type **p**
Type **Superscript**
Press **Right Arrow**
Type **characters**
Press **Enter**
Press **Ctrl-F8**
Type **s**
Type **b**
Type **Subscript**
Press **Right Arrow**
Type **characters**
Press **Enter**
Press **Ctrl-F8**
Type **s**
Type **f**
Type **Fine characters**
Press **Right Arrow**
Press **Enter**
Press **Ctrl-F8**
Type **s**
Type **s**
Type **Small characters**
Press **Right Arrow**
Press **Enter**
Press **Ctrl-F8**
Type **s**
Type **L**
Type **Large characters**
Press **Right Arrow**
Press **Enter**
Press **Ctrl-F8**
Type **s**
Type **v**
Type **Very Large characters**
Press **Right Arrow**
Press **Enter**

Press   **Ctrl-F8**
Type   **s**
Type   **e**
Type   **Extra Large characters**
Press   **Right Arrow**
Press   **Enter**

Selecting a Size option inserts size codes into the document before and after the text you type, just like the Underline command. Pressing the Right Arrow key after typing text in a particular size moves the cursor past the second size code and returns to the default size. To see what you have done, print the document:

Press   **Shift-F7**
Type   **f**

You can also use the View Document feature to examine the results. Note that some of the sizes turn out the same, depending upon your printer. A dot-matrix printer, for example, may have only two or three different sizes. A laser printer, on the other hand, can probably produce all of the different character sizes.

Step 4: Select the Appearance Option

Activate the Font menu and select the Appearance option:

Press   **Ctrl-F8**
Type   **a**

WordPerfect will display the Appearance menu, which has nine options: Bold, Underline, Double Underline, Italic, Outline, Shadow, Small Caps, Redline, and Strikeout. This menu allows you to change character formats, as you learned in the Beginning WordPerfect chapter. Execute the Exit command:

Press   **F7**

Step 5: Select the Normal Option

The Normal option of the Font menu turns off all size and appearance attributes for the next characters you type. It returns to the default character size and format.

Press   **Ctrl-F8**
Type   **n**

Step 6: Select the Base Font Option

The Base Font option of the Font menu displays the fonts available with your printer and allows you to change the font you are using.

Press   **Ctrl-F8**
Type   **f**

Figure 12 shows the result for an Epson LQ-850 dot-matrix printer. The list you see on your screen may be different. The font highlighted and marked with an asterisk is the base font, the default typeface used for normal characters. If more fonts are available than fit on the screen, they can be viewed by pressing Up Arrow or Down Arrow to scroll through the list. The list presents the name of each font and its size. Sizes are given in points (pt) or characters per inch (CPI).

Figure 12 The Base Font Menu for the Epson LQ-850 Printer

```
Base Font

    Roman (10 CPI)
    Roman (12 CPI)
    Roman (15 CPI)
    Roman (17 CPI)
    Roman (20 CPI)
    Roman 12pt (PS)
    Roman 12pt (PS) Condensed
    Roman 12pt (PS) Dbl-Wide
    Roman 12pt (PS) Italic
    Roman Italic ( 5 CPI)
    Roman Italic ( 6 CPI)
    Roman Italic ( 7 CPI)
    Roman Italic (10 CPI)
    Roman Italic (12 CPI)
    Roman Italic (15 CPI)
    Roman Italic (17 CPI)
    Roman Italic (20 CPI)
    San Serif ( 5 CPI)
    San Serif ( 6 CPI)
    San Serif ( 7 CPI)
  * San Serif (10 CPI)

  1 Select; N Name search: 1
```

A **point** is a typographic measure equal to about $\frac{1}{72}$-inch. Ten characters per inch (10 CPI), the most common default size, is equivalent to the type produced by pica typewriters. Elite typewriters produce 12-CPI type. The abbreviation PS stands for "proportionally spaced," which refers to fonts that use different amounts of horizontal space for each character.

The two options at the bottom of the screen allow you to select a different base font or search through the list for a particular font name. Let's just leave the base font the same. Execute the Exit command to leave the Base Font menu:

Press   **F7**

Step 7: Select the Print Color Option

If you have a color printer, you can use the Print Color option to change the color of printed text.

Press   **Ctrl-F8**
Type   **c**

Most printers cannot produce colors, only black and white. If you have a color printer, however, the table presented by the Print Color option lets you compose print colors by specifying the mixture percentages of the primary colors red, green, and blue. Leave the table the same and return to the editing screen:

Press   **F7**

Practice

1. Move the cursor to the beginning of the document and execute the Reveal Codes command. Note the following codes for character sizes: [SUPRSCPT], [SUBSCPT], [FINE], [SMALL], [LARGE], [VRY LARGE], and [EXT LARGE]. Return to the editing screen.

2. Reproduce these expressions in your document:

   H_2O
   2×10^3
   $e = mc^2$

3. Use the Help facility to read about all of the Font menu options. When you are finished, return to the editing screen.

4. Change the base font, type some new text, and print out the document to see the result. Then change the base font back to what it was before. Clear the screen without saving the document:

   Press　**F7**
   Type　　**n**
   Type　　**n**

Lesson 6: Adding Headers and Footers

A **header** is one or more lines of text printed at the top of every page. A **footer** is one or more lines of text printed at the bottom of every page. Headers and footers are most often used to print titles, chapters, page numbers, or other identification on every page. WordPerfect makes it easy to create headers and footers.

Step 1: Retrieve NEWS.DOC

As an example, let's add a header to the document NEWS.DOC. Your editing screen should be empty. If it is not, use the Exit command to clear it. Then retrieve NEWS.DOC from the LESSONS subdirectory:

   Press　**Shift-F10**
   Type　　**c:\lessons\news.doc**
   Press　**Enter**

Step 2: Select the Headers Option

To create a header, execute the Format command, select the Page option, and then select the Header option:

   Press　**Shift-F8**
   Type　　**p**
   Type　　**h**

Step 3: Select the Header

Another menu will appear with two options: Header A and Header B. Word-Perfect lets you create up to two headers. Select Header A:

   Type　**a**

Step 4: Select the Pages

Another menu will appear with five options: Discontinue, Every Page, Odd Pages, Even Pages, and Edit. Select the Every Page option to have the header printed at the top of every page:

   Type　**p**

Step 5: Enter the Header Text

The screen will temporarily clear so you can enter the text of the header. Suppose you want the header to be "Newsletter" followed by the page number. Follow these instructions:

Type   **Newsletter**
Press **Space Bar**
Press **Ctrl-b**
Press **F7** (2 times)

The Ctrl-b is a code that tells WordPerfect to insert the current page number.

Step 6: Print or View the Document

Headers show up only when the document is printed or examined with View Document. If you have a printer, you can print the document:

Press **Shift-F7**
Type   **f**

Or you can use the View Document feature:

Press **Shift-F7**
Type   **v**

The header will appear in the upper left corner of every page (see Figure 13).

Step 7: Examine the Other Options

The process for creating footers is the same, except you choose the Footers option from the Page menu of the Format command. The Discontinue option allows you to remove an existing header or footer. The Edit option allows you to make changes to an existing header or footer.

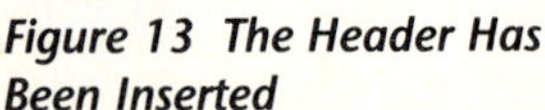

Figure 13 The Header Has Been Inserted

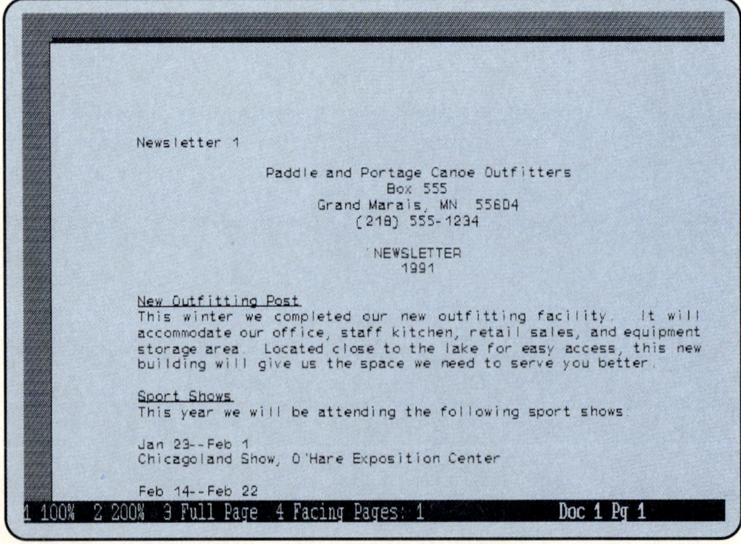

Practice

1. Discontinue the header you have created for NEWS.DOC.
2. Create a footer for NEWS.DOC. Print the document or examine it with View Document.
3. Use the Edit option to alter the footer in some way.
4. Discontinue the footer.

Lesson 7: Creating Text Columns

WordPerfect can create two types of text columns in a printed document: newspaper-style and parallel. **Newspaper-style columns** contain text that continues from the bottom of one column on the left to the top of the next column on the right on the same page. **Parallel columns** contain text that continues in the same column on the next page. Columns are often used in newsletters, magazines, newspapers, and for narrow lists of items in books. As an example, let's reformat NEWS.DOC so that it contains two newspaper-style columns.

Step 1: Move the Cursor

The first step is to move the cursor to the place in the document where columns are to begin. In NEWS.DOC, columns should begin on the line that contains the title "New Outfitting Post."

Press   **Home** (2 times)
Press   **Up Arrow**
Press   **Down Arrow** (8 times)

Step 2: Turn On Automatic Hyphenation

It is usually necessary to hyphenate some words when text is arranged in columns. Turn on automatic hyphenation:

Press   **Shift-F8**
Type   **L**
Type   **y**
Type   **a**
Press   **F7**

Step 3: Define the Columns

Next, you must tell WordPerfect the number of columns you want and their spacing on the page. Execute the Math/Columns command and select the Column Definition option:

Press   **Alt-F7**
Type   **d**

WordPerfect will display the Text Column Definition menu, as shown in Figure 14. The default type of columns is newspaper-style, with two three-inch-wide columns spaced ½-inch apart. These default settings are fine for our example, so tell WordPerfect to accept them:

Press   **Enter**

*Figure 14 The Text Col-
umn Definition Menu*

```
Text Column Definition

   1 - Type                               Newspaper

   2 - Number of Columns                  2

   3 - Distance Between Columns

   4 - Margins

   Column   Left    Right    Column   Left      Right
     1:      1"      4"         13:
     2:      4.5"    7.5"       14:
     3:                         15:
     4:                         16:
     5:                         17:
     6:                         18:
     7:                         19:
     8:                         20:
     9:                         21:
    10:                         22:
    11:                         23:
    12:                         24:

Selection: 0
```

Step 4: Turn On Columns

The columns are now defined, but you still have to turn them on. Select the Column On/Off option from the Math/Columns menu:

> Type   **c**

After you turn on columns, any new text you type will automatically be arranged in columns. You can turn off columns at any time by executing the Column On/Off command again. Then you can type text that you don't want split into columns.

Step 5: Scroll Through the Text

Now that columns are turned on, you can use the Down Arrow key to scroll through the text and WordPerfect will create the columns on your screen.

> Press   **Down Arrow** (to the end of the document)

The program will prompt you to manually hyphenate words that it cannot hyphenate automatically. If you cannot hyphenate the word correctly, execute the Cancel command (press F1) to wrap the entire word to the next line.

Step 6: Move to the Other Column

The normal cursor movement commands work only within the current column. You must use a variation of the Go To command to move to another column. Execute this command to move to the right column:

> Press   **Ctrl-Home**
> Press   **Right Arrow**

Now, move back to the left column:

> Press   **Ctrl-Home**
> Press   **Left Arrow**

Step 7: Print or View the Document

The screen shows the two columns, but you can see the document better by printing it or using the View Document feature. If you have a printer, you can print the document:

Press   **Shift-F7**
Type   **f**

Or you can use the View Document feature:

Press   **Shift-F7**
Type   **v**

The newsletter will appear in two newspaper-style columns (see Figure 15). Don't worry about the tables, which do not line up or are split between the pages. The tab stops were set too wide for the narrow columns. If this were an actual newsletter, you would have to fix the tables and any other minor formatting problems.

Step 8: Exit and Retrieve NEWS.DOC

Let's abandon the columns you have created and leave NEWS.DOC the way it was before this lesson. Exit the file without saving it and then retrieve NEWS.DOC again:

Press   **F7**
Type   **n**
Type   **n**
Press   **Shift-F10**
Type   **c:\lessons\news.doc**
Press   **Enter**

Practice   Invoke the Help facility and read about the commands and options you have used in this lesson.

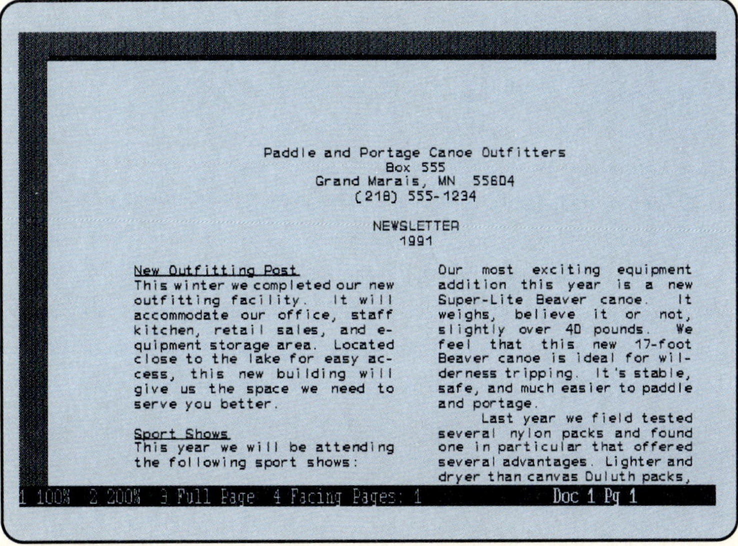

Figure 15 Two Newspaper-Style Text Columns

 Lesson 8: Adding Footnotes and Endnotes

Anyone who has written a term paper or technical report has faced the problem of placing footnotes. A **footnote** is a numbered comment or explanation at the bottom of a page. Footnotes are used to list sources or provide more detailed information about items in the text. A footnote must appear at the bottom of the page that contains its number. Placing footnotes at the bottom of the appropriate pages is difficult with a typewriter and some word processing programs. If text is added or deleted, existing footnotes may have to be moved to a different page. Fortunately, WordPerfect automatically numbers footnotes and keeps them at the bottom of the appropriate page. An **endnote** is similar to a footnote, except that comments are collected and placed at the end of the document instead of at the bottom of each page. You can have footnotes and endnotes in the same document. Although newsletters usually don't have footnotes or endnotes, let's add a footnote to NEWS.DOC just to see how they work.

Step 1: Move the Cursor

The cursor must be moved to the location in the document where the note number is to be inserted. Let's put a footnote number at the end of the New Outfitting Post paragraph.

    Press   **Home** (2 times)
    Press   **Up Arrow**
    Press   **Down Arrow** (12 times)
    Press   **End**

Step 2: Execute the Footnote Command

Footnotes and endnotes are created by executing the Footnote command.

    Press   **Ctrl-F7**

WordPerfect will present a menu at the bottom of the screen with three options: Footnote, Endnote, and Endnote Placement. Select the Footnote option:

    Type   **f**

Step 3: Create the Footnote

The Footnote menu will appear at the bottom of the screen with four options: Create, Edit, New Number, and Options. Select the Create option to begin creating the footnote:

    Type   **c**

WordPerfect will present a special screen for editing footnotes. The footnote number, in this case 1, is automatically created. Simply type the text of the footnote:

    Type   **See last year's newsletter for a photo.**

Your screen should look like Figure 16. Execute the Exit command to save the footnote and return to the document editing screen:

    Press   **F7**

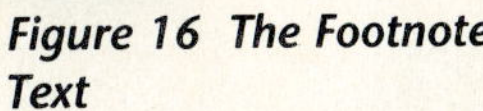

Figure 16 The Footnote Text

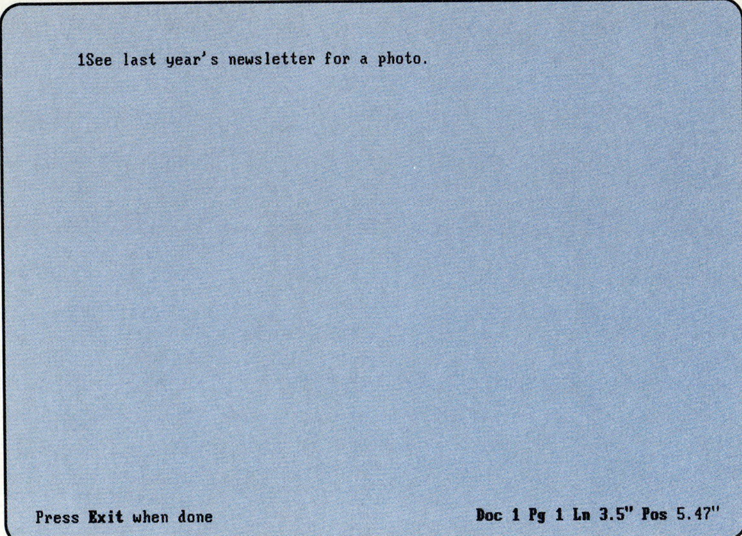

Step 4: View the Document

When you return to the editing screen, you can immediately see the footnote number WordPerfect placed at the end of the first paragraph. The footnote text, however, only appears when the document is printed or examined with View Document. Use the View Document feature to look at the footnote you have created:

Press   **Shift-F7**
Type   **v**
Type   **1**
Press   **Grey Plus** (2 times)

Your screen should look like Figure 17. The footnote appears at the bottom of the first page beneath a line separating it from the document text. Return to the editing screen:

Press   **F7**

Step 5: Examine Other Options

Creating endnotes is just like creating footnotes, except that you select the Endnote option instead of the Footnote option after you execute the Footnote command. In addition, you have to tell WordPerfect where you want the endnotes placed in the document. This is done by moving the cursor to the desired location, executing the Footnote command, and then selecting the Endnote Placement option.

To edit existing footnotes or endnotes, you select the Edit option from the Footnote or Endnote menu. The New Number option lets you start numbering notes with a new number. This option is useful when you have a document broken up between two files and you want the note numbers in the second file to continue after the numbers in the first file instead of starting from 1. The Options option in the Footnote or Endnote menu lets you specify attributes such as footnote spacing and the numbering style.

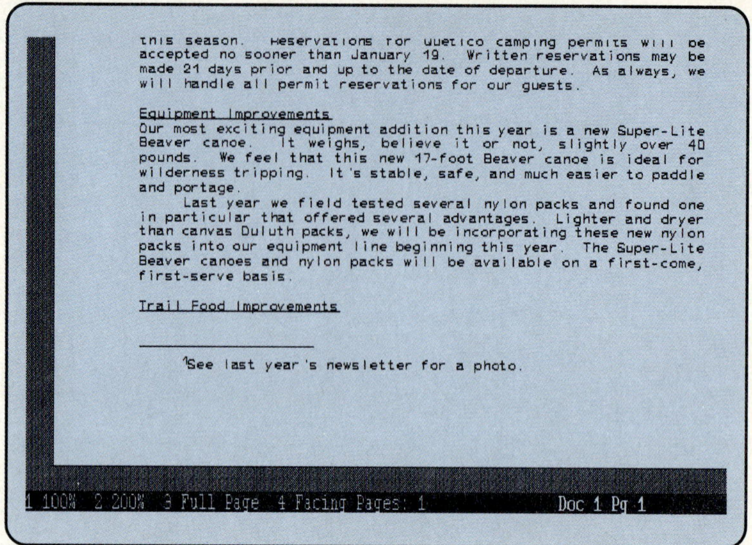

Figure 17 The Footnote Has Been Added at the Bottom

1. Add the following footnote at the end of the New Regulations paragraph:

   Write to the Ontario Ministry of Natural Resources for more information.

2. Add a couple of endnotes and place them at the end of the document. Use the View Document feature to examine the endnotes you have created.

3. Delete all of the footnotes and endnotes you have created by deleting each note number in the document text. Answer "yes" to the confirmation prompt displayed by WordPerfect each time you delete a note number. Move the cursor to the beginning of the document.

Lesson 9: Sorting Text

Sorting is arranging items in some particular order. WordPerfect makes it easy to sort lines of text or paragraphs. This feature is handy for alphabetizing names or any list of words or phrases. Sorting is also used to arrange numbers, such as dates and ZIP codes, into ascending or descending order. As an example, let's sort the list of fishing records on the second page of NEWS.DOC.

Step 1: Mark the Lines As a Block

The first step is to mark the lines of text to be sorted as a block. Follow these directions to move the cursor with the Search command and then mark the fishing records as a block:

Press	**Home** (2 times)
Press	**Up Arrow**
Press	**F2**
Type	**Bluegill**
Press	**F2**

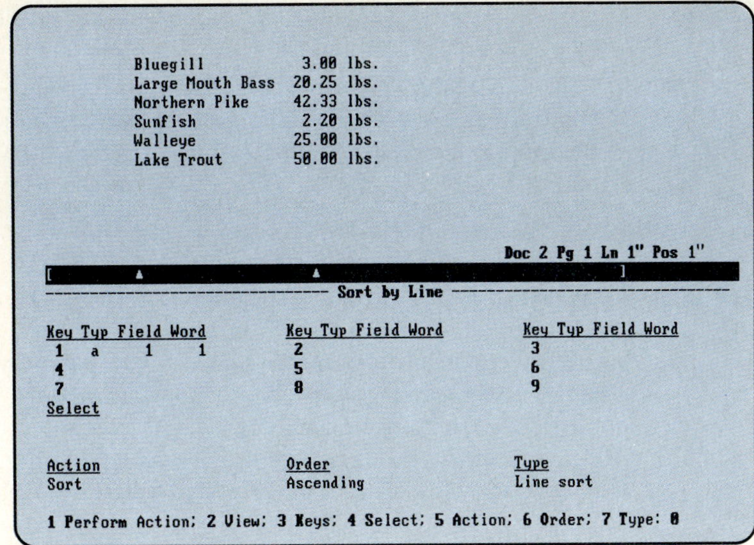

Figure 18 The Sort Menu

> Press   **Home**
> Press   **Left Arrow**
> Press   **Alt-F4**
> Press   **Down Arrow** (6 times)

The table of fishing records will be marked as a block and displayed in reverse video.

Step 2: Execute the Merge/Sort Command

The table of fish names and records is almost sorted. The only name out of order is Lake Trout. Let's sort the table by fish name. Execute the Merge/Sort command:

> Press   **Ctrl-F9**

WordPerfect will display the Sort menu shown in Figure 18. Each line in the marked block is a **record** to be sorted. Each word separated by tabs or spaces is a **field.** The **key** is a field on which the records are to be sorted. WordPerfect lets you specify up to nine keys, but in most cases you need only one. The key in this case will be the first word of the fish names. But because all of the lines in this table begin with a tab, you must tell WordPerfect that the second field in each record is to be the key. Select the Keys option and change the key field from 1 to 2:

> Type   **k**
> Press   **Right Arrow**
> Type   **2**
> Press   **F7**

The default sort order is Ascending, which will sort items in alphabetical order from A to Z. Select the Perform Action option to complete the sort:

> Type   **p**

The table will be rearranged, with Lake Trout coming after Bluegill.

1. Sort the Fishing Records table in descending order. Select the Order option from the Sort menu and then select the Descending option.
2. Sort the Fishing Records table in ascending order again. Save NEWS.DOC to the disk to preserve the changes you have made. Move the cursor to the beginning of the document.

Lesson 10: Performing Math

WordPerfect has a Math feature that lets you perform calculations in your documents. The most common use of the Math feature is to add up a column of numbers. As an example, let's add up the weights in the Fishing Records table. Although adding these numbers does not make much sense in the context of this table, it will serve as a useful illustration of the Math feature.

Step 1: Move the Cursor

The first step is to move the cursor to the line that contains the first number to be totaled. Follow these directions to move to the beginning of the Fishing Records table.

Press	**Home** (2 times)
Press	**Up Arrow**
Press	**F2**
Type	**Bluegill**
Press	**F2**
Press	**Home**
Press	**Left Arrow**

Step 2: Define the Math Columns

You already have the numbers arranged in a column created with tab stops. The next step is to define the math columns. Execute the Math/Columns command:

    Press **Alt-F7**

WordPerfect will display the Math/Columns menu at the bottom of the screen. Select the Math Definition option:

    Type **e**

WordPerfect will then display the Math Definition menu. By default, all columns are assumed to be math columns, negative numbers will appear in parentheses, and two digits will appear to the right of the decimal point. The default settings are fine, so just execute the Exit command:

    Press **F7**

Step 3: Turn On Math

WordPerfect will return to the Math/Columns menu at the bottom of the screen. Select the Math On option to turn on the Math feature:

    Type **m**

WordPerfect will return to the editing screen, and the word "Math" will appear in the status line to remind you that the Math feature is turned on.

Step 4: Insert the Math Operator

You must insert the math operator + below the numbers to tell WordPerfect to compute their total. Move the cursor to the end of the last line in the table:

Press   **Down Arrow** (5 times)
Press   **End**

Now, insert a label and the operator to compute the total:

Press   **Enter**
Press   **Tab**
Type   **Total**
Press   **Tab**
Type   **+**

Note that the Tab key acts like the Tab Align command (Ctrl-F6) when the Math feature is turned on. This ensures that the total will line up with the numbers above.

Step 5: Select the Calculate Option

Execute the Math/Columns command and select the Calculate option to actually compute the total:

Press   **Alt-F7**
Type   **a**

The total will be computed and inserted before the plus sign. You can now delete the operator:

Press   **Backspace**

Your screen should look like Figure 19.

Figure 19 The Computed Total

```
          1 to 3 persons      $31.00
          4 to 6 persons      $29.25
          7 to 9 persons      $28.50

     1990 Fishing Records
          Bluegill             3.00 lbs.
          Lake Trout          50.00 lbs.
          Large Mouth Bass    20.25 lbs.
          Northern Pike       42.33 lbs.
          Sunfish              2.20 lbs.
          Walleye             25.00 lbs.
       Total                 142.78_

     Trips
     This fall we took a trip into the Cherry Lake area for some lake
     trout fishing.  We had our usual quota of rain, but did enjoy two
     beautiful crisp autumn days.  Mornings we awoke to clear, deep blue
     skies with heavy, white steam rising from Cherry Lake.  On shore
     we could look up into the blue sky, but as we paddled into the
     steam we disappeared into white nothingness.  It was a trip we'll
     long remember.
          We extended our camping into winter this year with several
     overnight trips in December.  From our house we have easy access
     to about 15 kilometers of cross-country ski trails that lead to
     Math                                    Doc 1 Pg 2 Ln 4.17" Pos 4.3"
```

Step 6: Turn Off Math

After you have performed the calculation, you should turn off the Math feature.

> Press **Alt-F7**
> Type   **m**

The word "Math" will disappear from the status line, indicating that the Math feature is now off for the text below the table.

Step 7: Delete the Total Line

Computing a total of the weights in the Fishing Records table makes little sense. It was done just to illustrate the use of the Math feature. So delete the Total line to restore the table to the way it was before:

> Press **Home**
> Press **Left Arrow**
> Press **Ctrl-End**
> Press **Delete**

 Use the Help facility to read more about the Math feature.

Lesson 11: Outlining a Document

An outline is an invaluable tool for organizing topics before you type the text of a document. Many word processing programs include outlining facilities to help you plan your documents. WordPerfect's Outline feature is simple and easy to use. Let's illustrate this helpful feature by creating part of the outline of a quick reference guide to WordPerfect.

Step 1: Clear the Screen

Exit and save NEWS.DOC to clear the editing screen:

> Press **F7**
> Type   **y**
> Press **Enter**
> Type   **y**
> Type   **n**

Step 2: Select the Outline Option

Execute the Date/Outline command and then select the Outline option:

> Press **Shift-F5**
> Type   **o**

WordPerfect will display the word "Outline" on the status line to indicate the Outline feature is turned on.

Step 3: Enter the Outline

The default outline style used by WordPerfect can be summarized as follows: I., A., 1., a., (1), (a), 1), and a). In other words, the first level headings are assigned Roman numerals, the second level headings are assigned capital letters, the third level headings are assigned Arabic numerals, and so on. Up to eight heading levels can be used. The first level headings begin at the left margin. You press the Tab key to move in to the next level heading. Headings are automatically numbered or lettered by WordPerfect. Follow these directions to enter part of the outline of our quick reference guide:

Press   **Enter**
Press   **Space Bar**
Type   **`Function Key Commands`**
Press   **Enter**
Press   **Tab**
Press   **Space Bar**
Type   **`F1 Key Commands`**
Press   **Enter**
Press   **Tab** (2 times)
Press   **Space Bar**
Type   **`Cancel (F1)`**
Press   **Enter**
Press   **Tab** (2 times)
Press   **Space Bar**
Type   **`Thesaurus (Alt-F1)`**
Press   **Enter**
Press   **Tab** (2 times)
Press   **Space Bar**
Type   **`Shell (Ctrl-F1)`**
Press   **Enter**
Press   **Tab** (2 times)
Press   **Space Bar**
Type   **`Setup (Shift-F1)`**
Press   **Enter**
Press   **Tab**
Press   **Space Bar**
Type   **`F2 Key Commands`**
Press   **Enter**

Your screen should look like Figure 20. You can edit an outline and add or delete headings. You can press Shift-Tab to move back to a previous heading level after pressing Tab too many times.

Step 4: Turn Off the Outline Feature

When you are finished creating your outline, execute the Date/Outline command and select the Outline option again to turn off the feature:

Press   **Shift-F5**
Type   **o**

WordPerfect will remove the word "Outline" from the status line, indicating that the Outline feature has been turned off.

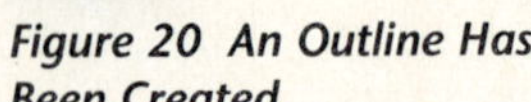

Figure 20 An Outline Has Been Created

Practice

1. Turn on the Outline feature again and enter headings that go below "F2 Key Commands":

   Search Forward (F2)
   Replace (Alt-F2)
   Spell (Ctrl-F2)
   Search Backward (Shift-F2)

2. Turn off the Outline feature. Save the document in a file named OUT-LINE.DOC in the LESSONS subdirectory.

Lesson 12: Generating a Table of Contents

Many long documents, such as reports and books, require a table of contents. The purpose of a table of contents is to list the chapter titles and other headings along with their page numbers. WordPerfect, like many advanced word processing packages, can automatically generate a table of contents. All you have to do is mark the headings to be included in the table of contents, define a numbering style for the table, and tell WordPerfect to generate the table. The headings will be copied from the existing text and the correct page numbers will be inserted by the program. Although it is rather short, let's generate a table of contents for the document NEWS.DOC.

Step 1: Retrieve NEWS.DOC

Clear the editing screen and retrieve the document NEWS.DOC:

Press	**F7**
Type	**n**
Type	**n**
Press	**Shift-F10**
Type	**c:\lessons\news.doc**
Press	**Enter**

Step 2: Mark the Heading as a Block

Each title or heading from the document to be included in the table of contents must be marked as a block and then flagged as a table entry. Follow these steps to mark the "New Outfitting Post" heading as a block:

Press	**Down Arrow** (8 times)
Press	**Alt-F4**
Press	**End**

Step 3: Select the ToC Option

Now, flag the marked block as a table of contents entry by executing the Mark Text command and selecting the ToC option:

Press	**Alt-F5**
Type	**c**

WordPerfect will display the prompt

```
ToC Level:
```

Up to five levels of headings can be created in the table of contents. In this simple document, all of the table of contents entries will be at the first level.

Type	**1**

Step 4: Mark the Remaining Headings

Repeat the two previous steps for the remaining headings in the document. First, mark each heading as a block. Then execute the Mark Text command, select the ToC option, and type 1 as the level.

Step 5: Insert a New Page for the Table

The table of contents will come before the text of the document. So, move the cursor to the beginning of the document, insert a new page, and type a title for the table:

Press	**Home** (2 times)
Press	**Up Arrow**
Press	**Ctrl-Enter**
Press	**Up Arrow**
Type	**Paddle and Portage Newsletter**
Press	**Enter**
Type	**Table of Contents**
Press	**Enter** (2 times)

Step 6: Define the Table

After the headings have been marked and a page has been inserted for the table of contents, you must define a numbering style. Follow these directions to execute the Mark Text command and specify the default settings for defining the table of contents:

Press	**Alt-F5**
Type	**d**

Figure 21 The Generated Table of Contents

```
Paddle and Portage Newsletter
Table of Contents


New Outfitting Post. . . . . . . . . . . . . . . . . . . . . . . .   2

Sport Shows. . . . . . . . . . . . . . . . . . . . . . . . . . .   2

New Regulations. . . . . . . . . . . . . . . . . . . . . . . .   2

Equipment Improvements . . . . . . . . . . . . . . . . . .   2

Trail Food Improvements. . . . . . . . . . . . . . . . . .   2

Current Outfitting Rates . . . . . . . . . . . . . . . . . .   3

1990 Fishing Records . . . . . . . . . . . . . . . . . . . .   3

Trips. . . . . . . . . . . . . . . . . . . . . . . . . . . . . . .   3

A Final Note. . . . . . . . . . . . . . . . . . . . . . . . . .   3


=====================================================================
               Paddle and Portage Canoe Outfitters
C:\LESSONS\NEWS.DOC                              Doc 1 Pg 1 Ln 1" Pos 1"
```

    Type   **c**
    Press **Enter**

When the table is generated, WordPerfect will use one level of headings and present page numbers flush right with dot leaders.

Step 7: Generate the Table

The final step is to tell WordPerfect to generate the table of contents. Follow these directions to execute the Mark Text command and generate the table:

    Press **Alt-F5**
    Type   **g**
    Type   **g**
    Type   **y**
    Press **Home** (2 times)
    Press **Up Arrow**

Your screen should look like Figure 21.

Practice

1. Use the Help facility to read about the Mark Text command and its various options.

2. Move the cursor to the "New Outfitting Post" heading in the document on page 2. Execute the Reveal Codes command and examine the codes that mark the heading as a table of contents entry.

3. You can remove a heading from the table of contents as follows. Delete the code [Mark:ToC,1] in front of the heading "New Outfitting Post." Execute the Reveal Codes command again to return to the full editing screen. Move the cursor to the beginning of the document. Repeat Step 7 in this lesson to regenerate the table of contents. The new table of contents will omit the heading "New Outfitting Post."

4. Mark the heading "New Outfitting Post" as a table of contents entry again. Then regenerate the table of contents.

Lesson 13: Generating an Index

An index lists important terms and their page numbers in alphabetical order at the end of a document. Generating an index with WordPerfect is similar to generating a table of contents. As an example, let's create an index containing a few terms for the document NEWS.DOC.

Step 1: Move the Cursor to a Term

If a term to be included in the index is a single word, you can simply move the cursor to the word. If the term is a phrase, it must be marked as a block. Move the cursor to the word "building" in the New Outfitting Post paragraph:

    Press   **F2**
    Type   `building`
    Press   **F2**
    Press   **Left Arrow**

Step 2: Select the Index Option

To flag the word as an index entry, execute the Mark Text command and select the Index option:

    Press   **Alt-F5**
    Type   **i**

WordPerfect will display the prompt

    `Index heading: Building`

At this point, you can enter a more descriptive index entry or simply press the Enter key twice to accept the entry as is and without a subheading:

    Press   **Enter** (2 times)

Step 3: Mark the Remaining Index Entries

To create a comprehensive index, you would have to go through the entire document and mark all the significant terms. For the purpose of this example, however, just mark each of the following terms by moving the cursor to the term and repeating Step 2:

Shows

Regulations

Equipment

Food

Rates

Fishing

Trips

Step 4: Insert a New Page for the Index

The index will come after the text of the document. So, move the cursor to the end of the document, insert a new page, and type a title for the index:

Press	**Home** (2 times)
Press	**Down Arrow**
Press	**Ctrl-Enter**
Type	`Newsletter Index`
Press	**Enter** (2 times)

Step 5: Define the Index

After the entries have been marked and a page has been inserted for the index, you must define a numbering style. Follow these directions to execute the Mark Text command and specify that page numbers are to be flush right with dot leaders:

Press	**Alt-F5**
Type	**d**
Type	**i**
Press	**Enter**
Type	**L**

Step 6: Generate the Index

The final step is to tell WordPerfect to generate the index. Follow these directions to execute the Mark Text command and generate the index:

Press	**Alt-F5**
Type	**g**
Type	**g**
Type	**y**
Press	**Home** (2 times)
Press	**Down Arrow**

Your screen should look like Figure 22.

Practice

1. Mark a few more terms as index entries. Try some phrases instead of single words. Remember that you must mark a phrase as a block before you can mark it as an index entry. Also, try entering a slightly different entry when WordPerfect prompts you for the index heading.

2. Move the cursor to a term you have marked as an index entry. Execute the Reveal Codes command and examine the code that designates a term as an index entry. You can delete the index code to unmark the term as an index entry. Return to the full editing screen.

3. Regenerate the index. Save the document to preserve the changes you have made.

Lesson 14: Adding Graphics

With WordPerfect you can incorporate horizontal and vertical lines, boxes, and pictures in documents. These features can greatly improve the appearance of documents such as newsletters, reports, ads, and tutorials. This lesson will intro-

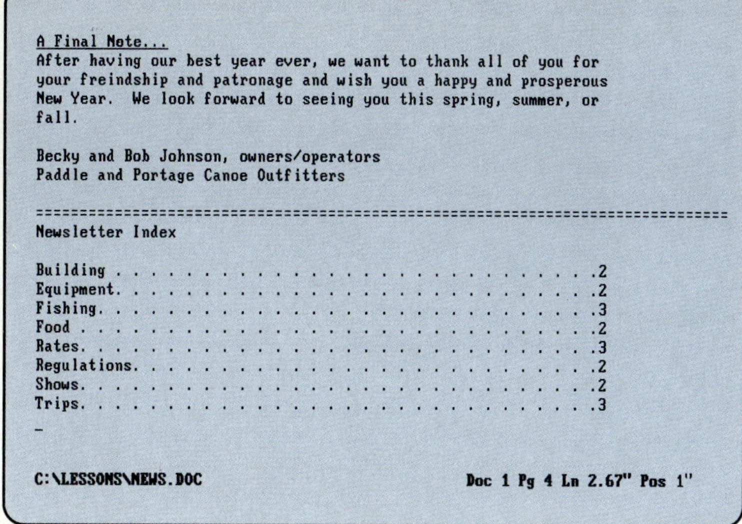

Figure 22 The Generated Index

duce some of WordPerfect's graphics capabilities. In order to use them, however, you will need a computer with a graphics display or a dot-matrix or laser printer.

Step 1: Insert a Horizontal Line

The simplest application of graphics in a document is to add horizontal or vertical lines. Even basic elements such as lines can improve the appearance of a document. Horizontal lines are often used to separate sections of text. Let's insert a horizontal line between the heading and first paragraph of the newsletter. First, move the cursor to the proper position and insert a blank line:

> Press **Home** (2 times)
> Press **Up Arrow**
> Press **Page Down**
> Press **Down Arrow** (7 times)
> Press **Enter**
> Press **Up Arrow**

The cursor is now where you want the horizontal line to go. Next, execute the Graphics command, select the Line option, and then select the Horizontal Line option:

> Press **Alt-F9**
> Type **L**
> Type **h**

WordPerfect will present the Horizontal Line menu, which lets you specify the position, length, width, and gray shading of the line. The default settings are for a thin black line extending from the left margin to the right margin. Accept these settings and return to the editing screen:

> Press **Enter**

The line will be inserted, but you can see it only if you print the document or use the View Document feature.

> Press **Shift-F7**
> Type **v**

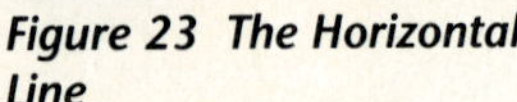

Figure 23 The Horizontal Line

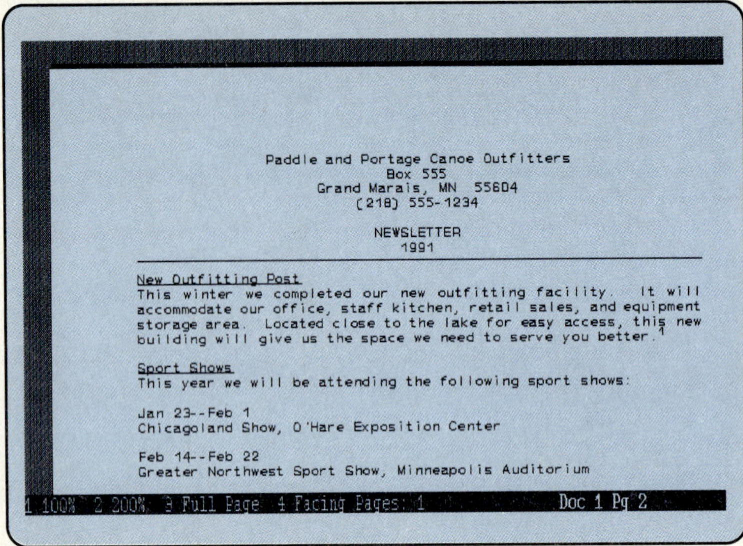

Your screen should look like Figure 23. When you are finished examining your work, return to the editing screen.

Press   **F7**

Step 2: Insert a Vertical Line

Vertical lines are often used to separate columns of text. Let's insert a vertical line between the columns of the Current Outfitting Rates table. Move the cursor between the columns in the first line of the table:

Press   **F2**
Type   **Number In Party**
Press   **F2**

Look in the status line. The cursor is 3.5 inches from the left edge of the paper. The next column begins 4 inches from the left edge of the paper. So, 3.75 inches from the left edge would be a good place to put the vertical line. Since the table is only four lines long and six lines equals an inch, the line should be about 0.67 inches long. Execute the Graphics command, select the Line option, and then select the Vertical Line option:

Press   **Alt-F9**
Type   **L**
Type   **v**

WordPerfect will present the Vertical Line menu on the screen. Follow these directions to specify a vertical line 0.67 inches long positioned 3.75 inches from the left edge of the paper:

Type   **h**
Type   **s**
Type   **3.75**
Press   **Enter**
Type   **v**

Current Outfitting Rates
　　　　　Number In Party　　|　Rate Per Person Per Day
　　　　　1 to 3 persons　　　|　$31.00
　　　　　4 to 6 persons　　　|　$29.25
　　　　　7 to 9 persons　　　|　$28.50

1990 Fishing Records
　　Bluegill　　　　　　3.00 lbs.
　　Lake Trout　　　　 50.00 lbs.
　　Large Mouth Bass　 20.25 lbs.
　　Northern Pike　　　42.33 lbs.
　　Sunfish　　　　　　 2.20 lbs.
　　Walleye　　　　　　25.00 lbs.

Trips
This fall we took a trip into the Cherry Lake area for some lake
trout fishing. We had our usual quota of rain, but did enjoy two
beautiful crisp autumn days. Mornings we awoke to clear, deep blue
skies with heavy, white steam rising from Cherry Lake. On shore
we could look up into the blue sky, but as we paddled into the
steam we disappeared into white nothingness. It was a trip we'll
long remember.
　　We extended our camping into winter this year with several
overnight trips in December. From our house we have easy access
to about 15 kilometers of cross-country ski trails that lead to
Boundary Waters Canoe Area campsites. After setting up a base
camp, we would typically venture out for exploring and ice fishing.
Nothing like twenty below temperatures to get you moving in the
morning!

1 100% 2 200% 3 Full Page 4 Facing Pages: 1　　　　　　Doc 1 Pg 3

Type　　**s**
Press　　**Enter**
Type　　**L**
Type　　**0.67**
Press　　**Enter** (2 times)

To see the vertical line you have created, use the View Document feature:

Press　　**Shift-F7**
Type　　**v**

Your screen should look like Figure 24. When you are finished examining your work, return to the editing screen:

Press　　**F7**

Step 3: Insert a Box Around Text

Text is often enclosed in a box to draw the reader's eye. As an example, let's enclose the letterhead of the newsletter in a box. First, move the cursor to the first line of the letterhead and insert a blank line:

Press　　**Home** (2 times)
Press　　**Up Arrow**
Press　　**Page Down**
Press　　**Enter**

Insert another blank line after the letterhead and move back up to the top of the page:

Press　　**Down Arrow** (4 times)
Press　　**Enter**
Press　　**Grey Minus**

Execute the Graphics command, select the Text Box option, and then select the Options option:

    Press   **Alt-F9**
    Type   **b**
    Type   **o**

WordPerfect will display a menu of options for designing a text box. By default, a text box has no sides. Follow these directions to add thick lines to the sides of the box:

    Type   **b**
    Type   **t**
    Type   **t**
    Press   **F7** (2 times)

Execute the Graphics command again, select the Text Box option, and then select the Create option:

    Press   **Alt-F9**
    Type   **b**
    Type   **c**

WordPerfect will display the Text Box Definition menu. Specify the type, position, and size of the box as follows:

    Type   **t**
    Type   **a**
    Type   **h**
    Type   **s**
    Type   **2.25**
    Press   **Enter**
    Type   **s**
    Type   **b**
    Type   **4**
    Press   **Enter**
    Type   **1**
    Press   **Enter**
    Type   **w**
    Type   **n**
    Press   **F7**

WordPerfect will return to the editing screen, but you will not see the box. You must print the document or use the View Document feature to see the box you have created:

    Press   **Shift-F7**
    Type   **v**

Figure 25 shows the result. Note that the inside of the box is lightly shaded, due to the default Gray Shading setting of 10%. When you are finished examining your work, return to the editing screen:

    Press   **F7**

Step 4: Insert a Picture

You cannot create pictures with WordPerfect, but you can import images created with many painting, drawing, and graphing packages. In fact, WordPerfect comes with a number of sample graphics files on the diskette labeled Graphics. These

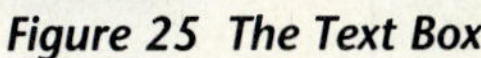

Figure 25 The Text Box

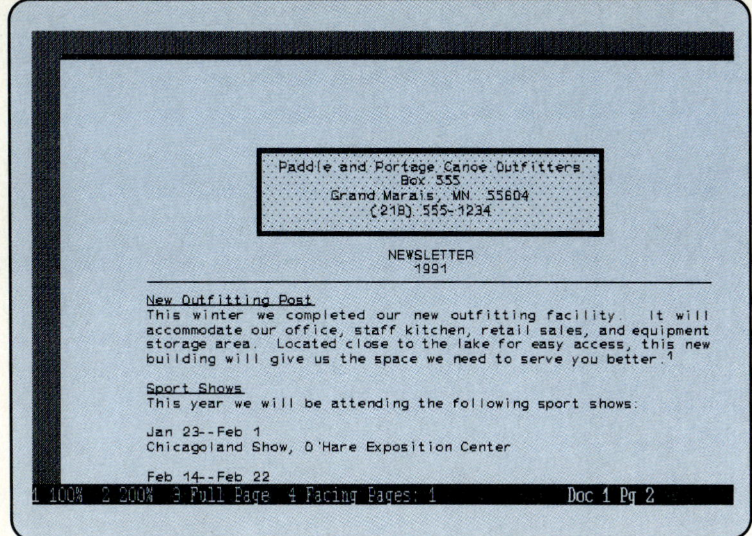

files are identified by the extension WPG, which stands for WordPerfect Graphics format. This lesson assumes that you have at least one of these WPG files on your hard disk in the WP50 subdirectory. As an example, let's insert a picture on a new page before the index. The graphics file we will use is USAMAP.WPG, which contains a line drawing map of the United States. If you like, you can substitute another WPG file or a picture file from some other program, such as PC Paintbrush, Microsoft Windows Paint, or Lotus 1-2-3. Use the List Files command to examine your disk to find the name of a graphics file if you are not going to use USAMAP.WPG in the WP50 subdirectory.

Move the cursor to the end of the page before the index and insert a new page:

Press   **Home** (2 times)
Press   **End**
Press   **Page Up**
Press   **Ctrl-Home**
Press   **Down Arrow**
Press   **Ctrl-Enter**

Next, execute the Graphics command, select the Figure option, and then select the Create option:

Press   **Alt-F9**
Type   **f**
Type   **c**

WordPerfect will display the Figure Definition screen. All of the default settings are fine for our example, but you must specify the name of the graphics file.

Type   **f**
Type   **usamap.wpg**
Press   **Enter**
Press   **F7**

If you do not have USAMAP.WPG in your WP50 subdirectory, type the path and name of a graphics file you do have. When WordPerfect returns to the editing

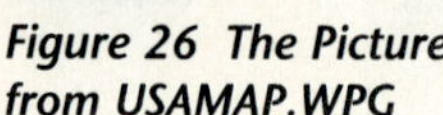

Figure 26 The Picture from USAMAP.WPG

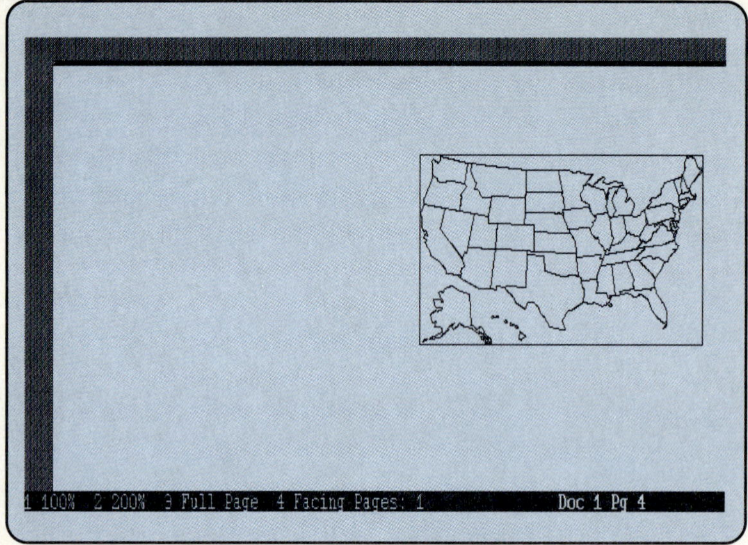

screen, you will not see the picture. You must print the document or use the View Document feature to see the picture you have inserted.

> Press   **Shift-F7**
> Type   **v**

Your screen should look like Figure 26. When you are finished examining your work, return to the editing screen:

> Press   **F7**

WordPerfect has many other options for inserting graphics into your documents. You can resize pictures, specify their exact position on the page, and wrap text around them. You can also automatically number figures and create captions for them.

Practice

1. Insert a horizontal line in the newsletter after the line "Becky and Bob Johnson."

2. Insert a vertical line in the newsletter separating the columns of the Fishing Records table.

3. Use the List Files command to see the names of any WPG files you may have in your WP50 subdirectory. Choose a name and insert this picture file into the newsletter. Print the document or examine it with the View Document feature.

4. Use the Reveal Codes command to examine the document. Graphic elements such as lines, boxes, and pictures can be removed by deleting their codes. Delete the code for the picture you just inserted and examine the newsletter with the View Document feature.

Lesson 15: Using Macros

A **macro** is a sequence of keystrokes that can be recorded, stored, and replayed. The keystrokes may include function keys, menu selections, and ordinary text. Macros are handy for automating frequent actions that require many keystrokes. For instance, suppose you must often type the phrase "Paddle and Portage Canoe

Outfitters" in a document. WordPerfect lets you assign this entire phrase to an abbreviated command, such as Alt-P. Once you define the macro, you can simply press Alt-P instead of typing the phrase. Instead of having to type 35 characters, you need only press two keys at the same time. The phrase will be automatically inserted at the current cursor location. You can use the macro as often as you like. As an example, let's create such a macro.

Step 1: Move the Cursor

When you create a macro, the keys you press will be executed. So, you must first move the cursor to the place where you want to perform the action the first time. In this case, you can move the cursor to the end of the document:

> Press   **Home** (2 times)
> Press   **Down Arrow**

Step 2: Name the Macro

Before you can use a macro, you must name it and then record it. Execute the Macro Define command:

> Press   **Ctrl-F10**

WordPerfect will display the prompt:

```
Define Macro:
```

This is where you choose a name for the macro. You can enter a name up to eight characters long, press Enter to have WordPerfect choose a name for you, or hold down the Alternate key and type any letter from A to Z. The last method is the easiest to use, but you get only a single letter with which to name your macro. Name your macro Alt-P, for Paddle and Portage:

> Press   **Alt-P**

Step 3: Describe the Macro

WordPerfect will display the prompt

```
Description:
```

Now you can enter an optional explanation of the function of your macro. A description is helpful for complex macros, but our simple example hardly requires a comment. Leave the description blank:

> Press   **Enter**

Step 4: Record the Macro

The macro recorder will be turned on and WordPerfect will display a blinking "Macro Def" message on the status line. Now you press the keys that will make up the macro—the keystrokes that will be activated when you press Alt-P later. To specify our simple macro, type the phrase and then execute the Macro Define command again:

> Type   **`Paddle and Portage Canoe Outfitters`**
> Press   **Ctrl-F10**

Step 5: Use the Macro

The macro can now be used anywhere in the document. To see how it works, move down a line and execute the macro:

　　Press **Enter**
　　Press **Alt-P**

The phrase "Paddle and Portage Canoe Outfitters" will be inserted at the current cursor location. Try it again:

　　Press **Enter**
　　Press **Alt-P**

This simple macro merely inserts text, but it can save you a lot of time if you must type the same phrase over and over again. Remember that macros can record any series of keys, including commands and menu selections. They can be a powerful tool for repeating complex sequences of commands.

Practice

1. Create a macro named Alt-N to type your name. Try the macro a number of times.

2. Create a macro named Alt-B to move the cursor to the beginning of the document and then execute the List Files command on the current directory. Exit the List Files menu, move the cursor to the end of the document, and try the macro you have created.

Lesson 16: Creating Form Letters

WordPerfect's Merge feature allows you to print form letters or other personalized text by combining a document with a data file. This feature, sometimes called **mail-merge,** is very useful to businesses and organizations that send letters or bills to various individuals. As an example, let's modify the document HOLMES.DOC, which you created in the previous chapter, so that it can be used to print personalized form letters to a number of different customers.

Step 1: Create the Address File

Form letters are generated by combining names and addresses from a data file with a generic letter. The letter contains codes that indicate where the names and addresses are to go. The data file is sometimes called the **secondary merge file** or **address file.** Let's create the address file first. Execute the Exit command and save the current file to clear the screen:

　　Press　**F7**
　　Type　　**y**
　　Press　**Enter**
　　Type　　**y**
　　Type　　**n**

Suppose form letters are to be sent to four customers. The address file will consist of one record for each customer. Each record consists of five fields: the name, street address, city, state, and ZIP code. Each field is typed on its own line and is terminated by pressing F9 to insert a Merge R code. A record is terminated by pressing Shift-F9 and then selecting the Merge E code option. Follow these directions to enter the four customer records:

Type	`Oscar Griffith`
Press	**F9**
Type	`805 Florida`
Press	**F9**
Type	`Urbana`
Press	**F9**
Type	`IL`
Press	**F9**
Type	`61801`
Press	**F9**
Press	**Shift-F9**
Type	`e`
Type	`George Carver`
Press	**F9**
Type	`906 Busey`
Press	**F9**
Type	`Brainerd`
Press	**F9**
Type	`MN`
Press	**F9**
Type	`56401`
Press	**F9**
Press	**Shift-F9**
Type	`e`
Type	`David Banks`
Press	**F9**
Type	`604 Armory`
Press	**F9**
Type	`Green Bay`
Press	**F9**
Type	`WI`
Press	**F9**
Type	`54305`
Press	**F9**
Press	**Shift-F9**
Type	`e`
Type	`Susan Young`
Press	**F9**
Type	`1104 Grand`
Press	**F9**
Type	`Anchorage`
Press	**F9**
Type	`AK`
Press	**F9**
Type	`99502`
Press	**F9**
Press	**Shift-F9**
Type	`e`

At this point, your screen should look like Figure 27. Save the document in the LESSONS subdirectory in a file named CUSTOMER:

Press   **F10**
Type   `c:\lessons\customer`
Press   **Enter**

Step 2: Create the Primary File

The **primary file** is the text of the form letter containing special merge codes. In this case, you can simply modify the existing document HOLMES.DOC to create the primary file. Clear the screen and retrieve HOLMES.DOC:

Press   **F7**
Type   **n**
Type   **n**
Press   **Shift-F10**
Type   `c:\lessons\holmes.doc`
Press   **Enter**

Move the cursor to the line that contains "Mr. Richard Holmes" and delete to the end of the line:

Press   **Down Arrow** (7 times)
Press   **Ctrl-End**

Instead of an explicit name, you will insert the merge code ^F1^. This code stands for the first field of the data file, which contains the customer's name. Follow these directions to execute the Merge Codes command, select the ^F merge code, and then enter the field number.

Press   **Shift-F9**
Type   **f**
Type   **1**
Press   **Enter**

When the letter is merged with the address file, the ^F1^ codes will be replaced with customer names. Now, follow these directions to delete the remaining address items and replace them with the appropriate merge codes:

Press   **Home**
Press   **Left Arrow**
Press   **Down Arrow**
Press   **Ctrl-End**
Press   **Shift-F9**
Type   **f**
Type   **2**
Press   **Enter**
Press   **Home**
Press   **Left Arrow**
Press   **Down Arrow**
Press   **Ctrl-End**
Press   **Shift-F9**
Type   **f**
Type   **3**
Press   **Enter**
Type   **,**

Figure 27 The Address File

```
^E
=================================================
George Carver^R
906 Busey^R
Brainerd^R
MN^R
56401^R
^E
=================================================
David Banks^R
604 Armory^R
Green Bay^R
WI^R
54305^R
^E
=================================================
Susan Young^R
1104 Grand^R
Anchorage^R
AK^R
99502^R
^E
=================================================
_
                                    Doc 1 Pg 5 Ln 1" Pos 1"
```

Press	**Space Bar**
Press	**Shift-F9**
Type	**f**
Type	**4**
Press	**Enter**
Press	**Space Bar** (2 times)
Press	**Shift-F9**
Type	**f**
Type	**5**
Press	**Enter**
Press	**Home**
Press	**Left Arrow**
Press	**Down Arrow** (2 times)
Press	**Right Arrow** (5 times)
Press	**Ctrl-End**
Press	**Shift-F9**
Type	**f**
Type	**1**
Press	**Enter**
Type	**:**

When you are finished, your screen should look like Figure 28. Save the document in the LESSONS subdirectory and name the file LETTER.DOC:

Press	**F10**
Type	`c:\lessons\letter.doc`
Press	**Enter**

Step 3: Merge the Primary File and Address File

The address file and primary file are now complete. When they are merged, WordPerfect will substitute items from the address file for the ^F1^ through ^F5^ merge codes in the letter. A new document will be created containing four separate letters, each one addressed to a different customer. Clear the screen, execute

Figure 28 The Primary File

```
                              Paddle and Portage Canoe Outfitters
                                            Box 555
                                   Grand Marais, MN  55604
                                      (218) 555-1234

                                         January 2, 1990

^F1^
^F2^
^F3^, ^F4^  ^F5^

Dear ^F1^:_

Here is our sport show schedule for 1991.  We hope to see you soon!

Jan 23--Feb 1
Chicagoland Show, O'Hare Exposition Center

Feb 14--Feb 22
Greater Northwest Sport Show, Minneapolis Auditorium

Mar 13--Mar 22
Milwaukee Sentinel Sport Show, MECCA Building

C:\LESSONS\HOLMES.DOC                      Doc 1 Pg 1 Ln 2.83" Pos 2"
```

the Merge/Sort command, select the Merge option, enter the names of the primary and secondary merge files, and move to the beginning of the document:

Press   **F7**
Type   **n**
Type   **n**
Press   **Ctrl-F9**
Type   **m**
Type   **c:\lessons\letter.doc**
Press   **Enter**
Type   **c:\lessons\customer**
Press   **Enter**
Press   **Home** (2 times)
Press   **Up Arrow**

Your screen should look like Figure 29. Examine the other three letters:

Press   **Page Down**
Press   **Page Down**
Press   **Page Down**

You could now save the new document or print it to produce the four separate letters.

Practice   1. Clear the screen without saving the document containing the four form letters. Retrieve the CUSTOMER file and add another record:

Richard Holmes
444 Adams Street
Green Bay
WI
54301

Save the updated CUSTOMER file and clear the screen. Note that you can add any number of records to the address file.

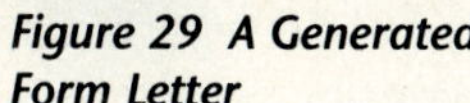

Figure 29 A Generated Form Letter

```
                              Paddle and Portage Canoe Outfitters
_                                                       Box 555
                                           Grand Marais, MN  55604
                                                 (218) 555-1234

                                            January 2, 1990

Oscar Griffith
805 Florida
Urbana, IL  61801

Dear Oscar Griffith:

Here is our sport show schedule for 1991.  We hope to see you soon!

Jan 23--Feb 1
Chicagoland Show, O'Hare Exposition Center

Feb 14--Feb 22
Greater Northwest Sport Show, Minneapolis Auditorium

Mar 13--Mar 22
Milwaukee Sentinel Sport Show, MECCA Building

                                          Doc 1 Pg 1 Ln 1" Pos 1"
```

2. Merge LETTER.DOC with the new CUSTOMER file to create five form letters.
3. Print the full document to output the five form letters.

Lesson 17: Using Styles

A **style** is a collection of formatting codes and possibly text that can be created, saved, and inserted into documents to automate formatting and provide a consistent appearance to documents. Styles are often used for book chapters, newsletters, and other long documents whose format settings are used over and over again. For example, three styles might be used for a book. One style could include the margin and tab stop settings and be inserted at the beginning of each chapter. Another style could contain formatting codes for the chapter headings. A third style could include formatting codes for the multiple choice questions that appear at the end of each chapter. As an example, let's create a style that sets margins, justification, and tab stops.

Step 1: Clear the Screen

Clear your current editing screen:

Press   **F7**
Type   **n**
Type   **n**

Step 2: Name the Style

Execute the Style command, select the Create option, select the Name option, and then enter a name for the style:

Press   **Alt-F8**
Type   **c**
Type   **n**
Type   **Settings**
Press   **Enter**

Step 3: Select the Style Type

Two types of styles are available, paired and open. A **paired style** type has a beginning and ending code. A style to underline text, for example, would be a paired style because a code is required before and after the underlined text. An **open style** has just a beginning code and is often used to set formats for an entire document. A style to set margins, justification, and tab stops would be an open style. Select Open as the type of the style:

> Type **t**
> Type **o**

Step 4: Describe the Style

The style description is text that explains the purpose of the style. This description appears in the Styles menu to help you remember what the style does. Enter a description for the style:

> Type **d**
> Type `Margins, justification, and tab stop settings`
> Press **Enter**

Step 5: Enter the Codes

A style can contain WordPerfect codes and text. To include codes in a style, you select the Codes option and then execute the commands to create those codes. Follow these directions to enter the codes to set margins, justification, and tab stops:

> Type   **c**
> Press **Shift-F8**
> Type   **L**
> Type   **m**
> Type   **1.25**
> Press **Enter**
> Type   **1.25**
> Press **Enter**
> Type   **j**
> Type   **n**
> Type   **t**
> Press **Home** (2 times)
> Press **Left Arrow**
> Press **Ctrl-End**
> Type   **L**
> Type   **0,1**
> Press **Enter**
> Press **F7** (4 times)

WordPerfect will return to the Styles menu, shown in Figure 30. The Settings style that you have created will set the left and right margins to 1.25 inches, turn off justification, and set tab stops at 1-inch intervals beginning at the left edge of the page.

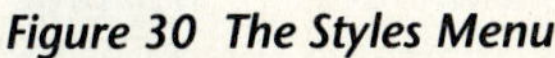

Figure 30 The Styles Menu

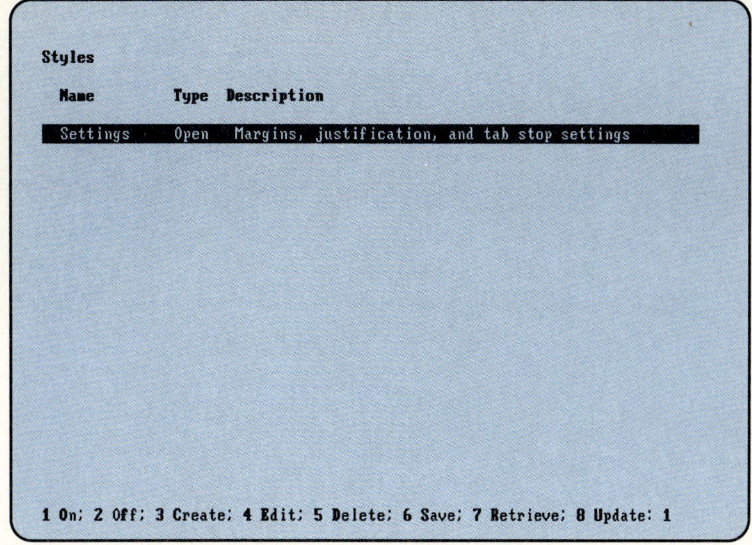

Step 6: Save the Style

By default, a style is saved with the document in which it was created. You can, however, save the styles you create separately and use them in any document. Select the Save option and then enter a file name to hold your styles:

> Type　**s**
> Type　**c:\lessons\styles**
> Press　**Enter**

The style Settings is now saved in a file named STYLES in the LESSONS subdirectory. Return to the editing screen:

> Press　**F7**

Step 7: Use the Style

After you have created and saved a style, you can use it in any document. Move the cursor to the place where the style is to be inserted, execute the Style command, and retrieve the style file:

> Press　**Home** (2 times)
> Press　**Up Arrow**
> Press　**Alt-F8**
> Type　**r**
> Type　**c:\lessons\styles**
> Press　**Enter**
> Type　**y**

WordPerfect will present the Styles menu. In this case, only one style is listed. You can, however, create and save a number of different styles. Then you would use Up Arrow or Down Arrow to highlight the style you want to use. When the style is highlighted, select the On option:

> Type　**o**

The Settings style is now inserted at the beginning of the current document. You don't have to set the margins, justification, and tab stops individually. Any time you need these particular format settings, you can simply retrieve the STYLES file and select the Settings style.

Practice

1. Execute the Reveal Codes command to confirm that the Settings style has indeed been inserted. When you are finished, return to the full editing screen.
2. Execute the Format command and select the Line option to confirm that the margins, justification, and tab stops have indeed been set. When you are finished, return to the editing screen.

Lesson 18: Customizing WordPerfect

When you start WordPerfect, you can begin typing immediately. The program has already been set up for speed and efficiency. The default settings in effect are adequate for most users. You can, however, tailor WordPerfect to your specific needs by using the Setup command to change various settings. These changes will then remain in effect each time you start WordPerfect. Let's examine the settings you can change with the Setup command.

Step 1: Execute the Setup Command

To examine or change various WordPerfect options, execute the Setup command:

    Press **Shift-F1**

The program will display the Setup menu, shown in Figure 31.

Figure 31 The Setup Menu

```
Setup

     1 - Backup

     2 - Cursor Speed              30 cps

     3 - Display

     4 - Fast Save (unformatted)   No

     5 - Initial Settings

     6 - Keyboard Layout

     7 - Location of Auxiliary Files

     8 - Units of Measure




 Selection: 0
```

Step 2: Examine the Backup Option

Select the Backup option:

> Type   **b**

Two automatic Backup options will be described on the screen. The Timed Document Backup option will automatically save your document to the disk without you having to execute the Save command. The default interval for Timed Document Backup is every 30 minutes. The Original Document Backup option will save the original document in a file with the extension BK! whenever you replace it during a Save or Exit command. Both of these Backup options can help safeguard against power failures and mistakes, but they are no substitute for saving your documents frequently as you edit them. Return to the Setup menu:

> Press   **F1**

Step 3: Examine the Cursor Speed Option

Most keys repeat when you hold them down for more than a second. The Cursor Speed option lets you change the rate at which a key repeats when it is held down. The speed is given in characters per second (cps). Note that many computers can repeat keys no faster than ten times per second, even if the Cursor Speed option is set higher.

Step 4: Examine the Display Option

Select the Display option:

> Type   **d**

A menu of display options will appear on the screen. These options let you change the way in which WordPerfect displays text and graphics on the screen. Return to the Setup menu:

> Press   **F1**

Step 5: Examine the Fast Save Option

When the Fast Save option is turned on, WordPerfect saves a document to the disk without formatting it. Although this option saves time, it prevents you from printing a document from the disk unless that document is currently on your editing screen.

Step 6: Examine the Initial Settings Option

Select the Initial Settings option:

> Type   **i**

The Initial Settings menu allows you to change a number of default settings to be in effect each time you start WordPerfect. For example, you can specify whether WordPerfect will beep when error messages are displayed and whether the program will prompt you for a document summary whenever you save or exit a document. Return to the Setup menu:

> Press   **F1**

Step 7: Examine the Keyboard Layout Option

Select the Keyboard Layout option:

> Type   **k**

This option lets you change the commands and even the characters assigned to keys. For example, you can create a keyboard layout that makes the F1 key execute the Help command instead of the Cancel command. You can use the Keyboard Layout feature to make WordPerfect simulate some other word processing program by executing its commands. You can even reassign the letter keys if you want to try an alternate keyboard arrangement, such as the Dvorak system. Unlike the more popular QWERTY arrangement, the Dvorak keyboard layout places the most frequently used letters in the center for use by the strongest fingers to increase speed and comfort, while reducing errors. Return to the Setup menu:

> Press   **F1**

Step 8: Examine the Location of Auxiliary Files Option

Select the Location of Auxiliary Files option:

> Type   **L**

Auxiliary files are files that WordPerfect needs for features such as the spelling checker, thesaurus, macros, printer, and so on. The Location of Auxiliary Files option lets you specify the disk drives and subdirectories of these various files. Return to the Setup menu:

> Press   **F1**

Step 9: Examine the Units of Measure Option

Select the Units of Measure option:

> Type   **u**

The Units of Measure option lets you specify the units for the presentation of cursor position, margins, tab stops, and other measurements. The default unit of measure is inches, but WordPerfect can use centimeters, points, or line and column numbers instead. Return to the Setup menu:

> Press   **F1**

Step 10: Exit the Program

This concludes the WordPerfect lessons. Exit the program and return to DOS:

> Press   **F7** (2 times)
> Type   **n**
> Type   **y**

Practice   Use the Help facility to read more about the various Setup command options.

Summary

- *Using the Print menu.* Press Shift-F7 to activate the Print menu and then select Full Document, Page, Document on Disk, Control Printer, Type Through, View Document, Initialize Printer, Select Printer, Binding, Number of Copies, Graphics Quality, or Text Quality.

- *Hyphenating words.* Press Shift-F8 to activate the Format menu, select Line, select Hyphenation, and then select Manual or Automatic.

- *Avoiding orphans and widows.* Press Shift-F8 to activate the Format menu, select Line, and then select Widow/Orphan Protection.

- *Avoiding splitting paragraphs between pages.* Press Shift-F8 to activate the Format menu, select Other, and then select Conditional End of Page.

- *Using the Font menu.* Press Ctrl-F8 to activate the Font menu and then select Size, Appearance, Normal, Base Font, or Print Color.

- *Adding headers and footers.* Press Shift-F8 to activate the Format menu, select Page, and then select Header or Footer.

- *Creating text columns.* Press Alt-F7 to activate the Math/Columns menu, select Column Definition, specify the column settings, select Column On/Off, and type the text. Press Ctrl-Home followed by an arrow key to move to another column.

- *Adding footnotes and endnotes.* Press Ctrl-F7 to activate the Footnote menu, select Footnote or Endnote, select Create, and type the note.

- *Sorting text.* Mark the lines to be sorted as a block, press Ctrl-F9 to activate the Sort menu, specify the keys, specify the sort order, and select Perform Action.

- *Performing math.* Press Alt-F7 to activate the Math/Columns menu, select Math Definition, specify the settings, select Math On, insert the operator, press Alt-F7 again, select Calculate.

- *Outlining a document.* Press Shift-F5 to activate the Date/Outline menu, select, Outline, and enter the headings. Press Tab to move in to the next level heading.

- *Generating a table of contents.* Mark each heading as a block, press Alt-F5 to activate the Mark Text menu, select the ToC option, and enter the heading level. Press Alt-F5 again, select Define, and select Table of Contents. Press Alt-F5 again, select Generate, and then select Generate Tables.

- *Generating an index.* Move the cursor to each word to be in the index, press Alt-F5 to activate the Mark Text menu, and select Index. Press Alt-F5 again, select Define, and select Index. Press Alt-F5 again, select Generate, and then select Generate Tables.

- *Adding graphics.* Press Alt-F9 to activate the Graphics menu, and then select Line, Text Box, or Figure.

- *Using macros.* Press Ctrl-F10 to execute the Macro Define command, name the macro, describe the macro, and record the macro. Use the macro by pressing Alternate along with its key.

- *Creating form letters.* Create the address file, separating fields with Merge R codes and records with Merge E codes. Create the primary file containing merge codes ˆF1ˆ, ˆF2ˆ, ˆF3ˆ, and so on to represent field contents. Press Ctrl-F9 to activate the Merge/Sort menu, select Merge, and enter the names of the primary and address files to generate the form letters.

- *Using styles*. Press Alt-F8 to activate the Style menu, select Create, specify the name, type, description, and codes of the style, and then save the style. Press Alt-F8 again, select Retrieve, enter the file name, highlight the style name, and select On.

- *Customizing WordPerfect*. Press Shift-F1 to activate the Setup menu and then select Backup, Cursor Speed, Display, Fast Save, Initial Settings, Keyboard Layout, Location of Auxiliary Files, or Units of Measure.

Key Terms

As an extra review of this chapter, try defining the following terms.

automatic hyphenation	open style
endnote	orphan
field	paired style
footer	parallel columns
footnote	point
greeking	primary file
header	print queue
hyphenation	record
key	secondary merge file (address file)
macro	sorting
mail-merge	style
manual hyphenation	widow
newspaper-style columns	

Multiple Choice

Choose the best selection to complete each statement.

1. WordPerfect lets you specify several documents to be printed by using a
   - (a) display adapter.
   - (b) function key.
   - (c) print queue.
   - (d) View Document feature.

2. Which feature do you use to see how your document will look when it is printed?
   - (a) Setup
   - (b) Reveal Codes
   - (c) Screen
   - (d) View Document

3. Which feature can make justified text more attractive by reducing large gaps between words?
   - (a) hyphenation
   - (b) indentation
   - (c) mail-merge
   - (d) word wrap

4. What term is used to describe the last line of a paragraph that appears at the top of a page?
   - (a) orphan
   - (b) widow
   - (c) header
   - (d) footer

5. Which feature is handy for keeping titles or headings together with their first paragraphs?

   (a) Merge

   (b) Block

   (c) Mark Text

   (d) Conditional End of Page

6. Which command would you use to change the size of characters?

   (a) Bold

   (b) Macro

   (c) Font

   (d) Screen

7. One or more lines of text printed at the top of every page is called a(n)

   (a) orphan.

   (b) widow.

   (c) header.

   (d) footer.

8. Which type of column continues text from the bottom of one column on the left to the top of the next column on the right on the same page?

   (a) parallel

   (b) newspaper style

   (c) horizontal

   (d) vertical

9. A numbered comment or explanation at the bottom of a page is a(n)

   (a) footnote.

   (b) endnote.

   (c) header.

   (d) footer.

10. Which of the following sequences is an example of descending sort order?

    (a) A to Z

    (b) Z to A

    (c) 0 to 9

    (d) X, Y, Z

11. What is the most common use of the WordPerfect Math feature?

    (a) computing π (pi)

    (b) computing square roots

    (c) adding columns of numbers

    (d) multiplying columns of numbers

12. After the Outline feature is turned on, which key do you press to move in to the next level heading?

    (a) Enter

    (b) Shift

    (c) Space Bar

    (d) Tab

13. After a phrase has been marked as a block, what command do you execute to flag it as a table of contents or index entry?

    (a) Text In/Out

    (b) Merge/Sort

    (c) Macro Define

    (d) Mark Text

14. How do you remove a term from an index?

    (a) Execute the Cancel command.

    (b) Execute Reveal Codes and delete the index code.

    (c) Execute the Macro command and delete the line.

    (d) Execute the Merge R command.

15. Which command do you use to insert lines and boxes into a document?

    (a) Underline

    (b) Graphics

    (c) Date/Outline

    (d) Format

16. Which file name extension identifies the sample graphics files that come with WordPerfect?

    (a) GRA

    (b) DOC

    (c) PIX

    (d) WPG

17. Which key, along with a letter key, is often used to name and execute WordPerfect macros?

    (a) Alternate   (b) Control

    (c) Shift   (d) Tab

18. Which feature allows you to create personalized form letters?

    (a) List Files   (b) Macro

    (c) Merge   (d) Style

19. Which term describes a collection of formatting codes that can be created, saved, and inserted into documents to provide a consistent appearance?

    (a) Format   (b) Macro

    (c) Outline   (d) Style

20. What command would you use to have WordPerfect automatically back up your current document every 30 minutes?

    (a) Date   (b) Replace

    (c) Save   (d) Setup

Fill-In

1. The View Document option of the _______ menu allows you to see on the screen how your document will look when it is printed.

2. WordPerfect offers two types of hyphenation: _______ and _______.

3. To avoid orphans and widows, execute the _______ command, select the Line option, and then select the Widow/Orphan Protection option.

4. The Conditional End of Page feature is a way to keep text from being _______ between pages.

5. The _______ option of the Font menu displays the fonts available with your printer and allows you to change the font you are using.

6. A _______ or _______ is often used to print a title, chapter number, page number, or other identification on every page.

7. Press _______ and then Right Arrow to move the cursor to the right column in a document set up with newspaper-style or parallel columns.

8. An _______ is similar to a footnote, except that comments are collected and placed at the end of the document instead of at the bottom of each page.

9. The _______ command is handy for alphabetizing names or any list of words or phrases.

10. After math columns have been defined and the math feature has been turned on, the math operator _______ is inserted below a column of numbers to tell WordPerfect to compute their total.

11. An _______ is an invaluable tool for organizing topics before you type the text of a document.

12. A table of contents entry is flagged by executing the Mark Text command and selecting the _______ option.

13. Generating an _______ with WordPerfect is similar to generating a table of contents.

14. Text may be enclosed in a box by executing the _______ command and selecting the _______ option.

15. The Figure option of the Graphics menu lets you insert a previously created ________ in your document.

16. A macro is a sequence of ________ that can be recorded, stored, and replayed.

17. The Merge command allows you to combine a primary file, containing text and merge codes, with an address file, containing fields and records, to create ________ letters.

18. An ________ style has just a beginning code and is often used to set formats for an entire document.

19. You can tailor WordPerfect to your specific needs by using the ________ command to change various default settings.

20. You would use the ________ option from the Setup menu to have the cursor position on the status line reported in column and line numbers.

Short Problems

1. Start WordPerfect and retrieve the file MEMO.DOC from the LESSONS subdirectory. Activate the Print menu and change the Text Quality option to Draft. Print the file and compare its quality to previous printouts of the memo. Change the Text Quality option back to High.

2. Clear the screen and retrieve NEWS.DOC from the LESSONS subdirectory. Use the Conditional End of Page feature to ensure that no headings are separated from their paragraphs.

3. Clear the screen. Use the Base Font option of the Font menu to create a document that demonstrates at least five different fonts available with your printer. Print the document to see the results.

4. Clear the screen. Type the following words, pressing **Enter** after each one:

   ```
   couch
   zebra
   donkey
   turtle
   frog
   apple
   gate
   vine
   ball
   uncle
   horse
   whistle
   elephant
   x-ray
   ivy
   reindeer
   kangaroo
   parrot
   lobby
   neighbor
   soda
   melody
   ```

   Use the Sort feature to alphabetize this list of words.

5. Clear the screen. Use the Graphics Line options to create a sheet for playing Tic-Tac-Toe. Print two copies using the Number of Copies option in the Print menu.

6. Clear the screen. Use the Graphics Figure option to import one or two WPG files from the WP50 subdirectory or the WordPerfect Graphics diskette. Examine the pictures with View Document. Activate the Print menu, set Graphics Quality to High, and print the document.

7. Clear the screen. Use the math feature to add up the following column of numbers:

   16.34
   25.00
   127.35
   57.70
   50.00
   75.00
   22.00
   19.97
   906.51
   209.12

8. Create a macro named Alt-D that will move the cursor to the end of the document and execute the Reveal Codes command. Return to the full editing screen, move the cursor to the beginning of the document, and try your new macro.

9. Create a style named Letterhead that will set the left and right margins to 1.5 inches. In addition, have the style insert a centered letterhead containing your name and address, and the current date flush right two lines below the letterhead. Save the style in the file LHEAD in the LESSONS subdirectory. Clear the screen, execute the Style command, retrieve LHEAD from LESSONS, and apply the Letterhead style to your new document.

10. Execute the Setup command, select the Units of Measure option, and change the status line display so that it reports the current cursor position in line and column numbers. Return to the editing screen, move the cursor, and observe the status line. Now, change the setting back to inches.

Long Problems

1. Create a quick reference guide to WordPerfect that includes all of the commands covered in this chapter and the previous two chapters.

2. Use WordPerfect's Outline feature to organize the topics of a term paper, report, speech, or presentation you must do for school or work.

3. Use WordPerfect to type a term paper or report, complete with footnotes or endnotes, for school or work.

4. Use the Line options of the Graphics command to create a calendar page for the month of January.

5. Create an address file containing ten friends' names and addresses. Remember to separate the fields with Merge R codes and the records with Merge E codes. Create a primary file that contains the text and appropriate merge codes of an invitation to your birthday party. Use the Merge feature to generate and print the form letters for all ten friends.

6. Suppose you are moving. Create a form letter informing your friends of your new address. You can use the address file you created in the previous exercise.

7. Select an article from a newspaper or magazine. Reproduce this article in a WordPerfect document with two newspaper-style columns.

8. Create a document that demonstrates how text can wrap around a picture. Import a WPG file from the WP50 subdirectory or WordPerfect Graphics diskette. Examine the picture with View Document. Make up a couple of paragraphs to go with the picture and type the text so that it wraps around the picture. Print the document when you are finished.

9. Suppose you want to sell your stereo, bike, car, or some other possession. Use what you have learned about drawing lines and text boxes and changing character sizes to create an attractive and eye-catching flyer to put up on bulletin boards.

10. Use what you have learned about drawing boxes and lines to create a chart showing your family tree going back at least two generations.

SELECTING A SYSTEM

More and more people are buying microcomputers for business and home use. Most companies already have at least one microcomputer, and they are continually acquiring more. Schools at all levels have been purchasing microcomputers for both students and faculty. It's been estimated that at least 20% of all U.S. households will ultimately have some type of microcomputer. Just as most of you will eventually purchase stereo systems, video systems, other high-tech home appliances, and automobiles, it's likely that in the near future you may be investing in a computer system, too. Perhaps you won't be buying a computer for your home, but you might still be involved in the process of selecting a system for your school or work. This appendix offers some guidelines that can help both individuals and organizations in their process of computerization.

Computers are complicated equipment. Although their prices have been steadily dropping, computers still represent a substantial investment for most people. With so many different computer models and an overwhelming array of software packages on the market, unless you're wealthy or are already a computer expert, purchasing a system is no trivial task. The choices you make can have profound effects on the quantity and quality of work you will accomplish with your computer. To make good choices, you need to have a plan.

Selecting a computer system is somewhat like selecting a stereo system or automobile. If you buy on irrational impulses, you risk regretting your decision for years to come. If, on the other hand, you follow a well-thought-out, step-by-step selection process, chances are good that you'll end up with an economical labor-saving system. One such approach involves six basic steps:

1. Learn about computers.
2. Define your needs.
3. Select the software.
4. Select the hardware.
5. Purchase the system.
6. Install the system.

A1

Step 1: Learn About Computers

You need not be a computer scientist to effectively select and use computers. Some basic knowledge, however, can help a great deal. The first step in selecting a system is to become familiar with the capabilities and limitations of computers. In other words, you need to know what computers can and cannot do for you. The chapters in this book are designed to provide you with an understanding of the capabilities and limitations of microcomputers.

Of course, this book can by no means cover all relevant microcomputer topics. Although learning more is not absolutely required, the more you do know the better prepared you'll be to take advantage of what computers have to offer. Fortunately, there are many opportunities for you to learn more about computers. Some of the possibilities include books, periodicals, organizations, shows, courses, conferences, and workshops.

Books

An astonishing number of computer books are available in local bookstores, libraries, and computer stores. Some are quite technical, but many others have been written especially for novices. Some of the most common books you'll find are "How to" books that cover specific computer models or software packages. Others teach programming in certain languages or deal with the philosophical and sociological aspects of using computers. You can even buy books that discuss how to select a computer system.

Periodicals

In 1975, only two magazines were devoted solely to microcomputers. Today, hundreds of microcomputer newspapers, newsletters, and magazines are available. Although books can cover topics in great detail, they're usually somewhat out of date by the time they actually hit the shelves. Newspapers, newsletters, and magazines reveal what's happening in the marketplace *now*. They frequently contain reviews and in-depth evaluations of hardware and software products. Periodicals also contain informative articles and columns that answer questions and provide tips from other computer users. They are crammed with ads from manufacturers, retailers, and mail-order outfits. Many owners have at least one subscription to a microcomputer periodical. Some of the more popular publications include *A+*, *BYTE*, *Infoworld*, *Macworld*, and *PC Magazine*.

In addition to traditional periodicals printed on paper, *disk magazines* have been gaining popularity recently. These publications are issued on floppy disks and are aimed at users of particular computer models. They uniquely provide subscribers with tested programs for business, education, entertainment, and home use.

Organizations

Computer users, it seems, are a very sociable lot. At regular intervals, thousands of folks gather in societies, clubs, and user groups to share computer experiences, help solve each others' problems, and trade software. Although most people don't join such organizations until after they purchase a computer system, joining before buying can be advantageous. Many user groups are centered around a particular computer model or type of popular software. Group members can usually offer advice on where to get the best deals. Joining a computer organization may even qualify you for certain group discounts off the retail prices of selected hardware and software products. Once you have your system, a computer organization can put you in contact with people who have the same hardware and software. These colleagues can be an invaluable source of information because it's likely that they've already solved problems you might be having as a beginning user.

Computer organizations offer fellowship, support, general information, and answers to those tricky questions not answered in any manuals. Many groups have been established since the advent of microcomputers in the mid-1970s. For example, more than 850 groups in the United States serve Apple computer users. Some groups have remained local, small, and dedicated to one particular type of computer, like the Champaign-Urbana, Illinois Apple II Users Group with its 40 or so members. Other groups have grown immense and wield a good deal of influence over the microcomputer industry. The Boston Computer Society, for instance, was founded in 1977 by Jonathan Rotenberg when he was thirteen years old. Today, with about 24,000 members, it's perhaps the nation's largest microcomputer users group. The Boston Computer Society has its own magazine, *Computer Update*, sponsors around 100 monthly events, and has approximately 40 special-interest subgroups, each of which publishes its own newsletter.

Shows

Every year, computer shows are held in various cities across the United States. These events may be sponsored by individual entrepreneurs, manufacturers, retail stores, magazine publishers, or other associations that deal with computers. Although many shows specifically target manufacturers and retailers, others are open to the general computer-buying public. They are typically held in large exhibit halls, with booth space rented to hardware manufacturers, software manufacturers, dealers, distributors, retailers, computer clubs, publishers, and any other organizations that want to sell or advertise products. Admission is often charged. Besides exhibiting new products and services, many shows also offer short talks, seminars, and classes for attendees, frequently given by well-known computer personalities. These shows may last several days and attract thousands of people who come from all over the country.

Computer shows can offer the following opportunities:

- *See new products*. Manufacturers often introduce products at computer shows, so it may be an early chance to see what's new in the market. Furthermore, most shows exhibit a wider variety of products than you can usually find in the typical computer store. It's easy to collect all kinds of brochures, product descriptions, advertisements, and other handouts.
- *Try out products*. Many computer show exhibits are specifically designed to let you "test drive" hardware and software products. This may be your only chance to get hands-on experience with an item before you actually buy it.
- *Buy products*. Frequently, computer shows allow exhibitors to sell their products directly to consumers. At some shows, you can buy anything from a single diskette to an entire microcomputer system. Prices are generally less than retail and it's possible to get some good bargains at computer shows, especially as closing time nears.
- *Learn more*. As we mentioned before, many computer shows sponsor lectures and seminars. Subjects may include very specific topics, such as how to use a particular feature of a software package, or more general matters, such as the role of microcomputers in our society.

- *Meet people*. Computer shows offer excellent opportunities to come into contact with other people who have similar interests. You may meet just one person at a booth looking for the same product, or you may discover an entire users group that you want to join. The people you meet can offer advice, answer questions, and share some of their computer experiences with you.
- *Talk to manufacturers*. Since many hardware and software manufacturers send representatives to computer shows, you may get an opportunity to ask questions, get more information, or even complain about a particular product.

Courses

For people who seek a more structured approach to learning about computers, a wide variety of formal courses is offered to both students and the general public. Traditional educational institutions, like high schools, community colleges, and universities, hold classes aimed primarily at those seeking diplomas. Many community colleges and university continuing education and extension services also offer computer courses for non-degree students. Classes range from simple, non-technical introductions for novices to in-depth studies for those pursuing computer careers. Alternative learning centers, such as those affiliated with local churches, libraries, and park districts, often conduct classes taught by computer experts in their spare time. Although such courses may be less academic than those run by traditional educational institutions, they may be more accessible to the general public. Computer stores often teach courses about particular hardware and software products, but these courses may be limited to customers. Several proprietary (for-profit) schools also offer computer-related coursework. Many accredited home study schools as well as colleges and universities have correspondence courses that teach computer subjects by mail. Finally, some private individuals offer computer courses too. Before you enroll in any course, however, be sure to investigate it thoroughly to determine just what is being offered and how much it will cost.

Conferences and Workshops

Many organizations offer conferences and workshops covering particular computer topics. Some of these events are expensive, intensive training sessions aimed specifically at computer professionals. Others are less technical and attract novice computer users. They typically last from several hours to several days, and are held in various cities across the country.

Step 2: Define Your Needs

Once you have a general picture of what microcomputers can do, you can begin to examine how you might use one. It's important to carefully consider exactly what you want to do with a computer before you purchase anything. Of course, you probably can't anticipate every possible use you'll find for your computer once you get it, but you should have some clearly stated, specific reasons for investing in a system. A good approach is to make a list. Write down, in order of importance, all of the uses you expect to have for a computer. At this stage, try not to think too much about costs, but keep your ideas realistic. As a sample, your list might look something like this:

1. *Word Processing*. For term papers, reports, class notes, and letters.
2. *Record Keeping*. For addresses, phone numbers, personal property inventory, bank account numbers, credit cards, and tax-deductible expenses.
3. *Calculating*. For bills, budgets, and income taxes.
4. *Education*. For math review, foreign language study, college entrance test review, and learning about computer programming.
5. *Entertainment*. For fun with computer games and simulations.

This list is probably fairly typical of the uses a student or other individual might have for a computer at home or school. A business, however, might have a more specific list of computer needs, especially if it is computerizing for the first time, or perhaps considering replacing an existing system. A small business, for example, might have the following uses for a microcomputer system:

1. *General Ledger*. To keep track of financial records and produce reports, such as balance sheets and profit and loss statements, that summarize the financial status of the firm.
2. *Accounts Receivable*. To keep track of the money owed to the company and when payments are due.
3. *Accounts Payable*. To keep track of money the company owes to its suppliers.
4. *Payroll*. To calculate each employee's gross pay, withhold taxes, subtract deductions, print paychecks, and maintain necessary payroll records.
5. *Inventory*. To monitor the goods on hand and make sure enough are in stock for production and customer requests.
6. *Mailing List*. To prepare direct mailing of ads and notices.
7. *Word Processing*. To create letters, reports, newsletters, and memos.
8. *Personnel Files*. To hold information for insurance, retirement, and governmental regulations.

Step 3: Select the Software

Now comes perhaps the most difficult step in acquiring a computer system: selecting the software. First of all, from the user's standpoint, software is much more important than hardware. Software is what makes the computer accomplish useful work. Without programs, computer hardware is utterly worthless. It's likely that you'll pay much more for all the software you'll eventually buy than the hardware. If you have a stereo system, this probably doesn't surprise you, since most people have more money invested in records, tapes, or compact discs than they originally paid for the stereo components. Shopping for software is also more difficult than shopping for hardware, because there is so much more software on the market than hardware. Some software companies sell only by mail, so it may be difficult to obtain information about their programs. A thorough evaluation of software requires using it in your own particular situation for a substantial amount of time. This may be difficult, if not impossible, to do by running a program at a single sitting in your local computer store. Finally, because software usually has a smaller profit margin than hardware, computer salespeople may not be as enthusiastic or helpful about selling a program as they would an entire computer system.

All those difficulties aside, it really is possible, even for novices, to make good software selections. First, go back to your list of computer uses. For each item, come up with at least three different software packages. Here you'll need some of those learning resources we talked about previously. Perhaps the best source of possible selections may be people you know from school, work, clubs, user groups, or computer shows. See if you can arrange to try a potential software selection for an extended period of time. Perhaps a friend or relative has a computer and software you can use. If your school has a computer lab, you may be able to use it at times when classes aren't in session. Many school labs have software you can check out and run on a computer at your own pace.

Probably the best source of information comparing various software packages are computer magazines. Most have reviews of new software products; some even devote entire issues to comparing all the major competitors in a particular application. The publications extensively test each package by using it for a predetermined set of activities, and then quantitatively rate how each one does. Often, the reviewers will conclude with one or more "editor's choices," and give their reasons for selecting these packages as the best of the lot. Scanning the magazine stands and going through back issues in the library are excellent ways to find out more about specific application packages.

As you begin to compile your list of potential software selections, make your own evaluations and rank the packages, if possible. As you talk to people and read product reviews, note the following characteristics of good software:

- *Competent*. Capable of performing an important job well.
- *Easy to Learn*. Can be mastered with moderate effort in a reasonable amount of time.
- *Easy to Use*. Intrudes as little as possible between the user and getting the job done.
- *Tolerant*. Gently and sensibly handles errors made by the user.
- *Layered*. Simple and self-evident on the outside for beginners, and progressively more complex and powerful as internal features are mastered.
- *Flexible*. Can be adapted to handle variations in its basic task.
- *Compatible*. Works well with other software by using standard conventions and being able to share files.
- *Well-Documented*. Comes with clearly written, correct instruction and reference manuals designed with both novices and experts in mind.
- *Supported*. Backed by its manufacturer, which conscientiously fixes errors, provides updated versions, and answers users' questions.
- *Reasonably-Priced*. Provides value comparable to its cost.

Once you complete this process, you'll have a list of computer uses ordered according to your priorities, within which will be sublists of potential software packages ranked by preference. You're not ready to buy anything yet, and you haven't singled out the exact packages you'll eventually get, but you have a pretty good idea of the field of contenders.

Step 4: Select the Hardware

By seriously considering software first, the selection of hardware is much easier. The idea is to choose hardware that can run the software packages you've selected. This helps you put together a system that really matches your needs.

Computer

Some of the software packages you've selected have versions that run on different computers, but many will only work on a single machine. This is where you begin to determine the most important hardware decision facing you: which computer to get. Although there are hundreds of different companies making microcomputers, the great majority of machines fit into one of just a few categories. Today, these categories are IBM and IBM-compatible computers, Apple Macintoshes, Apple II computers, and all others. This is not to belittle all those "other" computers. There are quite a few great machines with large numbers of devoted users. However, there's no doubt that the microcomputers in the first three categories far outnumber all the rest, especially in businesses, offices, and schools.

IBM and IBM-Compatible Computers

IBM is the recognized leader in the microcomputer industry. They sell more microcomputers than any other single manufacturer. People who prefer other computers may not concede that IBM sells the "best" computers, but the fact remains that they sell the most. Although IBM no longer manufactures members of its original Personal Computer line (PC Jrs, PCs, PC Portables, XTs, and ATs), millions of these machines remain in use and some dealers are still selling new ones. The current IBM Personal System/2 line of computers improves on the previous models while still being able to run all the old software. IBM computers tend to be solidly-built, reliable machines that have been traditionally popular in the business world. Even though IBM computers might be a bit more expensive than comparable machines from other manufacturers, they have been getting more price-competitive lately. It's been said that "no manager ever got fired for buying IBM."

A true **IBM-compatible** computer is one that can run all the software and accept all the expansion boards and peripheral units that IBM microcomputers can use. Because IBM chose standard parts, published detailed design descriptions in technical references, and used an operating system designed and also sold by Microsoft, it was relatively easy for other manufacturers to produce compatible computers. Although there may still be some exceptions, most IBM-compatibles produced today do a very good job of mimicking the way IBM computers work. Many such "clones" offer more advanced features at a significantly lower price than IBM computers. Some IBM-compatible manufacturers, such as COMPAQ, have become highly-respected microcomputer industry leaders in their own right. Many well-established computer and electronic companies, like Tandy and Zenith, have expanded their lines to include IBM-compatible machines. In addition, quite a few mail-order firms, such as Dell Computer Corporation and Northgate Computer Systems, sell IBM-compatibles that they construct themselves from standard components. In fact, many more IBM-compatibles are sold today than IBM microcomputers.

Although IBMs and IBM-compatibles have their critics, selecting such computers has many advantages. American businesses have over $80 billion invested in IBM and IBM-compatible computers. This includes over 72 million software and hardware products, and hundreds of millions of hours of training. Books, magazines, and user groups devoted solely to IBM-compatible computers abound. Chances are good that you can find experts nearby to help you if you have problems. Most IBM and IBM-compatible systems can be easily expanded if you need to add more capabilities later.

Apple Macintosh Computers   In the early days of IBM microcomputers, many people considered them to be powerful and expandable, but not particularly easy to set up and use. Apple, building on their great success with the Apple II line, decided to address these concerns and build a computer "for the rest of us." In 1984, Apple introduced the Macintosh. Easy to learn and fun to use, the Macintosh has changed the way people perceive computers. Today's models preserve the philosophy of simplicity, yet have become more powerful and expandable. The Macintosh is becoming increasingly popular in businesses, especially for word processing, graphics, and desktop publishing applications. Many individuals and schools are also purchasing Macintoshes in ever greater numbers. Hundreds of software packages and a variety of optional peripherals are now available for this machine.

Apple II Computers   The original Apple II computer was introduced in 1977. Since then, several million of the Apple II family (including the Apple II +, Apple IIe, Apple III, Apple IIc, and Apple IIGS) have been sold. These computers have done very well in elementary and secondary schools. The Apple II's share of sales in this market is currently around 50%, although some schools are turning more toward Macintoshes and low-cost IBM-compatibles. Apple II computers have also been quite popular as home computers and were common in businesses before the introduction of the IBM Personal Computers. At least 10,000 software packages run on Apple II computers and a wide variety of expansion devices and peripherals are available. Although this family of computers is not as powerful and fast as Macintoshes and IBM-compatibles, they are still viable machines with a large number of devoted users.

Memory

In the early days of microcomputers, RAM was expensive and most machines could have no more than 64K. This situation has changed dramatically. Many microcomputers now have the potential to use up to 4 gigabytes of RAM, and memory chips are less expensive. For many people, the memory that comes with the computer will be sufficient for most of their needs. For example, most IBM microcomputers now come with at least 640K standard and all Macintoshes come with at least one megabyte installed. On other machines, you'll have to make sure you get enough memory to run the application packages you've selected. Since most software manufacturers state how much memory is required for their programs, figuring out how much memory to buy should be fairly simple. If you can, try to choose a computer system that can accept more RAM than you may initially need. Then if you later purchase software that requires more memory, you can add more RAM to upgrade your system.

Disk Drives

When it comes to secondary storage, you have several choices to make. The first one is whether you need the high capacity and rapid data access of a hard disk. This depends on the types of applications you'll run and the quantity of data you'll be working with. Some application packages require a hard disk. Others don't actually require one, but would work much better and faster with a hard disk. If the application programs you run and the data files you'll work with won't each fit on a single floppy disk, you probably need a hard disk. If you're not sure if you want to invest the extra few hundred dollars in a hard disk, make sure that you get a computer system that can accommodate a hard disk if you decide to add one later.

The other most common secondary storage decisions involve what kind and how many floppy drives to get. The 5¼-inch diskette drives are still more common, less expensive, and use less expensive floppies than 3½-inch drives. However, many computers, like the Macintosh and IBM Personal System/2 computers, come with only 3½-inch disk drives standard. Most software is now distributed on either type of disk. Each type of floppy drive has its advantages, but your major concern should be whether you can trade diskettes with colleagues, co-workers, and friends. It's best to get the same type of diskette drives as people with whom you'll be frequently exchanging programs and data. If you do get a hard disk, one floppy drive will probably be sufficient. However, if you often need to copy entire diskettes, it might be worth investing in two drives. In systems without hard disks, having two floppy drives is the most practical arrangement.

Display

With some computers, you have no choice as to what kind of display to get. The Apple Macintosh Plus and Macintosh SE, for example, come with a built-in 9-inch monochrome graphics display. On most computers, however, you have a choice among several alternatives. Older and less-expensive computers give you a choice among monochrome text, monochrome graphics, and color graphics monitors. Many newer microcomputers, like the IBM Personal System/2 series, support only graphics monitors, but you do have a choice between monochrome and color. To complicate matters more, many computers can accept several different display adapters, each of which may support several video modes.

To resolve your display dilemma, first look at your software selections. If you want to run software that uses graphics, you'll need a graphics display. On the other hand, if you're *positive* that you'll only be working with text, you may want to opt for a less expensive monochrome text monitor. Although in most cases color is not absolutely necessary, many people find that color monitors are more pleasant to work with, despite the added expense. If you are planning to use software that manipulates detailed graphics, you'll need a high-resolution display. As with most hardware selections, try to choose a system that can be upgraded later, if possible. Your needs may expand and prices may fall to a point where you would like to invest in a more sophisticated display. It's much easier and less expensive to replace a display adapter and monitor than an entire computer system.

Printer

Literally hundreds of microcomputer printers are on the market. Before you choose a particular model, you must first decide on what type of printer you need. Most microcomputer users have 9-pin dot-matrix printers. These printers can do graphics and can print fairly rapidly in draft mode, yet also have a more attractive, but much slower, near-letter-quality mode. If you will be printing letters on bond or letterhead paper, be sure to look for models that can easily accept single sheets as well as the fan-fold, pin-feed computer paper most dot-matrix printers use. For true letter quality, you might want to get a daisy-wheel printer. These printers produce text that looks just like that from typewriters, but they are quite slow. Applications that produce very high-quality text and graphics may require a 24-pin dot-matrix printer or perhaps even an expensive laser printer. Before you make your final decision on any printer, be sure to see samples of the text and graphics it can produce. Also consider the cost of supplies like paper, ribbons, toner cartridges (for laser printers) and additional typefaces.

Other Peripherals

A wide range of optional peripheral devices can be connected to a microcomputer. In your selection of a system, you should try to choose initially only those devices that will be absolutely necessary. You can always add more peripherals later, provided that you've chosen a system that can be expanded. If you'll be accessing remote computers, you'll need to select a modem. Many graphics applications require the use of a mouse. Some computer games use joysticks or trackballs. Examine your software selections carefully to make sure that you understand exactly what hardware devices are necessary.

Specifications and Benchmarks

In the preceding sections, we've briefly described the hardware you need to select. But, how do you pick the exact models to buy? Just as in making software selections, one method is to look carefully at what people around you have purchased. Some experts have even suggested that you get a system exactly like another one you have access to, perhaps at school, work, or a friend's. This way, you can become familiar with the components before you buy, and after you get your system, you have access to an exact duplicate in case your system isn't working. Although it definitely helps to have access to a similar system, if you only buy what someone else has, you're depending a great deal on their judgment, which may or may not be better than your own.

Another method of selecting hardware is to read reviews published in computer and consumer magazines. Just like software reviews, hardware reviews compare and evaluate actual products. For computers, hardware reviews can provide in-depth information about how they are constructed and how they work. For devices like displays, printers, and modems, reviews can compare models quantitatively and tabulate their features. Be forewarned, however, that these reviews are often saturated with specifications and benchmarks.

Specifications are a detailed list of the exact components, options, and capabilities of a particular hardware device. Microcomputer specifications typically list the manufacturer, exact size, microprocessor, coprocessors, system clock speed, amount of standard RAM, total possible RAM, amount of ROM, disk drives and capacities, number and type of expansion slots, number and type of interfaces, retail list price, and many other details. Sometimes, specifications include measures of performance. For example, many printer specifications include the number of characters printed per second. Although specifications can be one way to compare different devices, they may be misleading. Performance measurements are often made under ideal conditions. So, a printer advertised at 200 characters per second, may not actually be that fast when printing a document from your word processor, especially if it contains underlining, boldface, and italics.

A **benchmark** is an objective, reproducible measure of hardware or software performance, typically the amount of time it takes to run a standard program or process a particular set of data. Just like specifications, benchmarks are one way to compare hardware, but they can also be misleading. For example, a common benchmark for computer performance is one cycle of a calculation known as the *Sieve of Eratosthenes*. This is a method of finding prime numbers (numbers only evenly divisible by themselves and 1) that has been adapted to computers. Although benchmarks such as these may be useful for measuring the time required for certain very specific kinds of computer operations, they provide little or no information about ease of use, reliability, maintainability, the amount of manufacturer support for a product, or other equally important attributes. Sometimes, magazines like *BYTE* and *PC Magazine* develop their own benchmarks for reviewing products. Although these benchmarks are designed to measure performance under typical conditions, they may still not reflect how fast your software will run on your machine. Benchmark results, like specifications, should be taken with a grain of salt.

Step 5: Purchase the System

After selecting your hardware, you may have to go back and modify your list of software packages so that you have ones that will all run on the machine you've chosen. Before you even think of buying anything, you should have a fairly complete list of the exact software and hardware products you'll need. Since most product reviews and ads contain prices, you should also have a good notion of how much all this will cost. This is the time to look at your budget and make some realistic choices. You may not be able to afford all the software packages and optional peripherals you want to get. Fortunately, some of these purchases can be postponed. If you've listed your selections by priority, you can initially buy only those most essential items.

When to Buy

For many people, the most disconcerting circumstances of microcomputer shopping are the rate at which technology advances and how quickly prices can drop. Computer newspapers and magazines are filled with rumors, educated guesses, and pre-release previews about new products and upgrades to existing ones. Most manufacturers, it would seem, are constantly on the verge of releasing a computer, peripheral, or software package that will render every preceding product hopelessly obsolete. Even worse, what you pay $4,000 for this year may cost less than $1,000 two years from now. This perpetual anticipation can immobilize some potential computer shoppers.

Unfortunately, you must simply accept the facts that whichever hardware and software you choose, prices will drop and new versions will be released. There may be some prudence in waiting one or two months if a product is about to be released that will truly meet your needs. However, production often lags behind the demand for new products and it's sometimes best not to be one of the first owners of a brand-new piece of hardware or software. New technology, such as automobiles, stereos, hardware, and software, frequently has unsuspected flaws. It's nearly impossible to detect all of the potential problems in a complex product that's being rushed out of the factory into a highly competitive marketplace. Although it's tempting to be one of the first to get the latest hardware or software, you may wind up as a guinea pig whose complaints contribute to the design of Version 2.0.

In most cases, the time to buy is *now*. If you truly need a computer, you probably can't afford to wait months for the release and delivery of a brand-new product. A great deal of hardware and software is currently available that will provide years of valuable service, even if new versions are released after your purchase. Assuming you've done your homework and selected a system that fulfills your requirements, it shouldn't matter that less expensive, more powerful alternatives will eventually be released. Even if your computing needs grow, you can most likely expand your current system later. Someday, you may even want to select a completely new system, but in the meantime you will have a computer that can help you now.

Where to Buy

Nowadays, computer hardware and software can be purchased from a variety of sources. The outlet you select often depends upon such factors as how much you know about computers, how much money you want to save, how soon you need a system, whether you're buying a well-established brand name product, and whether you're buying hardware or software. You can purchase a computer system from computer stores, department stores, school stores, manufacturers, mail-order firms, and used equipment dealers.

Computer Stores   Local retail outlets that specialize in computers, such as Computerland and Radio Shack Computer Centers, are the traditional source of hardware and software products for many shoppers, especially novices. Salespeople are usually knowledgeable and can help a great deal in putting together a system that meets your needs. Most computer stores can also service your hardware should it need repair after the purchase. Many items are in stock or can be ordered and obtained in a few days. Unfortunately, many computer stores sell only a few brands. Although the brands tend to be from a select group of well-established manufacturers, your choices may be somewhat limited at a computer store. Items are usually sold at retail list prices, but there may be occasional sales or discounts given to certain groups of people. It may cost a bit more to buy a computer or peripheral device at a computer store, but dealers are nearby, accessible, and stand behind the hardware they sell.

Despite the additional cost, it often makes sense to buy hardware from a computer store. There is less advantage, however, to buying brand name software from a computer store. Software doesn't break down in the sense that hardware does, so a computer store technician can't repair a program. For most software packages, any problems or questions you have must usually be taken directly to the manufacturer. Although computer store salespeople may be able to answer some of your software questions, they simply can't be experts on every program they sell. In many cases, brand name software can be purchased for less from other sources.

Department Stores   Sometimes, retail department stores like Sears, Target, and Service Merchandise sell computers and software. List prices are usually discounted and you can get items immediately if they are in stock. Unfortunately, department store salespeople may not be very knowledgeable about computers. Furthermore, each store typically only carries a single computer brand. In most cases, service after the sale may only be obtained from the original manufacturer. However, if you're fairly knowledgeable about computers and a local department store has exactly what you want, you may be able to get a good bargain.

School Stores   If you're a student, faculty, or staff member of a college or university and in the market for a computer system, you may be in luck. Many schools have special deals with computer hardware and software manufacturers enabling them to offer products to qualified buyers at substantial savings. Hardware and software may be sold through a university bookstore, student union, educational consortium, or local computer center at discounts of up to 50% for students, faculty, and staff. Computer manufacturers like Apple, IBM, Hewlett-Packard, and Zenith often make deals with schools to sell their equipment at very low prices. In many cases, sales agents are knowledgeable and schools may also have their own service centers.

Manufacturers   Sometimes, there's no dealer in the area that sells the computer you want. Or, you may qualify for a volume discount by wanting to purchase a number of systems all at once. In such situations it may be advantageous to go directly to the manufacturer of a particular hardware or software product. Unless you're purchasing in volume, you'll probably pay the list price and it may take several days or weeks for the item to be shipped to you. However, at least you know that you're going directly to the source and eliminating the middleman. Some large manufacturers, like IBM, may even have a local office through which you can purchase products and get equipment serviced after the sale.

Mail-Order Firms   In the past, computer mail-order firms have had a somewhat less than prestigious reputation. With very few exceptions, that reputation is no longer justified. In fact, the seventh largest domestic microcomputer manufacturer, Dell Computer Corporation, is strictly a mail-order firm. This particular company even offers an optional next-day, on-site service contract for most major metropolitan areas and unlimited access to technicians over toll-free phone lines. Although most mail-order firms may not be this accommodating, a great many individuals, schools, and businesses buy computer hardware and software through the mail. Mail-order buying can save you money, and, in this day of overnight package delivery, can also be very convenient.

Still, the rule is "let the buyer beware" when it comes to mail-order purchasing. Ordering hardware over the phone can be daunting to computer novices. Many mail-order firms put together their own computers from standard components. These computers can be fantastic machines, but unless you know exactly what you're doing, it's probably best to stick to established brand names. Although, as we said, some mail-order firms offer repair service, most of them don't. Many advertise technical support over the phone, but it can sometimes be difficult to get through and have your questions answered politely, quickly, and accurately. Make sure that any mail-order firm you do choose has been in business for awhile.

Buying brand name software through the mail, however, offers several advantages. Discounts are usually substantial and the package you get in the mail is identical to what you would get from your local computer store or directly from the manufacturer. Large mail-order firms may have many items in stock and can often deliver them the next day via an overnight carrier for a modest extra charge.

Used Equipment Dealers   A recent market study showed that most people buying new computers have owned at least one computer before. What's happening to all those computers that are being replaced? Some are winding up at used computer dealers. As the microcomputer industry ages, more and more used computer stores are opening. Sometimes you can find real bargains at such stores but, like buying a used car, purchasing a pre-owned computer or hardware component can be somewhat risky. Many of the machines in used computer stores are obsolete. They may still be quite useful, but it might be difficult to get parts, service, and software for computers no longer in production. If, on the other hand, a used computer is being sold because its owner simply upgraded to a more powerful system, there may be no reason not to buy it as long as it's been thoroughly tested and guaranteed by the dealer.

 ## Step 6: Install the System

You've chosen and purchased your software and hardware. The system was delivered today and now it's at home still in the boxes. What do you do? Well, first open all the boxes and get out the instructions. Make sure all the components, cables, disks, and other items are there. Follow the directions and set up the machine. Some computers come with tutorial programs you can run to teach you the basics of using the hardware and running the operating system. Besides being entertaining, these tutorials are usually quite informative and well worth the time. Once you feel comfortable with the fundamentals, you can follow the instructions to install your software on your computer. Don't be surprised if you have problems or if things don't work exactly as the tutorials and manuals indicate. Reread the instructions and try again. If you're still having problems, call your dealer or the manufacturer's customer service department. If you still can't get your system running, you may have an honest-to-goodness defect and will have to return your system.

Once you do get your system up and running, try out all of the hardware and software components as soon as possible. Read your warranties and mail in the cards that register you with the manufacturers as a new owner. Not only will this validate your warranties, it will also put you on mailing lists so that you can get information about new versions and upgrades. At this time you might be thinking about insurance and service contracts. If your computer system represents a substantial investment to you, and you come to need it on a daily basis, you'll want make sure that it's insured and that you can get it repaired if it breaks down.

Finally, consider the surroundings in which you set up your system. A sturdy, roomy table or desktop and a well-designed, comfortable chair are musts if you expect to use your computer system for hours at a time. Keep your system clean and free from dust, spills, food crumbs, and other foreign materials. Try to keep any cooling vents unobstructed so that your system won't overheat. Unplug your hardware when not in use and try not to run it during electrical storms. Computer equipment, like other electronic devices, can be easily damaged or even destroyed by electrical surges caused by lightning or other power line disturbances. It might be prudent to plug all of your equipment into a **surge protector**. This is a relatively inexpensive device with a main switch, several electrical sockets, and circuitry to rapidly cut off power when a voltage surge occurs. Careful installation of your computer system can help ensure its reliability and usefulness for years to come.

SOFTWARE INSTALLATION

Most operating systems and application packages must be **installed** on your computer before you can use them. This typically involves running a special installation or setup program included with the software. Installation programs often create a new subdirectory on your hard disk, copy the files from the floppy disks included with the package to that subdirectory, and let you specify what kind of hardware you have. At most school microcomputer labs, this has already been done for you by the attendants. If you own a computer, however, you will probably have to install any new software you purchase yourself. The documentation that comes with the software should explain, step-by-step, how to run the installation program and answer any questions that may be asked about your hardware and software. Let's briefly go over the steps necessary to install the software discussed in this book: PC-DOS and MS-DOS Version 3.30, IBM DOS 4.00, MS-DOS 4.01, WordPerfect Version 5.0, Lotus 1-2-3 Release 2.01, Lotus 1-2-3 Release 2.2, Lotus 1-2-3 Release 3.0, and dBASE IV Version 1.0.

PC-DOS and MS-DOS Version 3.30

MS-DOS 3.30 and PC-DOS 3.30 are very similar. The MS-DOS package comes with two manuals entitled *MS-DOS User's Guide* and *MS-DOS User's Reference*. The first one contains the instructions for installing the system. The package can be purchased on either 3½-inch, 720K floppy disks, or 5¼-inch, 360K floppy disks. The 5¼-inch package comes with two disks, one labeled *Startup* and the other *Operating*.

Although the DOS 3.30 *Startup* diskette can be copied to another diskette to routinely boot up the computer from drive A, many people install the operating system on their hard disk C, if they have one. To install DOS 3.30 on a hard disk, follow these steps:

1. Insert the DOS 3.30 Startup disk into drive A.

2. Turn on the computer. If it is already on, press **Ctrl-Alt-Del** to reboot.

3. If the hard disk is not formatted (e.g., if you have a brand new computer), enter **format c: /s**. WARNING: Do not use this command if your hard disk is already formatted, or you will lose all files stored on it.

4. If the hard disk is already formatted with a previous version of DOS, enter **sys c:** instead of using the FORMAT command.

5. Enter **copy command.com c:** to copy the command processor to the hard disk.

6. If a subdirectory named DOS already exists on the hard disk, enter **del c:\dos*.*** to delete its contents. If such a subdirectory does not exist, enter **md c:\dos** to create it.

7. Enter **copy *.* c:\dos** to copy all the files from the Startup diskette to the DOS subdirectory on the hard disk.

8. Take the Startup diskette out of drive A, replace it with the Operating diskette, press **F3**, and press **Enter** to repeat the previous command and copy all of the files from the Operating diskette to the DOS subdirectory on the hard disk.

9. Remove the diskette from drive A, store all your original DOS diskettes in a safe place, and press **Ctrl-Alt-Del** to reboot your computer from the hard disk with DOS 3.30.

10. Enter **path c:\;c:\dos;** to set up the search paths for the root directory and the DOS subdirectory. You can add other search paths on the end of this command if you like. Ideally, this path command should be put in your AUTOEXEC.BAT file.

IBM DOS Version 4.00

The IBM DOS 4.00 package comes with two short manuals entitled *Getting Started with Disk Operating System Version 4.00* and *Using Disk Operating System Version 4.00*. The first one contains the instructions for installing the system. The package can be purchased on either 3½-inch, 720K floppy disks or 5¼-inch, 360K floppy disks. You should get the package with disks that match your floppy drive A. The 3½-inch package comes with two disks, one labeled *Install* and the other *Operating*. The 5¼-inch package comes with five disks labeled *Install, Select, Operating 1, Operating 2,* and *Operating 3*.

Although DOS 4.00 can be installed on floppy disks to boot up the computer from drive A, most people install the operating system on their hard disk C, if they have one. To install DOS 4.00 on a hard disk, follow these steps:

1. Insert the DOS 4.00 Install disk into drive A.

2. Turn on the computer. If it is already on, press **Ctrl-Alt-Del** to reboot.

3. After the copyright screen appears, press **Enter** and follow the instructions given by the installation program, which is called Select.

4. When you are finished with the installation program, remove the DOS floppy disk from drive A, store all your DOS disks in a safe place, and press **Ctrl-Alt-Del** to reboot your computer from the hard disk with DOS 4.00.

MS-DOS Version 4.01

The MS-DOS 4.01 package comes with three manuals entitled *MS-DOS User's Guide*, *MS-DOS User's Reference*, and *MS-DOS Shell User's Guide*. The first one contains the instructions for installing the system. The package can be purchased on either 3½-inch, 720K floppy disks or 5¼-inch, 360K floppy disks. You should get the package with disks that match your floppy drive A. The 3½-inch package comes with two disks, one labeled *Install* and the other *Operating*. The 5¼-inch package comes with six disks labeled *Install*, *Select*, *Operating 1*, *Operating 2*, *Operating 3*, and *Shell*.

Although MS-DOS 4.01 can be installed on floppy disks to boot up the computer from drive A, most people install the operating system on their hard disk C, if they have one. To install MS-DOS 4.01 on a hard disk, follow these steps:

1. Insert the MS-DOS 4.01 Install disk into drive A.

2. Turn on the computer. If it is already on, press **Ctrl-Alt-Del** to reboot.

3. After the copyright screen appears, press **Enter** and follow the instructions given by the installation program, which is called Select.

4. When you are finished with the installation program, remove the DOS floppy disk from drive A, store all your DOS disks in a safe place, and press **Ctrl-Alt-Del** to reboot your computer from the hard disk with MS-DOS 4.01.

WordPerfect Version 5.0

When you purchase WordPerfect Version 5.0, you get a softcover book entitled *WordPerfect Workbook*, and a three-ring reference manual. Also included are various keyboard templates and a quick reference card. The 5¼-inch package contains twelve floppy disks:

- *WordPerfect 1* and *WordPerfect 2*. These disks hold the files that make up the main WordPerfect program.
- *Fonts/Graphics*. This disk holds the WordPerfect character sets, fonts, clip art images, and screen capture utility.
- *Learning*. This disk contains the Install program that lets you set up WordPerfect on your computer and the on-line tutorial program that teaches you to use the package.
- *Printer 1* through *Printer 4*. These disks contain printer drivers, the files needed to use WordPerfect with many different kinds of printers.
- *PTR Program*. This disk holds PTR, a program that lets you create a driver for a printer not included on the Printer disks.
- *Speller*. This disk holds the spelling checker dictionary and Spell, a utility that lets you add words to or delete words from the dictionary and create specialized user dictionaries.
- *Thesaurus*. This disk holds the thesaurus program.
- *Conversion*. This disk holds Convert, a program that converts files from selected programs, such as WordStar and MultiMate, to WordPerfect format and vice versa.

To install WordPerfect on a hard disk, follow these steps:

1. Turn on your computer and boot up DOS.

2. Insert the WordPerfect Learning diskette into drive A.

3. Type **a:** and press **Enter** to switch to drive A.

4. Type **install** and press **Enter.**

5. Answer the questions and follow the directions given by the Install program.

6. Remove the Learning diskette from drive A.

7. Now you have to run WordPerfect to install and select your printer driver. Type **wp** and press **Enter** to start WordPerfect.

8. Hold down the **Shift** key and press the **F7** function key to activate the Print menu.

9. Type **s** to choose the Select Printer option.

10. Type **2** to select the Additional Printers option.

11. Type **2** to select the Other Disk option, put the Printer 1 diskette into drive A, type **a:**, and press **Enter.** (If you have a dot-matrix printer, you can save time by inserting the Printer 3 diskette instead.)

12. Press **Up Arrow** or **Down Arrow** to highlight the name of your printer or of a model that works similarly. If you can't find your printer in the list, put a different Printer diskette into drive A, type **2** to select the Other Disk option, type **a:**, and press **Enter.**

13. After you have highlighted your printer, type **1** to choose the Select option and then press **Enter.**

14. Keep pressing the **F7** key until you return to the editing screen. Now you can continue using WordPerfect or press **F7** again to return to DOS.

15. Remove the Printer diskette from drive A and put away all of your original WordPerfect diskettes in a safe place.

COMMAND SUMMARIES

MS-DOS Version 4.01

DOS Keys

Keypress	Description
Ctrl-Alt-Del	Reboots DOS.
Ctrl-Break	Cancels a command.
Ctrl-PrtSc	Echoes to the printer.
Enter	Processes a command.
Esc	Cancels the current line.
Pause	Pauses screen scrolling (Enhanced keyboards).
Ctrl-Num Lock	Pauses screen scrolling (PC and AT keyboards).
Print Screen	Prints the contents of the screen (Enhanced keyboards).
Shift-PrtSc	Prints the contents of the screen (PC and AT keyboards).
F1	Retypes one character from the previous command.
F2	Retypes previous command up to the specified character.
F3	Retypes all of the previous command.
F4	Deletes previous command up to the specified character.
F5	Saves current command as if it were the previous command.
F6	Inserts an end-of-file code (Ctrl-Z).
Del	Skips over a character from the previous command.
Ins	Switches insert/overwrite mode in the command line.
>	Redirects output.
>>	Redirects and appends output.
<	Redirects input.
|	Pipes output.

DOS Commands

These conventions are used in the list of DOS commands that follows.

Command Format Conventions	
[ ]	optional command switch or parameter, such as [/a]
or	either/or choice, such as DEL **or** ERASE
...	optional repetition of the previous item as necessary
italics	name or value you must enter, such as the following:
drive:	disk drive name, such as A: or B:
path	directory name, such as \WP\LETTERS\WORK
filename	file name, including extension, such as JIM.DOC
pathname	path plus a *filename*, such as \WP\LETTERS\WORK\JIM.DOC
(Internal)	indicates an internal (resident) DOS command.
(External)	indicates an external (transient) DOS command.
(No Network)	indicates a command that does not work over a network.

You can specify a drive and/or path before any external command in the table below.

DOS Command	Formats and Description
APPEND	APPEND [/x] [/e] [;] **or** APPEND [*drive:*]*path*[;[*drive:*][*path*]...] **or** APPEND [*path*] [/x:[off **or** on]] [/path:[off **or** on]] Specifies the paths to be searched for files with extensions other than BAT, COM, and EXE. (External) /x — Searches for BAT, COM, and EXE files, too. /e — Stores appended paths in the DOS environment. /path — If on, searches for files in the appended paths even if the files have drive or path prefixes.
ASSIGN	ASSIGN [*x* [=] *y*] ... Reassigns a disk drive letter to another drive. (External)
ATTRIB	ATTRIB [+r **or** -r] [+a **or** -a] [*drive:*]*pathname* [/s] Changes a file's read-only or archive attribute. (External) +r — Turns on read-only attribute. -r — Turns off read-only attribute. +a — Turns on archive attribute. -a — Turns off archive attribute. /s — Processes files in subdirectories.
BACKUP	BACKUP [*drive1:*][*path*][*filename*] [*drive2:*] [/s] [/m] [/a] [/f:*size*] [/d:*date*] [/t:*time*] [/L:[[*drive:*][*path*]*filename*]] Backs up one or more files from one disk to another. (External)

DOS Command	Formats and Description
BACKUP *(continued)*	/s Backs up subdirectories. /m Backs up only changed files. /a Adds files without erasing backup disks. /f: Formats target disks if necessary; *size* indicates type of disk (160K, 180K, 320K, 360K, 720K, 1.2M, or 1.44M) /d: Backs up only those files modified on or after *date*. /t: Backs up only those files modified on or after *time*. /L: Makes a backup log entry in the specified file.
BREAK	BREAK [off **or** on] Turns Ctrl-Break off or on for certain operations. (Internal)
CD or CHDIR	CD **or** CHDIR [*path*] Switches between subdirectories or displays the current directory. (Internal)
CHCP	CHCP [*nnn*] Displays or changes the current code page, where *nnn* is the code page. (Internal)
CHKDSK	CHKDSK [*drive:*][*pathname*] [/f] [/v] Displays a disk and memory status report and checks for errors. (External) (No Network) /f Fixes lost cluster chains on the disk. /v Displays the name of every file on the disk.
CLS	CLS Clears the screen. (Internal)
COMMAND	COMMAND [*drive:*][*path*] [*device*] [/e:*nnnnn*] [/p] [/c *string*] Starts a new command processor. (External) /e: Specifies the environment size, where *nnnnn* is the size in bytes. /p Keeps the secondary command processor in memory. /c Performs the commands specified in *string* and then returns to the primary command processor.
COMP	COMP [*drive:*][*pathname1*] [*drive:*][*pathname2*] Compares the contents of two sets of files. (External)
COPY	COPY [*drive:*]*pathname1* [*drive:*][*pathname2*] [/v] [/a] [/b] **or** COPY [*drive:*]*pathname1* [/v] [/a] [/b] [*drive:*][*pathname2*] **or** COPY *pathname1* + *pathname2* ... *pathnameN* Duplicates one or more files. Also appends files. (Internal)

DOS Command	Formats and Description
COPY *(continued)*	/v Turns on the verify switch. /a Copies ASCII files. /b Copies binary files.
CTTY	CTTY *device* Changes the console (terminal) to another device. (Internal)
DATE	DATE [*mm-dd-yy*] Displays or sets the date. (Internal)
DEL or ERASE	DEL **or** ERASE [*drive:*] *pathname* [/p] Removes one or more files from a disk. (Internal) /p Prompts user before each deletion.
DIR	DIR [*drive:*][*pathname*] [/p] [/w] Lists the files on a disk or in a subdirectory. (Internal) /p Pauses after each screen. /w Displays a wide listing.
DISKCOMP	DISKCOMP [*drive1:*] [*drive2*] [/1] [/8] Compares two diskettes. (External) (No Network) /1 Compares just the first sides. /8 Compares just the first 8 sectors of each track.
DISKCOPY	DISKCOPY [*drive1:*] [*drive2:*] [/1] Duplicates an entire floppy disk. (External) (No Network) /1 Copies only one side.
DOSSHELL	DOSSHELL Starts the DOS Shell. (Batch File)
EXE2BIN	EXE2BIN [*drive:*]*pathname1* [*drive:*]*pathname2* Converts EXE files to BIN or COM files. (External)
EXIT	EXIT Exits the COMMAND.COM program. Also, returns to the DOS Shell from the DOS prompt. (Internal)
FASTOPEN	FASTOPEN [*drive:*[= *n*][...]] /x **or** FASTOPEN [*drive:*[= (*n,m*)][...]] /x **or** FASTOPEN [*drive:*[= ([*n*],*m*)][...]] /x Speeds up disk access by storing directory and file names and locations in a memory cache. (External) (No Network) *n* The number of files FASTOPEN will work with (10–999). *m* The number of file extent entries (1–999). /x Puts the cache in expanded memory.
FDISK	FDISK Partitions a hard disk. (External) (No Network)
FIND	FIND [/v] [/c] [/n] "*string*" [[*drive:*][*pathname*] ...] Searches for a text string in one or more files. (External)

DOS Command	Formats and Description
FIND *(continued)*	/v — Displays all lines *not* containing the string. /c — Displays only the number of lines that contain the string. /n — Precedes each line with its line number in the file.
FORMAT	FORMAT *drive:* [/1] [/4] [/8] [/n:*sectors*] [/t:*tracks*] [/v[:*label*]] [/s] **or** FORMAT *drive:* [/1] [/b] [/n:*sectors*] [/t:*tracks*] **or** FORMAT *drive:* [/v[:*label*]] [/f:*size*] [/s] Prepares a disk for use. (External) (No Network) /1 — Formats only one side. /4 — Formats a 360K disk in a 1.2M drive. /8 — Formats 8 sectors per track. /n: — Specifies the number of sectors. /t: — Specifies the number of tracks. /v: — Specifies the disk name (volume label). /b — Leaves room for the DOS hidden system files. /s — Creates a bootup disk. /f: — Specifies the disk size (160K, 180K, 320K, 360K, 720K, 1.2M, 1.44M)
GRAFTABL	GRAFTABL [*xxx*] **or** /status **or** [?] Enhances the display of graphics characters on a Color Graphics Adapter. (External) *xxx* — The code page id number. /status — Displays the active character set. ? — Displays instructions for using GRAFTABL.
GRAPHICS	GRAPHICS *type* [*profile*] [/r] [/b] [/lcd] [/printbox:*id*] Allows printing of graphics screens. (External) /r — Prints black on the screen as black on the page. /b — Prints the background in color. /lcd — Uses aspect ratio of LCD screens. /printbox — Selects the printbox size.
JOIN	JOIN [*drive: drive:path*] **or** *drive:* /d Treats a disk drive as if it were a subdirectory. (External) (No Network) /d — Unjoins a previous JOIN.
KEYB	KEYB [*xx*[,[*yyy*],[[*drive:*][*path*]*filename*]]] [/ID:*nnn*] Loads a keyboard-translation table for a country, where *xx* is a two-letter country code and *yyy* is the code page that defines the character set. (External) /ID: — Specifies the keyboard in use to be *nnn*.
LABEL	LABEL [*drive:*][*label*] Creates or changes a disk's name (volume label). (External) (No Network)

DOS Command	Formats and Description
MD or MKDIR	MD **or** MKDIR [*drive:*]*path* Creates a new subdirectory. (Internal)
MEM	MEM [/program **or** /debug] Displays a memory report. (External) /program Displays programs in memory. /debug Displays technical information.
MODE	MODE [*device*] [/status] **or** MODE LPT*n*[:][*c*][,[*l*][,*r*]] **or** MODE LPT*n* [cols=*c*] [lines=*l*] [retry=r] **or** MODE COM*m*[:]*b*,[,*p*[,*d*[,*s*[,*r*]]]] **or** MODE COM*m* baud=*b* [data=*d*] [stop=*s*] [parity=*p*] [retry=r] **or** MODE *display, n* **or** MODE [*display*], *shift* **or** MODE CON[:] [cols=*m*] [lines=*n*] **or** MODE CON[:] rate=*r* delay=*d* **or** MODE *device* codepage prepare=((*yyy*)[*drive:*][*path*]*filename*) **or** MODE *device* codepage select=*yyy* **or** MODE *device* codepage refresh **or** MODE *device* codepage [/status] **or** MODE LPT*n*[:]=COM*m*[:] Establishes settings for various input/output devices. See the *MS-DOS User's Reference* for detailed information. (External)
MORE	MORE < *source* **or** *source*	MORE Accepts input and presents it one screen at a time as output. (External)
NLSFUNC	NLSFUNC [[*drive:*][*path*]*filename*] Specifies country-specific language and code page. (External)
PATH	PATH [*drive:*[*path*][;[*drive:*][*path*]...] **or** PATH [;] Tells DOS where to search for BAT, COM, and EXE files, or displays the current path. (Internal)
PRINT	PRINT [/d:*device*] [/b:*size*] [/u:*value1*] [/m:*value2*] [/s:*timeslice*] [/q:*qsize*] [/t] [*drive:*][*pathname*] [/c] [/p] Prints a text file. (External) /d: Specifies the device name. /b: Specifies the size of the internal buffer in bytes. /u: Specifies the number of clock ticks PRINT will wait for a printer. /m: Specifies the number of clock ticks PRINT can take to print a character. /s: Specifies the timeslice for background printing.

DOS Command	Formats and Description	
PRINT *(continued)*	/q:	Specifies the number of files allowed in the print queue.
	/t	Deletes all files in the print queue.
	/c	Removes the preceding file and all following files from the print queue.
	/p	Adds the preceding file and all following files to the print queue.
PROMPT	PROMPT [[*text*][$*character*]...] Changes the format of the DOS prompt. (Internal) The *character* may be one of the following:	
	q	The = character.
	$	The $ character.
	t	The current time.
	d	The current date.
	p	The current directory.
	v	The DOS version number.
	n	The default drive.
	g	The > character.
	l	The < character.
	b	The | character.
	—	The Enter key.
	e	The Escape key.
	h	The Backspace key.
RD or RMDIR	RD **or** RMDIR [*drive:*]*path* Removes an empty subdirectory. (Internal)	
RECOVER	RECOVER [*drive:*][*path*]*filename* **or** RECOVER *drive* Reconstructs damaged files or disks. (External) (No Network)	
RENAME or REN	RENAME **or** REN [*drive:*][*path*]*filename1 filename2* Changes the name of one or more files. (Internal)	
REPLACE	REPLACE [*drive:*]*pathname1* [*drive:*][*pathname2*] [/a] [/p] [/r] [/s] [/w] [/u] Updates a set of files. (External)	
	/a	Adds new files to the target instead of replacing existing ones.
	/p	Prompts user before replacing each file.
	/r	Replaces read-only files.
	/s	Searches all subdirectories.
	/u	Replaces only older files.
	/w	Prompts user before beginning.
RESTORE	RESTORE *drive1:* [*drive2:*][*pathname*] [/s] [/p] [/b:*date*] [/a:*date*] [/e:*time*] [/L:*time*] [/m] [/n] Restores files backed up with the BACKUP command. (External)	
	/s	Restores subdirectories.
	/p	Prompts the user before restoring read-only files or files that have been changed.

DOS Command	Formats and Description
RESTORE *(continued)*	/b: Restores only files modified on or before *date*. /a: Restores only files modified on or after *date*. /e: Restores only files modified at or earlier than *time*. /L: Restores only files modified at or later than *time*. /m Restores only files modified since the last backup. /n Restores only files that no longer exist on the target disk.
SELECT	SELECT menu Installs DOS. SELECT is usually executed by inserting the MS-DOS Install diskette in drive A and pressing Ctrl-Alt-Del. (External)
SET	SET [*string* = [*string*]] Displays or changes the contents of the DOS environment. (Internal)
SHARE	SHARE [/f:*space*] [/L:*locks*] Permits file sharing and locking on network systems. (External) /f: Specifies the storage space used to record file sharing information. /L: Specifies the number of locks to allow.
SORT	[*source*] | SORT [/r] [/ + *n*] **or** SORT [/r] [/ + *n*] *source* Accepts input, arranges it in order, and writes it out. (External) /r Reverses the sort (Z–A, 9–0). / + *n* Sorts the file according to the character in column *n*.
SUBST	SUBST [*drive*: *drive:path*] **or** SUBST *drive:* /d Treats a subdirectory as if it were a disk drive. (External) (No Network) /d Cancels a previous substitution.
SYS	SYS *drive*: Installs hidden system files on a properly formatted disk. (External) (No Network)
TIME	TIME [*hour:minute*[:*second*][.*centisecond*]]] Displays or sets the time of day. (Internal)
TREE	TREE [*pathname*:] [/f] [/a] Displays the directory structure of a disk. (External) /f Displays the names of the files in each directory. /a Uses only characters that can be output on any display or printer.

DOS Command	Formats and Description
TYPE	TYPE [*drive:*]*filename* Displays a text file on the screen. (Internal)
VER	VER Displays the DOS version number. (Internal)
VERIFY	VERIFY [off **or** on] Turns verification off or on when copying files. (Internal)
VOL	VOL [*drive:*] Displays the disk name (volume label). (Internal)
XCOPY	XCOPY [*drive:*]*pathname* [*drive:*][*pathname*] [/a] [/d:*date*] [/e] [/m] [/p] [/s] [/v] [/w] **or** XCOPY *drive:*[*pathname*] [*drive:*][*pathname*] [/a] [/d:*date*] [/e] [/m] [/p] [/s] [/v] [/w] Duplicates files faster and more flexibly than COPY. (External) <table><tr><td>/a</td><td>Copies files that have their archive bit set.</td></tr><tr><td>/d:</td><td>Copies files modified on or after *date*.</td></tr><tr><td>/e</td><td>Copies subdirectories, even if they are empty.</td></tr><tr><td>/m</td><td>Same as /a, but turns off archive bit.</td></tr><tr><td>/p</td><td>Prompts user before copying each file.</td></tr><tr><td>/s</td><td>Copies subdirectories, unless they are empty.</td></tr><tr><td>/v</td><td>Turns on the verify switch.</td></tr><tr><td>/w</td><td>Waits before copying files.</td></tr></table>

Batch File Command	Formats and Description
CALL	CALL [*drive:*][*path*]*batchfile* [*argument*] Invokes *batchfile* from within the current batch file. The *argument* is the command in the current batch file that will be run following *batchfile*. (Internal)
ECHO	ECHO [off **or** on **or** *message*] Turns screen messages off or on, or displays *message*. (Internal)
FOR	FOR %%*c* in *set* do *command* **or** FOR %*c* in *set* do *command* Sets up a repeating loop in a batch file to perform a command for a set of files. The character *c* represents a variable name, the *set* is a set of files, and the *command* is a DOS command or program. (Internal)
GOTO	GOTO [:]*label* Transfers execution in a batch file to the line after *label*. (Internal)

Batch File Command	Formats and Description
IF	IF [not] errorlevel *number command* **or** IF [not] *string1* = = *string2 command* **or** IF [not] exist *filename command* Executes a command based on the result of a condition. (Internal)
PAUSE	PAUSE [*message*] Temporarily suspends the execution of a batch file until the user presses a key. (Internal)
REM	REM [*comment*] Identifies a batch file comment or remark. (Internal)
SHIFT	SHIFT Sets up more than nine batch file parameters. (Internal)

CONFIG.SYS Command	Formats and Description
BREAK	BREAK = [off **or** on] Turns Ctrl-Break off or on for certain operations.
BUFFERS	BUFFERS = *n*[,*m*] [/x] Sets the number of disk buffers. *n* The number of disk buffers (1–99). *m* The maximum number of sectors that can be read or written in one input/output operation (1–8). /x Sets the maximum number of disk buffers to 10,000 or the largest number of buffers that will fit in memory, whichever is less.
COUNTRY	COUNTRY = *xxx*[,[*yyy*][,[*drive:*]*filename*]] Changes country-specific information. *xxx* The country code. *yyy* The code page for the country. *filename* The file containing country information.
DEVICE	DEVICE = [*drive:*][*path*]*filename* [*argument*] Installs a device driver.
DRIVEPARM	DRIVEPARM = /d:*number* [/c] [/f:*factor*] [/h:*heads*] [/i] [/n] [/s:*sectors*] [/t:*tracks*] Defines parameters for block devices such as disk and tape drives. /d: Specifies the physical drive number (0–255). /c Indicates that the drive can sense if its door has been opened. /f: Specifies the device type or form factor (0–7).

CONFIG.SYS Command	Formats and Description	
DRIVEPARM *(continued)*	/h:	Specifies the maximum head number (1–99).
	/i	Specifies an electrically-compatible 3½-inch disk drive.
	/n	Specifies a nonremovable block device.
	/s:	Specifies the number of sectors per track (1–99).
	/t:	Specifies the number of tracks per side (1–999).
FCBS	FCBS = x,y Allows access to file control blocks.	
	x	The number of files that can be open at one time.
	y	The number of files that DOS cannot close automatically.
FILES	FILES = x Specifies the maximum number of open files (x).	
INSTALL	INSTALL = [*drive:*][*path*]*filename* [*parameters*] Installs RAM-resident features. The *filename* must be FASTOPEN.EXE, KEY.EXE, NLSFUNC.EXE, or SHARE.EXE.	
LASTDRIVE	LASTDRIVE = x Specifies the last accessible drive, where x is the drive letter (A–Z).	
REM	REM *comment* Allows a comment or remark to be entered in the CONFIG.SYS file.	
SHELL	SHELL = [*drive:*][*path*]*filename* [*parameters*] Begins execution of the top-level command processor.	
STACKS	STACKS = n,s Supports the dynamic use of data stacks.	
	n	The number of stacks (0–64).
	s	The size of each stack (0–512).

WordPerfect Version 5.0

Cursor Movement Commands

Up one line	Up Arrow
Down one line	Down Arrow
Left one character	Left Arrow
Right one character	Right Arrow
Left one word	Ctrl-Left Arrow
Right one word	Ctrl-Right Arrow
Next tab stop	Tab
End of line	End
Up one screen	Grey Minus (num. keypad)
Down one screen	Grey Plus (num. keypad)
Up one page	Page Up
Down one page	Page Down
Right edge of screen	Home, Right Arrow
Left edge of screen	Home, Left Arrow
Beginning of Line (Before Text)	Home, Home, Left Arrow
Beginning of Line (Before Codes)	Home, Home, Home, Left Arrow
Beginning of document	Home, Home, Up Arrow
End of document	Home, Home, Down Arrow
Go to specified page	Ctrl-Home

Insert and Delete Commands

Switch insert/typeover mode	Insert
Insert hard return	Enter
Insert page break	Ctrl-Enter
Insert hard space	Home, Space Bar
Delete character or block	Delete
Delete character left of cursor	Backspace
Delete word at cursor	Ctrl-Backspace
Delete word left	Home, Backspace
Delete word right	Home, Delete
Delete to end of line	Ctrl-End
Delete to end of page	Ctrl-PgDn

Function Key Commands

Cancel last command	F1
Temporarily return to DOS	Ctrl-F1
Invoke Setup Menu	Shift-F1
Invoke thesaurus	Alt-F1
Search forward for text	F2
Invoke spelling checker	Ctrl-F2
Search backward for text	Shift-F2
Global search and replace	Alt-F2
Invoke Help facility	F3
Split screen into windows	Ctrl-F3
Switch to other window	Shift-F3
Reveal hidden formatting codes	Alt-F3

Indent paragraph	F4
Move, copy, or delete text	Ctrl-F4
Center paragraph	Shift-F4
Turn on block marking	Alt-F4
Invoke List Files menu	F5
Save or load ASCII text file	Ctrl-F5
Invoke Date/Outline menu	Shift-F5
Invoke Mark Text menu	Alt-F5
Boldface text	F6
Align text to tab stop	Ctrl-F6
Center text	Shift-F6
Align text flush right	Alt-F6
Exit menu, document, or program	F7
Create footnotes	Ctrl-F7
Invoke Print menu	Shift-F7
Invoke Math/Columns menu	Alt-F7
Underline text	F8
Invoke Font menu	Ctrl-F8
Invoke Format menu	Shift-F8
Invoke Style menu	Alt-F8
End-of-field merge code (^R)	F9
Invoke Merge/Sort menu	Ctrl-F9
Invoke Merge Codes menu	Shift-F9
Incorporate graphics	Alt-F9
Save current document	F10
Define new keyboard macro	Ctrl-F10
Retrieve existing document	Shift-F10
Invoke macro	Alt-F10

Alphabetical List of Features

In the table below, the Keypresses column lists the keys to press and characters to type to invoke the feature. For example, to invoke the Advance feature (to advance the printer), press **Shift-F8**, type **4**, then type **1**.

Feature	Keypresses
Advance	Shift-F8, 4, 1
Appearance Attributes	Ctrl-F8, 2
Automatic Reference	Alt-F5, 1
Automatically Format and Rewrite	Shift-F1, 3, 1
Backup	Shift-F1, 1
Base Font	Ctrl-F8, 4
Beep Options	Shift-F1, 5, 1
Binding	Shift-F7, B
Block	Alt-F4
Block Protect (Block on)	Shift-F8
Boldface	F6
^C (Text from Keyboard)	Shift-F9, C
Cancel	F1
Cancel Print Jobs	Shift-F7, 4, 1
Cartridges and Fonts	Shift-F7, S, 3, 5

Feature	Keypresses
Case Conversion (Block on)	Shift-F3
Center	Shift-F6
Center Page Top to Bottom	Shift-F8, 2, 1
Colors/Fonts/Attributes	Shift-F1, 3, 2
Columns (Text and Parallel)	Alt-F7
Compose	Ctrl-2
Concordance	Alt-F5, 5, 3
Conditional End of Page	Shift-F8, 4, 2
Control Printer	Shift-F7, 4
Copy File	F5, Enter, 8
Create Directory	F5, =
^D (Date)	Shift-F9, D
Date Code	Shift-F5, 2
Date Format	Shift-F5, 3
Date Text	Shift-F5, 1
Date/Outline	Shift-F5
Decimal/Align Character	Shift-F8, 4, 3
Define (Mark Text)	Alt-F5, 5
Delete Directory or File	F5, Enter, 2
Display All Print Jobs	Shift-F7, 4, 3
Display Pitch	Shift-F8, 3, 1
Display Setup	Shift-F1, 3
Document Comments	Ctrl-F5, 5
Document Compare	Alt-F6, 6, 2
Document Format	Shift-F8, 3
Document Summary	Shift-F8, 3, 4
DOS Text File Retrieve	Ctrl-F5, 1, 2
DOS Text File Save	Ctrl-F5, 1, 1
Double Underline	Ctrl-F8, 2, 3
^E (End of Record)	Shift-F9, E
Edit Table of Authorities	Alt-F5, 5, 5
Endnote	Ctrl-F7, 2
Endnote Placement Code	Ctrl-F7, 3
Exit	F7
Extra Large Print	Ctrl-F8, 1, 7
^F (Field)	Shift-F9, F
Fast Save	Shift-F1, 4
Figure (Graphics)	Alt-F9, 1
Filename on Status Line	Shift-F1, 3, 4
Fine Print	Ctrl-F8, 1, 3
Flush Right	Alt-F6
Footers	Shift-F8, 2, 4
Footnote	Ctrl-F7, 1
Force Odd/Even Page	Shift-F8, 2, 2
Format	Shift-F8
Forms	Shift-F7, S, 3, 4
^G (Start Macro)	Shift-F9, G
Generate (Mark Text)	Alt-F5, 6
Generate Tables	Alt-F5, 6, 5
Generic Word Processor Format	Ctrl-F5, 3
Go (Start Printer)	Shift-F7, 4, 4

Feature	Keypresses
Go to DOS	Ctrl-F1, 1
Graphics	Alt-F9
Graphics Quality	Shift-F7, G
Graphics Screen Type	Shift-F1, 3, 5
Headers	Shift-F8, 2, 3
Help	F3
Horizontal Line (Graphics)	Alt-F9, 5, 1
Hyphenation	Shift-F8, 1, 1
Hyphenation Zone	Shift-F8, 1, 2
Indent Paragraph	F4
Indent (Center) Paragraph	Shift-F4
Index Define	Alt-F5, 5, 3
Index Mark	Alt-F5, 3
Initial Settings (Format)	Shift-F8, 3, 2
Initial Settings (Setup)	Shift-F1, 5
Italics	Ctrl-F8, 2, 4
Justification	Shift-F8, 1, 3
Kerning	Shift-F8, 4, 6, 1
Keyboard Layout	Shift-F1, 6
Language	Shift-F8, 4, 4
Large Print	Ctrl-F8, 1, 5
Line Draw	Ctrl-F3, 2
Line Format	Shift-F8, 1
Line Height	Shift-F8, 1, 4
Line Numbering	Shift-F8, 1, 5
Line Spacing	Shift-F8, 1, 6
List Define	Alt-F5, 5, 2
List Mark (Block on)	Alt-F5, 2
List Files	F5, Enter
Location of Auxiliary Files	Shift-F1, 7
Look	F5, Enter, 6
Macro	Alt-F10
Macro Define	Ctrl-F10
Margin Release	Shift-Tab
Margins Left/Right	Shift-F8, 1, 7
Margins Top/Bottom	Shift-F8, 2, 5
Mark Text	Alt-F5
Master Document Condense	Alt-F5, 6, 4
Master Document Expand	Alt-F5, 6, 3
Master Document Subdocument	Alt-F5, 2
Math/Columns	Alt-F7
Menu Letter Display	Shift-F1, 3, 7
Merge	Ctrl-F9, 1
Merge Codes	Shift-F9
Move	Ctrl-F4
Move Block (Block on)	Ctrl-F4, 1
Move Page	Ctrl-F4, 3
Move Paragraph	Ctrl-F4, 2
Move Rectangle (Block on)	Ctrl-F4, 3
Move/Rename (List Files)	F5, Enter, 3
Move Sentence	Ctrl-F4, 1

Feature	Keypresses
Move Tabular Column (Block on)	Ctrl-F4, 2
^N (Next Record)	Shift-F9, N
Name Search (List Files)	F5, Enter, N
New Page Number	Shift-F8, 2, 6
Normal Text (Attributes off)	Ctrl-F8, 3
Number of Copies	Shift-F7, N
^O (Display Message)	Shift-F9, O
Other Directory	F5, Enter, 7
Outline	Shift-F5, 4
Outline (Attribute)	Ctrl-F8, 2, 5
Overstrike	Shift-F8, 4, 5
^P (Primary File)	Shift-F9, P
Page Format	Shift-F8, 2
Page Numbering	Shift-F8, 2, 7
Paragraph Number	Shift-F5, 5
Paragraph Numbering Definition	Shift-F5, 6
Paper Size/Type	Shift-F8, 2, 8
Password	Ctrl-F5, 2
Print	Shift-F7
Print Block (Block on)	Shift-F7, Y
Print Color	Ctrl-F8, 5
Print Full Document	Shift-F7, 1
Print List Files	F5, Enter, 4
Print Page	Shift-F7, 2
Printer Command	Shift-F8, 4, 6, 2
Printer Settings	Shift-F7, S, 3
^Q (Stop Merge)	Shift-F9, Q
^R (End of Field)	Shift-F9, R
Redline	Ctrl-F8, 2, 8
Redline Method	Shift-F8, 3, 3
Remove Redline/Strikeout	Alt-F5, 6, 1
Repeat Value	Escape
Replace	Alt-F2
Replace, Extended	Home, Alt-F2
Retrieve Block (Move)	Ctrl-F4, 4, 1
Retrieve Document	Shift-F10
Retrieve List Files	F5, Enter, 1
Retrieve Rectangle (Move)	Ctrl-F4, 4, 3
Retrieve Tabular Column (Move)	Ctrl-F4, 4, 2
Reveal Codes	Alt-F3
Rewrite	Ctrl-F3, 0
Rush Print Job	Shift-F7, 4, 2
^S (Secondary File)	Shift-F9, S
Save	F10
Screen	Ctrl-F3
Search Forward	F2
Search Forward Extended	Home, F2
Search Backward	Shift-F2
Search Backward Extended	Home, Shift-F2
Select Printer	Shift-F7, S
Setup	Shift-F1

Feature	Keypresses
Shadow	Ctrl-F8, 2, 6
Shell	Ctrl-F1
Side-by-side Column Display	Shift-F1, 3, 8
Size Attribute	Ctrl-F8, 1
Small Caps	Ctrl-F8, 2, 7
Small Print	Ctrl-F8, 1, 4
Sort	Ctrl-F9, 2
Spell	Ctrl-F2
Split Screen	Ctrl-F3, 1
Stop Printing	Shift-F7, 4, 5
Strikeout	Ctrl-F8, 2, 9
Style	Alt-F8
Subscript	Ctrl-F8, 1, 2
Superscript	Ctrl-F8, 1, 1
Suppress (Page Format)	Shift-F8, 2, 9
Switch	Shift-F3
^T (Send to Printer)	Shift-F9, T
Tab Align	Ctrl-F6
Tab Set	Shift-F8, 1, 8
Table (Graphics)	Alt-F9, 2
Table of Authorities Define	Alt-F5, 5, 4
Table of Authorities Edit Full Form	Alt-F5, 5, 5
Table of Authorities Full (Block on)	Alt-F5, 4
Table of Authorities Short Form	Alt-F5, 4
Table of Contents Define	Alt-F5, 5, 1
Table of Contents Mark (Block on)	Alt-F5, 1
Text Box (Graphics)	Alt-F9, 3
Text In (List Files)	F5, Enter, 5
Text In In/Out	Ctrl-F5
Text Quality	Shift-F7, T
Thesaurus	Alt-F1
Thousand's Separator	Shift-F8, 4, 3
Type Through	Shift-F7, 5
^U (Rewrite Screen)	Shift-F9, U
Undelete	F1
Underline	F8
Underline Spaces/Tabs	Shift-F8, 4, 7
Units of Measure	Shift-F1, 8
User-Defined Box (Graphics)	Alt-F9, 4
^V (Insert Merge Code)	Shift-F9, V
Vertical Line (Graphics)	Alt-F9, 5, 2
Very Large Print	Ctrl-F8, 1, 6
View Document	Shift-F7, 6
Widow/Orphan Protection	Shift-F8, 1, 9
Window	Ctrl-F3, 1
Word/Letter Spacing	Shift-F8, 4, 6, 3
Word Search	F5, Enter, 9
Word Spacing Justification Limits	Shift-F8, 4, 6, 4
WordPerfect 4.2 Format	Ctrl-F5, 4

GLOSSARY

absolute reference   a cell address that does not change when it is moved or copied

access arm   a mechanical extension in a disk drive that moves the read-write head toward or away from the center of the disk

account   a file containing financial information

accounting package   software that manages an organization's finances

accounts payable   the accounting subsystem that records the purchases of goods and services from each vendor

accounts receivable   the accounting subsystem that records all sales of goods and services

action line   in dBASE III PLUS, the line above the status bar that shows the command generated by the current Assistant operation

active cell   see *current cell*

Ada   a powerful, comprehensive high-level programming language applicable to a wide range of problems

adapter   see *expansion board*

address   a unique identifying number for a storage location in memory

address file   see *secondary merge file*

aggregate operator   see *summary operator*

alias   in dBASE, a number, letter, or name that refers to a work area or data base file

allocation unit   in DOS, a group of contiguous sectors, also known as a cluster

alphanumeric characters   letters, numbers, and punctuation marks

alternate operating environment   see *windowing environment*

American Standard Code for Information Interchange (ASCII)   the code used by most microcomputers for representing text in binary form

application   see *application software*

application generator   see *fourth generation language*

application package   see *application software*

application software   a program or set of programs that applies the computer to useful tasks like helping you write letters, figure taxes, maintain mailing lists, and draw charts

Applications Generator   in dBASE, an easy-to-use tool for creating a customized data base system without programming

archive attribute   the file attribute that indicates if a file has been changed since it was last saved with the DOS BACKUP command

artificial intelligence (AI)   a field of study combining aspects of computer science, mathematics, philosophy, psychology, and linguistics whose main goal is to mimic human learning and decision making

ascending order   the arrangement of numbers from smallest to largest, and of text alphabetically from A to Z

ASCII file   see *text file*

assembler   a program that translates assembly language instructions into the binary numbers of machine language

assembly language   a programming language that substitutes meaningful abbreviations for the numerically coded instructions of a machine language

Autokey macro   A VP-Planner Plus macro created by recording keystrokes

automated vision   a type of software that allows computers to distinguish and interpret images from optical sensors

automatic hyphenation   a word processing feature that uses a set of built-in rules to split words at the ends of lines when necessary without confirmation from the user

automatic recalculation   the ability of a spreadsheet program to immediately update the entire worksheet whenever the contents of a cell are changed

background   in OS/2, where an application that does not have control of the physical console is running

backup   an extra copy of vital programs or data; to make such a copy

balance sheet   a report that summarizes the assets, liabilities, and capital of a business

bar graph   a chart in which numeric values are represented by evenly spaced, thick vertical lines

BASIC   (Beginners' All-purpose Symbolic Instruction Code) a simple, interactive programming language originally designed to teach students about computer programming

Basic Input/Output System (BIOS)   on some computers, the hardware interface that controls physical components such as disk drives, monitor, keyboard, and printer

batch file   a text file that lists operating system commands to be performed automatically when the name of the batch file is entered

batch processing   using batch files to reduce several frequently used operating system commands to just one command to save time and effort

batch processing commands   a special set of internal DOS commands, such as CALL and ECHO, that add power and flexibility to batch files

benchmark   an objective, reproducible measure of hardware or software performance

Bernoulli box   see *Bernoulli disk drive*

Bernoulli disk drive   a secondary storage device that combines the advantages of both floppy and hard disk drives

billing   the accounting subsystem that prepares and records invoices

binary file   a file that contains programs or data that are not encoded as ASCII characters

binary point   the period that separates the whole part from the fractional part of a mixed binary number

bit   the basic unit of data processing; a single binary digit, 0 or 1, off or on

bit-mapped   see *pixel-based*

bits per second (bps)   unit of modem transmission speed

block   a contiguous section of text—can consist of a single character up to an entire document

booting up   initially loading and executing the operating system

border palette   a menu of line thicknesses used to draw lines and outline shapes

branching   altering the order in which batch file commands are executed using IF and GOTO commands

briefcase computer   see *laptop computer*

browse   to casually scan the records of a data base

bug   an error or problem in a computer program

built-in dictionary   an automatic proofreading feature that looks for spelling errors

bus   a set of wires and connectors that link the CPU to memory and other computer components

bus network   a topology in which each workstation is connected to a single cable running past all the workstations

byte   a contiguous group of eight bits; the amount of memory it takes to store a single character or a numeric quantity from 0 to 255

C   a concise, yet powerful programming language frequently used for the development of system software and application packages

cache   an intermediary storage place

calculated field   a field that contains the result of an expression instead of a value entered directly in a data base file

capture   to gather incoming data from a host computer and save it in a disk file

carrier sense multiple access (CSMA)   a protocol that requires each network workstation to listen before sending messages or data

catalog   in dBASE, a list of files

cathode ray tube (CRT)   a display that uses an electronic gun to paint images on a phosphor-coated glass screen

cell   the box at the intersection of a row and a column in a worksheet

cell address   a designation that specifies a cell's exact location within a worksheet

cell pointer   the highlighted cell that marks the current location in a worksheet

cell reference   see *cell address*

central processing unit (CPU)   the part of a computer that performs calculations, logic, and control operations

chaining   executing a batch file as the last command in another batch file

chamfer   a CAD feature that joins two lines with another straight line

character formatting   specifying the way individual letters or words are presented

charting program   a program that produces graphs, plots, and charts from data entered directly or imported from a spreadsheet or data base file

chassis   a metal and plastic frame that houses all of the internal components of a computer

child file   the more specific file in a relation that contains the information to be looked up by the parent file

chip   see *integrated circuit chip*

circular reference   the result of a formula in a cell being either directly or indirectly dependent on the value in that very same cell

clicking   moving the mouse pointer on top of an item to be selected and briefly pressing and releasing the mouse button

clipboard   a temporary storage area for copying data

clone   a computer that works just like, or very similar to, another computer

coaxial cable   a center conductor surrounded by a shield or wire braid, used for cable television and local area networks

COBOL   a high-level programming language introduced in 1960 especially for business data processing

code   in WordPerfect, a hidden formatting indicator generated when you press a key such as Enter or Tab, or execute a command that changes a document's appearance, such as Center or Bold

code page   a conversion table that tells DOS how to translate data stored as numeric values into letters, numbers, punctuation, and other symbols to be displayed or printed

color graphics monitor   a monitor that can display both text and graphics in more than one color

column   a field in an SQL table

column-wise recalculation   the order of worksheet recalculation that begins with cell A1 and proceeds down column A, goes on to cell B1 and proceeds down column B, and so on

combining   see *merging*

command   a directive that is issued to a program

command-line interface (CLI)   a user interface, such as DOS without the DOS Shell, that presents a prompt and accepts commands instead of using menus, icons, and windows

comment out   temporarily shut off a command in a program or batch file by inserting a comment in front of it on the same line

communications package   software that lets a computer transfer messages, programs, and data to other computers

communications parameters   the settings that specify the technical details of how a computer will communicate with another computer

communications server   a network workstation that lets users communicate with computers outside the network via serial ports and a high-speed modem

compact disc read-only memory (CD-ROM)   an optical disk drive that allows access to previously recorded data, but not storage of any new data

compiler   a program that translates high-level language instructions into machine language

complex instruction set computer (CISC)   a microprocessor, such as the Intel 80486 or Motorola 68040, that incorporates many relatively slow instructions especially designed for high-level languages

computer   an electronic device that performs calculations and processes data into information

computer-aided design (CAD)   a type of software package for drafting complex plans, blueprints, models, schematics, and other detailed drawings of parts, mechanisms, and buildings

computer-aided engineering (CAE)   a system that allows engineers to simulate and test their designs on a computer before they are built

computer-aided manufacturing (CAM)   a system in which a computer controls the machines that make or assemble products

computer-assisted instruction (CAI)   a system that uses computers to teach students at their own pace

computer graphics   the presentation of images such as figures, charts, graphs, maps, diagrams, and other pictures on a display screen

computer-managed instruction (CMI)   a system that uses computers to help with school administrative tasks

computer matching   a technique that involves comparing records in various data bases to identify individuals who meet overlapping sets of criteria

computer virus   a hidden program that secretly copies itself from disk to disk and across networks, often causing mischief or outright destruction of data

computerized axial tomography (CAT or CT)   a computer-controlled, three-dimensional X-ray machine

context-sensitive   the ability of a help facility to display information specifically relevant to the current activity

Control Center   the menu system of dBASE IV

control panel   the space on the screen that displays cell information, menus, messages, and the operating mode

coprocessor   integrated circuit chip designed to perform a specialized task for the main microprocessor

copy-and-paste   a word processing operation in which a section of text is reproduced in another location

copy-protection   a way to prepare diskettes so that it is difficult or impossible to copy them with ordinary operating system commands

CP/M   a single-user, single-tasking generic microcomputer operating system sold by Digital Research

criteria   requirements that a record must fulfill to be retrieved by a search or query

Critical Path Method (CPM)   a scheduling method that focuses on the sequence of critical activities that must be performed to complete a project

crosshair   two lines that intersect on the screen to indicate the current cursor position

current cell   the cell marked by the cell pointer, where you can enter data or initiate commands

cursor   a small, blinking underscore or box that marks the position where characters will appear on the screen when typed

cut-and-paste   a word processing operation in which a section of text is moved from one location to another

daisy-wheel printer   a printer with solid, raised characters embossed on the ends of little arms arranged like the spokes of a wheel, for producing slow, but letter-quality output

data   numbers, text, pictures, and sounds that are to be processed into information; in a spreadsheet program, data can be numbers, labels, or formulas

data base   an organized collection of one or more files of related data

data base management package   software that lets you organize large quantities of information, such as mailing lists and inventories

data bus   the pathway connecting the microprocessor to memory

data encryption   a security method that encodes information so that it can be read and changed only by authorized users who know the password

data entry form   a listing of each field in a record, accompanied by an empty box for each field's contents

debug   to remove the errors from a computer program

debugger   a program that helps to detect errors in software under development

decision support system (DSS)   a computer system that helps managers make decisions by applying statistical models and mathematical simulation

dedicated server   a network workstation reserved solely as a file, printer, or communications server

dedicated word processor   a microcomputer system expressly designed and solely used to prepare, store, and print documents *de facto* **standard** a standard that emerges from many manufacturers voluntarily making products that will work together

default predefined settings for certain features (margins, line spacing, column widths, etc.) that a software package uses automatically if the user does not explicitly establish settings

default drive the disk drive where DOS will look for programs and data files unless otherwise specified

delete to remove, erase, or destroy one or more pieces of information

delimiter a space, comma, semicolon, equal sign, or tab

descending order the arrangement of numbers from largest to smallest, and of text alphabetically from Z to A

desk accessory a utility program that provides commonly used desk functions such as a calculator, calendar, or address book

desktop computer the most common type of microcomputer, small enough to fit on top of a table or desk

desktop organizer see *desk accessory*

desktop publishing using a computer and laser printer to produce near-typeset-quality documents

desktop publishing package software that combines the results of word processing and graphics to produce near-typeset-quality documents

device controller a set of chips or a circuit board that operates a piece of computer equipment such as a disk drive, display, keyboard, mouse, or printer

device driver a file that contains the programming code needed to attach and use a special device, such as a nonstandard disk drive, memory board, mouse, monitor, or printer

digitizer see *graphics tablet*

direct access medium storage medium, such as magnetic disk, that allows data items to be retrieved in any order

direct-connect modem see *external modem*

directory a list of the files stored on a disk; another term for subdirectory

disk a medium used by computers to store information, consisting of one or more flat surfaces on which bits are recorded magnetically or optically

disk backup utility a program that facilitates making backup copies of a hard disk on floppy disks

disk buffer an area of memory DOS uses to temporarily hold data being read from or written to a disk

disk caching utility a program that reserves part of memory as an intermediary storage place to speed up the retrieval of frequently used software and data

disk copying utility a program that specializes in duplicating files and disks, especially those that are copy protected

disk drive a computer system component that reads and writes programs and data on disks

diskette see *floppy disk*

Disk Operating System (DOS) see *PC-DOS*

disk optimizing utility a program that makes secondary storage devices operate more efficiently

display output screen on which the computer presents text and graphic images

display adapter a circuit board or set of chips that controls a monitor

display-only field see *read-only field*

document the paper output of a word processor

documentation the user manual or technical information about a computer or software package

document file a collection of text created by a word processing program in such a way that the text includes embedded formatting codes

DOS a generic name for PC-DOS and MS-DOS

DOS Compatibility Box see *DOS Session*

DOS environment a special area of memory, like a scratch pad for DOS, that some programs use to hold variables, values, and text

DOS prompt a symbol that identifies the current default drive and indicates that DOS is waiting for a command

DOS Session the special environment in OS/2 that can run a single DOS application at a time

DOS shell a menu-driven addition to DOS that helps manage disk files and directories

DOS Shell the DOS shell developed by IBM and Microsoft and included with DOS versions 4.0 and newer

dot-matrix printer a common type of printer that constructs character images by repeatedly striking pins against the ribbon and paper

dot pitch the distance between the illuminated centers of any two adjacent dots on a display screen

dot prompt the dBASE command-line interface

dot prompt command a dBASE command entered in response to the dot prompt and not selected from a menu

double clicking pressing and releasing a mouse button twice in rapid succession

downloading transferring a file from a host computer to your computer

draft mode the fastest print mode in which low-quality characters are formed by a single pass of the printhead

dragging holding down the mouse button while moving the mouse—used to pull down menus, outline parts of a picture, move selections, and stretch objects

drive specifier a disk drive letter immediately followed by a colon

edit to make changes in a file

electronic mail (E-mail) a way to send and receive messages with a computer

electronic typewriter an electric typewriter with a built-in microprocessor

Encapsulated PostScript (EPS) file a graphics file containing gray-shade information that can be imported and printed by page layout programs that use the PostScript language

encryption a method of protecting sensitive data by scrambling it so that it cannot be read without the proper key

end user see *user*

endnote   a numbered comment or explanation similar to a footnote, except that it appears at the end of the document instead of at the bottom of each page

erasable optical disk drive   a disk drive that uses optical disks that can be written to and read from any number of times

ergonomics   the science of designing objects so that they can be most easily, effectively, comfortably, and safely used by people

example variable   in dBASE IV, a place holder for the value of a field entered in the link field to link two data base files

expansion board   a circuit board that plugs into an expansion slot

expansion card   see *expansion board*

expansion slot   an internal connector that allows you to plug an additional circuit board into the motherboard; an extension of the bus

expert   an experienced computer user

expert system   a computer program that contains both a collection of facts and a list of rules for making inferences about those facts

expert system shell   microcomputer software that contains an inference engine and lets nonprogrammers set up expert systems by supplying (1) their own facts to create knowledge bases and (2) rules to create rule bases

exponent   in scientific notation, the number indicating the power of ten to be multiplied by the mantissa

exporting   writing data in a format that can be accepted by a different program

extension   the second part of a DOS file's name

external command   a DOS command that is kept in disk storage and temporarily loaded into memory only when needed or specifically requested

external modem   a modem built into its own separate housing

fiber-optic cable   glass filaments that transmit data in the form of extremely rapid pulses of light generated by lasers, used for high-speed local area networks

field   a group of related characters in a data base record; a single data item, such as a number, character, word, or phrase

field template   in dBASE, a representation of the width and contents of a data field to be displayed in a form

file   a collection of information kept in secondary storage and loaded into primary memory when needed by a program; in a data base, a group of related records

file attribute   a characteristic of a file, such as read-only or archive

file compression utility   a program that squeezes files into less disk space by eliminating waste and redundant data

file control block (FCB)   a data structure used by early versions of DOS to manage open files

file conversion utility   a program that modifies files from one application so that they can be used by another application

file locking   allowing only one person or program to use the same file at the same time on a network

filename   the primary part of a DOS file's name

file recovery utility   a program that can reinstate accidentally erased files, restore reformatted hard disks, or perform other useful file operations

file server   a network workstation used to store shared program and data files on a large-capacity, high-speed hard disk

file sharing   allowing two or more people or programs to use the same file at the same time on a network

file skeleton   a graphic representation of a data base file

file specification   the combination of a disk drive specifier, a filename, and an extension

file transfer utility   a program that can move data among different types of computers

fillet   a CAD feature that joins two lines to create a rounded corner

film recorder   a graphics output device that turns screen images into 35-mm slides

filter   a DOS command (FIND, MORE, or SORT) that normally reads input from the keyboard, changes it in some way, and then displays it as output on the screen

filter condition   in dBASE, an expression that determines which records are to be selected for a view

Finder   a part of the Apple Macintosh operating system that allows users to run application programs, set up disks, and organize, copy, and delete files

firmware   low-level, system software stored in ROM chips, such as the BIOS

first line indent   a format in which only the first line of the paragraph is moved in from the left margin

fixed currency format   a worksheet format in which two places are to the right of the decimal point, thousands are separated by commas, and each number is preceded by a dollar sign

fixed disk drive   see *hard disk drive*

fixed-point number   a number whose decimal or binary point is in a fixed place in relation to the digits

flat-file data base manager   a program that works with one file of structured data at a time

floating-point number   a number in which the position of the decimal or binary point can vary

floor model   a powerful, expensive microcomputer with a system unit larger than that of the typical desktop computer and designed to accommodate more add-in hardware components

floppy disk   an inexpensive, flexible magnetic medium for storing computer programs and data that can be removed from the disk drive when not in use

floppy disk drive   a disk drive that accepts floppy disks

font   a set of letters, numbers, punctuation marks, and other symbols with a consistent appearance

footer   one or more lines of text printed at the bottom of every page

footnote   a numbered comment or explanation at the bottom of a page

foreground   in OS/2, where the application that has control of the physical console is running

form   a screen or printout that shows the fields of an individual record

formatting   initializing a disk so that files can be stored on it

formula   an expression that instructs a spreadsheet program to perform calculations or other manipulations on numbers, labels, or the contents of cells

FORTRAN   one of the first high-level programming languages, designed to fulfill the computational needs of scientists, engineers, and mathematicians

fourth generation language (4GL)   the most abstract type of programming language, designed to make it as easy as possible for users to tell a computer what to do

free-form data base manager   a program designed to handle narrative text and irregular pieces of data, such as paragraphs, pages, articles, notes, discussions, and instructions

full-duplex   a communications mode in which the characters sent to the host computer are echoed back to the terminal's screen

function   a ready-made procedure that performs tedious, complex, or often-used computations or other manipulations

function keys   on an IBM-compatible computer, the keys on the left side or top of the keyboard labeled F1 through F10 or F12, used to perform common operations

game adapter   a circuit board or set of chips that allows the use of joysticks or trackballs

Gantt chart   a horizontal bar graph that shows the major tasks of a project, when each task must be performed, and how long each task will take to perform

general ledger   the main listing of the accounts of a business

generic operating system   an operating system that can be adapted to almost any type of computer

gigabyte (G)   1,073,741,824 bytes

global   pertaining to or acting upon an entire document, spreadsheet, or data base file

global delete   the ability to remove all those records that meet certain criteria

global filename character   the * (which matches any group of characters) or the ? (which matches any single character) used in a DOS file specification to indicate names with one or more characters in common

global modify   the ability to change all those records that meet certain criteria

global search and replace   changing a word or phrase automatically throughout an entire document

graphical user interface (GUI)   a sophisticated, easy-to-use system that includes pull-down menus, icons, windows, and a simulated desktop

graphics   any kind of graphs, plots, drawings, and other images not restricted to text characters

graphics adapter   a display adapter that can produce graphics

graphics-based windowing environment   a windowing environment that can work with programs that display pictures and characters of all different sizes, styles, and fonts

graphics package   software that can produce graphs, plots, drawings, pictures, or charts

graphics tablet   a flat surface on which the user draws with a stylus, pen, or some other pointing device

greeking   representing text too small to be distinguished by tiny characters or shaded bars to show its position on a page

grid   criss-crossed lines used to keep objects lined up with each other on the screen; a visual aid for placing objects in a drawing

hacker   a hardware designer or programmer with an obsession for computing

half-duplex   a communications mode in which the characters sent to the host computer are not echoed back to the terminal's screen

hand-held computer   the smallest type of microcomputer, smaller than a paperback book and weighing less than a pound

handle   a little black square on the boundary of a selected object, used to drag or resize the object

hanging indent   a format in which all lines of a paragraph except for the first are moved in from the left margin

hard disk   a circular platter of rigid aluminum or glass covered with a thin magnetic coating for storing computer programs and data

hard disk drive   a disk drive that contains one or more hard disks

hard hyphen   a hyphen created by pressing the - key

hard page break   in WordPerfect, a division between two pages that is manually generated by pressing Ctrl-Enter

hard return   in WordPerfect, a new line or paragraph begun by pressing the Enter key

hard space   in WordPerfect, a blank created by pressing the Space Bar

hardware   the physical components of a computer system

Hayes-compatible modem   a modem that operates like a Hayes Smartmodem

head crash   the result of a disk drive's read-write head colliding with a minute obstruction or hitting the surface of a disk

header   one or more lines of text printed at the top of every page

headword   in WordPerfect, a word that can be looked up in the thesaurus

hexadecimal system base 16 number system

hidden column a worksheet column that exists and contains data, but is not displayed or printed

hidden file a special file used by DOS or some other program that does not appear in the disk directory

hierarchical a method of organizing files into rank-ordered groups

high-level language an abstract programming language that facilitates the expression of complex data processing operations

host computer the computer being called by another computer

hypermedia the nonsequential organization and presentation of information, including graphics, audio, and video

hypertext the nonsequential organization and presentation of information with a computer

hyphenation the division of certain words at the ends of lines to improve the appearance of text

IBM-compatible a microcomputer that works just like, or in some ways better than, an IBM microcomputer, and can run the same software

icon a small pictorial symbol that represents a file, a file folder, an action to be performed, or a program to be run

importing reading and, if necessary, translating data originally created with some other program

income statement a report that summarizes the revenues and expenses of a business for a given period of time

incremental backup a backup procedure that copies only those files that have been changed since the last backup

indenting moving text away from the margin toward the center of the page

index file a file that contains record numbers listed in a particular order

indexing a way to reorder the records of a data base without actually duplicating the data in a new file or rearranging the actual records in the original file

information a more organized and useful form of input data

ink-jet printer a printer with a mechanism for squirting tiny droplets of ink to form text and graphics on paper

input any data or information entered into a computer

insertion point another term for *cursor*; where text is inserted with a word processing package

insert mode a typing mode in which all characters typed at the current cursor location push aside existing text to the right

installed when a software package is copied to a hard or floppy disk and set up to be run

instruction set a limited collection of low-level tasks a computer can do with a single instruction

integrated circuit chip a thin slice of semiconductor material, such as pure silicon crystal, impregnated with carefully selected impurities, commonly used in computers and many other electronic devices

integrated software a software package that includes word processing, spreadsheet, data base, graphics, and communications capabilities

intelligent recalculation see *smart recalculation*

interface a connection between a computer's CPU and an external device operated under its control

internal command an essential or frequently used DOS command that is kept in memory

internal modem a modem built onto an expansion board or directly onto the motherboard

interpreter a program that translates and runs one high-level language instruction at a time as it is entered into a computer

interrupt a signal that suspends the current program to tell the CPU that some critical event has occurred

inventory control the accounting subsystem that tracks products and materials on hand

invoice a bill sent to a customer

iteration a way to obtain an approximate result to an indirect circular reference in a worksheet by recomputing the formulas a number of times

journal a chronological listing of transactions

joystick a vertical lever that can be tilted in any direction to control a cursor or steer a simulated vehicle

justified a type of text alignment in which text is flush to both the left and right margins

key a field used to sort or index the records of a data base

keyboard the primary input device with which you enter data and tell a computer what to do

keyboard macro see *macro*

keyboard template a plastic or cardboard guide that fits over or near the function keys on the keyboard listing the most common keyboard commands

kilobyte (K) 1,024 bytes

knowledge-based system see *expert system*

label in a DOS batch file, a place for a GOTO command to branch to; in a spreadsheet program, any kind of text, such as a heading, title, name, address, or note in a worksheet cell

label macro a macro created by entering the labels that represent the keystrokes to be performed when the macro is run

label prefix character a special character (', ^, ", \) that tells the program that the following item is a label and not a number or formula, and indicates how to align labels within cells or if a character is to be repeated within a cell

laptop computer a full-fledged microcomputer squeezed into a 4- to 15-pound housing smaller than most briefcases

laser printer a high-quality printer that uses tightly focused beams of light to transfer images to paper

layer a CAD feature like a transparent overlay sheet that can be created separately and superimposed on top of other layers

learn feature in Lotus 1-2-3, a way to create a macro by recording keystrokes

learn mode an easy-to-use method of defining a macro by recording keystrokes

learn range in Lotus 1-2-3, the single-column range of cells where keystrokes will be recorded for a macro definition

left indent a format in which all lines of a paragraph are moved in from the left margin

letter-quality like the output of a good electric typewriter

light pen a rod used to point at or draw on a computer display screen

line editor a simple program that can only work with a single line of text at a time

line graph a plot that represents each data value by a point at an appropriate distance above the horizontal axis and connects the points by line segments

line height in WordPerfect, the distance between lines of printed text

link field a common field that connects two data base files

linker a program that combines the output files of programming language translators into a single executable program file

liquid crystal display (LCD) a flat-panel screen that presents black characters against a grey background, commonly used in watches, clocks, calculators, and hand-held and laptop microcomputers

load to copy a program or data file from disk into memory

local area network (LAN) several microcomputers connected together within the same building, or nearby buildings, to share hardware, software, and data

locked cell see *protected cell*

logged the current disk drive or directory

logical formula in a worksheet, a formula that compares values and produces a result of 1 for true or 0 for false

logical operator in dBASE, an operator (.AND., .OR., or .NOT.) that modifies the true or false result of one or two conditions

log-in to enter the assigned group name, user name, and password to gain access to a system

Lotus Access System a program called Lotus that lets you start 1-2-3 or any of the other programs that come with the Lotus 1-2-3 package

machine language the only programming language that can be directly used by a computer, consisting of binary numbers that represent CPU instructions, memory addresses, and data

machine learning a method by which computers can program themselves, through trial and error, to accomplish a particular task

macro a sequence of keystrokes that can be recorded, stored, and replayed

magnetic disk a semipermanent storage medium that can be erased and written over and over again

magnetic resonance imaging (MRI) a medical scanning method that produces high-quality cross-sectional pictures of the body without X-rays or other radiation

magnetic tape a long strip of thin plastic covered with a magnetic coating

magnetic tape drive a secondary storage device that uses magnetic tape to hold programs and data

mail-merge a word processing or data base feature that lets you combine a master document with a data file of names and addresses to create personalized form letters

mainframe a big, powerful, fast, expensive computer

management information system (MIS) a computer system that provides managers with the information they need to do their jobs more effectively

mantissa in scientific notation, the decimal part of the number that is to be multiplied by the power of ten indicated by the exponent

manual hyphenation a hyphenation method that requires you to confirm the splitting of each word as you scroll through the document

manual recalculation a feature that causes the formulas in a worksheet to be recalculated only when explicitly directed to do so

many-to-many link a type of link that connects multiple records to other multiple records in data base files

master document a document containing text and special commands to be mail-merged with a data file

master index file the index file that specifies the order in which all records will be displayed unless otherwise specified

megabyte (M) 1,048,576 bytes

megahertz (MHz) a unit of frequency equal to one million cycles per second

memo marker in dBASE IV, an indicator that appears in a record to show if the associated memo field contains any text

memory a computer's internal storage for temporarily holding programs and data

memory-resident a type of program that allows a user to temporarily suspend an activity and switch to another one under a single-tasking operating system such as DOS

memory variable in dBASE, a place in RAM that temporarily holds a data value

menu a list showing options available in a program

menu bar a list of the names of pull-down menus across the top of the screen

menu pointer the highlighted block that shows the command that will be invoked if you press the Enter key

merging combining two worksheets into one

message line in dBASE, a line near the bottom of the screen that displays messages

Micro Channel Architecture the high-performance bus (underlying circuit) design of IBM's Personal System/2 Models 50 through 80 microcomputers

microcomputer a small computer that uses a single microprocessor chip as its central processing unit

microcomputer standard a generally accepted set of rules by which hardware and software operate

microprocessor a central processing unit made up of a single integrated circuit chip

million instructions per second (MIPS) a unit of computer performance that represents the execution of computer instructions

minicomputer a medium-sized computer that simultaneously serves several users or controls complex equipment

minimal recalculation a spreadsheet program feature that increases speed by recalculating only those cells that have changed, and the cells that depend on them, since the worksheet was last recalculated

mixed reference a cell address that is half-relative and half-absolute, in which either a row or column is absolute, but not both

mnemonic an easy-to-remember abbreviation for a computer operation, such as ADD

mode indicator the highlighted block in the upper right corner of the control panel that describes the current operating mode, such as READY or MENU

modem a device that allows a computer to transmit and receive programs and data over ordinary phone lines

modem cable a cable that connects an external modem to a serial interface socket at the back of a computer

modular phone jack a socket that accepts the little plastic plug on the end of a telephone cord

monitor a computer display screen (see *display*)

monochrome graphics monitor a single-color screen that can display both text and graphics

monochrome text monitor a single-color screen that displays sharply-defined characters, but no graphics

motherboard the main circuit board of a computer

mouse an input device consisting of a small box with one or more buttons that is slid across the tabletop to manipulate objects on the screen, draw, and select menu options

MS-DOS see *PC-DOS*

multidimensional spreadsheet a spreadsheet program that allows every cell in a worksheet to be connected to corresponding cells in other worksheets

MultiFinder an addition to the Apple Macintosh operating system that allows some multitasking capabilities and lets users run application programs, set up disks, and organize, copy, and delete files

multifunction board an expansion board that includes several add-on options, such as memory, a real-time clock, a game adapter, a display adapter, and serial and parallel interfaces

multiple index file in dBASE IV, a file with an extension of MDX that can contain up to 47 separate indexes of a data base file

multiprocessing the ability to run several programs simultaneously by using more than one processing unit

multiscan monitor a monitor that can change its resolution to match a number of different display adapters

multitasking the ability to run more than one program concurrently

natural language processing getting computers to understand portions of ordinary human languages such as English

natural recalculation the order of worksheet recalculation that updates a cell only after evaluating any cells on which it depends

navigation line in dBASE, a line near the bottom of the screen that lists some of the available keystrokes

near letter-quality (NLQ) a dot-matrix print mode that produces attractive output by having the printhead make two or more passes over each character

nesting in DOS, using the CALL command to invoke one batch file from within another batch file without ending the first batch file

NETBIOS (Network Basic Input/Output System) low-level programs that send and receive data to and from the network adapter

network computers connected to share hardware, software, and data

network adapter a sophisticated expansion board that connects a microcomputer to a local area network

network interface the adapter and connector that link a workstation to a network

network media the cables that connect network workstations

network server a network workstation that handles special chores

network software a set of programs, mostly on the file server, that moves data and messages between the workstations and servers, and controls the sharing of files and hardware devices

network workstation an ordinary microcomputer used to run software, transfer files, and send messages on a network

neural network a type of computer or a software simulation loosely modeled after the interconnection of neurons, or nerve cells, in the human brain

newspaper-style columns text that continues from the bottom of one column on the left to the top of the next column to the right on the same page

nonprocedural language see *fourth generation language*

novice a beginning computer user

null-modem cable a cable for directly connecting the serial ports of two computers

number a numeric quantity, such as 100, 52.34, or 0.05

numeric formula in a worksheet, a mathematical expression that calculates using numeric values and produces a numeric result

numeric keypad on an IBM-compatible computer, the area on the right side of the keyboard arranged like the number keys on a calculator

object code   software that has been translated into machine language

object-oriented   a package that lets you create and manipulate images made up of only discrete geometric objects such as lines, curves, rectangles, ovals, irregular outlines, polygons, and text

octal system   base 8 number system

one-to-many link   a type of link that connects a single record in one file to multiple records in one or more other files

one-to-one link   a type of link that connects a single record in one file to a single record in another file

on-line   connected to and controlled by the computer

on-line help   information about how a program works that you can display on the screen, without your having to look it up in a printed reference manual

on-line information service   a service that allows computers equipped with a modem to retrieve vast quantities of information and communicate with other users

on-line reference   a program such as a spelling checker, thesaurus, or user manual that you can use while running another program

open style   in WordPerfect, a style that has just a beginning code, often used to set formats for an entire document

operand   a number on which an operation is to be performed

operating system   a set of programs that controls a computer's hardware and manages the use of software

operation code (opcode)   the part of a machine language instruction that indicates which operation is to be performed

operator   a symbol that represents an action to be performed in a formula, such as + or *

optical disk drive   a secondary storage device that uses a laser to read or write data on a plastic disk

optimal recalculation   see *minimal recalculation*

orphan   the first line of a paragraph that appears at the bottom of a page

OS/2   a single-user, multitasking operating system, developed by IBM and Microsoft, for IBM and IBM-compatible microcomputers that use the Intel 80286, 80386, and 80486 microprocessors

output   any information produced by the computer; the computer's responses to your input

overwrite mode   a typing mode in which characters typed at the current cursor location replace existing characters

packet-switching network   see *public data network*

page break   a division between two pages

page description language   a specialized computer programming language for defining the size, format, and position of text and graphic elements on a printed page

page formatting   specifying the general organization of an entire page of text

page layout software   a package for arranging text and graphics on pages before they are printed

painting program   a pixel-based program for producing pictures on a computer screen

paired style   in WordPerfect, a style that has a beginning and ending code

palette   the total number of colors to choose from in a particular video mode

pan   a CAD feature that lets you move the viewing window up, down, left, or right

paragraph formatting   specifying the appearance of individual blocks of text

parallel columns   text that continues in the same column on the next page

parallel interface   a connection that transmits data, an entire byte at a time, between a computer and an external device, such as a printer

parallel port   see *parallel interface*

parameter   an entry that designates possible alternate actions

parent file   the more general file in a relation that looks up the information in the child file

parity   a method of error checking used to help ensure that all of the data bits of a character were received correctly after a transmission

partition   a separate section of a hard disk that may contain its own operating system

Pascal   a general-purpose, high-level language originally designed to teach students the principles of good programming

patent   an exclusive right to produce or sell an invention for a given time

path   a drive specifier followed by a list of subdirectory names, separated by backslashes, that describes the route to a particular subdirectory

pattern palette   a menu of patterns that can be used with drawing tools to create objects and to fill in enclosed areas on the screen

payroll   the accounting subsystem that maintains personnel information, generates paychecks, computes tax withholdings, and creates summary reports of employee earnings

PC-DOS   a single-user, single-tasking operating system developed by Microsoft for IBM microcomputers

pel   see *pixel*

personal computer   see *microcomputer*

physical console   the display and keyboard

pie chart   a graph that represents values as wedges of a circle, used to show the parts of a whole

piping   a DOS feature, symbolized by the | (vertical bar), that takes the output of one command, which would normally go to the display screen, and feeds it as input to another command

pixel   picture element; a tiny dot on a computer display

pixel-based   a package that has control over every dot on the screen

plotter   an output device that uses one or more pens to draw on paper

point   a typographical measure equal to about 1/72-inch

pointer movement keys keys that you press to move the cell pointer

polling a protocol in which a controlling workstation sends messages to other workstations on the network, asking each one in turn if it has any messages or data to transmit

pop-up menu a list of options that appears on the screen only when a user issues a special command

pop-up utility see *desk accessory*

portable computer a microcomputer about the size of a small suitcase, designed to be moved, but not used, in transit

positron emission tomography (PET) a medical scanning technique that produces images by detecting positively charged particles emitted from radioactive substances injected into the bloodstream

PostScript a page description language for high-resolution printers and typesetters

power supply a refined source of electrical power for a computer that contains a transformer to lower and regulate the voltage level

power user see *expert*

Presentation Manager the graphical user interface of OS/2

primary file in WordPerfect, the text of a form letter containing special mail-merge codes

primary key the field on which records are sorted first

primary storage a computer's internal memory

print buffering see *print spooling*

printer a device for producing permanent copies of computer output on paper

printer setup string a group of special control codes directing the printer to turn on such options as compressed print

print queue a list of files to be printed in the background

print server a network workstation used to control a printer shared by other workstations on a network

print spooler a utility program that reduces or eliminates waiting for a printer to produce documents

print spooling the ability to print one document while working on another

procedure file see *batch file*

ProDOS a single-user, single-tasking proprietary operating system for the Apple II family of microcomputers

program a sequence of step-by-step instructions that tell a computer what to do

Program Evaluation and Review Technique (PERT) a scheduling method for tasks whose completion times are difficult to estimate

programmable data base manager a relational or flat-file data base manager that includes its own programming language or works with a standard programming language such as BASIC, C, COBOL, FORTRAN, or Pascal

programmer a person who creates computer programs

programming language a set of symbols and rules that direct the operations of a computer

project management software a package that helps to formally plan and control complex undertakings

prompt a symbol or statement that indicates the computer is waiting for a response from the user

proportional spacing allotting different amounts of space for different characters

proprietary hardware or software, with tightly controlled patents or copyrights, that cannot be legally duplicated without being licensed by the originator

proprietary operating system an operating system designed specifically for a single model or line of computers

protected cell a cell that cannot be altered, deleted, or moved unless its protection is first turned off

protocol a set of rules that govern how computers communicate

public data network a way to call a distant communications service from a local telephone number

pull-down menu a list of options that appears when the list's title or symbol is selected from the top of the screen

query a search for records that meet one or more specific criteria; in dBASE, a set of instructions to retrieve, display, organize, or edit data

Query-by-Example (QBE) a highly interactive query language that makes it easy for a user to extract information from a data base

query file in dBASE III PLUS, a special type of file that filters a data base to display or print only those records that meet specific criteria

query language a specialized set of commands for rearranging or extracting data from data bases

QuickDraw laser printer a laser printer designed especially for Apple Macintosh computers as a lower-cost alternative to PostScript printers

RAM cache a part of memory specially reserved for data that must be frequently retrieved

RAM disk an area of memory that is set up to simulate a disk drive

RAM resident see *memory resident*

random access memory (RAM) storage in which all addresses are equally accessible; the portion of a computer's primary storage used to hold programs and data temporarily

range a block of adjacent cells in a worksheet, indicated by the address of the upper left cell, two periods, and the address of the lower right cell

read-only attribute the file attribute that determines if a file can be written, modified, or deleted

read-only field a data base field whose contents can be viewed but not altered

read-only memory (ROM) permanent primary storage that is encoded with programs and data at the factory, retains its contents when the power is turned off, and can be read and used but never erased, changed, or augmented

read-write head   a tiny electromagnet on a disk drive's access arm that can create or erase minuscule magnetic spots on the disk directly below

real number   see *floating-point number*

real-time clock   a built-in clock that keeps the date and time-of-day for a computer

record   an array of related fields that contains all the data about a particular person or object

record buffer   in Lotus 1-2-3 Release 3.0, a 512-byte area of memory that stores the most recent keystrokes

record feature   in Lotus 1-2-3 Release 3.0, a way to create a macro by copying keystrokes saved in the record buffer

record locking   preventing the deletion or modification of an individual record currently being used by another person on the same network

record number   a unique number assigned to each record in a data base file

record pointer   in dBASE, an invisible pointer that keeps track of the current record

redirection   changing the normal source or destination of information processed by a DOS command by using the >, <, or >> symbols

redirector   a layer of software that acts as a traffic controller for the data and messages transmitted over a network

reduced instruction set computer (RISC)   a microprocessor that has a relatively small number of simple instructions that all execute very quickly

reformatting   erasing and reinitializing a previously formatted disk

register   a storage compartment inside the CPU for temporarily holding numbers that are currently being manipulated

relate   to link two or more data base files

relational data base   a data base that includes two or more files with at least one field in common

relational data base manager   a program that allows you to create, maintain, reorganize, and print structured data from more than one file at a time

relational operator   a symbol or word that specifies how items are to be compared

relative reference   a cell address that pertains to a cell's position relative to the current cell, and changes when the cell is moved or copied

replace   a word processing feature used to automatically substitute one word or phrase for another throughout a document

replaceable parameter   a special code inserted into a batch file that allows the user to pass information to the batch file while it is running

report   a printed listing of the contents of a data base

report band   in dBASE IV, a logical piece of a report design

resident routine   see *internal command*

resolution   the sharpness of a display screen

ring network   a topology in which each workstation is connected to a single cable that runs past all of the workstations, with the two ends of the central cable hooked together

robot   a computer-controlled machine that performs mechanical tasks

root directory   the main directory on every DOS disk

row   a record in an SQL table

row-wise recalculation   the order of worksheet recalculation that begins with cell A1 and proceeds across row 1, then row 2, and so on

ruler guide   in a page layout program, a dotted line that helps keep text and graphics aligned

ruler line   a line that shows the positions of the margins and tab stops

rules   dividing lines placed to separate columns and offset blocks of text

running head   the same title printed on every page

sans serif   a kind of plain typeface without serifs

scanner   an input device that can read text and/or graphics from paper and enter it directly into the computer

scatterplot   see *XY graph*

scroll bar   an on-screen tool used to allow movement within a document, usually found in word processing packages with graphics interfaces

scrolling   the upward movement of text on a display screen

search   a word processing feature used to locate a name or topic within a document

secondary key   the field on which records are sorted second, after the primary key

secondary merge file   in WordPerfect, the data file that contains the names and addresses for a mail-merge

secondary storage   storage that supplements primary storage by providing a place to keep programs and data when they are not needed

sector   a division of a disk track

semiconductor   a substance that conducts electricity poorly at low temperatures, but well at high temperatures, and is used to make integrated circuit chips

sequential access medium   storage medium, such as magnetic tape, on which data items can be retrieved only in the order in which they were recorded

serial interface   a connection that transmits bytes of data, one bit at a time, between a computer and an external device, such as a modem

serial port   see *serial interface*

serif   a kind of typeface that has lines crossing and finishing off the main strokes of the characters

service program   low-level program in the BIOS or DOS that can be invoked by other software to perform hardware-related tasks

shared word processor   a word processing system on a large, multiuser computer

single-tasking   the simplest type of operating system that accommodates a single user and runs a single program at a time

site license   permission to make copies of software for internal use at a reduced fee for each copy

slide show program   a program that allows you to present a sequence of pictures on a computer screen, either automatically timed or directly controlled

Small Computer System Interface (SCSI)   a connection that provides high-speed access to peripheral devices such as hard disks

smart recalculation   the ability of a spreadsheet program to automatically update only those cells, if any, that are affected when a new entry is made

snaking columns   see *newspaper-style columns*

snap   a CAD feature that automatically aligns objects to the nearest grid lines

soft hyphen   a hyphen generated by the auto-hyphenation feature

soft page break   a division between two pages automatically generated by the word processing software

soft return   a new line begun by the word wrap feature

soft space   an extra blank generated by a word processing program to justify text

software   a program or set of programs that tells a computer system what to do

software licensing   a legal agreement in which a program is not actually sold, but licensed to a user with limits on what can be done with the program

software piracy   the practice of illegally copying software

sorting   arranging items in some particular order

Soundex search   a search technique that finds words that sound like the specified word

source   a disk or file to be copied

source code   software in an assembly language or a high-level language before it is translated into machine language

specifications   a detailed list of the exact components, options, and capabilities of a particular hardware device

speech synthesizer   an output device that either mimics human speech or constructs it out of prerecorded sounds

spelling checker   see *built-in dictionary*

spooling   multitasking technique that prints files in the background while the computer is used for other work

spreadsheet   see *worksheet*

spreadsheet package   software that helps you manipulate tables of numbers

stack   a data structure used by the CPU, operating system, or application program as a temporary storage area

stacked bar graph   a variation of the basic bar graph that shows components and total amounts for each category by dividing each bar into sections

stackware   information systems created with the Hypertalk language of Apple's Hypercard program

star network   a topology in which an individual cable is run from a central server to each workstation

startup directory   the disk drive and directory automatically used to store and retrieve worksheet files unless otherwise specified

static menu   a list of options that usually remains on the screen in a fixed position

status bar   in dBASE, a line near the bottom of the screen that displays information about the operation you have chosen

status line   in WordPerfect, the line at the bottom of the screen that displays messages and warnings

stop bits   bits that mark the end of an individual data character transmission

string combination operator   the & (ampersand), which joins two labels

Structured Query Language (SQL)   a standardized language for extracting information from a relational data base

style   in WordPerfect, a collection of formatting codes and possibly text that can be created, saved, and inserted into documents to automate formatting and provide a consistent appearance to documents

style sheet   a collection of formatting instructions that can be saved in a file and applied to different documents

subdirectory   a group of files on a disk organized under a single name

submenu   a menu that is activated by selecting an option from a higher-level menu

summary operator   in dBASE IV, an operator for performing operations in view queries such as SUM, AVERAGE, and COUNT

supercomputer   an extremely fast mainframe

supermicro   see *workstation*

supermini   a powerful minicomputer with capabilities similar to those of some mainframes

surge protector   a device that rapidly cuts off the electricity when a voltage surge occurs

switching drives   telling DOS to use a different disk drive as the default

symbolic addressing   the assignment of meaningful names, such as TOTAL, to computer memory locations

system board   see *motherboard*

system call   see *service program*

system clock   a crystal, oscillating several million times per second, that synchronizes the internal operations of the microprocessor and other computer components

system prompt   see *DOS prompt*

system software   the software that handles the many details of managing a computer system

system unit   in many microcomputers, the box that houses the central processing unit, control circuitry, expansion boards, memory, and disk drives

table   a screen that displays a record in each row and a field in each column; the basic component of an SQL data base

tag   in dBASE IV, the name of an index in a multiple index file

target   a disk or file copy to be created

telecommute   to work at home using a microcomputer or a terminal connected to a computer at the office

teleconference   an electronic forum that allows computer users who share special interests to communicate and hold on-line meetings

template a general-purpose, ready-made worksheet in which the user fills in the blanks or changes selected entries

terminal a computer input/output station consisting of a keyboard and a display

terminal emulation a communications software feature that lets you use a microcomputer as a computer terminal

text area in WordPerfect, the area on the screen where you enter text and edit a document

text-based windowing environment a windowing environment that uses only the standard character set built into the computer and that cannot work with graphics programs

text file a file, also known as an ASCII file, that contains only ordinary letters, numbers, and punctuation marks

time-sharing an operating system that rapidly switches among several users at fixed intervals of time

token-passing a protocol that uses a control signal called a token that determines which workstation is allowed to transmit messages or data

tool palette a menu of icons for drawing, adding text, moving about, and selecting parts of a picture created with a painting or drawing program

topology the way hardware components are arranged in a network

touch screen an input device built into or over a display screen that uses infrared light beams or an electrically conductive surface to identify the position of a finger as it points to the screen

track a ring on a disk where data can be stored

trackball a box that contains a protruding ball that can be freely rotated in any direction and is often used as an alternative to a mouse

trademark a legal protection for creative expression, usually limited to a word, phrase, or graphic symbol representing a company or product

transient routine see *external command*

Transputer a special microprocessor that can be connected with other Transputers to construct a fast, powerful multiprocessing computer

twisted-pair wire two wires that have been partially wrapped around each other, used for ordinary telephone lines and inexpensive local area networks

typeface see *font*

ultrasound scanner a medical imaging device that uses very high-frequency sound waves

undo a feature that lets you cancel your most recently performed operation

UNIX a multiuser, multitasking generic operating system originally developed at AT&T's Bell Laboratories

update query in dBASE IV, a query used to add, modify, or delete data in a data base file

uploading transferring a file from your computer to a host computer

upwardly compatible the ability of a new software product to handle every official command that worked with previous versions of it

user a person who runs software on a computer to accomplish some task

user friendly easy-to-learn; can be used by people who don't have a lot of computer experience

user interface how a user directs the actions of software and how the software responds to these requests

utility a small, specific program that adds handy features to a particular operating system or application package

value-added network see *public data network*

very high level language see *fourth generation language*

video mode a combination of screen resolution and number of colors that can be used at one time

view in dBASE, an arrangement of data on the screen

view file in dBASE III PLUS, a file that displays data from two or more data base files

view query in dBASE IV, a set of instructions that displays selected data on the screen

view skeleton in dBASE IV, a graphic representation of the fields that will be displayed by the view query

virtual console a simulated display and keyboard used by programs that run in the background under OS/2

voice recognition system an input device that can recognize a finite number of isolated sounds, words, and phrases

volume label in DOS, the name of a disk

widow the last line of a paragraph that appears at the top of a page

wildcard character in WordPerfect and dBASE, the * (which represents any group of characters) or the ? (which represents any single character) used in search and replace operations

what-you-see-is-what-you-get (WYSIWYG) a feature in which a document is printed on paper exactly as it appears on the screen

window a boxed-in area on the screen that shows the activity of a particular software program

windowing environment system software that lets you divide your screen into a number of different boxes and run a separate program in each one

word processing a common computer application that allows you to produce documents, such as letters and reports, with a computer

word processing package a software package used to create, enter, edit, format, store, and print documents

word wrap a word processing feature that automatically begins new lines when necessary without the user having to press the Enter key (carriage return)

work area in dBASE, a place in memory that holds an open data base file

worksheet   a table of columns and rows of numbers, text labels, and formulas used in a spreadsheet package for the manipulation of numerical, financial, and accounting data

workstation   a small, yet powerful computer generally used by only one person at a time, traditionally used by scientists and engineers for drafting, design, and map-making

write once, read many (times) (WORM)   an optical disk drive that allows users to record data once, and then only read it thereafter

write-protection   a diskette feature that can be used to prevent the contents from being erased or altered

write-protect notch   a small rectangle cut out of one side of a 5¼-inch diskette that can be covered with a gummed tab to write-protect the disk

write-protect switch   a tab on a 3½-inch diskette that can be slid to open a little hole in the disk's plastic case, thereby write-protecting the disk

XY graph   a plot that shows the relationship between two or more variables

PHOTO CREDITS

Chapter 1
2 IBM; 3 IBM; 4 Intel; 5 Memorex; 6 Seagate Technologies;
7 IBM; 8 IBM; 10 Hewlett-Packard; 11 Hewlett-Packard

Chapter 2
8 IBM.

MS-DOS® 4.01 (function-key template)

F1	F2	F3	F4	F5	F6	F7	F8	F9	F10
Retype one character from previous command	Retype previous command up to specified character	Retype all of previous command	Delete previous command up to specified character	Save current command as previous command	Insert End-of-file code Ctrl-Z				

MS-DOS® 4.01

Ctrl–Alt–Del	Reboot	Enter	Process cmd.
Ctrl–Break	Cancel	Esc	Cancel line
Ctrl–Print Screen	Echo	Del	Skip char.
Print Screen	Print	Ins	Toggle insert

D.C. Heath

WordPerfect® 5.0 (function-key template)

Ctrl (red) / *Alt* (blue) / *Shift* (green) / plain (black)

	F1	F2	F3	F4	F5	F6	F7	F8	F9	F10
Ctrl	Shell	Spell	Screen	Move	Text In/Out	Tab Align	Footnote	Font	Merge/Sort	Macro Define
Alt	Thesaurus	Replace	Reveal Codes	Block	Mark Text	Flush Right	Math/Columns	Style	Graphics	Macro
Shift	Setup	◄Search	Switch	◄Indent	Date/Outline	Center	Print	Format	Merge Codes	Retrieve
plain	Cancel	►Search	Help	►Indent	List Files	Bold	Exit	Underline	Merge R	Save

WordPerfect® 5.0
for IBM Personal Computers

Delete to End of Ln/Pg	End/Pg Dn	◄Margin Release	Tab
Delete Word	Backspace	Screen Up/Down	-/+ (num)
Go To	Home	Soft Hyphen	–
Hard Page	Enter	Word Left/Right	←/→

© WordPerfect Corp. 1988
D.C. Heath

Cut here

MS-DOS® 4.01

Ctrl Shift Alt		D.C. Heath
Retype one character from previous command		Retype previous command up to specified character
Retype all of previous command	Cut here →	Delete previous command up to specified character
Save current command as previous command		Insert End-of-file code Ctrl–Z

MS–DOS® 4.01

Ctrl-Alt-Del	Reboot	Enter	Process cmd.
Ctrl-Break	Cancel	Esc	Cancel line
Ctrl-Prt Sc	Echo	Del	Skip char.
PrtSc	Print Screen	Ins	Toggle insert

WordPerfect® 5.0

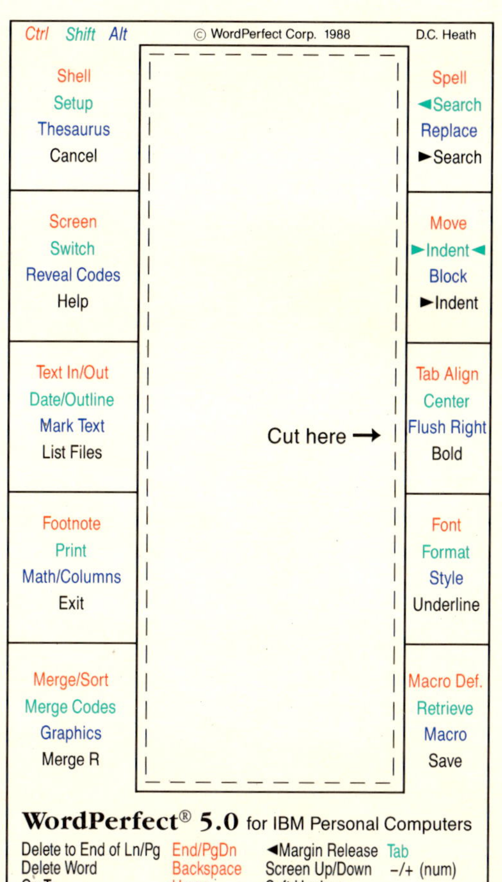

Ctrl Shift Alt	© WordPerfect Corp. 1988	D.C. Heath
Shell / Setup / Thesaurus / Cancel		Spell / ◄Search / Replace / ►Search
Screen / Switch / Reveal Codes / Help		Move / ►Indent◄ / Block / ►Indent
Text In/Out / Date/Outline / Mark Text / List Files	Cut here →	Tab Align / Center / Flush Right / Bold
Footnote / Print / Math/Columns / Exit		Font / Format / Style / Underline
Merge/Sort / Merge Codes / Graphics / Merge R		Macro Def. / Retrieve / Macro / Save

WordPerfect® 5.0 for IBM Personal Computers

Delete to End of Ln/Pg	End/PgDn	◄Margin Release	Tab
Delete Word	Backspace	Screen Up/Down	-/+ (num)
Go To	Home	Soft Hyphen	–
Hard Page	Enter	Word Left/Right	←/→